Dharma of the Dead

Contributions to Zombie Studies

White Zombie: *Anatomy of a Horror Film*. Gary D. Rhodes. 2001

The Zombie Movie Encyclopedia. Peter Dendle. 2001

American Zombie Gothic: The Rise and Fall (and Rise) of the Walking Dead in Popular Culture. Kyle William Bishop. 2010

Back from the Dead: Remakes of the Romero Zombie Films as Markers of Their Times. Kevin J. Wetmore, Jr. 2011

Generation Zombie: Essays on the Living Dead in Modern Culture. Edited by Stephanie Boluk and Wylie Lenz. 2011

Race, Oppression and the Zombie: Essays on Cross-Cultural Appropriations of the Caribbean Tradition. Edited by Christopher M. Moreman and Cory James Rushton. 2011

Zombies Are Us: Essays on the Humanity of the Walking Dead. Edited by Christopher M. Moreman and Cory James Rushton. 2011

The Zombie Movie Encyclopedia, Volume 2: 2000–2010. Peter Dendle. 2012

Great Zombies in History. Edited by Joe Sergi. 2013 (graphic novel)

Unraveling Resident Evil: *Essays on the Complex Universe of the Games and Films*. Edited by Nadine Farghaly. 2014

"We're All Infected": Essays on AMC's The Walking Dead *and the Fate of the Human*. Edited by Dawn Keetley. 2014

Zombies and Sexuality: Essays on Desire and the Living Dead. Edited by Shaka McGlotten and Steve Jones. 2014

...But If a Zombie Apocalypse Did Occur: *Essays on Medical, Military, Governmental, Ethical, Economic and Other Implications*. Edited by Amy L. Thompson and Antonio S. Thompson. 2015

How Zombies Conquered Popular Culture: The Multifarious Walking Dead in the 21st Century. Kyle William Bishop. 2015

Zombifying a Nation: Race, Gender and the Haitian Loas on Screen. Toni Pressley-Sanon. 2016

Living with Zombies: Society in Apocalypse in Film, Literature and Other Media. Chase Pielak and Alexander H. Cohen. 2017

Romancing the Zombie: Essays on the Undead as Significant "Other." Edited by Ashley Szanter and Jessica K. Richards. 2017

The Written Dead: Essays on the Literary Zombie. Edited by Kyle William Bishop and Angela Tenga. 2017

The Collected Sonnets of William Shakespeare, Zombie. William Shakespeare and Chase Pielak. 2018

Dharma of the Dead: Zombies, Mortality and Buddhist Philosophy. Christopher M. Moreman. 2018

The Subversive Zombie: Social Protest and Gender in Undead Cinema and Television. Elizabeth Aiossa. 2018

Dharma of the Dead

Zombies, Mortality and Buddhist Philosophy

CHRISTOPHER M. MOREMAN

CONTRIBUTIONS TO ZOMBIE STUDIES
Series Editor Kyle William Bishop

McFarland & Company, Inc., Publishers
Jefferson, North Carolina

ALSO BY CHRISTOPHER M. MOREMAN
AND FROM MCFARLAND

Race, Oppression and the Zombie: Essays on Cross-Cultural Appropriations of the Caribbean Tradition (coeditor, with Cory James Rushton, 2011)

Zombies Are Us: Essays on the Humanity of the Walking Dead (coeditor, with Cory James Rushton, 2011)

ISBN (print) 978-1-4766-7249-6
ISBN (ebook) 978-1-4766-3296-4

LIBRARY OF CONGRESS CATALOGUING DATA ARE AVAILABLE

BRITISH LIBRARY CATALOGUING DATA ARE AVAILABLE

© 2018 Christopher M. Moreman. All rights reserved

No part of this book may be reproduced or transmitted in any form or by any means, electronic or mechanical, including photocopying or recording, or by any information storage and retrieval system, without permission in writing from the publisher.

Front cover images © 2018 iStock

Printed in the United States of America

McFarland & Company, Inc., Publishers
Box 611, Jefferson, North Carolina 28640
www.mcfarlandpub.com

For the gang in Montreal:
Mark, Andy, Beaver, Fiore, Rachel,
P-Timm, P-McLean, Eric, and Big Al

In memoriam
George A. Romero
1940–2017

Acknowledgments

This book has been a long time in coming, and many people have listened to my ideas, read some of my work, offered suggestions, and/or watched a lot of zombie fiction with me. Primary among these folks are my old friends in Montreal, to whom I dedicate the book. Other friends and colleagues that have also supported this project in a variety of ways include Jennifer Eagan, Andrew Pierson, Robert Farrow, Robert Kennedy, Dee Andrews, Barbara Hall, Craig Derksen and David Larson. Thanks to you all. Additionally, the participants of a writing circle at CSUEB also offered great insight in very early drafts of parts of this book, and thanks go out to them as well—Aline Soules, Christina Chin-Newman, E. Maxwell Davis, Monika Sommerhalter and Sarah Taylor.

Kathy Kaiser from Editcetera contributed some excellent editorial comment, and I am, as ever, grateful to the anonymous reviewers whose feedback helped to improve the finished product. My university, California State University, East Bay, has also offered much appreciated support in the form of two Faculty Support Grants, a summer stipend from the Dean of the College of Letters, Arts, and Social Sciences, and a sabbatical leave, all of which combined to make this work possible.

Of course, Deena Rymhs remains a rock of support and fount of inspiration.

Table of Contents

Acknowledgments vi
Introduction 1

CHAPTER ONE
The Haitian Origins of the Zombie   21

CHAPTER TWO
The Evolution of the Cinematic Zombie   42

CHAPTER THREE
Embodied Death   90

CHAPTER FOUR
Zombies and the Buddhist Meditation on Death   138

Chapter Notes   183
Bibliography   207
Filmography   225
Index   229

Introduction

I want to start out by getting directly to the point of my book, and to give you, the reader, a sense of just where I'm headed. There is a wide range of interpretations of the zombie. Many of the critics and scholars presenting these ideas nod to the fact that, on the surface, the zombie is a representation of death itself, but they go on to say that this is obvious and that, in fact, there is much more to the zombie. Most scholars apply one or more of a range of culturally and temporally specific fears, sometimes called "sociophobics" (not to be confused with a fear of social situations!), to the genre.[1] Some of these sociophobics include the collapse of the nuclear suburban family, the Vietnam War (or war in general), terrorism, AIDS, and on and on. Particularly, Marxist theorists argue that the zombie is *really* a condemnation of consumer society, an explanation supported directly by some filmmakers; George Romero intentionally adds such social commentary to his films, especially in his second and later *Dead* films. Critical theory also allows for subsequent arguments in terms of race and gender, both of which have been applied liberally to zombie films. The emphasis on reading bodies as inscribed by culture and society has led to the posthumanist turn, which, like postmodernism, is by its nature somewhat difficult to define succinctly. In "reading" the literally broken bodies of zombies, critical theorists and posthumanists use their particular lens(es) to see them as indicative of a breakage in sociocultural norms. Essentially, posthumanists see an evolution of the concept of the human beyond earlier humanist assumptions, which themselves grew out of a secularized Christian view of human exceptionalism. Typically, this evolution involves expanding human exceptionalism to other nonhuman agents, be they animal, robotic, spiritual, or divine.

Many of these various interpretations apply well to a set of zombie films more than they do to the zombie generally, and sometimes they only apply when forced into the critic's preconceived ideas. Overall, the sum of such zombie theories present what Sarah Juliet Lauro calls "zombie dialectics," the zombie both in the context of its Haitian tradition of colonialism and also its modern reflection in global capitalism, standing for a revolution of power dynamics.[2] For my part, I contend that all sociophobic fears boil down to one universal human fear—that of death. I agree with the many scholars who suggest that the connection of the zombie to death should be obvious, but I completely disagree that somehow the fact of its obviousness means that we should ignore it. As for posthumanists, they present some interesting perspectives on the interconnectivity of humans with the nonhuman world we inhabit. However, for me, their greatest contribution is to trouble the prevailing notion of self that has been comfortable within the Christian-humanist mindset for all too long. That said, I don't agree with the approach taken by most posthumanists, which ultimately boils down to an expansion of, adaptation of, or improvement upon the humanist ideals.

For my part, I turn to a completely alternative understanding of the self, that proposed by Buddhism, which, I will argue, presents not some kind of proto-posthumanist perspective, nor even an antihumanist one. Rather, it presents a different, albeit entirely coherent, perspective on human nature and the self that is perfectly reflected in zombie fiction. Not only is the zombie first and foremost about death, but, I argue, the existential crisis present in zombie apocalyptic fiction brings to the fore the central problem of humanity's search for meaning in life, especially in an increasingly global, secular world. In fact, all of the other interpretations offered can be seen as subsets of the existential quest for meaning that persists alongside the fear of death—terrorism, disease, and war are closest to driving home this fear; and then there are questions of how we should live our lives, and from what we should derive meaning. For example, is consumer culture desirable when you can't take any of it with you when you die?

As to the posthuman concern for the inclusion of nonhuman persons into our thinking, we can also look in the other direction and wonder at whether the underpinnings of our conception of personhood itself might not be wrong. By extending that which makes humans special to nonhumans, we still maintain the conceit that there *is* something special about humans. Scarier to contemplate, and closer to the existential angst of impending mortality, is the possibility that it isn't the problem that others are like us but that we are each individually like those others instead.

In this book, I will argue that the zombie's connection to death is paramount, and that Buddhist philosophy can allow us to consume zombie fiction in a way that can help us overcome existential angst and the fear of dying. Christian critics and scholars have looked for signs of their faith in film for some time, and Kim Paffenroth did a great job of placing the zombie into a Catholic framework in his *Gospel of the Living Dead*.[3] His work infers the place of God in the genre by remarking on God's absence from the zombie apocalypse. Comparing zombie fiction to Dante's *Inferno*, Paffenroth argues that the horror of the resurrected zombie equates directly to the absence of God just as a Catholic might describe Hell as a state of complete separation from God. The fact that God remains absent from the genre is actually critical to my understanding of it as well, especially in terms of contemplation of death, dying, and beyond. Rather than assuming the importance of the thing that is not there, however, the *absence* of God in this genre is essential to indicating the importance of those aspects that *are* present. A strong ambivalence to Christianity is present in the zombie from its Haitian origins, providing one of the clearest and yet least recognized bridges between the original zombie and its modern incarnation. I argue that the perverse, God-less resurrection depicted by zombies be understood not as a reflection of Catholic ideology but, rather, a rejection and a mockery of it.

Moreover, the zombie is not simply a representation of Buddhist ideas; I also argue that partaking of zombie fiction can become a form of meditation on death itself. By understanding the elements of Buddhism inherent in the zombie, audiences might take in zombie fiction as a lesson in Buddhist thought on mortality and the state of the person, thereby overcoming some existential angst and becoming a more compassionate and less selfish person in the process. For those who are willing and able, this presents a testable hypothesis as well. Perhaps some scholar so inclined can put my argument to the test—might watching zombie fiction after having been educated on the Buddhist elements of the zombie lower the audience members' fear and anxiety of death?

Why Zombies?

The walking dead have been shambling through the folklores of the world since time immemorial. Ghostly apparitions haunt spooky houses, ghouls skulk about dark cemeteries, mummies creak forth from dusty sarcophagi, skeleton armies rise up from the dust, and vampires now charm teenage girls. The zombie, however, has recently enjoyed a tremendous surge in popularity, rivaling, and at times surpassing, that of the vampire.

We are currently in the midst of a veritable zombie-craze now spanning almost two decades. Zombies can be found in every form of media from "high art" to pop culture. AMC's television series, *The Walking Dead*, based on an ongoing comic book, has become the highest rated basic cable drama among adults aged 18–49 in history.[4] Zombies are ever-present, infecting both the big and small screens, appearing in everything from video games and board games to literature and comic books. There are philosophical zombies, zombie computers possessed by hackers, zombie cocktails, zombie pot, zombie litigation, myriad "zombie categories,"[5] and zombie walks in which major cities across North America have seen sometimes hundreds of people dress as the risen dead and march (or lurch) en masse in gruesome flash-mobs, sometimes with political agendas but often just for fun. There have even been emergency-preparedness drills organized around the idea of a zombie apocalypse. And, of course, there are zombie films of every stripe imaginable, the outpouring of which since 2000 surpasses the volume of zombie films from all of the previous decades combined![6]

While some scholars have long maintained an interest in horror and the undead, it is only within the last decade and a half that a significant number of academics have begun to keep pace with the extraordinary public interest in horror, the undead, and in zombies in particular. Even with the long-standing bias against the academic study of pop culture as low-art, horror has received special disregard, and of all that appears in horror, zombies especially have been the victims of scholarly scorn and disdain. It appears that this tide is only now turning—perhaps the newest generation of scholars is not as afraid of the dark as those before?

I myself have been asked numerous times to explain just why zombies are so popular today.[7] As will be shown throughout this book, the equation of zombies with death is paramount. It seems more than coincidence that the current zombie craze has developed at a time when cultural secularization has encountered significant threats, including the events of 9/11 and the aging population of baby boomers. Many sources for fear have been linked to the zombie, but at the root of all of these are an existential dread brought on by death anxiety. Buddhism offers a solid yet unrealized means of understanding and coping with this fear as expressed in the metaphor presented by zombies, a metaphor that has captured the attention of wide swaths of the world's population through a variety of popular media.

Zombie Scholarship

When Gilles Deleuze and Felix Guattari went so far as to proclaim that "[t]he only modern myth is the myth of zombies,"[8] they were speaking within a particular philosophical perspective, but one that resonates, at least in part, with my own approach to the zombie. For one thing, building upon Freud's conception of a "death drive," that irrational aspect supposed in humans to account for acts against one's own best interests, Deleuze and Guattari recognized in the modern zombie the dichotomous tension between living and dying.[9] Deleuze and Guattari move to collapse the Freudian opposites of Eros and Thanatos, the procreative sex-drive and self-destructive death-drive. In their presentation of the concept of rhizome, the philosophers further collapse dualistic distinctions between one and other.

In *A Thousand Plateaus*, they propose a contrast between a solitary tree and its system of roots to a rhizome, a rootstalk that spreads underground to foster an array of interconnected sprouts.[10] Bamboo is an excellent example: a bamboo grove, while appearing from above ground to be a forest of individual stalks, is a single plant connected underground by the vast, interconnected system of rhizomes: "The rhizome is reducible neither to the One nor the multiple. It is not the One that becomes Two or even directly three, four, five, etc. [...] It is composed not of units but of dimensions, or rather directions in motion. It has neither beginning nor end, but always a middle (milieu) from which it grows and which it overspills."[11] Here, the two offer a perspective that will resonate with Buddhist thought in the latter's focus on the "Middle Path," a perspective contrasting common-sense perceptions of time with an emphasis on the present moment, which, when you consider it, is an ever-changing beginning and ending that occurs simultaneously while also remaining eternally present.[12] As one scholar has noted, "Viewed from the Buddhist perspective of the formation of things, material and mental, the rhizomatic conception assemblage is very similar to the Buddha's assertion that all things are comprised by the Five Aggregates."[13] That Deleuze and Guattari both recognized the centrality of the zombie to modern experience while simultaneously extruding Buddhist connections reflects the importance of the present study. The links between Buddhist thought, existential philosophy, and the zombie have simmered below the surface long enough.

Scholars have engaged with the image of the walking dead, whether of the Haitian-slave or the Romero-flesh-eating variety, from a wide range of fields and perspectives, arriving at myriad conclusions as to its meaning.

As Romero himself explained: "I always see the zombies as an external force [....] The story is happening around them and nobody is paying attention [....] There is some major shit going on out there, and in a distant way the zombies represent what we, the global community, should really be thinking about."[14] Just what it is that we should really be thinking about has changed from critic to critic over time. Ultimately, though, whatever problems there are in the world, whatever major shit is going on out there, Buddhism begins with the observation that our reactions to the world are entirely within our own control. The search for answers to the world's problems begins with an inward mindfulness aimed at changing perspective and behavior in the light of genuine truths about the human condition that are so often ignored by the vast majority of us in our day-to-day lives. Romero's *intention* to make people pay attention is on track, though even he is likely not entirely aware of the truths to which his works point. His films are like the finger pointing at the moon, and I aim in this book to help viewers distinguish the finger from the moon and learn a little bit about Buddhist philosophy in the process. Or, to return to Deleuze and Guattari, the various zombie-interpretations that have been offered are like the plants above the surface whose hidden rhizome links them all below—and that rhizome is mortality itself, the fact of death that is too often denied.

Noël Carroll, while skeptical of the widespread use of psychoanalytic theory, argues that horror generally seems to be an ideal place for just such interpretation. The act of willingly allowing oneself to be frightened, to him, presents a paradox, which might be resolved in seeing the act in a therapeutic light. As he puts it, "the horror film may release some part of the tensions that would otherwise eruct in nightmares. Perhaps we can say that [...] horror film fans go to the movies (in the afternoon) perchance to sleep (at night)."[15] In resolving the "paradox," Carroll points to the facts that the object of terror is not the depicted object itself, but rather the *thought* of that object; the audience is guided to react sympathetically to the characters in the film, to the point of shared physical responses (like screaming, shivering, or reacting in disgust). In some way, then, real anxieties are overcome by affecting physical (real) reactions to fictive horrors developed around horrible ideas. A real mental anxiety is fictionalized in horror, the fiction then affecting a real physical response from which the audience emerges unscathed, thereby releasing the audience from the preexisting anxiety.[16]

Cultural anxieties might be understood and, more importantly, "domesticated," to borrow Jeffrey Cohen's term.[17] In attempting to thus understand and domesticate anxiety, Eugene Thacker suggests that horror is not only open to philosophical analysis, but that horror is itself a kind of philosophical introspection: "'horror' is a non-philosophical attempt to think about the world-without-us philosophically."[18] Horror does important work, then, in providing a venue for the display of society's deepest fears, and allowing audiences to experience those fears as if real, but to then walk away unharmed. From horror, then, we should be able to draw a picture of the deepest fears of society; but, if these thinkers are correct, we should also have the means by which society might overcome these fears.

As to what the specific fears might be, there has been a wide range of suggestions. Many focus on slippages of normativity—intrusions of the Other into otherwise normative bourgeois life. For some, like Robin Wood, horror often serves as a conservative element in society, helping to maintain social norms.[19] In so-called "reactionary horror," the monstrous Other threatens, but is ultimately destroyed, with order restored. Through the 1970s, though, many horror films implemented a shock ending where the monster turns out not to have been vanquished after all (the ceaseless series of slasher sequels like *Friday the 13th*, *Nightmare on Elm Street*, or *Halloween*). Still, a great deal of horror can be seen to stand in the reactionary mold: monsters threatening the status quo, but being ultimately, even if only temporarily, vanquished and the normative order restored. Wood describes a minority of horror fiction as "revolutionary horror," in which the monstrous Other appears not only to live to threaten another day, but to actually win. The normative order (our current heteronormative, patriarchal, capitalist order) is threatened, but the monstrous Other is not destroyed and the normative structure is not restored, requiring a new world order to replace it. Examples of such cinema are few, but zombie fiction is a bastion of revolutionary horror. The genre often presents an apocalyptic scenario in which there is no restoration of the social order as the zombie horde slowly grows to consume everyone in its path. So, if the zombie is Other, zombie fiction, especially in Romero's iterations, provides a revolutionary turn wherein only protectors of a dying normativity feel horror where the growing masses of disaffected social Others take over. Herein, presumably, lies the zombie's popularity as witnessed in such spectacles as the massive Zombie Walks organized worldwide.

But there is more to the zombie than that. In this book, I do not hold simply to the zombie-as-Other interpretation that allows for myriad interpretations according to a given critic's preference of Otherness. I acknowledge that the zombie does fulfill this role, but so do a lot of other horrors.

I intend to get to the root meanings of the zombie specifically, differentiating it from other objects of analysis. Most important to my understanding of the zombie are its defining characteristics: it lacks agency; it blurs the boundary between life and death as a risen corpse; all humans are eligible to join their ranks and, in the modern iteration, inevitably will; and they are associated with cannibalism and animalistic drives. There are also important specific elements of the zombie's socio-cultural contexts, both in its origins in Haiti and its modern rebirth in the 1960s. Racial histories of slavery and ongoing social inequality, combined with the increased concentration of wealth among the richest all encourage questions of agency. Colonialism and dog-eat-dog capitalism both resonate with notions of cannibalism. The religious implications of a perverted resurrection stemming from anti–Christian and anti-establishment sentiments in the zombie's Haitian origins force further discussion of eschatological questions.

Defining the Zombie

Given the widespread popularity of the zombie today, it may seem as though everyone agrees on just what a zombie is, but this is far from certain. Before going any further, I must first establish the ground for what exactly we are talking about when we talk about a zombie.

In its most basic form, the zombie is a walking corpse, but that is not all that it is. Many have begun to use the term "zombie" to describe any corpse rising from the grave, most recently evidenced in popular discussion of archaeological discoveries of ancient Greek burials indicating corpses weighted down as if to prevent their returning from the grave. The "zombie," though, did not exist in ancient Greece, per se. Not all walking corpses are zombies. It may seem a trivial distinction, but it is critical to a full understanding of not just the history of the zombie, but of what it signifies for modern audiences. Vampires or mummies, for instance, are recognizably different from zombies, even to modern audiences, though all are technically walking corpses. And given popular discourse, such as that about the ancient Greek burials, there is no doubt that if Egyptian mummies were only discovered today, people would be calling them zombies, too. So, I must outline what differentiates a zombie from all of these other revenants before moving on.

Firstly, the term itself can be traced most directly to Haiti, and from there to Africa. In its African forms, zombies were identified as deceased spirits made into slaves by powerful magicians. Often, such ethereal zombies would be held captive in seemingly empty bottles, echoing tales of genies in lamps, the possessor of which could manipulate the imprisoned soul to perform magical duties. With the African slave trade's Haitian hub, the concept of the enslaved zombie took on more immediate, physical reality. In this light, magicians would still capture the soul of a dead person, but would animate the corpse to perform manual labor for financial gain. I will say more on this in the next chapter, but for now it is essential to realize that the core aspects of the zombie from its origins are not only that of a walking corpse, but of that corpse's lack of free will, the body being bound to mindless servitude to an evil master bent on riches.

The modern perspective on zombies was radically altered with George A. Romero's 1968 revolutionary horror film, *Night of the Living Dead*. For Romero's part, he was not making a zombie film. The creatures in *Night* are risen corpses, but they have no known cause for their resurrection, and do not obey any intentional master. The film never uses the term "zombie," and Romero himself has expressed surprise at critics and audiences later responding to the monsters by identifying them as such. So, it was not Romero's intention to portray zombies, or to reinvent the zombie genre. In fact, his film is broadly adapted from Richard Matheson's vampire novel, *I Am Legend*! Audiences familiar with the Haitian zombie, as well as other walking corpses like mummies and vampires, saw Romero's monsters as zombies, and this identification has stuck ever since.

Romero's creatures remain risen corpses, though the reason for their reanimation is unclear. *Night* suggests radiation from a Venus probe returned to Earth; later films offer a range of possibilities including (but not limited to) Voodoo (*Dawn of the Dead*), to God's wrath (*Day of the Dead*), to chemical-laced rain (*Return of the Living Dead*), and eventually a virus (*28 Days Later*). What is clear in these films is that there is no magician directing the dead. Instead, the new zombies are driven by a single-minded desire to consume living human flesh (the *Return* franchise is responsible for the specific desire for brains). Again, usually no reasons are given for this particular desire; *Day of the Dead*, for instance, includes scientific experiments that illustrate that the zombies will continue to eat even when their stomachs are removed and the flesh simply falls to the floor upon consumption. *Return* offers the explanation that being dead is tremendously painful and that eating brains allows for brief respite from the constant suffering, but it is Romero's "rules" that have defined the genre much more clearly.

The risen dead are also generally depicted as continuing to rot even as they act, allowing for increasingly gory special effects. The zombie's key weakness is in its brain, a shot to the head being the advised means of destruction. Fire works, too.

No zombies had ever been depicted as devouring human flesh before *Night*, so there must be something else about them that encouraged audiences to identify them as zombies. My sense is that it is the mindlessness of them that is the key, since this was a defining characteristic of the Haitian zombie with which people were familiar. Vampires have long been depicted as thinking agents, and the Mummy, though less vocal, has a clear motive for revenge in mind. Zombies, then, were and remain unique in lacking any individual will, motivation, or agency. Romero made his creatures eat human flesh, but if these creatures are zombies, then he also removed the slave-master as a source of evil. In its place, Romero planted only an irresistible drive to consume, and to consume without pleasure or satisfaction, and specifically to consume living (mainly) human flesh. These are the core characteristics that have defined the zombie. Many who use the term apply it metaphorically according to some combination of these characteristics—mindlessness; servitude to another; risen corpses; the eating of human flesh or brains; or endless consumption more generally. I argue that we cannot fully understand the zombie without taking all characteristics into account.

Consciousness and the P-Zombie

The problem of consciousness remains unresolved after thousands of years of philosophical energy spent on the subject. The materialism of modern scientific inquiry eliminates the possibility of a non-physical mind, relegating personal consciousness to epiphenomena of the human brain; essentially, however much we may feel as if we think or however well we can imagine leaving our bodies and existing in some non-physical state, scientifically speaking the only reality is one's brain, and without that we are lost. That we don't *feel* like we are a brain is simply how the brain works. Some philosophers maintain a dualist position arguing that there is a distinction between the immaterial mind, or perhaps soul, and the physical body.

Though the notion of unconscious automata has been around since at least Descartes, it is philosophers Robert Kirk (not to be confused with Robert Kirkman, creator of *The Walking Dead*)[20] and David Chalmers who have made the most effective use of the "zombie" as a creature that is completely identical to a human being in every way—in action, physiology, neurology, memory—except that it lacks consciousness.[21] What should be obvious immediately to any fan of zombie fiction is that what is being described by the philosophers of mind sounds nothing like the Romero-inspired undead, and bears little resemblance to even the Haitian zombie, which is immediately recognizable by its dull eyes, slow gait, and dim mind.[22]

Rather, a closer analog lies in the alien pod-people of *Invasion of the Body Snatchers* (1956; 1978; also remade as *Body Snatchers* [1993] and *The Invasion* [2007]). Association is sometimes made between zombies and the pod-people, probably due to the latter's loss of humanity and an assumed lack of individual will in favor of a collective motivation. Each of these films finds its horror in the notion that an alien life form is capable of replacing a human being by imitating us in every way except that they lack some crucial emotional element that marks them as distinctly unhuman. Chalmers distinguishes between the Hollywood zombie and what might better be labeled a pod-person by describing the former as "psychological zombies" and the latter as "phenomenal zombies."[23]

The phenomenal zombie, also called "p-zombie" or "philosophical zombie," offers us the conception of a complete physical replica of a human being but lacking consciousness, or experience. They are functionally identical in every way, but they do not experience the world as conscious beings. The crux of the argument comes down to assuming that since there is no logical error in the conception of a being that is physically identical to one's self, except for its lacking consciousness, and since one knows one's self to be conscious, then physical identity does not equate to consciousness. Dennett, in an effort to show the fruitlessness of such a thought experiment, uses a form of *reduction ad absurdum* in showing how we might conceive of a creature, which he calls a "zimbo," that is identical to us in every way, including displaying what *appears* to be conscious; if such a being is conceivable, then how can one know whether one is conscious or simply behaving as if conscious—and what would be the difference?[24] Though the p-zombie has found itself at the center of raging debate, it rests on one important assumption; as Chalmers himself states: "In the real world, it is likely that any replica of me would be conscious."[25] Of course, in the "real world" there are no such replicas to begin with, but Chalmers indicates that for a replica to be a true replica it would need to be exactly the same in every way, so that it really makes little sense to distinguish the replica from the original.

Epiphenomenalism, on the other hand, is the term used to describe the sense of consciousness as arising directly from activities of the brain, thereby making what seems to be the dualism of body and mind or spirit a mere illusion caused by physical activity. Basically, the suggestion goes, our sense of having a mind, of consciousness, is explained by the effect of the brain's activity. We don't feel like a brain working, but instead feel like a person thinking. The hard materialist view explains, though, that a brain working simply feels like a person thinking so there is no difference between the two and so no need to imagine that there really is a mind or spirit as conscious entity.

However this debate may work itself out, the use of the p-zombie seems to be fatally flawed by the fact that one is simply assuming a being that behaves as if conscious but is not. Such a being, one would expect, would similarly behave as if it had experiences, and how can one know whether another being actually has consciousness or simply behaves as if it has consciousness? And then, how can I know whether I have consciousness or whether I simply think I do? Here I agree with Daniel Dennett that "the literal truth about the mechanisms responsible for all the sworls and eddies in the stream [of consciousness], as well as the informational contents of the items passing by, is—*ex hypothesi*—utterly unaffected by whether or not the stream is conscious or unconscious."[26]

Cartesian dualism is founded on the observation *cogito ergo sum*, that while my senses may sometimes lead me astray about the nature of the material world, I think therefore I know that I am. Ambrose Bierce wryly turned the axiom on its head in a manner that is impossible to contravene in "improving" it to state: *cogito cogito ergo cogito sum*: I think that I think, therefore I think that I am.[27] And here we may come full circle to a Buddhist perspective on the self, and one that I will explain in more detail in chapter four. Essentially, the Buddha, in recognizing that all things, including selves, are changing all the time, from moment to moment, argued that the notion of a permanently ongoing self was an untenable illusion. Unlike the current epiphenomenalists, though, the Buddha also held that the material world was similarly illusory in its seeming permanence. He conceded that consciousness obviously occurred, since this is empirically observable in every waking experience, but an entirely new and different perspective on self-hood was necessary in order to understand the nature and place of this ever-changing, non-localized consciousness.

In traditional and Hollywood zombies, the absence of agency is sometimes also seen as a hallmark of their horror. Peter Dendle, for instance, suggests that "supplanted, stolen, or effaced consciousness" is the "essence of the 'zombie' at the most abstract level," and that the absence of consciousness is the "logical conclusion of human reductionism."[28] Kevin Boon agrees, arguing that the absence of consciousness "is more central to the zombie than death," and that "[i]f this were not the case, we might rightly refer to the stories of Lazarus and Jesus as zombie tales,"[29] given that both Lazarus and Jesus returned from death while retaining their essential agency. Kyle Bishop, approaching the topic from the view of the living characters in a zombie film, argues that the battle against the zombies can be seen as "humanity's struggle to retain its sense of humanity."[30] Of course, this last view of zombies ignores filmic attempts to imbue the zombie with empathy going all the way back to Romero's *Day of the Dead* (1985) and Dan O'Bannon's *Return of the Living Dead* (1985), both of which include zombies that express at least rudimentary emotional response to situations. Agency and the capacity to exercise one's will are often seen as important definers of living a quality human life.

Conflicts between family members and physicians often arise over the vitality of patients in a state of brain-death or irreversible coma, a definition of death which itself was introduced in 1968, the same year that the first modern zombie film, Romero's classic *Night of the Living Dead*, was released.[31] With an increasingly aging population, dementia is a more prevalent possibility in the lives of many. As Susan Behuniak laments of the treatment received by victims of Alzheimer's disease: "The slow shuffle, the inarticulate moans, the relentless walking, the disheveled appearance, and references made to the coming of the 'grey hordes' as the baby-boom generation ages make it easy to apply zombie descriptors to real people."[32] While Behuniak, and surely many others,[33] would have dementia patients treated with the respect any person deserves, their condition strikes at the heart of intuitions about what it means to be human.

Craig Derksen and Darren Hudson Hick speak of the fear, often expressed in zombie fiction, of becoming a zombie. This fear, they argue, is unfounded unless one assumes that the zombie is, in fact, still you, for if the zombie is not you, then there really is nothing to fear in terms of personal harm except for the extinction of the self, which would remain the same fear regardless of anything that might occur to your corpse after death.[34] The possibility of remaining you after the zombified resurrection of the corpse, though, they also recognize as a substantial fear, and one that echoes prominently with the very real concerns of Behuniak and many others:

> Whether you are "locked in" the zombie, a passive observer without any control over the body, or whether you retain some but not all of your memories and personality, it seems you have survived to at least some degree, and so you are being harmed. You

have become the locus of your own fears. Worse still, you have become the object of horror—a thing categorically both like and unlike you, a horror you cannot escape.[35]

What Lies Ahead

Since its origin in Haiti, the zombie has been a source of both fear and pity. Having been a hub of the slave trade, the real fear incorporated by the zombie is that of being enslaved, of returning to slavery. The fear of a loss of agency is central to the zombie concept, an especially terrifying possibility for individualistic Westerners accustomed to holding independence and self-reliance among the most crucial of values. The conflation of zombies with pod-people, mentioned above, highlights this crucial feature.

From the perspective of the slave-owner, however, and from the perspective of colonialist power, it is the slave itself which is feared—a fear which is all the more palpable coming from Haiti, the site of the most significant slave-revolt and establishment of the first independent black state in the New World. Becoming a slave is to lose one's agency, sense of self, and one's humanity. This loss is one akin to death, or perhaps a fate even worse than death in becoming a conscious object forced to witness one's own loss of humanity. The fear of the slave, though, is one that recognizes the consciousness within and the revenge that must be in the heart of that person who has had their personhood, their very life, denied. This dichotomous fear of slavery and the slave lies at the root of all of the anti-consumerist, anti-capitalist, anti-colonialist, Marxist, and feminist interpretations that have been made of the zombie. The one who lords power and privilege over another, debasing and dehumanizing them through denying the full expression of their agency must be afraid both of seeing the tables turned and having their own power to express agency revoked and also of the vengeance of those whom they have for so long oppressed.

In chapter one, I will develop the course of the zombie beginning with its origins in the unique history of Haitian folklore. Among the core characteristics that remain relevant to our modern understanding of the zombie but that are Haitian in origin are, of course, the liminal qualities of their lack of agency and slavish obeisance to some higher authority and that they are risen from the grave. I will outline some important historical elements of Haiti from its discovery by Europeans, to the ensuing encounters with native populations, to the slave trade that would come to dominate the island for some centuries.

More important, though less understood by many today, are the significant religious elements relating to Vodou and its relationship to both African spirituality and Catholicism. Vodou is often described as a syncretic religion, a synthesis of Catholicism and African spirituality. I will argue that the relationship between these two traditions has been strained at best, and that the zombie legend itself embodies many elements that can be seen as direct parodies of Catholicism or, at least, reflect resistance to some of the Christian beliefs that had been forced upon the slave population. These elements are echoed not only in the racial themes present in modern zombie fiction, but also in anti-establishment ideals and the presence of a dystopic apocalypse that presents a dark mirror image of that expected by Christianity.

In this chapter, I will also take some time to discuss the specific issue of cannibalism, a taboo that has a long and twisted history as a label by which groups de-humanize others. The earliest inhabitants of Haiti believed Columbus to be a potential cannibal, a term that was then later applied by Columbus and other European explorers to the inhabitants of the Caribbean themselves as an argument for their primitive state necessitating religious salvation and civilization through enslavement. The Haitian zombie tradition incorporates cannibalistic elements as a dark reflection of the Catholic communion—the ingestion of the transubstantiated flesh and blood of the resurrected Christ is contrasted with beliefs about the dangers of accidentally consuming zombie flesh. The modern zombie takes the concept to yet another level in moving the flesh eating to the zombies themselves.

I will then end with some reference to modern Haiti and its perspective on the ongoing popularity of the zombie myth. Though Hollywood has done much to distort the Haitian Vodou religion, some of the elements of modern depictions of both "Voodoo" and the zombie have been incorporated into modern Haitian legends, illustrating the continuing impact of colonial powers on Haiti, the resilience and adaptability of the Haitian people, and the changeability of the zombie in differing contexts.

Chapter two will trace the evolution of the zombie as it moved from Haiti to North-American popular culture in the nineteenth, twentieth, and early twenty-first centuries. From Bela Lugosi's turn as a capitalist sorcerer named Murder Legendre in 1932's *White Zombie* to the modern zombie of Romero's *Night of the Living Dead* and beyond, the monstrousness of the zombie for (White) America cannot be fully appreciated without reference to the strained political relationship of America to Haiti and its former slave population. Racism and a real fear of the Other are prominent in the earliest appearances of the zombie on American shores and helped to shape the zombie into what it has become, adopting aspects of its Haitian origins and then adapting them to American circumstances. The zombie has continued to relate to a racist power dynamic that dehumanizes expanding circles of people by denying the power to exercise one's agency.

Film scholar Richard Dyer describes all horror racially as a predominantly "White" genre.[36] Emphasizing the distinctions between black and white characters in horror films generally, he concludes that blacks represent a primitive form of life, whereas Whites stand in for death in the sense that they hold the power of life and death.[37] Dyer echoes the importance of theories of bio-politics—the power dynamic between the state and the various individual and collective bodies within it—arising from such luminaries as Hannah Arendt,[38] Michel Foucault,[39] and Giorgio Agamben.[40] Reading zombies through the lens of bio-politics has been widespread. Haitian poet René Despestre likens colonialism to a generalized "zombification" of humanity, marking Haiti as the eye of the storm.[41] Extending beyond an identification of zombies with the monster's African roots, the zombie has become a vessel in which any number of Others might be housed. Still, the zombie's roots in Haiti remain central to discussions of the modern zombie. Critics have argued that the zombie stands in for a range of displaced people echoing modern American anxieties: refugees as interstitial beings feared for their implied need to consume without contributing to society[42]; post-9/11 fears of the threat of domestic terrorism[43]; or the horror of genocide and dangerous power fantasies.[44] Ian Olney goes further in suggesting that European horror has been much more explicit in tackling racial victimization, and that it is this political reason, and not the excess gore and violence normally pointed to, which has resulted in the banning of zombie fiction in Europe (i.e., the anti-consumerist *Dawn of the Dead* [1978] was originally banned in France; anti-colonialist *Zombi 2* [1979] was available only illegally in England).[45]

The modern iteration, as contrived by Romero's *Night of the Living Dead*, changes the nature of the monster while maintaining the emphasis on its roots in starring an African American lead who winds up being mistaken for a zombie and killed by an all-white country posse. That the film was released in 1968, the very year of Martin Luther King, Jr.'s, assassination, brings further gravitas to the racial politics apparent in *Night*. Though Romero has always maintained that the main character was not scripted as either black or white, the casting of African-American Duane Jones made analyses of the film in terms of racial politics unavoidable.

Despite almost five decades having passed since *Night*'s release, the film, and the zombie it rejuvenated, continue to resonate in terms of ongoing racial politics. Elizabeth McAlister, for instance, argues that Barack Obama sits in a similar position to that of *Night*'s protagonist as a lone black man under siege by an army of old, conservative, white men.[46] Conservatives continue to use the zombie myth to cast racial aspersions, as with Jason Mattera's screed, *Obama Zombies: How the Liberal Machine Brainwashed My Generation*.[47]

Moving through the history of the evolving zombie through the decades, I will also take some time to discuss the critical role of Richard Matheson's *I Am Legend* in the development of the modern zombie myth. Matheson's novel, a vampire tale of cultural revolution, marks a radical shift in the portrayal of vampires, but one whose impact has been felt much more prominently on the innovations of the zombie genre than on that of vampires. George Romero's *Night* is admittedly an homage to, if not a direct adaptation of, Matheson's vampire story, and differs remarkably, and importantly, from what were supposed to have been direct film adaptations of *I Am Legend*. The differences between Romero and the Hollywood adaptations are striking for their religious implications, again contrasting traditional Christian expectations with alternative and Eastern spiritualities. Matheson himself was deeply interested in New Age and Theosophical ideas, and routinely included his spirituality in his writing. Matheson's influence on Romero included anti-establishment and non–Christian moral and spiritual elements that also echo those of the Haitian zombie such that audiences recognized Romero's monsters as zombies despite his own contention that they were something else.

Before discussing Romero and his films in some detail, I will also spend some time on the importance of the comic book industry in the evolution of the zombie. As an alternative visual medium, and often one derided as particularly low art, the increasingly gory aspects of the zombie found a home within the pages of such comics as *Tales from the Crypt* and others that would further inspire Romero and later filmmakers. Readers could take their time viewing and re-viewing the gory details depicted in the pages of horror comics in a way that would allow for much more in-depth contemplation than was ever possible in film before the advent of home video.

Moving through several decades of zombie fiction in film, literature, and comic book form, we will see the influences on George A. Romero, whose work has essentially defined the modern zombie. *Night of the Living Dead* changed the horror genre completely and ushered in an entirely new genre of zombie horror. The film's impact continues to be felt even today. The zombie, embodying as it does ideas of slavery, racism, oppression, and anti-authoritarianism, was the perfect monster for the 1960s' counterculture. A socially conscious fight for egalitarian access to the power to exert one's agency resonates throughout the history of the zombie myth. That Romero drew heavily upon Matheson's Theosophically-informed vision of the walking dead must be further examined in the context of the 60s' New Age as well. Romero rejected his own Catholic upbringing just as the Haitian zombie can be seen to reflect a rejection of core Catholic teachings. Matheson's revolutionary spiritual ideals meshed well with those of the 1960s, too. From here, all of the characteristics that would be recognizable as a zombie then, and now, will come together to demonstrate a complex creature incorporating existential and religious themes at the heart of human understanding.

With chapter three, I will switch gears and move into a much more in-depth exploration of the religious and existential elements of the zombie, especially in terms of reflections on mortality and the nature of the human body throughout history. Having argued in chapter one for the tense relationship between Vodou and Catholicism resulting from Haiti's history, I will turn here to addressing specifically Christian interpretations of the zombie. Kim Paffenroth is key among those scholars analyzing zombie fiction from this angle, and his work deserves special attention. His interpretations of zombie fiction present a Catholic apologetic that is both interesting and useful in many ways. I will argue, though, that the genre itself works against a Catholic message since its Haitian origins, and suggest alternative approaches, especially that of Buddhist existential philosophy.

Extending beyond Christian analyses of zombies, I will then discuss the tradition of *memento mori*, the remembrance of one's own mortality. It is obvious that the zombie can be seen as a reflection of this same tendency, the rotting corpses easily associated with medieval depictions of Death running rampant. Attitudes to the body express a disgust that is echoed in depictions of the modern zombie. Again, I will develop the connections while also pointing to discrepancies with ideas that are present in the zombie tradition that may not sit so easily in a strictly Christian interpretation of the genre.

Moving into more detailed examinations, so-called "body horror" in which human bodies are ignobly rent and destroyed in a variety of imaginative ways will take us into more secular perspectives on *memento mori*. David Cronenberg is often seen as a champion of body horror and sometimes called a misanthrope because of his treatment of bodies, but I will show how his work effectively enacts a forced remembrance of human frailty and mortality that can have positive outcomes for viewers. Cronenberg only references zombies in perhaps one of his films, but I will explore his work more broadly because the themes appearing in his treatment of bodies reflect that of zombie fiction, while his work has received a great deal of scholarly and critical attention that will be usefully applied to the zombie genre as well. Cronenberg, who expresses inspiration from the likes of Wittgenstein and Nietzsche, leads us into modern existential discussions of human mortality. Responding to Cronenberg, then, I will also engage with various theorists, as well as with existential thinkers like Albert Camus and Martin Heidegger. Thinkers such as these point to the need to reconcile oneself with one's mortality, but they do not offer guidelines beyond an individualistic search for personal meaning. Heidegger, at least, inspired as he was by some Buddhist philosophy, offers an indication of where we might seek just such guidelines.

At this point, we will reach the climax of my argument in presenting an alternative spiritual interpretation of the zombie using Buddhist philosophy to address the existential crises elicited by zombies. Chapter four will move into the relationship between the zombie and Buddhism. I will begin with an explanation of some core Buddhist conceptions, especially as these relate to general Buddhist views of life and death, living and dying. I will then discuss a number of meditative practices directed towards the recognition of personal mortality, akin to the Christian *memento mori* discussed earlier. Many of these practices will appear odd to non–Buddhists unfamiliar with them, but I will illustrate throughout just how the modern zombie might relate precisely to these kinds of rituals.

In fact, I will then move into a detailed discussion of how the zombie can be seen to reflect Buddhist precepts. Christian interpretations of the zombie fail for a variety of reasons, including the perversion of the resurrection that they represent, the absence of God required in zombie fiction, and the alternative spiritual roots of the zombie tradition from Haiti to Matheson and Romero. On the other hand, core Buddhist concepts such as *samsara* (that is, the cycle of birth, death), *anatta* (the concept of not-self as opposed to our common sense of permanent self), suffering, attachment, and others, all appear in the figures of both zombies and survivors. Here I will make reference directly to specific films in order to illustrate my points.

Finally, I will then discuss the possibilities that understanding the zombie in light of Buddhist teachings might provide audiences. I suggest that viewers might engage with zombie fiction as a form of meditation on death, which is itself a meditation on the truth of the human condition and the existential quest for meaning in life. Fiction can be used effectively as a teaching aid. Christian theological perspectives on and interpretations of film have been popular areas for scholarship for decades, while Buddhist scholars have only recently begun to engage with film in the same way.

Ultimately, by bringing a Buddhist light to bear upon the zombie, I hope to demonstrate how this creature and its popularity ought to be seen alongside the growing acceptance of Eastern spirituality, and Buddhist philosophy especially, which exploded in the counter-cultural movement of the 1960s and, I argue, continues today. By thus understanding the zombie genre, I hope that audiences might take a new appreciation into their enjoyment of it, and allow themselves to gaze into the existential darkness of human mortality and accept it as a real part of ourselves rather than casting it away as a threatening, abject Other. In this way, we might all learn to get over ourselves, become less selfish and have more compassion for others.

CHAPTER ONE

The Haitian Origins of the Zombie

Regardless of whether modern zombie fans have any knowledge of Haiti or Vodou or the origins of the zombie in African folklore, the fact remains that those who recognized George Romero's creatures in 1968 as zombies saw their similarity to the Haitian monster, the one with which they were *already* familiar. If modern zombies are identified for their similarity to Romero's creation, and Romero's creatures were identified as zombies for their similarity to the Haitian monster, then those historical roots remain relevant today. To understand that relevance, we must understand those roots, which are deep in the soil of Haiti and stretch back to Africa. Fed by the slave trade, and watered by the syncretism of African tradition and Catholic iconography, the zombie emerged as a creature embodying a range of anxieties.

History

The slave trade imported a multitude of African cultures and spiritualities to the New World, with Haiti as a central hub. Haitian slaves were forced to convert to Catholicism, but they did not give up their old beliefs or practices. The fusion of African spiritualities and Catholicism became Haitian Vodou. Over the history of Hispaniola since its discovery by colonialists, the beleaguered island has experienced a great deal of turmoil,[1] and the zombie myth grows directly out of Haiti's trauma. As Alexandra

Boutros argues, a full understanding of Vodou is "contingent on knowledge of Haiti," and even non–Haitian Vodouisants become "friends of Haiti," acknowledging the complete connection between the religion of Haiti and its politics.[2]

The island of Hispaniola, of which Haiti constitutes the western third (the eastern two-thirds being today the Dominican Republic), became a Spanish colony in 1492, when it was discovered by Christopher Columbus. In fact, Columbus was forced to build a fort on the island when one of his ships, the *Santa Maria*, ran aground, thereby creating the first European settlement in the New World since the Vikings. Portentously, Columbus noted of the Taino/Arawak natives that "they must be good servants" and that "with fifty men one could keep the whole population in subjection and make them do whatever one wanted."[3] Later, Europeans would come to believe that imported slaves were even better than indigenous ones.

Though his earliest settlement was found to have burned to the ground when Columbus returned from Spain in 1493, the Spanish nonetheless followed through with the colonization of Hispaniola. The native population waged a massive yet entirely unsuccessful defensive war. They were completely over-matched by the superior Spanish military, which went on to decimate the native population in less than fifty years.[4] From the beginning of the sixteenth century, the island received African slaves to aid in the colonization process.

San Domingue, as Haiti was then named, was ceded to France in the 1697 Treaty of Ryswick. Though Spain retained the larger, eastern portion of Hispaniola, Spanish interest in the island waned in favor of colonial interests in Latin America. San Domingue soon outstripped the Spanish Santo-Domingo (which is the present-day Dominican Republic), its larger neighbor, in both wealth and population, becoming the richest and most populous European colony in the Caribbean. Over the next century, the French imported huge numbers of slaves to the island. By the time of the French Revolution a hundred years later (1789–1799), San Domingue represented roughly 40 percent of France's overall foreign trade and was home to roughly half a million slaves. This massive slave population outnumbered their French masters by a ratio of more than 10 to 1.

Once enslaved, the life expectancy of a laborer was a mere seven years after their arrival to Haiti. Slaves were treated like livestock, or worse, being compelled not only to work in their owners' fields, but also to then work further to grow their own subsistence foods. Male slaves were turned into "studs," forced to mate with selected female slaves in an attempt to breed more for their owners, presumably to ensure a constant future stock workforce eliminating the need to import across the sea.[5] The slaves were completely de-humanized. Punishment for any perceived recalcitrance was severe, as lashings were often tantamount to a death sentence. Female slaves were frequently raped and pregnant women had to work right up until the birth of the child. Miscarriages were exceptionally common. The death rate among slaves required regular new imports from Africa, which meant that slaves were able to maintain much of their African culture despite the Europeans' efforts to disperse the tribes and enforce Catholicism. The extremely abusive nature of Haitian slavery ultimately worked to keep a sense of African identity strong, acting like a forge to strengthen the bonds through fire. Shared African spirituality became a cornerstone of the coming revolution, in fact, with a Vodou priest, Dutty Boukman, said to have taken a leading role in its earliest days.

This imbalance of power could not be maintained, especially in the face of revolution in France and the more geographically proximate American Revolutionary War (1775–1783). Rebellion erupted in Haiti in 1791. It took thirteen years of conflict, but in 1804 Haiti won independence from France. Haiti then became only the second independent nation in the New World, after the United States, and its first independent black state. This massive, and successful, slave revolt struck fear into slave owners throughout the New World, and in the United States in particular, affecting American attitudes toward Haiti to this day.

Catholicism and Vodou

The relationship of the Catholic Church, and of Christianity in general, to slavery is complex. Slave-owners, in Haiti and America both, sought to convert their slaves. On the one hand, conversion might be seen as providing salvation to otherwise ignorant and lost souls. On the other hand, conversion also served the more cynical purpose of containing the potential for religious fervor and the organizational impetus that an alternative spirituality might evoke as Africans found community with one another. Patrick Bellegarde-Smith notes that "[p]erhaps the most powerful instrument of resistance, [in Haiti], was the Vodou religion. The eradication of African religious ideas had been a priority of planters throughout the Americas because the planters understood that the African religion would undermine their colonial power and authority."[6]

One important example of Christian ambivalence toward slavery appears in the person of Dominican priest Bartolomé de Las Casas, one of the most heralded voices for the humanitarian treatment of the New World natives.[7] Las Casas traveled to Hispaniola as a soldier of fortune soon after Columbus' initial explorations, procuring land as well as his own native slaves. He underwent what some call a dual conversion. His first conversion occurred shortly after his arrival in Hispaniola, when he became a priest. Years later, Las Casas expressed disdain for the poor treatment of the natives that he witnessed, and gave up his own slaves, which was a kind of second conversion (it was neither uncommon nor frowned upon for priests to own slaves). In an effort to spare the natives severe abuse, however, Las Casas, "Protector of the Indians," proposed the importation of Africans to take up the burden of forced labor. The suggestion, which he also later came to regret, was obviously favorably received, as African slaves quickly became a staple in the New World. While some have tried to extend their criticisms of Las Casas to include blame for the inception of the slave trade, the reality is that his case provides a good illustration of the ambivalent attitude of the Church to slavery and to the people of Haiti. Las Casas, venerated as an early liberation theologian, must also be condemned for ignoring the suffering of the African diaspora.[8] Of course, the Church itself condemned open criticism of slavery in the colonies, often recalling or transferring individuals who spoke out, even removing the whole order of Jesuits from Haiti when their eagerness to properly educate the slaves in Christianity cut into the number of hours slaves could work.[9] The history of the Catholic Church includes many papal pronouncements on slavery, its uses and who may or may not be taken into slavery, but it was not until the late nineteenth and early twentieth centuries that the Vatican denounced slavery outright.

The slave population of Haiti, as large as it was, was composed of a wide array of African cultures. In the face of forced dispossession, the diverse groupings found common ground in their shared African identity. This shared identity was further cemented in a response to the forceful attempts at conversion made by the Catholic Church, legislated by the so-called *Code Noir*.[10] Among rules for the treatment of slaves, the *Code Noir* mandated Catholicism as the only acceptably practiced religion in French lands. "King Louis XIII rationalized that slavery would assure that the slaves became Christians,"[11] providing as it did a literally captive audience. Of course, Catholicism had already been long-known in Africa and the largely West-African slave population had become adept at mixing and matching spiritual beliefs, incorporating some Catholic ideas into other forms of traditional African spirituality. A spiritual melting pot appears here as a range of African spiritualities were brought together in one place, some of which had already incorporated Catholic elements, and were then subjected to (attempted) forced conversion. Haitian Vodou (the preferred spelling over the negatively tagged "Voodoo," which is more readily applicable to Hollywood perversions of the religion) is the result.

The Haitian slave population largely adopted Catholicism nominally and symbolically in the interest of self-preservation, while at the same time maintaining traditions carried with them from Africa. For the most part, Catholicism remained "the religion of colonial oppression,"[12] language that is still invoked today. One early slave prayer called for "throwing away the symbol of the god of the whites (the cross)."[13] It has often been noted that Vodou spirituality was central to leading the revolt.[14] The tension between traditional spirituality and the Catholic Church is palpable in the following speech delivered by the insurrectionist leader and Vodou priest, Dutty Boukman, delivered on the eve of the successful Haitian revolution:

> Hidden God in a cloud
> is there, watching us.
> He sees all the whites do;
> the Whitegod demands crimes
> ours wants good things.
> But our God that is so good
> orders vengeance, he will
> ride us, assist us.
> Throw away the thoughts of
> the Whitegod who thirsts
> for our tears, listen to
> freedom that speaks to our hearts.[15]

Clearly, there was no love among revolutionaries for Catholic teachings. With Haiti's revolution and independence, the Catholic Church pulled its priests out of the island nation and waged a war of words against the "heathenism" of its people, and, as Patrick Bellegarde-Smith has said, "the colonial distinction between Christian and 'uncivilized' slaves became the basis for the religious discrimination against Vodou that continues today."[16] Though demonized in the world at large, Haitian spirituality continued to incorporate Catholic ideas and symbols, allowing a unique Haitian Catholicism to survive despite fifty-six years of separation from the Holy See. The variegated waves of politics have since established Catholicism as the official state religion of Haiti despite the fact that the vast majority still practices Vodou. There is a saying that Haiti is 90 percent Catholic, and 100 percent Vodou. Though the Church officials, and the Protestant evangelicals who represent another wave of zealous missionaries, formally reject Vodou, most Haitians see no difficulty in practicing Christianity and Vodou side-by-side, the syncretism of spiritualities being so complete.

From the Catholic perspective, especially after the Haitian revolution, when Catholic missionaries were largely withdrawn, the Church has not held a favorable view of Vodou. Both Vodou and Catholicism share the notion of divine inspiration and revelation as the source for truth. They disagree, though, on the ultimate authority as Vodou allows much more democratic access to divine inspiration than does the hierarchical church. Just as the Church has long endeavored to contain mystics by forcing adherence to dogma, so too has she tried to restrain the uncontrolled inspirations of Vodouists. Believers might be "ridden" by the gods during rituals or might encounter the spirit world in nightly dreams.[17] The church would often denounce such experiences as demon-possession rather than inspired by the Holy Spirit, let alone accepting the existence of the *loas*.[18] Father Jean-Baptiste, writing in 1722, is illustrative of the suspicion with which the Church eyed even the participation of Haitians in Catholic ritual:

> The Negroes have no scruples [....] They intermix Dagon's ark and secretly keep all the superstitions of their ancient idolatrous cult with the ceremonies of the Christian religion [....] They eat [the communion wafer] only when they are ill, or when they are afraid of some danger. In regard to the holy water [...] it is rare that one finds one drop of it when the ceremony has ended; they carry it in little calabashes and drink some drops when they rise (in the morning) and pretend that it will guarantee their welfare against all the witchcraft that might befall them.[19]

Religious syncretism, like that between African spirituality and Catholicism that produced Vodou, has often been depicted as a process of positive spiritual communication between cultures. The syncretism that emerged in Haiti is a conflicted one, though, with the product reflecting ambivalence to the religion of colonial slaveholders that was foisted upon African slaves. Vodou is not a happy marriage of traditions by any stretch, but, in Leslie Desmangles words, is a *tertium quid* (a third thing) "indigenous to Haiti."[20] Central to Vodou metaphysics are the *loas*, divine spirits like angels that serve as intermediaries between humans and the spirit world. Note that the word, *loa*, is pronounced as the French word "*loi*," or law, as in the Laws of Nature or Natural Law, allowing these spirits to find equation with various spirits of nature and also with the Christian God. It is generally recognized that many of the traditional African *loas* can be found under the veneer of Catholic saints, the most prevalent association being one between their iconographies.[21] The powerful serpent-

loa, Damballah, is closely associated with St. Patrick, being celebrated on the popular saint's holy day; Papa Legba, the gatekeeper to the spirit world, is associated with St. Peter whose key unlocks the golden gates of heaven; and Erzulie, the great goddess of love and beauty relates to the Virgin Mary. More pertinent to our present discussion, however, is the powerful Baron Samedi, a *loa* of death and also of its obverse, life; mirror image and companion to Legba. He is a trickster figure, fond of rum and tobacco, crude jokes, and chasing women. As a spirit of death, he is feared, and often appears dressed in a black tuxedo and top hat with a stark white skull face. Importantly, he is normally represented by a cross—a symbol harking back to African cosmography and the Kongo "four moments of the sun," around which the world and spirits within it rotate.[22]

For most Christians, the cross conveys the story of the suffering, death, and most importantly, resurrection of Jesus Christ establishing the eternal hope that all might be saved from death and granted everlasting life. Baron Samedi, dark debauched trickster, stands in direct contrast to Christ, lamb of God. More than that, as expressed by Haitian artist André Pierre, "Bawon Samdi is Adam. Guardian of the cemetery. Guardian of all the dead. Everyone's father. [...] Bawon Samdi is Christ. Lord over the Dead."[23] Christ is adored because he died to give us life, Samedi is feared because he alone has the power to determine whether we live or die. The cross, as Samedi, suggests a liminal stasis between life and death—or more accurately, between death and renewed life, as Holy Saturday is the day Christ "descended into hell" before rising from the grave. Baron Samedi's cross, then, does not signify the certitude of Christ's resurrection but instead remains in skeptical tension.

As a syncretism, Vodou must be seen in the context of the Haitian history, as not simply a coequal merging of Catholicism with African and native beliefs; it is clear that Catholic dogma takes a backseat. As Jack Cosentino has said, "Catholicism does not eclipse African religion; it extends it,"[24] thereby allowing greater opportunities for Vodou to express itself.

Voodoo vs. Vodou

The term Voodoo is largely a creation of the American imagination. As Arthur Lehmann and James Myers have said, "Movies, television, and novels have been merciless in delivering to the public a highly distorted picture of what is a legitimate religious practice of 80 to 90 percent of the people of Haiti."[25] Voodoo, which we might take as a term of derision, ought to be taken not to refer to the Haitian religion but rather applies to the negative and racist construction of a savage people whose traditions exploit black magic, engage in child sacrifice, and worship the Devil. Another subset of Voodoo appears in the range of folk medicine, tradition, and tourist-baiting known as Hoodoo. Found especially in New Orleans, Hoodoo grew out of Southern African-American culture mixed with the burgeoning American Spiritualist movement. With a reliance on spirit-mediums who claimed to be able to communicate with spirits of the dead, its practice is waning.[26]

Far from being the object of Hollywood horror, these distortions of Haitian religion, long proffered by fearful American slaveholders and Christian clergy alike, still appear today. Adam McGee forcefully defends Vodou from the implicit racism of Voodoo constructions, and provides a striking example of the former's denigration with a photo of Vodou religious symbols used as decoration on the dividing wall between urinals in a New Orleans bar.[27] And, after the massive earthquake that ravaged Haiti in January 2010, evangelist Pat Robertson provided an even more explicit example when he explained to viewers of *The 700 Club* that Haiti's independence, and subsequent misery and poverty, were the result of devil worship. The Haitian people, according to Robertson, "swore a pact to the Devil" during their successful revolution of 1791–1804, "they said, 'we will serve you if you'll get us free from the French.' True story."[28] True story, indeed.

Practitioners themselves have only recently begun calling their tradition Voodoo, adopting the name that Americans have attached to a wide variety of spiritual practices and beliefs. The spiritual tradition more properly called Vodou is a loosely affiliated, syncretistic religion originating primarily in Haiti (though aspects of it can be found throughout the West Indies, and similarities exist with traditions such as Santeria and Candomblé). Vodou combines elements of a variety of African spiritualities, most prominently from the West African kingdom of Dahomey (modern-day Benin), with Roman Catholicism and "New World" native spirituality.

The word Vodou itself likely derives from *vodu*, a Fon word meaning spirit or deity.[29] The common core elements of African spirituality can be loosely described as animistic, including strong beliefs in the continuing existence, and participation in the world, of spirits of the dead—often referred to as an ancestral cult or a cult of the dead. Among African groups, a creator god is also accepted, though this High God is considered to have retreated from the world after creation leaving myriad spirit-beings to mediate between humans and the rest of creation. In Catholicism, Africans might easily have recognized the High God at the center of Christian monotheism, though would disagree with His level of involvement in the world. Further, the range of Catholic saints would be preferred intermediaries relating as they do to the intercessionary role of the *vodu* spirits, the *loa* or *lwa* (or even more generally, the *misté*) in Haiti.

Aside from the increased role of the Creator in this world, a more pressing theological difference between Christian and African belief relates to death and the afterlife. In an animistic system, the dead remain a part of this world, and a part of the immediate family. Judaeo-Christian scripture commands that contact with the dead be entirely avoided.[30] John MBiti describes how the "departed of up to five generations are [...] in the state of personal immortality and their process of dying is not yet complete."[31] These spirits, what MBiti calls "living-dead," remain a part of the family, even visiting the living for symbolic meals from time to time, and "are the closest links that men have with the spirit world." Certainly, the African and Christian beliefs cannot easily accommodate each other here. Further, many African societies accept at least partial reincarnation as certain spiritual aspects of a person might be reborn into a new child after death. This is different from a Hindu sense of reincarnation as there is not a single soul, or *atman*, that transmigrates from one incarnation to the next, but rather in the African context, the belief in multiple components of the spirit allows one aspect to be reborn while another aspect remains in a spiritual state, thus one might both become a "living-dead" ancestral spirit and be reincarnated at the same time.[32] The African notion of reincarnation also differs from Indian conceptions, and Platonic ones for that matter, in that the circle of birth, death, and rebirth is not considered as something that one ought to escape; instead, life is seen as a boon and so it is desirable to be reborn. Of course, the harsh living conditions and short lifespan of slaves in Haiti would have been enough to shake the belief in the desirability of rebirth—indeed, procreation, considered in Africa to be one of life's great rewards and responsibilities, was not a freedom enjoyed by the slave population with slave-masters intent only on breeding workers.

The Zombi

The Caribbean was described as a place of monsters from the reports of the first explorers to arrive there.[33] Most of these, like sea serpents, mermaids, or the giants of Patagonia, can be relegated to the fearful imaginations of explorers. Others, many of which still survive in island folklore, may have been inspired by European tales, like the *lougawou* (a vampiric riff on the French werewolf, or *loups garoux*), *djables* (simply, she-devils), and various blood-sucking vampire-like beings or otherwise fearsome spirits variously called *jumbies* (Jamaica), *fumbis* (Cuba), or *soucouyants* (Trinidad). The most commonly recognized, though, is the zombie, which, growing out of the unique background of Haiti, most fully embodies (literally) the spiritual tension and historical baggage of colonialism. As Joan Dayan remarks, "[t]he phantasm of the zombi—a soulless husk deprived of freedom—is the ultimate sign of loss and dispossession."[34] The wandering corpse that is usually associated with the term zombie is not all there is to this "phantasm," however. There is no small amount of debate surrounding the zombie, its origins, and its nature.

Though the Haitian manifestation garnered the most traction, at least until Romero, zombies also appear in Africa, in both spiritual and physical forms. It seems most likely that a tradition of soul-stealing existed in the magical traditions of many African tribes, and that these took on more immediate physical qualities when confronted with the reality of slavery. The reworked zombie as physical forced labor has returned to Africa, with examples dating to the turn of the twentieth century. Vampire-like bloodsuckers and zombie-like slaves both appear in pan–African tradition after European colonial contact.[35] Early examples include creatures called *vekongi* that appear as miners in Mozambique in the late nineteenth century, and in West Cameroon after World War I, as a means of explaining how it is that some people become wealthy while others cannot. Legend explains that the rich must gain their wealth through the magical enslavement of zombies. Similar tales appear in South Africa as explanations for economic inequality by the 1960s and 70s, just as Romero's zombies and the associated critiques of consumerism are gaining traction.[36]

A wide range of etymological roots have been suggested, including the West African words: *zumbi* (fetish); *nzambi* (spirit/god/ancestor); *fumbi* (spirit); *nsumbi* (devil); *zan bii* (bogeyman); *ndzumbi* (corpse); *nvumbi* (body without a soul); *mvumbi* (cataleptic person).[37] Other suggestions include the Louisiana Creole term *jumbie* (thought to itself derive from the Spanish, *sombra*, being a ghostly shade, or the French shadows—*les ombres*), which can signify either an evil curse or a ghost, and the native Arawak *zemi*, meaning spirit or shade. Most of these etymological suggestions, it will be noted, relate to terms that do not correspond to our idea of a zombie as a walking corpse. One can even imagine a French patois derivative of the words *sans vie*, particularly fitting when one considers the relationship between the zombie and the slave in Haiti, as will soon be discussed below. Many studies have found that the term, sometimes rendered as zombi without the "e" in order to differentiate it from the popular concept of shambling cadavers, has many uses, having "been subject to much cross-cultural appropriation, decontextualization, and recontextualization."[38]

Haitian psychiatrist Louis Mars explains that "zombi" might refer to magical beings who work in servitude to a particularly successful farmer or it may just as easily refer to the spirit of a person who has been deprived of the opportunity to be possessed by a spirit, or *loa*, as "Heaven is not opened to this kind of a soul."[39] Spirit possession, unlike the Christian view of demonic possession, is a central ritual in Vodou used as a means of communicating with the ancestors and spirit world. That one might be rejected by the *loas* could represent a significant spiritual loss proportionate to the loss of humanity experienced in enslavement. Evil sorcerers, called *bokor* (not to be confused with Vodou priests and priestesses, respectively termed *houngans* and *manbo*), can steal a part of the soul of a person. Haitians believe human souls are composed of at least two spiritual components called *gros bon ange* (big good angel) and *ti bon ange* (little good angel), which indicate different parts of being. Though sources differ on specifically which *bon ange* is which,[40] one is believed to be the basic animating principle and the other is the higher consciousness that we would more readily associate with the self.

It is this latter spiritual aspect that is the target of the evil magician. Once capturing the requisite *bon ange*, the *bokor* has a number of options for how it might be manipulated. One might transform the person into an animal, which can then be butchered and sold for meat; the animal would then be called zombi—of course, potential consumers ought to beware of what they are eating, and zombie flesh can be identified by its smell and foamy appearance.[41] Often, spirits, in this instance called *zombi astral* (or sometimes *zombi ti bon ange*, or *zombi effacé*—erased or fading zombi), are kept in jars and sold as charms or tokens which might be thought to provide good fortune or to ward off evil or illness, or that might insidiously be used to curse an enemy, or perhaps even cause them to become ill or die. In South Africa, it is said that witches can similarly capture the soul of a person and transform them into a kind of servile diminutive fairy-folk called *ditlotlwane*, translated officially as zombies.[42] Less supernatural uses of the term also appear in South Africa, including the designation of zombi for particularly bratty children while "a swinging single ... without family burdens but, preferably, with an apartment" may be called *zombi libre*, or free zombi.⁴³ Common to most of these descriptions is the capturing of the self, followed by its being forced into service of some kind.

Ancestral spirits and *loa* may occasionally reside in pots or jars called *govi*, and it is possible that an evil bokor might capture a spirit therein for nefarious ends, but far more common in Haiti is the so-called *zombi cadavre*, the walking corpse. Bodily zombies can be found alongside the spiritual ones in Africa,⁴⁴ but, while the latter also appear in Haitian folklore,⁴⁵ the former have come to dominate popular imagination. As the monster entered the Western thought via Haiti, the natural association between the zombie (of whatever stripe) and slavery has resulted in the zombie being intertwined with Haitian folklore to the extent that many argue that zombies are uniquely Haitian. Certainly, as Maximilien Laroche argues,⁴⁶ myths evolve as subsets of given mythologies, sometimes constructing altogether new mythologies. Haiti represents a crucible of African mythologies in which myths evolved, adapted, and changed as they became Haitianized, and ultimately formed a uniquely Haitian mythology similar to but distinct from its African heritage. For Laroche, with whom I agree, the zombie is the prime example of the metamorphosis from African to Haitian mythology.

The Haitian zombie is a person who has died and then been brought back to life by a dark magician known as a *bokor*.⁴⁷ In reviving the corpse, the magician casts the *bon ange* of the self (whether *gros* or *ti*) from the body, producing a literally soulless slave. However uncommon, reports of true zombies can be found, describing the appearance of individuals known to have died and been buried years earlier wandering mindlessly through the streets. Sensational images of Haitian zombies appeared in the early twentieth century with William Seabrooke's travelogue, *The Magic Island*⁴⁸ and Zora Neale Hurston's ethnography *Tell My Horse*.⁴⁹ Hurston famously included a photograph of a "live" zombie, known as Felicia Felix-Mentor. Mars condemns Hurston for her credulousness in this case, noting that he himself diagnosed the zombie in this instance as a schizophrenic,⁵⁰ while Rita Keresztesi defends Hurston's photo as a crafty ploy by which to expose an ongoing system of indentured servitude aided by Western psychiatric pharmaceuticals as a mode of control and antivodou biases.⁵¹ The anthropologist, Alfred Métraux, reports once having seen what he thought to be a zombie, but who turned out to be "a poor idiot girl who had escaped from the house in which her parents kept her shut up."⁵² Seabrooke, for his part, reports with gothic aplomb on his encounter with a number of zombies at work at night:

three supposed *zombies*, who continued dumbly at work ... there was something about them unnatural and strange. They were plodding like brutes, automatons. Without stooping down, I could not fully see their faces, which were bent expressionless over their work.... The eyes were the worst. It was not my imagination. They were in truth like the eyes of a dead man, not blind, but staring, unfocused, unseeing. The whole face, for that matter, was bad enough. It was vacant, as if there was nothing behind it. It seemed not only expressionless, but incapable of expression.[53]

Despite the shock value of such depictions for non–Haitians, in Haiti it is not the zombie itself that is the object of fear, however, but the possibility of being made a zombie. The fear is not of the mindless servant, but of once more becoming a slave toiling away for the benefit of someone else. Medical professionals in Haiti are accustomed to the appearance of zombies, believed to have somehow gained freedom from their captors. Louis Mars estimates that as many as a thousand new cases of purported zombification appear every year.[54] Medically, these "real" zombies display various symptoms of mental deficiency or illness,[55] possibly representing a form of culture-bound syndrome,[56] or at least a culturally determined explanation for otherwise diagnosable illness. Despite this explanation for Haitian incidences of zombies, physiological causes have also been suggested, most notably in the ethnobiological work of Wade Davis.[57]

Davis gathered a number of recipes for so-called zombie-powders, which were said to be used by *bokors* to transform people into zombies. Davis claims to have found tetrodotoxin in the zombie powder, a poison found in puffer-fish that can act as a psychoactive agent. Davis concludes that zombification, rather than being a culturally bound syndrome or diagnosis, is real and that the process by which it occurs is caused by contact with the poison. In the correct dosage, tetrodotoxin might cause a person to lapse into a temporary comatose state, with potential brain damage and psychotic episodes, from which they might later awake imagining they have passed through a zombification ritual and have become enslaved. Critics of Davis' work, and there have been many, point to, among the myriad avenues of attack, problems in the composition of the powders, and the methods of analysis Davis employed for them.[58] That Davis also allowed his research to be sensationalized in the form of a Hollywood horror film, *The Serpent and the Rainbow* (1988), directed by Wes Craven (of *Nightmare on Elm Street* fame), further undermines his credibility, however unfortunate that may be. On the other hand, the film brought even wider popularity to Davis' conclusions, making the zombie powder hypothesis a widely believed truism. Problematically for this physiological explanation, the amounts of tetrodotoxin varied in Davis' samples, even being completely absent from one. Further, some of the experts from whom Davis procured the powders explained their use in ways that would make the necessary contact with the powder impossible; for instance, one popular method for employing zombie powder is to sprinkle it on the ground where one might walk—this might have magical causative effect but could never poison the person who might later walk over the powder. Roland Littlewood reports: "Haitian medical practitioners I spoke with regard zombification as the very real consequence of poisoning; the clergy accept it as a magical product of sorcery."[59]

Another of Davis' controversial, yet influential, conclusions is that the production of a zombie serves a social corrective function as only deviants are made into zombies.[60] Davis argues that before a person can be subject to zombification, he or she must first be found to have broken some specific social norms, such as "stealing" the wife of another man, and thus it exerts a positive social control. Mysterious secret societies, like the notorious *Bizango*, are said to create zombies out of social deviants, thereby exercising a moral authority in Haiti. Whether or not this is the case, Haitians hold the possibility of one's being transformed into a zombie—a mindless slave risen from the dead by evil magic—as very real, even enacting laws prohibiting the practice of zombification. Hans Ackermann and Jeanin Gauthier are among those scholars who take exception with this social-control theory for zombie creation, arguing that zombification seems an inordinately harsh punishment for social crimes (like adultery) and that simply cracking someone's skull open would seem to be a much simpler approach if this level of severity was desired. They further point out that many of the legends (and there are many) of the supernaturally powerful yet unknown *Bizango* are likely fiction.[61] As far as a functionalist argument goes, accusations of zombie production are normally leveled at those who have been inexplicably successful so that a man whose crops grow more plentifully than his neighbors' or an old man who can keep a herd of cattle without help attract suspicion and jealousy—magic is essentially invoked as the cause for good luck.[62] The villain is always the master of zombies and not the zombies themselves, and the masters are not generally justified (despite Davis' suggestion otherwise) but rather are those who unfairly succeed where others do not. The notion that the use of such evil magics will inevitably come back to "devour" its user and subsequent generations represents the possibility of divine retribution for the injustice.[63]

The zombie-as-slave, while found in African tradition, takes on a more poignant significance given Haiti's role in the history of the slave trade. Zombies are not feared in Haiti, but are rather the object of pity.

Those believed to be zombies are taken in by relatives, with families sometimes wrongly identifying a zombie as a deceased relative when there is actually no biological connection between them. Rather than the zombie itself, what is truly feared is the possibility of being returned to slavery, cast in the folklore as occurring through the powers of a sorcerer. As Deleuze and Guattari observed earlier, the zombie/slave is de-humanized and so loses its self-hood. Having struggled mightily to gain freedom and recognition as independent people in their own right, the prospect of losing self-determination again remains an ever-present fear; the American occupation of Haiti (1915–1934) is a reminder of the possibility. The idea of becoming a slave can be equated with the fear of death in that both might represent a loss of freedom and ultimately of the self, and so the zombie is a person who has both died and become enslaved.

Given the Catholic history in Haiti, it is not surprising that some aspects of Christian symbolism would appear even in such a uniquely Haitian creature. Jack Corzani explains how this should come as no surprise, "since the West Indians generally associated the [...] horrors of their American slavery with the demons of Christianity."[64] In comparing death with slavery, the zombie/slave becomes a resurrected body, removed from life and raised again into a new and entirely different, substantially less desirable one. Through distinctly Christian symbolism, the zombie can be seen to represent a subversive rejection of an enforced Catholicism—Vodou's "antagonistic mentor," as Jack Cosentino describes the Church.[65] The slave-masters of Haiti were not solely economic or political but religious as well, with the Church in Haiti yet another arm of European oppression. The notion of a Christian resurrection foisted upon the slave population represents the possibility, if the Christian doctrine of a final resurrection is correct, for a return to eternal subjugation. Certainly, from the perspective of the Christian, the zombie blatantly smacks of blasphemy as a perversion of the resurrection. But there is a Haitian legend describing Jesus himself as the first zombie, some artworks depicting Christ being led from the cross chained by a *bokor*. One legend tells how two Haitian guards stood by the tomb when Jesus was resurrected by God; they overheard the secret word used to accomplish the feat, and sold it to a *bokor*, thereby allowing sorcerers to raise the dead on their own ever after.[66] It is well worth noting that the traditional African zombie does not necessarily appear as a risen corpse, but more often is an enslaved spirit. That the *zombi astral* has largely disappeared in the post–Haitian zombie folklore is significant, emphasizing the importance of the body.

Despite relatively recent popular Christian ideas of one's soul leaving the body at death to enter Heaven, official Catholic dogma also emphasizes the importance of a bodily resurrection. Far from the traditional view of syncretism as a happy coupling of beliefs, Christian doctrines are recognized and rejected in other areas as well. The possibility that a *bokor* might sell a zombie for food is disturbing not so much for the fate of the corpse, but for the belief that eating the flesh of a zombie might prove fatal, or will at least make one seriously ill. Communion is *the* central feature of Christian ritual practice, wherein the body and blood of Christ are eaten. In Catholicism, with the doctrine of transubstantiation, the eating of flesh and blood is to be taken literally—the bread and wine actually take on the substance of Christ's own flesh and blood. For Christians, this is a physical and spiritual communion with Jesus Christ, the savior who died and was raised for the sins of humankind. From an alternate perspective, this is the flesh and blood of a man who died and came back to life. The repulsion caused by the idea of eating the flesh of a zombie suggests a surreptitious rejection of the core ritual of Haiti's oppressors.

Cannibalism and De-Humanization

Cannibalism, moreover, has a very negative connotation in Haiti as racist slurs claimed the act among Caribbean natives and subsequent non–European inhabitants. Accusations of cannibalism generally have long been recognized as one of the most blatant (and paradoxical) forms of dehumanization and Othering.[67] Colonialists marked native groups as cannibals as a sign of their sub-human standing, allowing for subjugation under the guise of salvation. Today, cannibalistic language is used by the have-nots to designate social class in exactly the same way accusations of zombification are with the rich being called *gros manjeurs* (big eaters) and the poor described as being eaten.[68] Of course, cannibalism, by definition, is the eating of one human by another, so the fact that its practice is seen as performed by sub-humans presents a contradiction in terms.

When Columbus first encountered the Tainos people of the Caribbean, he found that they held a belief in a spiritual cannibal race that threatened to steal their people and devour them. He was first seen as a legendary threat that would literally consume them, but his legacy is one in which the people were figuratively devoured through colonization and enslavement. For Columbus, though, the notion that there were savage cannibals living in the New World, against all practical evidence of such practice, was a useful one as it provided validation of the natives' subhumanity and need for salvation from themselves, both facilitating commerce through forced labor of the population.[69] As such, all natives who expressed hostility to Columbus and other explorers earned the cannibalistic title of Caribs, what had previously been the name only of a mythical threat actually realized in the form of the explorers themselves.

Following the revolution in 1804, the Catholic Church retreated from Haiti but initiated what can be described as an anti–Haitian/anti–Vodou propaganda campaign that incited and encouraged fears latent in American and European slave-holders. The prospect of a slave revolt strong enough to establish its own independent nation reverberated throughout the United States, especially in the South. Stories of Haitian savagery spread throughout the United States, replete with tales of magic, child sacrifice, and cannibalism. James Hastings' *Encyclopaedia of Religion and Ethics*, published in the early twentieth century, reflects a repugnant colonial ignorance with long-lasting consequences. What would generally have been accepted as a reliable academic source pejoratively describes the Haitian religion, stating: "Voodoo is devil-worship and fetishism brought from the Gold Coast of Africa by negro captives to the United States and West Indies. Its chief sacrifice is a girl child, referred to by the initiates as 'the goat without horns' [....] There is a regular priesthood to intimidate and rob the devotees."[70] Depictions of Haiti as a Caribbean version of the "Dark Continent" heightened cultural anxieties towards the former slave colony, and eventually facilitated the American takeover of Haiti in 1915. Though Haiti had gained physical independence, neither the religious nor political masters who had controlled the former slave population ever fully ceded their authority, or their "moral" right to rule.

The U.S. invasion was ostensibly carried out in order to protect Haiti from the Germans, but it did nothing to ingratiate Haiti in the American mind. Neo-colonial rhetoric referring to the lack of civility among inhabitants and their inability to rule themselves was used to justify the continued occupation. A 1920 issue of *National Geographic* commented on the U.S. occupation in an article titled "Haiti and Its Regeneration by the United States." "Here," the magazine says of Haiti, "in the elemental wilderness, the natives rapidly forgot their thin veneer of Christian civilization and reverted to utter, unthinking animalism, swayed only by fear of local bandit chiefs and the black magic of voodoo witch doctors."[71] The selection of military personnel assigned to Haiti can be described as "racially prejudiced,"[72] as they were largely Southerners chosen for being "accustomed to blacks."[73] Among first-hand accounts from American soldiers during this time include such graphic elaborations as a marine's claim to have witnessed the murder and cannibalism of an American lieutenant, alleging without any basis in fact: "'They cut off his genitals, removed his heart and liver, opened his stomach, removed the intestines, and detached large pieces of flesh from his thighs. The liver and heart were eaten.'"[74]

The American High Commissioner, charged with overseeing the "restoration" of Haiti, declared that in 1923, "95% of the Haitian people were 'illiterate and a large per cent unmoral.'"[75] Two years later, the commissioner reported that not only were most Haitians illiterate, but that the vast majority "had the mentality of a child of not more than seven years of age reared under advantageous conditions."[76] Haitians did not take kindly to a re-imposed foreign rule, and civil unrest forced the Americans to withdraw earlier than had been originally planned. Haiti returned to self-rule in 1934, two years ahead of schedule. In the same year, Marine Captain John H. Craige published an "intimately personal history" of his experiences in Haiti tastelessly titled, *Cannibal Cousins*, which he dedicates to his fellow marines who "left comfortable homes to lay their bones in the jungles and hills of a land of barbarism and disease."[77] Zora Neale Hurston, whose *Tell My Horse* appeared shortly after the American withdrawal, "has the dubious distinction of being the only black writer who actually approved of the American Occupation," seeing Haiti as "a nightmare world fit only to be probed anthropologically and to be rehabilitated militarily."[78] And this in one of the first and most popularly successful introductions to Haitian religion published in English.

Modern Legacies

Modern Haitians have, in part, reclaimed some of the negative imagery that continues to be directed towards Haiti[79] by asserting the power of not only Vodou but of zombification as well. For instance, the zombie has become a sign of Haitian identity, held up by some as a magical equalizing threat in the face of larger, more powerful military nations, to the point of suggesting that only a Haitian with African ancestry could even hold the potential to properly wield and understand its power.[80] The Haitian penal code includes a law apparently geared towards outlawing the production of zombies according to the chemical process discovered by Davis, the administration of which constitutes attempted murder, the charge being upgraded to murder if the person is subsequently buried "no matter what result follows."[81] Madelaine Hron suggests that such laws were actually pressed by Americans, indicating one way in which Haitians have to some extent accepted external interpretations of their own national identity. She further exposes this bifurcated identity: on one hand, Vodou itself is a syncretic reaction to Catholic slavers, and misunderstandings of Vodou as Voodoo have framed perceptions of Haiti for generations, while on the other hand, vodou became a focal point for the manifestation of Haitian resistance and revolution. As such, vodou represents both "resistance to imperialist oppression and colonial slavery," and "also connotes cultural repression and political oppression,"[82] thereby embodying the interstitial black double-consciousness described by W. E. B DuBois.[83] And the tension persists, or is perhaps exacerbated, for emigrants of the Haitian diaspora, whose largest populations have shifted to large urban centers like New York, Montreal, and Miami. The recognition of the zombie as emblematic of a shared cultural experience as Haitian conflicts with the image of zombie as monstrous Other just as the Haitian immigrant seeks to both hold onto his or her national identity but overcome the stigma of being an immigrant in a new land.[84]

And the zombie remains an active piece of African lore, especially insofar as it offers some explanation for economic inequality. Nollywood, as the Nigerian (also third-largest global) film-industry is called, produces hundreds of films every year, the lion's share of which lie within the genre of "Voodoo horror" or "Juju cinema." Such films accept Hollywood distortions and the notion of zombie slaves, adapting these into the longer history of traditional African Juju magic.[85] But such tales are not considered to be only fiction—one urban legend reported in the *Globe and Mail* recounts the story of a taxi driver's use of a magic helmet that when worn turns the wearer into a zombie, mindlessly vomiting money, commodifying the customer and enriching the driver through his evil scheme![86]

The zombie, whether explicitly Haitian or derived from Romero's later innovations, retains its racial overtones. Richard Dyer, for example, describes horror as a predominantly "White" genre in which blacks represent a primitive form of life, whereas Whites stand in for death in the sense that they hold the power of life and death.[87] Here, Dyer echoes Giorgio Agamben's notion of "bare-life" as applied to black characters—they live, but only in the most basic sense of bodies being alive.[88] The other side of this coin, for both Agamben and Dyer, is Michel Foucault's discussion of bio-power by which the ruling class controls not only the means but the right to subjugate bodies and to determine who lives and who dies.[89] While clearly applicable to both African and Haitian settings, bio-power and bare-life have been more broadly applied beyond a simple black/white dialectic when used in analysis of modern zombie films. Some have argued that the modern zombie stands in for all displaced people, refugees as interstitial beings feared for their implied need to consume without contributing to society.[90] René Despestre likens colonialism to a generalized "zombification" of humanity, marking Haiti as the eye of the storm.[91]

Conclusion

The history of Haiti is plagued with ignorance, racism, and oppression. The spirituality of the Haitian people, which has served as the glue that bound disparate African people together and a catalyst for revolution, has survived enormous efforts to eradicate it. Noteworthy is the further failure of the Catholic *Campagne anti-superstitieuse* waged in 1941–42. Though Catholicism has now become the official state religion of Haiti, most Haitians see no dilemma in practicing Vodou alongside Catholicism. Though the syncretism of these two traditions is often described positively, I have shown above how many Christian symbols and Catholic dogmas must be seen in a more nuanced light in order to be adequately understood in their proper context, especially as they relate to the folklore of the zombie. It is worth noting that both George Romero and Lucio Fulci, who can be credited with spreading the lore of Romero's zombie to Europe, have noted the influence of their own Catholic upbringing on their films, especially in terms of their own religious doubts.[92] Cannibalism is attached to the zombie myth insofar as it was associated first with colonialism, both used by the colonists to justify oppression and by the oppressed to describe their own suffering, and then continuing more recently as a criticism of global consumerism and the ongoing subjugation of the less fortunate by the powerful. While I take to heart Priscilla Walton's warning that in a dog-eat-dog world, we risk seeing references to cannibalism everywhere, the ones evoked by Haiti's history and the zombie are fairly explicit.[93] And more than these, the dual nature of the zombie as alive and dead—as symbol of rebellion (in its connections to Vodou and Haitian revolution) and sign of subjugation, as indicative of the double-consciousness that is the legacy of slavery—is paramount.

As Sarah Juliet Lauro and Karen Embry have argued, the challenge of the zombie is one not of history, culture, or race, but one of human agency and the subject/object power dynamic, the solution of which, they suggest, can only be achieved by embracing a posthumanist perspective.[94]

The historical, cultural, and racial history of Haiti helped to develop the foundations of this particular monster—the zombie. The lasting essence of the zombie, though, transcends the Haitian context and moves beyond the specific history of slavery's racial de-humanization to encompass a larger field of de-humanization generally. Essentially, a Hegelian master-slave dialectic that pits agencies against one another for recognition must be replaced by the acceptance of the fluidity of movement between self and other, an embracing of the liminal and interstitial. As we will see in the next chapter, the zombie has moved into an array of new contexts, but retains core features reflecting on the nature of the self, distinctions between self and other, and the linkage of life and death. Only in the middle ground lies the means to accepting what otherwise appear disjointed, and troubling, dichotomies. This requires an unfamiliar mode of self-conception, one that does not presume a tension between personal self as a source of meaning, and freedom up against others as sources of constraint and obstacle.

Chapter Two

The Evolution of the Cinematic Zombie

Having laid the ground for an understanding of the cultural origins of the zombie, in this next chapter I want to trace the evolution of the monster as it moved into American popular culture, eventually emerging as the rotten, flesh-crazed horror prevalent today. Since George Romero is recognized as the godfather of the modern zombie, and *Night of the Living Dead* as the turning point, in what follows I want to not only explain how the zombie moved into American cinema, but also how these earlier zombie and horror films influenced Romero himself so that we can get a cross section of all the pieces that make up the modern zombie.

Pulp fiction had been introducing Americans to "Voodoo" since the nineteenth century in the typically spurious light of Christian superiority over ostensible savages. The zombie entered the United States first by way of highly sensationalized travelogues, but only began to take root with its first Hollywood appearance. As Haitian filmmaker Raoul Peck says, "Hollywood invented voodoo," thereby limiting the possibility of any true expression of vodou in film; "Any way I present voodoo, it will be exotic, it will fit into all the clichés [...] so I consciously take it out of my work."[1] When *White Zombie* was released in 1932, so new was the zombie that educational publicity was needed to prepare American audiences before the show.[2] Zombies soon became a relatively recognized staple of the horror genre, though its definition as a mindless walking corpse in the thrall of some evil overlord remained for decades; the controlling agent, while most often connected to Caribbean, African, or "primitive" magic, also came to include aliens from outer space and the mad scientist run amok by the 1950s. The fear of being overtaken by some alien Other echoes the Haitian fears of enslavement, though for American audiences the zombie became as much a source of fear as did its master. The fear of being enslaved must be universal. The fear of slaves' vengeance that the slave-master suffers from, however, reflects knowledge of the wrong they inflict. The equation of the average post-slavery Haitian with zombification allows the monster to stand in for the racist insecurities of White America.

When Romero's *Night of the Living Dead* was released in 1968, Romero himself was surprised to find audiences respond to his ghoulish monsters as zombies given the lack of a controlling agent, the absence of Voodoo magic (or true cause of any kind), and the addition of a hunger for flesh as the sole motivating factor. Yet, the creatures of *Night* have come to define the modern zombie. Though Peter Dendle has done an absolutely excellent job of cataloguing every zombie film ever made through 2010, complete with synopses for many of them, he fails to recognize the core elements connecting the modern flesh-eating zombie to its Haitian origins.[3] Now, I don't intend to offer anything close to a catalogue of zombie cinema (though anyone interested in zombies should certainly take advantage of the work done both by Dendle in his two volume *Zombie Movie Encyclopedia*, by Jamie Russell in his *Book of the Dead*, and Glenn Kay's *Zombie Movies: The Ultimate Guide*), but by tracing the path of the zombie through its Hollywood incarnations through specific and important examples, I will draw out exactly those core features that not only allowed audiences to recognize the zombie in Romero's creature, but that remain embedded within its resurrected flesh today.

Important themes also emerge when some of the specific inspirations for Romero are analyzed as well. Romero unintentionally created the template for the modern zombie, incorporating core elements of the Haitian zombie (such as issues of de-humanization, the ambiguity between self and other and between life and death, and also anti–Christian spiritual elements present in Vodou and also the 1960's counter-culture). Critics and scholars have suggested a range of direct sources for his inspiration, and Romero himself has offered others. Some of the films cited as influences include: *Invisible Invaders* (1959); *The Day the World Ended* (1955); *The Killer Shrews* (1959)[4]: *Psycho* (1960), *Plague of Zombies* (1966),[5] *Invasion of the Body Snatchers* (1956), based on Jack Finney's novella, *Body Snatchers* (1955)[6]; *The Thing from Another World* (1951), based on John Campbell's story, *Who Goes There?* (1938)[7]; *The Birds* (1963), based on Daphne DuMaurier's short story of the same name[8]; *Blood Feast* (1963)

& *Spider Baby* (1964)[9]; *Two Thousand Maniacs* (1964)[10]; *Carnival of Souls* (1963)[11]; and *The Last Man on Earth* (1964). On this last film, it is actually the novel upon which it is based, Richard Matheson's *I Am Legend*, that Romero cites most clearly as a direct inspiration to the point of explaining *Night* as an homage (if not an adaptation), and so I will reserve a section below for further elaboration on this connection. Of course, Romero also references a number of heavy-hitters as his greatest stylistic inspirations—Howard Hawks, Orson Welles, Michael Powell—but here I'm more interested in content than style.[12] In addition to film and literature, *EC Comics* represents yet another source for Romero's inspiration; I'll discuss some of the ways the visual imagery of these horror comics influenced Romero's own vision, and also how changing decency laws and censor regulations had a major impact not only on Romero but on the horror, and ultimately the zombie, genre.

Hollywood Zombies from the 1930s to Romero

The zombie entered the North American imagination first through sensational travel writings such as William Seabrook's *The Magic Island*, published in 1929,[13] but unlike other classic movie monsters like Dracula and Frankenstein, the zombie enjoyed no real literary life before appearing on the big screen.[14] In fact, as a silent monster (moans aside), the zombie is especially suited to visual media over text; the spectacle of a walking corpse is truly something that needs to be seen to be appreciated, even in the older films where today's gore is unheard of.[15] So, in the shadow of the other monster movies of the 1930s—*Dracula* (1931), *Frankenstein* (1931), *Dr. Jekyll and Mr. Hyde* (1931), *King Kong* (1933)—the release of Victor Halperin's film, *White Zombie* (1932) introduced America to zombies and quietly set the benchmark for all subsequent zombie movies through the 1960s. Both the film and the travel writing sensationalize Vodou, while essentially maintaining the same locus of fear surrounding the zombie as that found within Haiti itself—the evil magician is the enemy, and the zombie an innocent victim.

In the film, Bela Lugosi plays Murder Legendre, an evil businessman and sorcerer who uses wax Voodoo dolls to create a zombie workforce for his mill, presenting what Robin Means Coleman sees as "a fantasy of post-slavery docility."[16] The plot moves along with the heroine, Madeline, being captured, poisoned, and turned into a zombie to become the lustful villain's love-slave, only to be later saved by her fiancé with the aid of Dr.

Bruner, a figure modeled on Dracula's nemesis, Dr. Van Helsing. Together, these two men manage to force Lugosi over a cliff, followed by his small band of mindless servants, upon which Madeline awakens as if from a bad dream, one that Jennifer Fay likens to the bad dream of the Haitian occupation Americans would rather forget.[17] Fay argues that the film be read in light of the American occupation of Haiti, from which U.S. troops had begun withdrawing in 1932 as the film was released. In this context, white colonial economic interests are depicted as re-instituting a new slavery. David Skal sees the film as "a nightmare vision of a breadline."[18] Alongside the U.S. withdrawal from Haiti, the film also appeared in the midst of the Great Depression when the zombie-as-slave would uneasily resonate for many Americans feeling increasingly dispossessed in the face of capitalist exploitation (a connection observed by at least one contemporary critic).[19] An ambivalence is apparent as the film figures the Haitian zombie as victim to Western economic interests in the person of Legendre as the white capitalist with a small army of servile workers, but then moves quickly to victimize an innocent white woman and the stability of her impending marriage through the power of Haitian black magic, again wielded by Legendre in his lust for her.[20]

With his thick Hungarian accent, Lugosi is certainly no traditional *bokor*, and his zombie followers are divided along racial lines, with those of African descent seen working in his mill, while he keeps a handful of decidedly white zombies nearby as his personal entourage. The vast majority of the film's action involves white characters fighting amongst each other, albeit in Haiti with its stereotyped black magic as the villain's weapon of choice. Gary Rhodes argues that the film is not particularly racist or unfair to Haitians, but that it simply represents the conventions of Hollywood in the 1930s in relegating blacks to the background.[21] Still, the villain Legendre with his use of Voodoo and zombification is the embodiment of the frightful, unknown Other found in the African spirituality of the "magic island" of the first independent slave colony. Battle lines are drawn in *White Zombie* between civility, decency, the sacrament of marriage, and the innocent, white American couple on one side, and lust, sin, black magic, and the exotic on the other.

Interestingly, though the film itself was not particularly controversial (a review in *Harrison's Reports* recommended against screening the film, especially on Sundays, to avoid the possibility that some Christians would take offense to a kind of perverse resurrection),[22] the subsequent interest in zombie-horror resulted in an ironic "zombification" of its own. As Fay describes the incident, "a reenslavement" was committed "within the logic of intellectual property"[23] when an American corporation claimed ownership of the very term from Haitian folklore describing a dead slave returned to mindlessly work for its master. With the production of *Revolt of the Zombies* (1936), what was to be a sequel to *White Zombie*, a financial backer of the original film sued claiming that it owned the term "zombie." Though seeking to maintain ownership of "zombies" ever after, the plaintiff only won damages and prevented the film's being billed as a sequel, allowing zombies to break free onto future movie screens. More than being simply an ironic curiosity, though, *Revolt* also shows the extent to which the zombie as metaphor had quickly adapted in its new social context. The film, though ostensibly a sequel to *White Zombie*, moves the scene away from Haiti entirely, instead locating its action in the jungles of the Far East.

While most scholars have ignored *Revolt of the Zombies*, it is the first film to use zombies in an entirely non–Caribbean setting. One other film sometimes mentioned in this regard is the 1933 Boris Karloff film, *The Ghoul*, in which an Egyptologist, Prof. Morlant (played by Karloff) uses Egyptian rituals to return to life as a revenant to exact revenge on a family he blames for betraying him. No mindless zombie, though, Karloff's Morlant creeps about methodically, picking his moments to strike.

In fact, a number of films from this period are sometimes erroneously counted by critics as zombie films, likely a result of the recent expansion of the term to include any walking corpse as if it were a zombie. Films like *The Walking Dead* (1936), *The Living Dead* (1936), and *The Man They Could Not Hang* (1939) turn entirely away from Voodoo altogether, instead embracing the mad-scientist trope, in each case bringing a dead man back to life in order to exact revenge upon the living. Despite the similarity in titles of the first two with some modern zombie fiction, such films should more rightly be seen as continuing the tradition of Frankenstein monsters rather than zombies, easy enough to do given Boris Karloff's presence in so many of these examples. The tagline for *Living Dead* is explicit—"not a ghost. Not a Vampire. NOT A ZOMBIE!—What is The Living Dead?" And of the three, this is the one that comes closest to fulfilling the characteristics of a zombie in its depiction of an evil doctor injecting people with a drug that puts them into a death-like state. However, the "victims" are actually accomplices in a plot to scam life insurance companies—an interesting spin on the commodification of the body and to whom that value is due at any rate! Though this alone might be deemed by some an adequate connector back to the economic power dynamics inherent in the zombie as slave, many critics have suggested that the entire spate of

1930s monster movies was directly tied to the Great Depression. The figure of the zombie, in particular, appealed to American insecurities; just as the zombie represented Haitian fears of returning to slavery, so too it represented American economic fears of being subjugated by foreign entities.[24] But then, so many other monsters fulfilled this function as well.

In any event, for all its flaws—bad acting, pretentious dialogue, clichéd plot—*Revolt of the Zomb*ies does show that within only a few short years of being introduced to American audiences, the zombie as metaphor was already understood such that it could be taken out of its Haitian context and supplanted to another, albeit still foreign Other. In this case, Orientalist fascination replaces Darkest African Voodoo with Cambodian Buddhist Esoterica. A Buddhist monk is said to be the only living person to know the secret to creating zombies, a process which in this film involves some kind of ritual, a chemical concoction, and then telepathic mind control. None of the zombies are risen corpses, though an army of them can seemingly ignore a barrage of bullets puncturing their bodies. For fear of this dangerous dark art's falling into the wrong hands, the Allied nations (the film is set at the end of World War I) imprison the monk (where he is then murdered), and then set out to destroy any remnants of the secret that may be discovered at Angkor Wat. In the process, one among the expedition, a man jilted by the only female character, discovers the secret on his own, and decides to use it to take control of his own army all with the intent of winning the love of this woman. The film hammers on the idea that a man must be ruthless if he is to attain what he desires, with the end result being a pedantic lesson in the failure of just such a philosophy. A friend and mentor advises him that he's gone too far, quoting Mencius—"When right ways disappear, one's person must vanish along with one's principle."[25] The man finally releases his zombies to prove how much he loves this woman, and the army of Cambodian zombies that he had created then rises up as a mob to kill him.

Recognizable in this film are themes familiar from *White Zombie*: a critique of colonial expansionism as overreaching ambition "running roughshod" over everyone in its path and the abuse of racial others, alongside fears that these same Others have access to magical forces capable of dominating the West if allowed. The movement of action from Haiti to Cambodia foreshadows growing tensions in the face of Japanese imperialism, and the replacement of Voodoo ritual with telepathic mind control presages (by over 20 years) fears of Communist brainwashing à la *Manchurian Candidate* (1959). In any event, both of the Halperins's zombie films tie enslavement and the loss of agency to an evil master bent on seducing an innocent white woman to overarching ambition and the abuse of power concomitant with colonialism; and both ambivalently suggest that the oppressed Others have at their disposal the power to turn the tables on their masters, though such powers emanate from some unknown dark magic that needs to be destroyed lest it consume its user—and, indeed, society.

By the 1940s Hollywood had largely lost interest in the subject of Voodoo and zombies, the tradition being kept alive in a series of low-budget B-movies including *King of the Zombies* (1941), *Revenge of the Zombies* (1943), and *Voodoo Man* (1944). At least one scholar has suggested that the 40s marked a transformation in portrayals of blacks from sources of evil to objects of derision and comic props.[26] Certainly, *The Ghost Breakers* (1940), a comedy-horror starring Bob Hope, does just that, and the first in the line of 40s horror flicks that draw a distinct link between black servant characters and the zombies, suggesting that whatever threat posed to white America by either of these is not one that need be taken seriously.[27] Racial tensions were treated for laughs, and the zombie lost any pretentions it may have had to genuine horror.

One among these early films that did try to take its subject seriously is the little-known *I Walked with a Zombie* (1943). The movie depicts a young Canadian nurse who is hired by a man in Haiti to care for his incapacitated wife. As the story unfolds, the wife is found to have been turned into a zombie by her mother-in-law, who admits to having turned to Voodoo ritual to save her son's marriage by turning his wife into a zombie to prevent her from leaving him. Of particular interest is the way in which ideologies are debated throughout the film, namely those of the "superstitious" Haitians and the rationalist Westerners. It is clear that the natives believe the wife to be a zombie from the outset, though the main characters all look for physical explanations for her sickness. In the end, it is revealed that the mother, who is the strongest voice of rationalism, caused the woman's affliction by turning to the Voodoo spirits.

Aside from this curious departure, however, much of the thematic observations stemming from this film reflect the conventions of its time. The film contains some interesting and not entirely unrealistic portrayals of Vodou ceremony even though the film is set on the fictional island of Saint Sebastian as a stand in for Haiti, but the tradition itself forms merely the backdrop to the main story. Some have defended *I Walked With a Zombie* as providing a relatively fair portrayal of Haitian religion, but ambivalence is clear from the outset as an early scene has the heroine, a white Canadian nurse speaking with a local Haitian man as she arrives at the island for the first time:

COACHMAN (Clinton Rosemond, uncredited): The enormous boat brought the long ago fathers and mothers of us all chained to the bottom of the boat.
BETSY: They brought you to a beautiful place, didn't they?
COACHMAN: If you say, Miss, if you say.

This dialogue is most explicit in both emphasizing the painful history of Haiti, while at once watering down that history with a simple platitude.[28] It may be that the film makers felt compelled to dilute their message due to the Motion Picture Production Code, which, among many other things, proscribed against the denigration of any country's history.

Aside from the wife of the lead hero in the story, the only zombie on screen is also the most frightening visual in the entire movie—a tall, lanky black man (played by Darby Jones) with bulging eyes, the whites of which are prominent. This menacing figure appears a few times in the film, acting in every instance as the main source of fear. Still, the true "villain" of the film, though she is depicted as being forced into her role, is the mother who poisoned her son's young wife. From another perspective, the wife herself is the villain as it becomes apparent that her crime was the seduction of her husband's brother, with whom she drowns in the ocean whilst fleeing from the black zombie at the film's finale. As in *White Zombie*, the main characters, including those who turn to magic to further their evil agendas, are all white, due mainly to Hollywood conventions of the time. The Haitians themselves are relegated to supporting roles.

Horror in the 1950s has generally been seen as awash in conservative, post-war jingoism glorifying the virtues of science while warning against its potential for abuse, especially in the nuclear age of the Cold War.[29] This decade is often characterized as turning away from the Gothic, supernatural horror of preceding years, and positing a rationalistic, this-world view of horror. Several films of the 50s have been noted as influences on the zombie genre, especially insofar as they effected or affected Romero's work. The 1950s saw the zombie-controlling Other taken to an extreme as extraterrestrials create zombie armies with which to dominate Earth (*Plan 9 From Outer Space* [1958]; *Invisible Invaders* [1959]). In addition to these Others, there were also home-grown dangers, most notably the threat of nuclear radiation, which ultimately appeared as a means of turning once living humans into walking corpses (*Creature With the Atom Brain* [1955]). American audiences were increasingly drawn to science-fiction fare capitalizing on scientific, nuclear fears over supernatural ones.

Those films of the 50s that tried to keep "Voodoo" links alive were remarkably unsuccessful, though some provide continuity for future developments in the zombie genre. Among them, *Voodoo Island* (1957) casts

Boris Karloff as a mythbuster hired by a wealthy hotel magnate to explain a pastiche of Voodoo dolls, zombification, the "primitive religion" of a "Polynesian cult" in the South Pacific, and the additional threat of prehistoric carnivorous plants; if nothing else, the film offers yet another fairly clear critique of global capitalism as the natives use their magics to ward off the greedy capitalists willing to do whatever it might take to build the tourists' paradise. In the same year, *Zombies of Mora Tau* returns to the zombie's roots in being set off the coast of Africa where a zombie crew are cursed to defend a shipwrecked cargo of diamonds. Beginning with a prologue stating: "In the darkness of an ancient world—on a shore that time has forgotten—there is a twilight zone between life and death. Here dwell those nameless creatures who are condemned to prowl the land eternally—the walking dead," the film evokes reference to the bare-life left in the wake of colonial expansionism. The opening scene then shows a white American woman and her white American driver discussing the fact that Africa hasn't changed in fifty years, a state admired by the woman as she contemptuously remarks on superhighways and drive-ins. While complaining about the bumpy state of the road, the driver then runs over a motionless figure standing dumbly ahead of them, remorselessly claiming, "It wasn't a man, it was one of *them*!" The zombies are distinctly non–African, being the cursed crew of the shipwreck. The curse can only be ended, and the zombies thus released to eternal peace, once the diamonds are cast out to sea, a fact that calls to mind current politics of the blood diamond trade and of necropolitics generally. The colonial capitalist is as much likely to suffer as is the oppressed laborer. The film's final line is the half-hearted lament, "I'll probably never be rich again." Only the zombies are unrelenting in their pursuit of riches, freed once their treasure is dispersed and made worthless.

Though its bona fides as a zombie film are debated, *Invasion of the Body Snatchers* (1956) remains a strong influence on Romero's zombie. Based on Jack Finney's, *The Body Snatchers* (1955), this film version marks only the first of at least four adaptations that have been made over the years, testament to its themes' enduring resonance. In the story, an alien life form has arrived on Earth with the power to kill and replicate any person, thereby eventually colonizing the entire planet. People begin to become aware that something is up when they notice small changes in loved ones, changes so personal as to be unnoticeable by any but the closest relations. The hero, a psychiatrist named Dr. Bennell, becomes suspicious when he hears the same concerns raised by multiple patients. Bennell leads what ends in a winning endeavor of struggle against this subversive takeover, convincing the alien beings to move on in their colonial aims.

Though the aliens do not enslave the human population, instead replacing them with look-alikes, the connection to the zombie tradition lies largely in questions of the nature of a self, and the notion that this invasion might spread covertly, like a virus, such that anyone might be or become one of them. Of these, the question of personal identity is foremost: if a person looks like me, says they are me, and knows everything that I know, who can say whether it is not actually me? Am I something other than my body? And, ultimately, what then is the nature of identity at all? Such existentialist questions lie at the very heart not just of this film, but also the zombie genre most profoundly.[30]

The problem, while present in the 1956 film, is more explicitly expressed in a scene in the 1978 remake (or sequel, as described by its director, Philip Kaufman).[31] Jack (Jeff Goldblum) and David (Leonard Nimoy), who are actually pod-people-versions of the originals, try to convince Jack and David's friends, Matthew Bennell (Donald Sutherland) and Elizabeth (Brooke Adams) to simply relax and allow themselves to be similarly replicated. As Bennell is told in the book: "You'll *be* the same, in every thought, memory, habit, and mannerism, right down to the last little atom of your bodies. There's no difference. None."[32] Both Jack and David are convincing as they explain that they remain who they previously were, only now improved versions that no longer suffer the negative emotions of their former lives. Matthew and Elizabeth resist, crying and begging for their lives, fearfully clinging to the lives they know and rejecting the claims of those who appear in all other respects to be their friends. In all versions, the aliens replicate humans when they sleep, and human characters are encouraged to relax and simply allow themselves to sleep as they will be transformed upon awakening. In each case, the protagonists finally cannot resist the urge to sleep—reminding me of Gilgamesh's failure to achieve immortality and overcome death when he cannot even overcome the basic human need for sleep. As the 1956 Bennell remarks, "That moment's sleep was death to [his girlfriend] Becky and the rest."

The film depicts recognition of a "pod person" on the grounds that some ineffable quality is missing, some human-ness that the alien replica simply lacks, thereby supporting a kind of human exceptionalism.[33] The 1978 version is more explicit in naming emotions as the key distinction, the pod people being practically devoid of emotion. The original, though, leaves the difference as some vague, uncanny dissimilarity in character. That anyone might be one of "them" creates an atmosphere of paranoia that many have linked to the Red Scare of McCarthyism,[34] or, on the other hand, a scathing critique of the new suburban conformity.[35] If the film is conservative, though, it is self-consciously so in the sense that it appears to recognize a certain inevitability of change. As Barry Keith Grant says so well: "But in the end, while one might read the film as a right-wing endorsement of paranoia or a leftist warning about capitalist mass culture, it is above all a centrist nostalgic lament for the fact that [...] things ain't what they used to be."[36] It isn't simply about the uncanny change of personality at an individual level, but on a social one.

And on this theme, the book seems clear, too, as the narrator returns to laments about change and so-called progress. In one instance, Bennell (as narrator, perhaps giving voice to Finney himself) laments the "inhuman perfection" and "utter brainlessness" of "marvelously efficient" dial phones that have replaced human switchboard operators, "saving you a full second or more every time you call."[37] Though few of us today would prefer to return to switchboard operators, Bennell worries that "we're refining all humanity out of our lives." Paradoxically, the book also suggests that this very urge towards progress is the very thing missing from the pod people! In this way, change is both lamented and recognized as crucial to the human condition. We might note a resonance with the Buddhist attitude to attachment here—change is recognized as inevitable and that remaining attached to anything in the hopes that it will not change is sure to bring about suffering. Of course, the difficulty in accepting change and letting go is at the heart of being human and the key challenge for the Buddhist.

Of particular inspiration for Romero, though, is Howard Hawks's adaptation of John Campbell's novella, *Who Goes There?*, *The Thing from Another World* (1951).[38] Set in a small research base in Antarctica, Gothic elements are prevalent. Where *Invasion* casts its scene widely, suggesting the widespread threat of alien imposters, *The Thing* places the same fear in a claustrophobic setting from which there is no escaping the "alien among us." Interestingly, Romero appears to have combined aspects of both the *Thing*'s wish to use humans as food, and the *Body Snatcher*'s need to consume the very essence of what makes one human.[39]

The trend towards scientific horror in the 1950s is often taken at face value as representative of fears of nuclear annihilation and the expectation that the authorities, scientific, economic, and political, will defend the people. This is what Robin Wood calls "reactionary horror," representing a conservative push to retain the status quo.[40] In fact, it is precisely the rationalism of just such authorities that is more often critiqued, albeit subtly, in 1950s horror. In *The Body Snatchers*, for example, the pod-people are seen against stereotypically "feminine" qualities. The aliens can be identified by their lack of emotion, or humans might recognize the alien through intuitive feeling that the pod people are not who they claim to be.[41]

Though the first film adaptation of it (*The Last Man on Earth*) wouldn't come out for another ten years, Richard Matheson's *I Am Legend* (1954) follows a similar path in depicting its protagonist as a solitary survivor who trains himself in rational, scientific methods in his efforts to understand and defeat a worldwide virus that has turned the population into vampires. His lack of empathy for the vampires he hunts ends with his becoming the bogeyman to a new world order. A woman, Ruth, shows him compassion, befriends him, and in the end, although she facilitates his capture and execution, she also shows mercy by providing him the means to end his own life peacefully.

I Am Legend *and the Revolutionary Spirituality of Richard Matheson*

A deeper discussion of the most direct influence on Romero—Richard Matheson's *I Am Legend*—is in order. Matheson's spirituality (he was inspired by ideas of the power of positive thinking found in Christian Science and New Thought, and, especially, the possibilities of spiritual evolution provided by Theosophical thinking, which he actively included in his fiction) can be found even in his early works, including *I Am Legend*, and this spiritual influence appears clearly in Romero's self-professed homage, *Night of the Living Dead*. In fact, the three official film adaptations—*The Last Man on Earth* (1964), *The Omega Man* (1971), and *I Am Legend* (2007)—progressively invert Matheson's own spirituality beyond recognition. Tracing the spiritual lineage from the eastern-inspired Theosophical tradition through Matheson to Romero is an important part of illustrating the applicability of Buddhist philosophy to the zombie, especially over and above any Christian interpretation thereof.

Richard Matheson's book presents a revolutionary take on the vampire which has been largely underappreciated in the scholarship on horror, and that on vampires especially.[42] This might be a result of the way Matheson envisions his vampires as both animalistic monsters and as building a new world order that overcomes its need for blood absent of humankind, features unfamiliar in the previous lore of vampires as mainly solitary, aristocratic figures stalking human blood from the shadows. In fact, *I Am*

Legend foreshadows the societal transformations of the 1960s counterculture in its criticism of traditional authority structures, especially institutional Christian religion and scientific rationalization, and places the conservative protagonist, struggling for the survival of the past, as the legendary villain.

The novel centers on the story of a man, Robert Neville, who is the lone survivor of a virus that has transformed all humankind into vampires. Neville barricades himself within his house at night, protected by the traditional weapons effective in warding off vampires: garlic, mirrors, and crucifixes adorn the exterior of his home. As he tries to get through each night, swarms of vampires surround his house, taunting, teasing, and throwing rocks. By day, Neville scours the city's dilapidated buildings in search of sleeping vampires, armed with a mallet and home-made wooden stakes. The story draws to an end when, after three years in solitude with only nightly visits by the monstrous vampires to keep him company, Neville encounters a woman. Despite her appearance in the full light of day, a feat outside the bounds of normal vampiric biology, Neville remains skeptical. He brings her to his fortified home and subjects her to a number of tests. She is revolted when he presents her with garlic, for instance. Through the night, the two develop an emotional bond as Neville's need for companionship and his long-dormant sense of human empathy overcomes his pure survival instinct. When he finally decides to run a blood test on his guest he discovers that she is, in fact, infected by the vampire virus. Before he can react, however, she renders him unconscious with a mallet blow to the head. He wakes to find a note explaining that she is among a new society formed by vampires who have found the means to control and contain the virus.

Neville had previously observed that there were two types of vampire—those who had become infected while alive and had then become vampires, and those who had died before rising from the grave. The "living" vampires are those who have formed this new society, while the walking dead are the terrors threatening Neville every night. Although Neville had observed the distinction between the living and the dead vampires, he indiscriminately killed them all during his daily tours of the city. For this reason, the new society sees Neville as a monster upon whom the woman, Ruth, had been sent to spy. Shortly thereafter, a group of living vampires, armed with spotlights and guns, attacks his stronghold. They destroy the dead vampires that surround Neville's house and then burst into his home where he is critically wounded during a brief firefight. Imprisoned, Neville is visited by Ruth who provides him with poison with which to kill himself before he is to be publicly and painfully executed. The novel ends with Neville's realizing the nature of his status as legend, thereby troubling distinct notions of good and evil,[43] and definitions of Otherness, and the monstrous.

James Twitchell contends that "[a]side from the devil, the vampire is the most popular malefactor in Christianity."[44] Although the vampire's origins can be traced into pre–Christian history, with possible links to Indian folklore carried via gypsies, the monster has acquired particularly Christian associations since Bram Stoker's *Dracula*.[45] Vampirism has long stood in stark contrast to Christianity, and specifically Catholicism, by signifying a perversion of the Final Resurrection and the vampire is routinely held in abeyance by a faithfully grasped crucifix. Bruce McClelland traces the late seventeenth-century incursion of vampire lore into Western Europe where they had previously been little known outside of the Ottoman empire; these legends provided the embattled Catholic Church with a supernatural Other, akin to the witch, to act as a scapegoat by which to rally the faithful.[46]

I Am Legend's protagonist, Robert Neville, strikes an ambivalent relationship with Christianity throughout the novel. Neville is horrified by the government-enforced cremation of infected bodies, an attitude that is increasingly rare today, but was very common when Matheson wrote the story. Although it is set in the 1970s, it was written in 1954, nine years before the Vatican lifted its ban on cremation. Neville is guilt ridden at having had to throw his dead and infected daughter into the fire pits, and he refuses to allow his wife's body to be similarly treated. Instead, he surreptitiously buries her, which results in her rising from the grave as one of the monstrous undead. At times, Neville prays for help but then immediately derides himself for doing so. Early in the novel, Neville ponders the significance of a large cross he had had tattooed onto his chest one night while drunk: "What a fool I was in those days! he thought. Well, maybe that cross had saved his life."[47] He clings to some sense of Christian tradition, though he also expresses strong doubt in the usefulness of any of it.

The novel justifies his ambivalence as Neville comes to realize that it is not the power of the cross itself that keeps vampires at bay, but the religious convictions held by the individual vampires before infection. He finds, for instance, that the cross has no effect on his former neighbor and friend, Ben Cortman, a Jew, who recoils instead when a Torah is thrust before him. "But as far as the cross goes—well, neither a Jew nor a Hindu nor a Mohammedan nor an atheist, for that matter, would fear the cross."[48]

The power of institutionalized religion is thus shown to be rooted in the minds of individuals without any objective truth for their claims.

As the predominant religion of America, Christianity is a particular target for derision throughout the book. In one flashback to the early days of the vampire virus, Neville is forced into a revivalist tent service as a garlic-breathed man calls upon him to repent: "'Come, brother, come,' the man said, his voice a grating rasp. He saw the man's throat moving like clammy turkey skin, the red-splotched cheeks, the feverish eyes, the black suit, unpressed, unclean. 'Come and be saved, brother, saved.'"[49] Neville's contempt turns to the entire group as they are described in Pentecostalist fervor screaming "terrible hallelujahs" trapping Neville on a "treadmill of hopes."[50] These hopes are proven untenable in the face of Neville's observation that the cross has no power over those who did not themselves believe. Worse, Neville presumes that such hope actually heightened the suffering of those who in the end turned to what he calls "primitive worship" since the believers are the ones who have ultimately caused their own suffering at the sight of what they formerly believed to be holy symbols:

> Not only had they died as quickly as the rest of the people, but they had died with terror in their hearts, with a mortal dread flowing in their very veins. And then, Robert Neville thought, to have this hideous dread vindicated. To regain consciousness beneath hot, heavy soil and know that death had not brought rest.[51]

The message of the text comes through loudly: the Christian hope for salvation from outside one's self is futile; the power of the cross is naught but a neurotic delusion; and in that delusion, all established religions are equal. Both vampire and vampire hunter are shorn from the supernatural, as Neville becomes "a Van Helsing without hope."[52] Matheson's personal rejection of established religion, what he has himself mocked in interviews as "Churchianity"[53] couldn't be more clear.

One might be inclined to read the attack on established religion as a general attack on the supernatural in favor of some kind of materialistic atheism along the lines of many perspectives on 1950s sci-fi and horror, but there are several reasons to argue that this is not the case with *I Am Legend*. The book does include such elements as have been linked to the reactionary, including fears of atomic war and McCarthyism; the blood-borne, vampiric virus that has been carried by dust storms resulting from an unnamed future war can easily be seen as a veritable Red Menace. Recall, though, Mark Jancovich's argument that 1950s horror, especially when hybridized with science fiction—as is the case here—ought to be read in terms of increasing unease with the "rationalization"[54] of the 1950s favoring the use of science to control all aspects of social and economic life, essentially producing a "technocracy" that alienated the general population.

To read *I Am Legend* as reflecting a fear of either the bomb (wiping out humankind) or the Soviets (creating a new world order) is limiting since ultimately it is neither the virus nor the vampires who end up as the villains. Rather, it is the protagonist, Robert Neville himself, who is the true monster, acting as a conservative drag on the social evolution of the vampires. Throughout the story, Neville is steadfast in his support for the scientific method as he struggles to understand the virus and the vampire. He performs horrific "experiments" on the vampires that include dragging one woman out of bed by her hair and into the sunlight to watch her writhe in pain until dead on the sidewalk. It is in many of these moments that Neville feels the pangs of conscience, though his rationalizing need to figure out how the vampires tick forces him to ignore feelings of guilt or compassion. The path to understanding, the novel seems to suggest, does not follow that of moral correctness, and torturous experiments are a necessity. Matheson's, and Neville's, disregard for establishment Christianity ought not to be seen as reflective of a general tendency to favor science over religion, as the novel clearly ends up denigrating amoral science for creating the monster that Neville becomes.

The scholar of religion and popular culture Christopher Partridge offers an extensive argument for what he calls "occulturation," which has essentially filled the spiritual gaps opened by the rifts of secularism. Western culture is now permeated with ideas and beliefs formerly considered "occult"—as Partridge explains: "[i]nterest in direct experience of the divine, in secret gnosis, in alchemy, in theurgy, in a *philosophia perennis*, and in ancient religious and mythical figures, texts and civilizations are all evident in contemporary occulture."[55] In addition, Partridge seeks to broaden the range of "occulture" to include "beliefs and practices sourced by Eastern spirituality, Paganism, Spiritualism, theosophy, alternative science and medicine, popular psychology (usually Jungian), and a range of beliefs emanating out of the general cultural interest in the paranormal."[56] Exposure to previously unfamiliar ideas and spiritualities has always opened up new possibilities for religious syncretisms and the development of new sources of meaning, and the 1950s was rife with Asian spiritualities imported by American experience in World War II and by the popularity of Gandhi in his innovation of non-violent protest.[57] Many of these elements appear in the eclectic spirituality of Richard Matheson, who wrote *I Am Legend* at the same time that the Beat Generation "Dharma Bums,"[58] inspired by the predicted *Decline of the West*,⁵⁹ called for social evolution and a "second religiousness" akin to the spiritual heterogeneity of the Theosophists.

I Am Legend, though rife with apocalyptic themes, does not depict a nihilistic world without either humanity or hope. The narrator exaggeratedly asserts toward the novel's end that "[i]n the years that had passed [Neville] had never once considered the possibility that he was wrong. It took [Ruth's] presence to bring about such thoughts [...] 'Do you actually think I'm wrong?' [Neville] asked in an incredulous voice."⁶⁰ The narrator is unreliable at this point, as throughout the novel Neville does in fact struggle with the morality of his actions. As he prepares to stake a child-vampire, for example, he laments that all of the children look like his own dead daughter.⁶¹ While dragging another vampire into the sunlight in order to observe the effects, the text notes that "[u]sually he felt a twinge when he realized that, but for some affliction he didn't understand, these people were the same as he."⁶² This same twinge rises up during another of Neville's cruel experiments: "Once he might have termed it conscience. Now it was only an annoyance. Morality, after all, had fallen with society. He was his own ethic." He then chastises himself: "Makes a good excuse, doesn't it, Neville? Oh, shut up."⁶³

Finally, Neville recognizes his own depravity even as he sits with Ruth and considers simply killing her in order to avoid the hassles that might come with her being uninfected and so a part of his future. "Such thoughts were a hideous testimony to the world he had accepted; a world in which murder was easier than hope."⁶⁴ The most explicit evidence of Neville's recognition of his own wrongdoing appears in the following drunken moment as he questions whether the vampire is any different from humankind:

> But are his needs any more shocking than the needs of other animals and men? Are his deeds more outrageous than the deeds of the parent who drained the spirit from his child? The vampire may foster quickened heartbeats and levitated hair. But is he worse than the parent who gave to society a neurotic child who became a politician? Is he worse than the manufacturer who set up belated foundations with the money he made by handing bombs and guns to suicidal nationalists? [...] Really, now, search your soul, lovie—is the vampire so bad?

All he does is drink blood:

> Why, then, this unkind prejudice, this thoughtless bias? Why cannot the vampire live where he chooses? [...] Why do you wish him destroyed? Ah, see, you have turned the poor guileless innocent into a haunted animal [....] Robert Neville grunted a surly grunt. Sure, sure, he thought, but would you let your sister marry one? He shrugged. You got me there, buddy, you got me there.⁶⁵

The novel's conclusion, in which Neville is revealed to be the true monster, is the most profound aspect of the story, but moral tension is a recurring theme throughout. Ultimately, Neville's refusal to accept the possibility of a new society of living vampires that might be composed of people, however Other to his past experience, aligns him with the monstrous walking dead who surround his house instead. The living vampires have adapted to their condition and have constructed a new society, while the latter appear as nothing more than monstrous walking corpses driven by a quest for blood. Before Neville is captured, he watches in horror as the living vampires quickly slay the monsters surrounding his house with pikes and machine guns. Though they had long tormented him, he realizes that his years of trapped solitude with these creatures has led to his being distressed by the prospect of their elimination. He even roots for the escape of his one-time-friend-turned-undead-nemesis Ben Cortman as the creature clumsily tries to flee. Further building the association, Neville is shot in the chest as he is captured. Empathizing not with the vampires that he himself killed with stakes through the heart, but rather with the monsters who were just slain by the living vampires, Neville thinks to himself: "This is what they must have felt when the pikes went into them."[66] Though we can see Neville struggling with the ethics of his actions throughout the book, in the end he relates to the monstrous vampires just as he comes to realize that he has become the bogeyman to a new world order.

Once it becomes clear to Neville that he will die at the hands of this new world order, he resigns himself to death. Richard Matheson summarizes his own personal philosophy on life and death with the statement: "To die is nothing. To live is everything."[67] Neville claims not to fear death though he does not understand it. On the other hand, he had long before ceased to actually live. He existed only to run through mundane routinized tasks without meaning. Through the story he gradually loses his humanity only to have it reignited, however slowly and reluctantly, by the appearance of Ruth. As Neville empathizes with the walking dead after his encounter with Ruth, one can see that he has recognized himself as one of the walking dead—not yet dead but no longer truly living. Despite the years of his own brutality, once he is resigned to his own demise and the formation of the new society, he makes one request: "Don't let it get ... too brutal. Too heartless."[68]

For his part, in a very brief telephone conversation I once had with him, Matheson denied that there was anything spiritual in *I Am Legend*, though author intentions are so often unrelated to the meanings found within their finished works, and it is not at all unlikely that we misunderstood each other in terms of what "spirituality" might mean.[69] Richard Matheson was not only a prolific writer of horror and science fiction, but a professed spiritual seeker of a particularly eclectic bent. He has more than once acknowledged intentionally inserting his opinions into his stories. In a 1951 letter to a former professor of his, he admitted to inserting his own politics and personal philosophy into his writing, especially when set on another world or in the future (as is the case with *I Am Legend*).[70] Later, he described his protagonists as extensions of himself: "[W]hen I'm writing in first person, I don't think about the characterization, or how they are going to express themselves, I just express my own approach to these things."[71] If this is the case, then Neville presents Matheson's own ambivalent attitude to a world that reluctantly, yet hopefully, recognizes change a-coming—one that removes the embodiment of the liminality of life and death in the form of the vampire from its traditionally Christian roots and flips night and day to replace the conservative rationalism of Neville with the non-traditional occulture of the new world order to come. This expectation opens the door to Buddhist ideals to enter into the zombie by way of Matheson's vampire as inspiration to Romero.

Matheson first explicitly revealed his own spiritual leanings with the 1978 publication of *What Dreams May Come*, which describes an afterlife created by the mental life of the individual and the possibility of successive reincarnations leading to spiritual evolution into higher states of being. Though a work of fiction, Matheson includes an introduction that explains that the view of the afterlife described in his book is based upon his own active research rather than idle imagination, and that aside from the characters and their relationships, "with few exceptions, every other detail is derived exclusively from research."[72] Research he has also explained as covering "hundreds of books in every branch of parapsychology and metaphysics and in what I choose to call the 'supernormal'—not to be confused with the supernatural," and with which he had hoped to write something that would help people.[73] (I also think that his distinction here between the paranormal/metaphysics and the supernatural not only reflects his rejection of established religion, but also nuances his rejection of my suggestion of "spirituality" in his work).

The story is one of a man, Chris Nielsen, who dies but returns to his family in spirit form, struggling to communicate reassurance that he remains. His efforts largely fail, and his grief-stricken wife commits suicide, an act that condemns her to a hell-like state in the afterlife. A core aspect of the afterlife, and life in general, as described in the book (and the related research Matheson cites) is that a person effects the world in which one lives with their mind; Chris's wife's suffering is entirely self-inflicted, and Chris makes it his goal to show that fact to his wife, thereby freeing her from herself. The book ends with her realizing this truth, and then being reincarnated in a new life to continue her growth. Such a cyclical view of life and death is typical of South Asian philosophies like Hinduism and Buddhism, and is accepted by many Theosophists, Spiritualists, and other alternative spiritualities of the "occulture." Interestingly, the Robin Williams film adaptation (1998) removes most of the alternative spiritual aspects of the book—Chris's wife's reincarnation at the book's end; an afterlife called the "Summerland"; Chris's attempts to use a medium during a séance; and the notion that one must learn to use one's mind to create new realities, instead emphasizing more conservative ideals like that individual willpower can effect change in one's life and that there is, in fact, some form of both Heaven and Hell.[74] The book more clearly represents Matheson's sincere effort to spread his spiritual philosophy.

Matheson once said: "I think *What Dreams May Come* is the most important (read effective) book I've written. It has caused a number of readers to lose their fear of death—the finest tribute any writer could receive."[75] Following the success of the film version of *What Dreams May Come*, Matheson then followed in the tradition of Carlos Castaneda[76] and James Redfield[77] by publishing his own fictionalized encounter between a man and a mysterious figure who directs him toward spiritual enlightenment, *The Path: A New Look at Reality*.[78] He followed this with a second nonfiction metaphysical volume, *A Primer of Reality*,[79] which is a collection of quotations without narrative from Theosophist Harold W. Percival. Percival's opus, *Thinking and Destiny*, a massive book detailing his personal philosophy distilled from his experience with Theosophy, aims to explain "the purpose of life," which is "not merely to find happiness, either here or hereafter. Neither is it to 'save' one's soul. The real purpose of life," Percival says, "the purpose that will satisfy both sense and reason, is this: that each one of us will be progressively conscious in ever higher degrees in being conscious."[80] The acceptance of a universal evolution of human consciousness and society, and the dismissal of institutionalized Christian notions of salvation appear in both *What Dreams May Come* and *I Am Legend*.

All three of Hollywood's adaptations of *I Am Legend* have moved to obscure any sign of the cultural inversion suggested by Matheson's story. Far from Neville being revealed as the bogeyman, the two most recent adaptations, *The Omega Man* (1971) and *I Am Legend* (2007), go so far as to portray Neville as a Christ-figure, providing the means through which the past can be restored and change averted. The screenplay for *I Am Legend*'s first film adaptation, *The Last Man on Earth* (1964), was originally written by Matheson, and thus the film very closely follows the book through much of it. Matheson withdrew his name from the credits, however, once producers insisted on changing the ending of his story. Most explicitly different from the book, Robert Morgan (as he is called in this adaptation) is a scientist who successfully cures Ruth of the vampire virus so that she fully reverts to being human. Before she can warn the other living vampires that Morgan can save them all, they attack. Rather than being captured, Morgan flees to a church where he is shot and then impaled by a pike, dying at the foot of the altar. In his last moments, he screams defiantly, "You're freaks! Mutants!" He dies with Ruth crying over him that they simply did not understand that he could help.

The changes made here fundamentally alter the story's message. In *The Last Man on Earth*, Neville-cum-Morgan is a rejected savior killed by an ignorant mob. There is no recognition of Morgan's guilt let alone any suggestion of his being a regressive drag on social change. The notion of freakish mutation is emphasized over social evolution, thereby valuing the status quo. Absent also is any critique of Christianity. Instead, Morgan flees to a church for safe haven, and it is the vampires who transgress the sanctity of the place to murder him. Where the novel makes it clear that religious signs have power against those who, in life, believed in them, the film here makes clear that while Morgan seeks refuge in these signs, the vampires blasphemously ignore them. Here again the vampires are in the wrong, and rather than indicating a criticism of Christianity, the film presents the new society as barbaric and sacrilegious. While Matheson's novel ends with indictments of rational science and institutional Christianity as conservative throwbacks in the face of an evolving social order, the film winds up defending both the elite scientist who can find the cure for any ill *and* the Christian church as final refuge.

The Omega Man even more flagrantly transforms Matheson's story to the point that Matheson didn't mind it as much as the first, being "almost unrecognizable."[81] Here Neville, played by Charlton Heston, becomes a true Christ-figure. This Neville is not only a scientist but also a U.S. Army colonel, has the cure to the virus literally in his blood having been the only person vaccinated before social collapse. Through his blood he can save those who have not yet reached the most advanced stages of the virus. He has achieved legendary status among other survivors who have heard of his hunts through the city, and to them he is a hero. A happy survivor exclaims, "Christ, you could save the world!" and a child asks him if he is

God, a question which, in true biblical form, Heston's Neville demurs to answer. In the end, he dies impaled on a spear in a pool of his own blood sprawled in a strained cruciform pose. The survivors flee the city with his blood-derived vaccine in hand.[82] Obviously here there is none of the blurring between good and evil, and it is clear that there is no new society but rather the salvation of the former one. Neville, depicted as a military man and a scientist, as well as a Christ, wholly embodies those very conservative, rationalizing forces that were rejected in Matheson's book. Moreover, the virus in this film doesn't create vampires, but instead creates a delusional cult of apocalyptic Luddites calling themselves The Family, conjuring up Charles Manson and his own "family" of race-war-baiting murderers.[83] In *The Omega Man* there is no social evolution; instead the status quo is maintained by the military, scientific, and religious authorities.

Finally, the Will Smith vehicle, *I Am Legend*, is similar to the novel in name only. In truth, the film is more a remake of *The Omega Man* than an adaption of the novel. Smith takes on the role of Christ, though this time his immunity to the virus is innate—he truly is unique by his very nature. In the end, he also sacrifices himself after having given the antidote to a group of survivors. Like Heston's Neville, Smith is also a military man and a scientist. The distinction between humankind and the infected is radically delineated, as the creatures here are mindless and bestial, their lack of humanity further reinforced by their being completely computer generated without the use of real actors to portray them. As in *The Omega Man*, Smith's *I Am Legend* defends the status quo by placing the scientific, military elite in the position of hero, and Christianity in the role of savior. The film ends with the survivors entering a barricaded compound in which the central feature is a small, white church.[84]

One film that has managed to capture some of what Matheson's novel intended is George Romero's independently produced *Night of the Living Dead* (1968). The original screenplay, titled "Anubis," was written as an allegory for social revolution.[85] *Night* did not accomplish the full sequence envisioned, but the evolution of the zombie has been depicted progressively through Romero's subsequent films—*Dawn of the Dead* (1978) suggests residual memory; *Day of the Dead* (1985) includes a zombie re-learning to speak and using a gun; and *Land of the Dead* (2005) completes the original cycle with a zombie-led revolt against a facsimile of modern society. For what it's worth, Matheson didn't appreciate Romero's first film, feeling it was too gory and "kind of cornball," adding bitterly, "Later on they told me he did it as an homage to *I Am Legend*, which means, 'He gets it for nothing.'"[86] Still, Romero does capture the essence of *I Am Legend* better than any of the official screen adaptations. Remnants of modern society cling to the past, struggling fruitlessly to hold off the undead hordes that will ultimately usher in a new world order. Unlike the virus of *Legend*, *Night* does not provide any clue to the cause of the rising dead (the media, government, and scientists are all of no help whatsoever). Further, where Matheson lampoons traditional Christianity, Romero leaves religious speculation out entirely—*Dawn* offers only one reference to Vodou, though it conflates the Haitian tradition with Brazil's similarly syncretic Macumba, but claims it as a Trinidadian tradition. Peter (Ken Foree) remarks on the connection between the living and the undead, saying: "You know Macumba? Voodoo. My grandad was a priest in Trinidad. He used to tell us, 'When there's no more room in hell, the dead will walk the earth.'"

Though Romero's undead are unnamed in *Night*, and the story is based on Matheson's vampires, audiences received the monsters as zombies, recognizing in them something of the previous tradition. Matheson's work includes some resonance with Haitian history, though entirely coincidentally. Namely, his invocation of a new, syncretic spirituality that criticizes mainstream institutional Christianity echoes the development of Vodou. The notion of social evolution also corresponds to the revolutionary history of Haiti just as it did in the hopes of the Beat Generation writers and counter-culture-revolutionary flower children. *Legend*'s flipping of good and evil, hero and monster, also aligns with ways in which the zombie problematizes the distinctions between groups, especially in terms of power dynamics. All of these are retained by Romero, whose film has the added controversy of casting a black lead who engages in a power struggle with a belligerent white man in 1968, playing to racial tensions of the time that may also have encouraged identification with the Haitian tradition in a way that *Legend* does not.[87] In fact, the distributor played up the racial tensions in the film, marketing it to black audiences with images of Ben, the black lead, punching Harry, his white nemesis, and including it in a double-bill with *Slaves* (1969), starring Dionne Warwick in a story that imports 1960s black militancy to the antebellum American south. Before delving any more deeply into Romero's zombies, though, I want to turn to one other avenue for his inspiration first.

Comic Book Zombies

Alongside the developments of horror film there was another, even less respected, form of visual media entertainment that grew in popularity since the 1930s—the comic book.[88] Though World War II saw a range of still-recognizable superheroes, like Superman, Batman, and Capt. America, post-war audiences became more interested in other genres, like westerns, romance, crime, and horror. The companies that would become the powerhouses of Marvel and DC Comics today published across all of these genres, but prime among these in terms of horror was EC Comics (which itself also published sci-fi, crime, and westerns, and, of course, its most famous contribution, *Mad Magazine*). Said to have been stylistically ahead of its time for the 1950s, EC's comics inspired a range of horror and sci-fi film makers, with the likes of Robert Zemeckis, Joel Silver, and Ray Bradbury likening the comics to storyboards ready for film.[89] While horror was the moneymaker for EC, among its science-fiction titles, the most popular themes included alien invasion narratives and apocalyptic tales of the Earth's destruction.[90] The horror of EC Comics, *Tales from the Crypt* the best known among them, was hugely influential for post-war horror, not to mention highly controversial for its fearlessness in depictions of graphic violence (all relative, of course, these comics would easily be considered tame in today's market). Many young people turned to these graphic depictions of blood, guts, and corpses in a time when they were coping with the aftermath of the Second World War with its duck-and-cover drills and McCarthyist paranoia, and the unimaginable horrors of Hiroshima, Nagasaki, and the depths of the Holocaust.[91]

Just how therapeutically effective the form might be has been the subject of debate. There are those who see value in being able to confront violence and its effects through a visual medium like comics. Tom Savini, the iconic special effects artist whose work includes several important zombie films, explained his work in terms of his own experience in war. He says: "much of my work for *Dawn of the Dead* was a series of portraits of what I had seen for real in Vietnam. Perhaps that was one way of working out that experience."[92] Gerry Canavan in discussing the popularity of Robert Kirkman's *The Walking Dead* (both a comic book and a television series) argues that there is a loss of immediacy inherent in comic books actually "*de-horrors*" the narrative,[93] which might ultimately serve to help readers deal with the reality. June Pulliam alternatively recognizes a distinct advantage in the capacity comics allow the reader to meditatively linger over an image,[94] thereby serving to help digest images of death and bodily destruction.

The graphic nature of EC Comics, and the irreverence with which they treated their subject (punning narrators would often mock readers' taste in reading material, for instance), both in the spirit of the *Grand*

Guignol tradition,[95] were the very aspects which both drew a following (including a young George A. Romero)[96] and also the ire of legislative opponents worried about corruption of the youth. Psychiatrist Frederic Wertham railed against the negative effects of comic books on the minds of children, most effectively in his book, *Seduction of the Innocent* (1954),[97] which eventually led to a Comics Code (echoing the Hollywood Production Code) that essentially policed the kinds of content that might be permitted in comics.[98] Among those things that were outlawed were all tales of horror, terror, or "weird"-ness, with specific bans against vampires, zombies, and ghouls! The implementation of this code effectively led to the destruction of EC Comics, just as similar outrage had previously condemned the British *Grand Guignol* Theatre itself.[99] EC then focused almost entirely on *Mad Magazine* until the old *Tales from the Crypt* was revived for cinema in 1972, a resurgence spawning a total of five films—*The Vault of Horror* (1973); *Demon Knight* (1995), *Bordello of Blood* (1996), and *Ritual* (2001)—and a long-running HBO series (1989–1996) as well as a substantially toned-down children's cartoon, *Tales from the Cryptkeeper* (1993–1994, 1998). Romero himself worked with Stephen King to make the EC Comics film-homage, *Creepshow* (1982), in the same style as the comics.

By the 1960s, Marvel Comics revived the superhero genre by taking a revolutionary approach to, of all things, radiation and science gone wrong. Beginning with the creation of the *Fantastic Four* (1961), whose story involves four astronauts being mutated by gamma radiation in outer space, Marvel appealed to public fears of the Cold War nuclear threat not through the horrors of the monsters that might result (along the lines of Godzilla and the long line of radioactive monsters of the previous two decades), but rather that this power might be harnessed for good. Spiderman, the X-Men, and the Incredible Hulk soon followed, and other comic books followed suit with Negative Man and the re-imagined origins of the Flash. Most explicitly with characters like the Thing and the Hulk, comic books from the 60s problematized clear distinctions between hero and monster, blurring the clear lines between good and evil that had been previously maintained.

Zombies survived in comic-form through the Comics Code period in a few publications that circumvented the code by publishing in the form of black-and-white magazines. Warren Publishing issued titles like *Eerie* (1966–1983), *Creepy* (1964–1983), and the still-popular *Vampirella* (1969–1983), all of which catered to the audience for horror comics through the 1970s and into the early 1980s. Marvel Comics also revived its own Zombie character, Simon Garth (who had appeared in a single issue of *Menace* (1953) published by Marvel's pre-cursor, Atlas Comics) in such a format under the title *Tales of the Zombie* (1973–1975).[100] Though Simon Garth's origin story follows the Hollywood Voodoo tradition, *Tales of the Zombie* opens with an introduction explaining the importance of Romero to the genre, marking perhaps the first link appearing in print between Romero's ghouls and the new zombie.

As the Comic Code increasingly lost its influence over advertisers beginning in the 1970s and 80s, the zombie had moved to the silver screen for its visual presentation; the only other zombie comic of note from that time being the *Deadworld* series (1987–present). With the resurgence of zombie cinema at the turn of the twenty-first century, though, there was also a veritable explosion of new zombie comics and graphic novels.[101] Though *The Walking Dead* (2003–present) is likely the best known, other titles include *Remains* (2004), *Blackgas* (2006–2007), and *Crossed* (2008–present), all of which largely follow Romero's zombie "rules." There is also, of course, the *Marvel Zombies* series (2005–present), first written by Robert Kirkman himself, which effectively plays off both the current popularity of zombies and of superheroes by depicting a zombie apocalypse wherein only the super-human become zombies in a largely parodic series bearing witness to the ongoing bodily destruction of cherished heroes. (One memorable scene includes the explosion of a zombified Bruce Banner's stomach due to the amount of flesh consumed by his zombified Hulk alter ego, a state retained upon transformation back to Hulk, healing no longer an option for zombies). A range of international zombie comics have also appeared, most notably in an absolute deluge of zombie manga from Japan, which often, interestingly, merges the concept of the zombie with Japanese spiritual traditions of Shinto and Buddhism. Given my intention to show the connections between the zombie and Buddhism, we'll return to the importance of the Japanese influence later. For now, we'll return to the evolution of the cinematic zombie, inspired and influenced as it was by the visual art of 1950s horror comics.

The Birth of the Modern Zombie

Critical to the development of horror, and of the zombie in particular, was the loosening of the Hollywood Production Code, which had begun to come apart by the early 1960s, pushed to the limits as it was by innovative directors like Alfred Hitchcock with *Psycho* (1960), to finally be scrapped altogether by 1968, the year of *Night of the Living Dead*'s release.[102] A month after *Night*'s release, the MPAA film-rating system came into effect, and though updated, remains the familiar rating system used today. Also, related to the zombie in particular, by this point audiences were comfortable with the general concept of the zombie and filmmakers had no hesitation in removing it from its Haitian roots and dropping it into a variety of contexts.

By the mid to late 1960s, Voodoo had largely faded from view in terms of zombie-films. *The Earth Dies Screaming* (1964) continued a sci-fi approach to zombies, with alien robots animating the corpses of the humans they killed. In *War of the Zombies* (1964), John Barrymore, Jr., plays an evil wizard in ancient Rome who raises an undead army in service to a "mysterious divinity thirsting for blood," described only as "the goddess of gold," in the form of a huge statue that looks suspiciously like a slightly modified Buddha. Risen corpses called "plague spreaders" avenge the murder of a twisted scientist in *Terror-Creatures from the Grave* (1965) and a band of Nazis are brought back from a kind of cryogenic slumber in *The Frozen Dead* (1966). Hammer Films' *The Plague of the Zombies* (1966), though, evokes Voodoo in asserting that the mad landowner who has been murdering people and turning them into zombie workers for his mines had previously lived in Haiti. It's worth noting, too, that although so many modern writers have assumed some kind of virus as the cause for post–Romero zombies, even the "plague" of this film is a ruse as the villainous Squire Hamilton has been murdering townsfolk in order to work his dark arts. In any event, the zombie throughout the 60s can be seen to have spread globally, and to be easily removed from its original context, though in every instance there is some single agent responsible for the raising of the dead towards some selfish goal.

Some of the films mentioned in the previous paragraph capitalize on the relaxation of code restrictions with extravagant gore. Both *Frozen Dead* and *Terror-Creatures* include some chilling scenes of severed limbs moving autonomously, and the latter a couple shots of gruesome disfigurations. Pushing the envelope of "good taste" to its limits, though, are films like Herschell Gordon Lewis's so-called blood trilogy of *Blood Feast* (1963), *Two Thousand Maniacs* (1964),[103] and *Color Me Blood Red* (1965) which embraced the tradition of the *Grand Guignol* theatre and reveled in unrestrained, exaggerated, and even utterly ridiculous gore. Recall that films such as these and others have been recognized as heavily influencing Romero's own aesthetic, leading to many critics to express disgust at the gore of *Night of the Living Dead*. While some see Romero's *Night* in the tradition of these contemporary splatter films,[104] others, like gore-expert Philippe Rouyer,[105] argue that such schlock as these could never be confused with the craftsmanship of Romero—it is at least true that Romero's film defined a genre, while these other examples are largely relegated to cult status at best.

Jay Slater notes the influence on Romero of the bizarre and little-known *Spider Baby* (1964),[106] which fits within a paradigm of the violent, inbred, southern redneck along with Lewis's films above, an enduring theme best expressed in *The Texas Chainsaw Massacre* (1974) and *The Hills Have Eyes* (1977). Not really about zombies, in this film the Merrye family is inflicted with a congenital illness that causes severe mental regression to the point of "pre-human savagery and cannibalism," the eating of flesh problematically hastening the condition. Several visual similarities exist between *Spider Baby* and *Night*, though, like the bickering siblings driving along the country road, the young girl stabbing her victim repeatedly, taxidermied-animal décor, and a couple instances of bug-eating and genuine cannibalism as well—this last appearing only at the film's end when the most regressed family members devour their cousin, who's come to claim the property as her inheritance, when she stumbles into their basement lair. *Spider Baby's* greatest influence may simply lie in the fact that it takes aim at so many taboos—incest, pedophilia, cannibalism, voyeurism—while also offering a (perhaps ham-fisted) message of love and respect and a criticism of the callous ostracization and institutionalization of mental illness. This last point echoing the loss of self embodied in the zombie, and in its connections to Alzheimer's patients mentioned earlier.

Also in terms of visual effect, I might as well also mention the dreamlike visual quality of the low-budget *Carnival of Souls* (1962), which is apparent in Romero's camera work as well. Both films address the by-now familiar issues of mortality and the distinction, or lack thereof, between the body and soul. The souls of the dead haunting the protagonist take on an almost zombie-like appearance, with exaggerated dark rings around the eyes and otherwise pale white faces, and the image of them rising up from the sea is striking, but any influence on Romero's work is largely visual and stylistic.

Several critics have pointed to Alfred Hitchcock's *The Birds* as a source for *Night*.[107] Certainly, the gothic element of being trapped in a house surrounded by a mindless horde intent on devouring those inside is similar, but these ideas are hardly uncommon. Likewise, the fact that neither film offers any explanation for the cause of the attack is jarring, but represents a development in postmodern horror generally, of which both *The Birds* and *Night of the Living Dead* are early examples.[108] Beyond these, though, there is little resemblance. *The Birds* has none of the racial tension of *Night*, and no tie back to the Haitian zombie. Birds might hold some symbolic significance in connection with death, perhaps even holding a liminal place as creatures able to traverse land, sea, and air,[109] but the zombie is undeniably the better metaphor for the interconnection of death with life. Ultimately, most scholars who have offered complete interpretations of *The Birds* have tended towards psychoanalytic approaches, emphasizing feminine sexuality as central to the work, the most impressive of which remains Camille Paglia's essay for the British Film Institute.[110] For what it's worth, Daphne Du Maurier's short story upon which Hitchcock's film is based includes descriptions of the birds that might apply as easily to any zombie since Romero: "but even when they fed it was as though they did so without hunger, without desire. Restlessness drove them to the skies again [...] seeking some sort of liberation, never satisfied."[111] Further, such a description likewise ties back to Buddhist thought as well.

The Last Man on Earth (1964) is an obvious inspiration for *Night*, it being the first film adaptation of the source material and having appeared only four years earlier. Even more than the book, the film presents its vampires unlike any vampires that came before. Instead, the stiff-limbed, pale-faced monsters of *Last Man* bring to mind zombies like those in *Invisible Invaders* (1959) or *Plan 9 From Outer Space* (1959). *Last Man* follows the book in having its monsters talk, though it dumbs them down considerably, moaning and struggling to utter their ghostly threats quite unlike the verbosity of the vampires in Matheson's original text. Romero went further and completely eliminated any capacity to speak (at least until the evolution of the zombie Bub in *Day of the Dead*), though both *The Last Man* and *Night* show their monsters clumsily employing clubs. Certainly, for Romero, the original novel is much more clearly a thematic source than was this film, while the visuals may resonate across both.

George A. Romero's *Night of the Living Dead* (1968) forever transformed the zombie for modern audiences, and his influence on the subgenre cannot be understated. Since Romero, the Haitian "Voodoo" zombie has largely fallen by the wayside, replaced instead by the mysteriously risen master-less corpse, slave only to its need to kill and devour the living. In *Night*, the zombies have no master and no known cause for their creation. "Experts" depicted in the film speculate on the possibility of radioactivity or a returning satellite as potential causes for the zombies, but the authorities are at the same time shown to be confused, frustrated, and entirely untrustworthy on the subject. As Romero puts it, "when a lot of people synopsize the film they say, 'This returning Venus probe,' etc. But it has nothing to do with anything."[112] Further, these zombies eat people, though seemingly not for sustenance. As shown in *Day of the Dead*, the zombie will continue to eat even when its entire digestive tract is removed. Later zombie films, including Romero's sequels (*Dawn of the Dead* [1978]; *Day of the Dead* [1985]; *Land of the Dead* [2005]; *Diary of the Dead* [2007]; *Survival of the Dead* [2009]), generally adhere to the rules laid out in *Night of the Living Dead*: zombies rise from the grave with no other motivation than to devour the living; people who are killed also rise up again as zombies; they cannot think or speak except perhaps in a very primitive manner; they generally have no known cause for awakening; and the only way to stop them is by destroying their brain. And, though zombie nerds are wont to debate the merits of zombie speed, Romero's zombies, well, "they're dead; they're all messed up," and as such are comically slow and clumsy. Romero, following Matheson, points beyond the zombie's Haitian roots and the racial politics of America and offers an evolutionary vision that transcends what were till then traditional authority structures (i.e., science, militarism, government, the nuclear family, even race and gender).

As the 60s came to a close, so many social structures had come under suspicion that it is no surprise to find massive role reversals depicted in film. *Night* has been described as undercutting the nuclear family in its depiction of the unhappily married Coopers who are both partially eaten by their zombified daughter[113]; a representation of the American nightmare of the Vietnam war[114]; a landmark in race relations in film[115]; the embodiment of America's history rising up to demand respect in the face of modern challenges[116]; the embodiment of the notion of revolution itself[117]; or a representation of the basic struggle to maintain one's humanity in the face of chaos.[118] Not surprising given its ending, many having seen the film as a reflection of a frustrated nihilism.[119] R. H. W. Dillard, in one of the earliest critical analyses of *Night of the Living Dead*,[120] recognizes the overall impact of the film not merely as nihilistic, but rather that the fear induced by the film is, essentially, one of meaninglessness in the face of death. It isn't the zombies, the dead, themselves that are the ultimate source of fear—they are certainly the main threat to the film's characters—but rather the fear that all life is pointless and random, as indicated by the unrelenting and unavoidable prospect of death brought by the zombies, and in the end to Ben, the main protagonist who has survived the night only to be carelessly shot by would-be rescuers. Certainly, the existential search for meaning in the face of death leads to all manner of other questions about what one ought to do in life, how society ought to be constructed, what one ought to value in life, etc. The turmoil of the 1960s certainly shattered a great deal of societal trust in established authorities, and so the answers to these Big Questions of life became ever less clear. Zombie films following *Night* echoed these same tensions, which we will return to later in this book.

Dawn of the Dead (1978), situated in a mall, forever marked the zombie as the perfect metaphor for mindless consumption. While Karl Marx himself invoked the vampire as a metaphor for capitalism,[121] the zombie is in its origins slave labor. As people become de-humanized by commodification, they can increasingly look forward only to death. The zombie, then, comes to represent the de-humanized person oppressed by anonymous corporate overlords. Certainly, other movie monsters lend themselves to Marxist interpretation and can often be equally seen as representations of the oppression of the anonymous corporation. The aliens in John Carpenter's *They Live* (1988) are a particular favorite of Slavoj Zizek in this regard, for instance.[122] Francis Gooding's summary of the myriad interpretations of the zombie succinctly when he says:

> Completely overdetermined in its meanings, [the zombie] contains an allegory of the emptiness of consumer culture; a picture of the doomed fantasy that the privileged can maintain their control of the world's wealth; a commentary on class and race distinctions; a morality tale about cruelty; manifestations of a lingering fear of communism, and so on.[123]

Ultimately, though, Gooding asserts, the reversal of the indisputable roles of the living to live and the dead to remain dead marks the fundamental disintegration of any claim to social order. With the dead rising, all bets are off insofar as any other structure is concerned.

Beyond Romero's New Zombie

The importance of death itself becomes clearly apparent in the zombie following Romero's work, while still retaining a bridge back to the monster's Haitian roots. Bob Clark, of *Porky's* (1982) and *A Christmas Story* (1983) fame, made two interesting zombie movies, both in the early 1970s, between Romero's *Night* and *Dawn of the Dead*. The first, 1972's *Children Shouldn't Play with Dead Things*, takes a somewhat playful approach to Romero's zombie. Considered a spoof by some, the low-budget acting and pretentious script still offer some interesting topics. In the film, a group of young hippies decide to enact a Satanic ritual that is supposed to raise the dead. To their surprise and dismay, the ritual works and the island cemetery's inhabitants, some of them with quite effectively gory makeup, rise up to attack and devour the group. There is no mention of Voodoo or Haiti here; the island is within view of the bright city lights across some river, invoking instead the dark power of Satan himself—of course, as I've noted earlier, generations of Christians have linked vodou tradition with devil-worship. However, even when a character sees the error of their ways and begs God for forgiveness, the zombies keep on coming. Leading the group is a particularly pugnacious character who revels in a kind of materialist disdain for humans both living and dead— at one point he responds to a suggestion that they ought to respect the dead with "The dead are losers. If anybody hasn't earned the right for respect, it's the dead," and to the notion that everyone living or dead should be treated with dignity by flatly stating: "Man is a machine that manufactures manure." The movie thus offers an interesting meditation on meaning and human exceptionalism in the face of mortality.

Removing the campiness of many of Clark's other films, *Deathdream* (1974), also known as *Dead of Night*, tells a story in the tradition of *The Monkey's Paw* in which a young man is killed in Vietnam, but returns to his family as his mother simply refuses to let him go: "You can't die, Andy, you promised!" The returned Andy is not exactly a zombie, having agency and maintaining a normal, albeit paler and skinnier, appearance. He avoids daylight, but, more interestingly, he requires the flesh and blood of the living in order to prevent his own body from beginning to rot. After a murderous rampage, the film ends with him finally falling into his own grave, and body decaying badly, dies with his kneeling mother weeping beside him. Certainly a commentary on the Vietnam war,[124] the film also suggests a real problem in our capacity to overcome the denial of death, in this case the mother's clinging to the wish for her son's life being the ultimate source for his undead existence.

Jamie Russell sees a plurality of 70s zombie flicks as critiques of the hippie-generation's flower power with a strong anti-drug bent to them, citing such examples as *Blue Sunshine* (1977), *Garden of the Dead* (1972), and *Toxic Zombies* (1980).[125] Among these is also the Romero film, *The Crazies* (1973), which was remade in 2010, and which, though not about zombies, replays many of the same themes that will appear throughout the zombie genre. Certainly, it is no small influence on later "zombie" fiction that does not actually involve the risen dead like the immensely important *28 Days Later* (2002), which has a human-made virus (called Rage) turning people into homicidal maniacs, and Stephen King's *Cell*, where the same is caused by an electronic signal sent via cell phone.[126] It can also be seen as a key influence in zombie fiction that does include zombies, most explicitly in *Return of the Living Dead* (1985), in which an experimental military chemical raises up the dead who then crave nothing but brains. Creating further connections to several of the common themes already seen, the chemical in *Return* is called "2-4-5 Trioxin," recalling both the agent in *The Crazies* as well the infamous Agent Orange, which included the real chemical, "2,4,5 Trichlorophenoxyacetic acid." In *The Crazies*, an experimental military bio-chemical weapon, called "Trixie," is accidentally released and turns people into mindlessly violent maniacs. The military quarantines the entire small town at the center of the outbreak, with the deaths of all residents essentially the only solution when the antidote is lost in the chaos of incompetent leadership and confusion. The film ends with the indication that the human-made virus has already appeared in another town, suggesting the apocalyptic certainty that would become characteristic of the zombie genre.

Similarly, *The Living Dead and Manchester Morgue* (1974) offers a vision of the beginning of a zombie apocalypse caused by an experimental pesticide that uses sound instead of chemicals. Somehow, the new technique has the side effect of causing corpses to return to life with the single-minded desire to kill and eat the living. Echoing the sentiments of *Children Shouldn't Play with Dead Things*, a detective in this film blames a Satanic cult for the murders being perpetrated by the undead, and scientists stubbornly refuse to believe the word of a hippie that their machine could be doing something wrong. The film ends with the suggestion that their ignorance results in an increasing number of risen corpses.

Haitian influence does appear post–Romero, though rarely. *The Zombies of Sugar Hill* (1974) evokes the tradition as a woman, Sugar Hill (played by Marki Bey) turns to a Voodoo queen to elicit the aid of Baron Samedi to raise up a gang of zombies with which to exact revenge upon a group of white mobsters who had killed her boyfriend. This film, like other 70s "Blaxploitation" horror films including *Blacula* (1972) and its sequel, *Scream, Blacula, Scream* (1973), in which Blacula turns to "Voodoo" rituals in a failed attempt to cure himself of his affliction, valorize the monster. Blacula is a victim of European vampirism, forced to kill against his own will; Sugar's zombies, which are clearly identified as long dead former slaves, rise up from their graves not only to avenge the murder of one man but to force the mobsters to become scapegoats for years of oppression. On the other hand, *Sugar Hill* uses first-person perspective forcing the audience to view events from the perspective of the white victims in each scene of murder, thereby evoking a fear of the zombie despite framing them as avenger in the narrative. Though the film, as Blaxploitation, evokes a revenge narrative that might appeal to a particular audience, by forcing viewers to inhabit the perspective of the zombie's victims the film plays with distinctions between self and other, and between races.

Romero's second zombie film, *Dawn of the Dead* (1978) cemented his legacy and most firmly entrenched the zombie in its role as metaphor for mindless consumerism, taking place as it does in a mall. A small group of survivors find the mall occupied by zombies shuffling from store to store, which they then clear out and secure as their own private fortress. Of course, once inside, they too fall into the empty day-to-day meaninglessness offered by everything the mall has to offer them. Eventually, their mall is attacked by a roving motorcycle gang who take glee in destructively looting the mall, stealing any and everything (strings of pearls and television sets among the more useless of their loot). Rather than taking the rational path of least resistance, especially given the immensity of resources provided by the mall, the remaining inhabitants engage in a battle with the bikers resulting in utter chaos, ultimately handing the mall back over to the throngs of zombie shoppers who once again roam its halls. Attachment to the material goods of the mall ends in the destruction of those seeking to hold onto it all, harking to Buddhist prescriptions of nonattachment to be discussed later.

Dawn, called *Zombi* in parts of Europe, received an unofficial sequel in the form of Lucio Fulci's *Zombi 2*, AKA *Zombie Flesh Eaters* (1979),[127] which did more than any other film to encourage European zombie cinema (and was, in fact, more successful at the box office than Romero's film[128]). Fulci's zombies are significantly more gruesome than any before, their rotting eye sockets dripping with maggots, exposing the frailties of the body more explicitly than any zombie outside of comics until then. Fulci sees his emphasis on gore and exaggerated violence (one impressive scene in *Flesh Eaters* involves a woman's eyeball being impaled on a broken piece of wood, using a combination of close-ups and first-person perspectives from the view of the victim) as a necessary foil to real violence.[129] By making audiences witness to violence, Fulci aims to deter it in the real world. This recalls the possibilities for film and comic book gore as aids to coping with violence discussed earlier as well.

Aside from his expressed distaste for real-world violence, Fulci has also expressed a dislike for any form of social commentary being inserted into film,[130] an interesting perspective given his taking inspiration from Romero's *Dawn*. Here, Fulci agrees with John Russo, who co-wrote *Night of the Living Dead* with Romero and has since tried to remain relevant in zombie fiction with a series of fairly lackluster efforts including film, books, and graphic novels. In one interview, Russo summed up his opinion on the social commentary that has become ubiquitous in zombie fiction since Romero thus:

> A lot of the critics have jumped off the deep end in likening the ghouls to the silent majority and finding all sorts of implications that none of us ever intended. I think George wants to encourage that kind of thinking on the part of some critics. But I'd rather tell them they're full of shit.[131]

And, surely, some of them are, but there is also a lot of good work that has been done in revealing the socio-phobics of various times through the expressions zombies have taken. One effect of deliberately trying to obscure these, though, is that the emphasis on gore and the elimination of social critique bring the core elements of the zombie in terms of its embodiment of human frailty and the imminence of death to the fore. Russo agrees: "*Night of the Living Dead* struck an atavistic chord in people. It was the fear of death magnified exponentially."[132]

Moreover, Fulci also explains his use of body horror as a reflection of his own Catholicism, and more specifically, of his spiritual self-doubt, a theme echoed by Romero as well. While *Flesh Eaters* connects its zombie apocalypse to the Caribbean, and Fulci is clear in his recognition of the syncretism between vodou and Catholicism in the zombie folklore, *City of the Living Dead* (1980) provides the suicide of a Catholic priest as the catalyst for the dark resurrection. Fulci also inspired a veritable horde of European zombie films, many of which were in the vein of Italian spaghetti horrors. Such films often make clear the effect of Italy's being, in Stephen Thrower's words, "under the desiccated thrall of Catholicism,"[133] the Church itself like a zombie moving lifelessly across Europe.[134] Elsewhere, in Francoist Spain, where the dictator had cynically adopted Catholicism to political ends, Amando de Ossorio created a series of "blind dead" films—*Tombs of the Blind Dead* (1971), *Return of the Blind Dead* (1973), *Ghost Ship of the Blind Dead* (1974), and *Night of the Seagulls* (1975)—in which ancient Templars who had been murdered by the Church return from the dead to feast on the living. In addition to evoking the contrast between occult traditions and the violence of the Catholic history within the context of a dictatorial collaboration with the Church (which similarly led a crackdown on Freemasonry during Franco's reign), the films also "underline the zombie's role as an image of mortality,"[135] being cowled, skeletal creatures akin to medieval images of Death itself. In the next chapter, I will go into more detail on the ways in which the zombie has been examined through a particularly Catholic lens, beginning with the groundbreaking work of Kim Paffenroth. And I will also show how such a lens ultimately fails to adequately account for the existential angst produced by the confrontation with mortality wrought by the zombie in the anti–Christian contexts from which it has emerged.

The Absurdity of Zombies Against Materialist Excess

There were a huge number of zombie films being churned out by the early 80s, many of which turned increasingly towards campy laughs over true horror. To be sure, dark humor has been present in the zombie genre since Romero's *Night* (Reporter: "Are these things slow, Chief?" Chief: "Yeah, they're dead, they're all messed up."), but over the next two decades zombies turned cheeseball. There are some interesting films among those of the early 80s, like Lenzi's *Nightmare City* (1980), of which a remake by Tom Savini is said to be in production; *Cannibal Apocalypse* (1980), continuing the Vietnam war-turned zombie narrative; and Sam Raimi's *Evil Dead* (1982). Raimi's film, though its plot involves demon possession as the cause for "zombification," has spawned its own franchise, largely on the back of its sequel/remake, *Evil Dead II* (1989), essentially a retelling of the original but for laughs rather than chills. On one hand, zombie films were cheap to make and there were a huge number produced of such low-quality as to be difficult to take with any seriousness. Further, the increasing materialism of the 1980s may have led to a decrease in the amount of explicit social commentary audiences were willing to take. In response, bodies were destroyed in increasingly exaggerated ways, as if the excess was needed to force audiences to pay attention. In the next chapter, we'll examine the work of David Cronenberg as the kingpin of so-called "body horror," but here we first turn to look at the effects of the period on zombie films specifically.

Most prominent among the films of this decade is *Return of the Living Dead* (1985), which, released the same year as Romero's *Day of the Dead*, is a pinnacle of so-called splat-stick, effectively combining horror and comedy in what some have called a send-up of the zombie genre. Michael Jackson's famous *Thriller* (1983) video prefigured the imagery of *Return* in both the horror of the zombie makeup and the campiness of their dance routine, adding the classical horror dramatics of Vincent Price's "rap" for good measure. Originally based on a book written by John Russo set in the continuity of *Night of the Living Dead*, *Return* was completely re-written, essentially using only Russo's title. Whereas Russo claims to have innovated the flesh-eating zombie in his script for *Night*, Dan O'Bannon's re-written zombies of *Return* added the iconic need for "Braiiiiinnnssss." Though parodic in many ways, the zombies of *Return* would be truly horrific monsters if removed from the comedy. These zombies retain the single-minded pursuit of human flesh of Romero's zombies, but here the walking dead can speak with some intelligence (twice, zombies use police and ambulance radios to call for backup so as to attract more brains), move with a greater speed and dexterity, and are essentially indestructible (early on referencing Romero's works with characters complaining that "the movie" lied when it said to shoot them in the head). While Romero's zombies present a slow and steady fatalism that at least allows some opportunity for brief respite, O'Bannon's creatures are absolute juggernauts of death. In fact, the film ends with the army's decision to drop a nuclear bomb on the infested town, unwittingly creating an atomic winter raining zombie-making chemicals in an ever-wider area. Romero's films have retained a subtle humor and have incrementally allowed for some small glimpse of hope at the end of each film (1985's *Day* sees three protagonists flee to a desert island as likely to be a dream as to be real). *Return of the Living Dead* and its sequels depict an utterly horrifying worldwide destruction, though seemingly only so long as it is all played for laughs.

Monster theorist, Jeffrey Cohen, believes that comedy serves to neutralize the monstrous, essentially disempowering it through mockery.[136] I'm not convinced that the matter is so cut-and-dry. From ancient Greece, tragedy and comedy represented two sides of a coin determined primarily by the story's ending being happy or not. This distinction fails in the present context, though, as films like *Return of the Living Dead* encourage audiences to laugh at the tragedy of military and government incompetence. In fact, the comedy encouraged by such a film is itself unsettling. As Bruce Hallenbeck notes in his history of comedy-horror films, "[a]udiences aren't sure if they should laugh, scream or throw up. Eventually, [*Return of the Living Dead*] settles on a tone that calls for all of those reactions."[137]

The distinction between comedy, horror, and disgust has always been blurry, in fact. On Kubrick's *The Shining*, Caterina Fugazzola and I follow Larry Caldwell and Samuel Umland's suggestion of the importance of play in Kubrick's films and argue for the film's being seen as comedy, aligning it more closely to the playfulness of Zen and Shugendō Buddhism.[138] Robin Wood notes the unavoidable comedy of *The Texas Chainsaw Massacre*, especially as focused on Leatherface, which has the effect of making the film all the more unsettling.[139] David Cronenberg, in the words of film scholar Maurice Yacawar, is a "comic philosopher," recognizing the absurdity of life in the face of death while echoing his own discomfort with existential angst: "He can see the serious and the trivial in the same moment of the human condition, death as at once the most important and the silliest fact of life, man with his dream in the ether and his hangnail in the slime, man at once the magnificence and the speck."[140] Even Alfred Hitchcock, whose *Psycho* (1960) is often seen as the first slasher film, described his horror masterpiece as "tongue-in-cheek" and "rather amusing [...] a big joke," and was horrified himself that audiences took it seriously.[141]

Where comedy, especially parody, appears, many will recall notions of the carnivalesque, particularly when looking for reflections of social and political criticism.[142] Mikhail Bakhtin saw the carnival as a source of societal renewal, embodying both death and rebirth together. His humanist perspective, though, caused him to worry that moderns had lost the capacity for renewal, and would certainly have seen the sadistic humor of zombie nihilism as proof of his fears. His discussion of the grotesque body, taken up by Julia Kristeva in her notion of the abject, will be more usefully discussed in the next chapter in the context of the body as a site of death, but his framing of death as the beginning of rebirth fails to take a long enough view of the human condition. On one hand, he emphasizes the fact that any individual death is unimportant in the face of the ongoing society, the survival of the race relying on a cycle of birth, death, and renewal. On the other hand, though, and this brings us closer to the existential crisis presented here, is the knowledge that even societies die, and, in fact, at some point it is inevitable that humanity will cease to exist just as planets, suns, and solar systems all must end. The utter ridiculousness of personal cares and the importance with which they weigh upon us is, in this long view, laughable. Any renewal present in zombie fiction is embedded in the body of the zombie, a sign of revolution and evolution. In that sense, death itself is the renewal point, inverting Bakhtin's intention when he notes, "Death is included in life."[143]

Ultimately, it isn't that comedy-horror mocks its subject matter— impending death—but rather that laughter and fear ought to go hand in hand. The Theatre of the Absurd, a designation for absurdist works from the likes of Samuel Beckett, Eugène Ionescu, Jean Genet, and others link the absurd with total despair. One cannot properly live life in fear of death; but one cannot laughingly ignore its reality either. Presented with the inevitable, though, one is encouraged by the existential absurdist to chuckle, shrug, and carry on.

Also, given the verisimilitude aimed for in the production of special effects, comedy may also be a useful tool to mask imperfections. For anyone who has watched an unbelievable monster in a film trying to take itself seriously can attest, the natural response is laughter. Unfortunately for the filmmakers in these cases, though, when they present a poor facsimile of a monster as if the thing were realistically scary, laughter indicates their failure. In that case, audience response might accurately be read as mockery, but of the makers of the film itself. On the other hand, lacing the horror with comedy, with tongue-in-cheek as it were, brings the audience on board with the laughs, which has the counter-intuitive result that audiences will be more forgiving of poor makeup and effects. Comedy, then, does not neutralize the films' monsters, but instead disarms the potential hostility of the audience. There is a delicate balance that must be maintained with both horror and comedy, though, as one does not want to scare audiences so much that they flee, and one does not want to move too far in the direction of laughs for fear of becoming a self-parody.[144]

One can see something similar to this idea in ongoing attempts at creating lifelike robots, prosthetics, and artificial intelligence. Researchers have found that people react poorly to a prosthetic when it is close to looking human, inducing an uncomfortable sense of the uncanny—recognizable but unfamiliar at once. On the other hand, people respond much more favorably to a prosthetic when it is purposefully designed to look different while still functioning practically.[145] Eyeglasses represent the most obvious illustration of a prosthetic device designed to look in no way similar to the human body. Likewise, organizations like the Alternative Limb Project create artistically designed limbs that look purposefully like skeletal, robotic, or artistic limbs, to positive response. The choice of prosthetics is one of whether one wants to conceal or admit one's bodily limitations. The desire to conceal a missing limb, say, with a realistic prosthetic runs the risk of inducing the sense of the uncanny; embracing the absence, though, by showing it off in a graphically designed prosthetic brings acceptance and curiosity. The modern popularity of Zombie Walks, where people gather to shamble *en masse* while dressed as zombies might also suggest a desire to revel in the fragility of the human condition. The desire to "play zombie" may provide, as Dave Beisecker suggests, "a welcome chance to laugh at our own ineptness."[146] We will return to the Absurdist response to existential angst in the next chapter, especially in terms of Albert Camus.

The Post-Millennial Zombie Boom

The new millennium marked a resurgence of the zombie as an object of horror more than one of humor. In the lead-up to 2000, the home of zombie horror actually lay in video games, especially Sony's immensely popular (and still-ongoing) *Resident Evil* franchise, which first appeared in 1996, with sequels in each of 1998 and 1999 (and more since), and Sega's successful, and also still-ongoing, *House of the Dead* series of first-person shooters (1996–2013). While some scholars have linked the surge in popularity of the zombie genre to the terrorist threat and 9/11, the two films that set the stage for the zombie outbreak were produced before the attacks despite being released shortly thereafter in 2002. *Resident Evil* (2002) capitalized on its namesake video game's popularity, earning big profits and spawning several sequels of its own despite fairly poor critical reviews. *28 Days Later* (2002), however, set a new standard for zombie horror.

Here we find an effectively grim apocalypse as Jim, the protagonist (played by Cillian Murphy), wakes from a 28-day-long coma to find London entirely vacant. After a hauntingly powerful stroll through the empty streets of London, Jim enters a church seeking help. Passing a scrawled message—"The end is really fucking nigh"—he enters a nave full of dead bodies from among which a number of people leap up to attack him, led by the shambolic priest himself. Though not technically risen dead, the monsters here are people infected by a fast-acting virus called Rage that almost instantly turns people into homicidal maniacs more ferocious than any in *The Crazies*.

Director Danny Boyle includes copious reference to Romero, though, clearly indicating an intention to be included within the zombie genre despite the film's innovations. Aside from general thematic similarities to the zombie genre, viewers will recognize references to, say, *Dawn of the Dead* in the joyous shopping pit stop, or *Day of the Dead* in the violent military keeping a chained infected for experimentation, or to the *Dead* films as a whole in the casting of a black lead.[147] On the other hand, despite being perhaps only tangentially a zombie film proper, it has proven highly influential in its own right.

For one thing, zombie contagion has become so prevalent that many modern scholars assume it to have been a recurring trope of the genre from the beginning when, in fact, it isn't present in Romero at all, showing up sporadically in some films but not others. In Fulci's work, for example, the zombies first rise up due to varying supernatural causes (*Zombie Flesh*

Eaters, 1979; *City of the Living Dead*, 1980) and later are caused by an infectious serum called Death One (*Zombi 3*, 1988). *28 Days Later*, though not exactly the first "zombie" film to feature spry monsters (*Return*'s juggernaut zombies were mighty spry themselves), certainly sparked the debate around slow vs. fast zombies. Most importantly, though, *28 Days* brought zombies back into a wide media attention, allowing Romero to return to the genre in 2005 with *Land of the Dead*, followed later by *Diary of the Dead* (2007) and *Survival of the Dead* (2009).

In the flurry of zombie fiction produced in the twenty-first century, film makers, writers, and video game designers have tended to stay within the general framework outlined by Romero's *Dead* films, the *Return of the Living Dead* series, and the infected of *The Crazies* and *28 Days Later*, though they have often mixed-and-matched a few core aspects. The cause for zombies often remains a mystery, and this is especially true for Romero. In fact, even when the virus is suggested only as a red herring many audiences aren't aware that it is intended only as a distraction. In Robert Kirkman's *The Walking Dead*, for instance, the protagonists become convinced that a virus is to blame when they are informed of the fact by the lone remaining scientist at a CDC lab in Washington. Most audiences take this character at his word despite the fact that he is later shown to be completely mad. Hardly an all-knowing narrator, it is as likely as anything that this character is mistaken or even lying. In any event, the notion that they are infected with a virus that will turn them all into zombies upon death causes the characters in *The Walking Dead* to recognize that it is they themselves who are the titular walking dead, aligning them all the more clearly with the zombies, the living dead, and the dying living. This important connection between humans and zombies has been pointed at not only since Romero's explicit juxtaposition of the corpse of *Night*'s final protagonist, Ben, thrown into a pile of bodies alongside the first zombie seen in the film. From Haitian slavery, the question of personhood for the slaves was paramount—people ought not to be enslaved, unless, it was suggested, those enslaved were subhuman but might still be capable of become fully human in terms of achieving civilization and salvation from the colonist and his religion.

Many have suggested that the wave of fast-moving zombies reflects a need for greater intensity of action or the fact that real-world threats have become more immediate and dire. Following *28 Days Later*, the 2004 *Dawn of the Dead* remake kept the fast zombie, though returned to their being risen corpses. Interestingly, though, the film portrays its zombies as slow and shuffling when not aroused by the presence of living flesh, a dynamic often employed in video games like *Left 4 Dead*, *The Last of Us*, and the *Resident Evil* games, a medium in which the speed of the monster has a huge impact on gameplay. In terms of the relation of the human to the zombie, though, the increased speed of the monsters serves to distance the association. In *Dawn of the Dead* (2004), it is telling that the protagonists reflect on the similarities between the dead and the living (while playing a game of guess-the-celebrity-look-alike-and-shoot-it-in-the-head) only when the dead are shambling slowly in the parking lot.

In other scenes, the quickness of the zombie serves as clear indicator of difference. Unlike *Return of the Living Dead*'s fast zombies that are played against comedy, there are few laughs mediating the fear of those of the new *Dawn*. Anna (Sarah Polley) first sees a neighbor's child standing in her house. The girl lunges at Anna's husband, ripping out a chunk of his neck, before Anna throws the girl off of him. She is forced to react at once, though, when the girl literally jumps to her feet and charges anew. Almost immediately, Anna is then again forced to fight and flee her now dead husband who rises instantaneously as a ferocious monster. What follows is an intense action sequence that eventually sees Anna in her car speeding away from her sprinting late husband. There is no time for reflection on either of these zombies as people; they are clearly monsters.

Other instances of fast-moving zombies drive the wedge between zombie and human ever deeper. Will Smith's turn in *I Am Legend* (2007) refers to its monsters as Infected and depicts them as not only superhumanly fast, but entirely computer-generated, allowing no opportunity to reflect on them as even once human. Even scenes in which Smith relates to the monsters on an individual basis we find that they all look completely alike as well, removing any sense that these are even individuals let alone people. The lamentable *Day of the Dead* (2008) has zombies so agile that they can, spider-like, cling to ceilings in their pursuit, a fact that entirely undermines a central premise of its namesake Romero film in which a captured zombie is found to retain memories of its former life. And the adaptation of *World War Z* (2013), which diverges from the book that stayed with the shambling zombie of Romero, has zombies so quick that they practically fly through the air as they hurl their mouths at their targets and form a living-dead tower of corpses like a swarm of ants enabling them to ascend the walled city of Jerusalem before its inhabitants have time to react. These all serve the desire for nail-biting action, but they miss a core component of the zombie genre—that "they're us," as Peter (Ken Foree) observes in the original *Dawn*.

The connection between the living and the dead is played out fairly explicitly in most zombie films, with characters themselves often remarking on the association. Sometimes it will be idle observation accompanied by close-ups of the face of some dimly searching zombie, and in other instances it is the result of a character's loved one becoming a zombie. The question whether the zombie is still the person in any way comes up time again, often with terrible consequences. Hershel, in *The Walking Dead*, keeps zombified loved ones in the barn, even feeding them in the hopes they might one day be cured. His Christian faith is challenged when the barn doors are sundered and his family violently emerges and must each be destroyed before his eyes. Also in *The Walking Dead*, the villainous Governor is humanized in his relationship to his living-dead daughter, whom he hopes to discipline into behaving. Comically, *Shaun of the Dead* (2004) has its protagonist (Simon Pegg) mistaking several zombies for late-night revelers and early-morning commuters. In *Night of the Living Dead*, several characters die when they mistake a zombie for a loved one and are unable to muster a defense, absent the clear monstrosity of the creatures in the *Dawn* remake.

Romero, inspired by Matheson's new vampire society, depicts a progression of agency in his zombies, though. Vestigial memories are indicated as the reason for zombies converging on the mall, an idea picked up in his later films, most pronouncedly in the forms of Bub in *Day of the Dead* and in Big Daddy's leading a zombie army in *Land of the Dead* (2005). That the zombies might retain some sense of agency has also been toyed with by others, though primarily in the realm of comedy. *Shaun of the Dead* ends with the zombies being domesticated and forced into menial labor for the living. Likewise, *Fido* (2006) is another zombie-comedy wherein the undead retain some slight agency and can be domesticated into menial laborers. The fact that they remain a victim of their own hunger for flesh, though, recalls the horror-comedy of *Return of the Living Dead* as well. *Zombie Honeymoon* (2004) tells the tale of newlyweds who must deal with the zombification of the groom; both husband and wife work together to try and overcome his cannibalistic desires, which eventually win out as he murders and devours several people close to them before attacking his wife. He retains enough agency, though, to stop himself at the last second, choosing to die himself in order to save his beloved. *Zombies Anonymous* (2006) also has its zombies struggling with their addiction to human flesh, but the undead here retain all of their wits and complete agency, effectively retaining their personhood, though they are severely discriminated against by the still-living population. At this point, the tendency to view the zombie as downtrodden Other is clearly being played out in reverse with the zombie literally the victim of violent intolerance. The television series, *iZombie* (2015–present), based on the comic of the same title, centers on a woman who becomes infected with a zombie-causing virus that she must keep secret from the world while using her new-found state to advantage in solving crimes.

In *Zombie Strippers* (2008) the strippers become more powerful and attractive when they become zombies, again playing with the revolutionary associations of the zombie, here in service of overturning heteronormative sexual power dynamics. The female zombie strippers retain their agency, selecting male audience members on whom to feed; willingly sacrificing themselves, believing something more titillating is in store for them, the men actually become mindless zombies that must be locked in the cellar. Taking the agency of zombies even further, *Warm Bodies* (2013), based on Isaac Marion's novel of the same name, tells a Romeo & Juliet tale of love between a human and a zombie. Shot from the perspective of the zombie, the audience witnesses the inner thoughts of troubled zombies unable to communicate with the living despite their desire for closeness. The film's tagline, "He's still dead, but he's getting warmer," effectively summarizes the story as the protagonist zombie, R (Nicholas Hoult), slowly regains the capacity to speak and express himself to a living woman, Julie (Teresa Palmer), and together they overcome human bias against the zombies. The film ends with the protagonist effectively coming back to life. This film proves the trajectory of the previous examples of zombie agency—whereas the horror of the zombie comes from the fear of death itself, each of these comedies allows for the zombies to have agency, thereby distracting from or downright denying their power as *memento mori*, reminders of mortality.

My point may be clearer if I put this in the context of those scholars who have equated Alzheimer's patients with the walking dead. Many whose loved ones have suffered from dementia will have at times wondered about whether any of the person they once knew still resides within the body of their loved one. Likewise for victims of comas. Though known since the 1960s, locked-in syndrome has only recently entered into popular consciousness with autobiographies of victims like Martin Pistorius's *Ghost Boy* (2011), Richard Marsh's *Locked In* (2014), and Jean-Dominique Bauby's *The Diving Bell and the Butterfly* (1997), which was also made into a motion picture in 2007. All of these memoirs describe the horrifying experience of being entirely conscious inside an entirely paralyzed body thought by those outside to be comatose and therefore completely unconscious and potentially even brain dead. In fact, a great many people must have witnessed themselves being removed from life-saving machines while in this state before its being discovered. Stories like this give hope to families of comatose patients who argue that their loved ones react to them despite doctors' assertions of brain death. Such instances bring into question our very definitions of death. Several high profile cases like those of Jahi McMath and Terri Schiavo, have raised questions about the persistence of consciousness, and selfhood, in states of so-called brain-death or persistent vegetative comas. Instances of locked-in syndrome prove that the medical establishment may be wrong in determining when a person is lost, encouraging some to hold onto loved ones as long as the body can be maintained. On the other hand, as perhaps most saliently recalled in the Schiavo case, many see the fate of those in a coma to be one worse than death.[148] As for those with Alzheimer's, the matter is even less clear as some degree of agency is apparent, though the patient may not behave as the person their family remembers. These conditions all present an ambiguity of consciousness in relation to the body, just as does the typical zombie.

After the success of his groundbreaking Catholic study of the zombie, *Gospel of the Living Dead*, theologian Kim Paffenroth has embarked on a successful career as a horror fiction writer. His *Dying to Live* series of novels adds yet another innovation to the genre, and one that corresponds with his own Christian understanding of the genre. Briefly, the first of the series, *Dying to Live: A Novel of Life among the Undead* (2007), introduces a salvific figure that is alive and yet also somehow zombie, giving him the power to influence the zombies, keeping them at bay, thereby saving his fellows from death. Like the comedies above, such an approach to zombies also ignores them as representatives for the inevitability of death, replacing it with the Christian equation of death with sin and Jesus with life. This is exactly Paffenroth's interpretation of the zombie genre, too, describing the zombie apocalypse as a vision of Hell like Dante's *Inferno*. While the films he discusses either completely ignore religion, or even mock it, offering no hint that there may be any God offering salvation, Paffenroth persists in seeing the zombies as a call to turn to God. Interestingly, the tongue-in-cheek television series, *Z Nation* (2015–present) incorporates something similar to Paffenroth's savior (though the series aims to hit on possibly every zombie trope possible) as its team of protagonists attempt to transport a former prisoner who wields power over the zombies and is somewhat resistant to the zombie virus, though he slowly begins to give signs of decay. Clearly, then, the films and show above share in common with the Christian understanding of needing a particular kind of happy ending—one that denies death as a permanent end.

Whether recent audiences might have responded to fears of terrorism or to ongoing fears of viral outbreak, such fears were not exactly new to the twenty-first century. Certainly, 9/11 had a profound effect on the sense of American safety at home, but even John Russo acknowledged terrorist fears thirty years earlier.[149] And whether disease or violence, the core fear remains that of death. It is true that more zombie fiction has been produced since 9/11 than was produced in all the decades before. It is certainly more than possible that the events of 9/11 exacerbated existential fears, but the important thing to note is that terrorism alone cannot account for the love of zombie fiction.

Also, since the seeds of the zombie resurgence were already rumbling through the 90s, I expect that millenarian concerns played a role in the zombie resurgence, especially given the fact that watershed films *28 Days Later* and *Resident Evil*, while released after 9/11, were produced before the terrorist attack. If Y2K was supposed to mark the end times, then we truly are living in a post-apocalyptic world. Alongside the brewing zombie storm, the late 1990s also saw the beginning of Tim LaHaye and Jerry Jenkins's best-selling *Left Behind* series, which has grown to include sixteen novels, a video game series, and four feature-films (*Left Behind: The Movie*, 2000; *Left Behind II: Tribulation Force*, 2002; *Left Behind: World at War*, 2005; and the Nick Cage reboot, *Left Behind*, 2014). However poor the films have been, the *Left Behind* series has been hugely influential in spreading the dispensationalist notion of the millennial End Times and rapture. While both zombie cinema and the *Left Behind* series depict apocalyptic worlds in which people are left on Earth to suffer the tribulations of the end of the world, only the latter refers to the possibility that any of the former earthly inhabitants might have been saved from this fate through a rapture to God. As such, the zombie genre reflects the same millennial fears as the rapture crowd, but without God's being involved in any positive, salvific way.

Reflecting the secularist perspective inherent in zombie fiction, Max Brooks's *The Zombie Survival Guide*, published in 2003, offers readers advice for "complete protection from the living dead." The book was a New York Times best seller, as was his follow-up novel, *World War Z: An Oral History of the Zombie War* (2006), and its realistic tone, furthered by a series of lectures Brooks has given, encouraged zombie-survivalist attitudes to go mainstream. While many zombie fans may have imagined escape or survival scenarios for themselves in the event of apocalypse, there are many others who take the enterprise seriously. National Geographic profiles various survivalist strategies, and their visions on what will cause the impending fall of civilization, in its four-season series, *Doomsday Preppers* (2012–2014), and Discovery Channel ran a special titled "Zombie Apocalypse" featuring survivalists claiming that a zombie apocalypse isn't a question of if, but when, and offers scientific justifications for the reality of just such an occurrence. The Center for Disease Control still maintains its "Zombie Preparedness" website[150]; while admittedly tongue-in-cheek, they've found it a useful outreach tool, but the association of the CDC to the idea of zombie pandemic lends the idea credibility to some. I've been asked by students more than once, in all seriousness, if I think a zombie apocalypse can happen. Some have even reacted with surprise when I've answered, "No, of course not."

Though I have already mentioned the influence of Sega and Sony as seeds of the new surge of interest in zombies, alongside the explosion of manga dedicated to zombies, there is a massive range of Japanese zombie cinema as well.[151] The vast majority of these productions fall squarely within the realm of the ridiculous as opposed to the horrific, but they feature elements of exaggeration and an emphasis on the destruction of the body that have come to define much of Japanese cinema. Titles like *Battle Girl: The Living Dead in Tokyo Bay* (1992); *Attack Girls' Swim Team vs. Undead* (2007); *Big Tits Zombie* (2010); and *Zombie Ass: Toilet of the Dead* (2011) all juxtapose sexualized-schoolgirl fetishism with myriad bodily abjections of shit, vomit, and corpses—a Freudians stew of Eros and Thanatos. Though the Japanese approach lies much more on the side of comedy, the emphasis on the zombie as embodied death remains. As a character in *Zombie Ass* resignedly remarks: "You fart and fart until you die. That's your fate." The parasite that creates the farting zombies of this film were an experimental attempt by a mad scientist to slow the cancer killing his daughter. Ultimately, though, the film ends when the heroine accepts her flatulence and uses it to defeat the villainous scientist. Though a ridiculous premise, the theme of accepting one's mortality and the absurdity of life as nothing but a fart in the wind is clear. The seemingly nonsensical approach is one familiar to the Japanese mindset, though, especially in reference to Zen, to be further discussed in chapter four later.

The zombie offers not a purely secular view of the end of the world since it requires a suspension of scientific laws in order to raise dead corpses seeking to destroy the living. But the zombie likewise does not offer a Christian view of the End Times, including no respite from suffering and no rapture of the faithful. Again, then, we see here the influence of occulture, a recognition of the numinous in the body of the zombie. I'll return to this idea in the next chapter, as well as an examination of how an emphasis on the body in both Christian and secular terms might blur in an occultural and popular imagination to present the problem of human identity and bodily corruptibility in the form of the quasi-supernatural zombie. At this point, we have traced the evolution of the zombie from Haiti through to today. The core feature of the zombie remains its loss of agency, and retains the texture of standing against traditional Christian resurrection as a revolutionary spiritual figure. A figure that speaks to the equality of all people in the face of death, and forces existential questions about what is important in life.

Chapter Three

Embodied Death

Applying so-called "sociophobics," various interpretations of the zombie have been proposed, especially in pointing to the fears of certain groups of people at different points in history.[1] For his part, Romero has waffled on his metaphorical use of zombies, seemingly settling on them as an outlet for his personal social commentary.[2] At first, with *Night*, Romero himself expressed skepticism at there being any message or deeper meaning intended, though he admits to the possibility: "I was just making a horror film, and I think the anger and the attitude and all that's there is just there because it was 1968. We lived at the farmhouse, so we were always into raps about the implication and the meaning, and stuff like that, so maybe some crept in."[3] Romero explains: "There is some major shit going on out there, and in a distant way the zombies represent what we, the global community, should really be thinking about."[4] On many of the interpretations suggested by critics and scholars, though, he is less convinced: "I find, oddly, occasionally you come across something and you say, gee, maybe I was thinking that or maybe this does represent that, but most of the time I think a lot of it's just way overanalyzed."[5] For his part, Fulci suggested that social comments had no place in fantasy fiction, and claimed that only amateurs couched their work in polemics in order to hide its artistic weakness.[6] And, as I have mentioned before, John Russo is more to the point: "I'd rather tell them they're full of shit."[7]

One area upon which there is general agreement, though, is on the relation of the gore inflicted by, upon, and manifest in the form of the zombie to its physical form and that of its victims—eliciting the label, "body horror." Zombies are dead, and, in the words of *Night*'s sheriff, they are "all messed up." Whatever other metaphorical representations might be hung on the zombie, it is above all a reminder of the inevitability of death, a *memento mori* of a particularly aggressive sort. Zombie scholarship will often nod to the obvious fear of death inherent in the genre, but then move on to some other specific agenda. Whatever aspect of society one might want to look at, though, it cannot be denied that death is a central concern. Those who want to argue over whether the zombie best embodies a fear of disease or, say, a fear of terrorists, are missing the point that death is core to any of these other fears.

It is worth noting the timing of Romero's first film, coming as it does soon before the publication of Elisabeth Kübler-Ross's highly influential *On Death and Dying* (1969). The success of her work stems not only from her own charismatic style, but also from the fact that the public was ready to engage death in a more open way than it had been for decades previous. Arguing for a view of zombie fiction as a critique of consumerism or of the nuclear family, or as revealing racial tensions and inequalities, or any other of the many critical perspectives available, is fine, and, in fact, commendable. But even these issues have at the heart existential questions about meaning and how we ought to live our lives. The fact of death, of its unquestioned yet uncertain imminence and pervasive immanence, forces us to consider meaning in life every day, so long as we accept reality and face it head-on. Recognizing horror's recurrent themes of "human finitude in general and their own personal mortality in particular," I agree with lawyer and philosopher, Juneko Robinson, in seeing this genre as especially ripe for existential analysis, the popularity of the genre, in fact, suggesting audiences' eagerness for just such contemplation.[8] Zombie fiction relentlessly forces audiences to face the existential fact of mortality. More than other genres, like war or westerns where death is ever-present, zombie fiction (largely) removes any capacity for escape and survival, and outmatches other horror (and even body horror) in its focus on the corpse, in realistically gruesome fashion.[9]

In this chapter I want to emphasize the importance of death in the zombie genre—the zombie is death itself, and it is coming for us all, and there is absolutely no escape. Though most commentators focus on how the zombie reflects on aspects of life and society, all of these concerns are secondary to core human existentialism in the face of mortality. It may be no surprise that the one group of scholars who approach the zombie with existential concerns in mind are also scholars of religion, the Catholic theologian, Kim Paffenroth, chief among them. Certainly, the Catholic tradition has a rich history of *ars moriendi* (art of death), and *memento mori* in particular. The short-lived Paulist congregation of the Brothers of Death, for example, met each other with the exhortation, "Remember that you must die," and meditated upon the death's head in solitary. Of course, Christianity also has an ambivalent relationship with the mortal body which leads Paffenroth and others to certain conclusions about how one ought to read the zombie. I'll argue in the following pages, though, that this perspective only works within a Christian framework that forces the zombie into a Procrustean bed of doctrine and ignores so many other aspects of the creature and the genre. Also, it finds itself in conflict with the Haitian tradition from which the creature came to prominence as a parody of the doctrine of resurrection.

For the Christian hermit, meditation on the mortality of the body was inflected by notions of sin on one hand, and eternal life in a glorified resurrected body on the other. The rotting corpse as object of meditation in this context does not reflect death, per se, but rather points to the sinful nature of the human being. The body, in essence, presents a physical metaphor for the rotting, sinful nature we have inherited as beings born into a world of Original Sin. Incorporating Christian doctrines into one's meditation will direct one's attention to the fact that death is, in fact, entirely avoidable through the cleansing of the sin which causes decay and death. That cleansing comes specifically through the life and teachings of Jesus Christ. Death is not a thing to be feared since it is but a stop along the way to further life. The real fear is sin, and the possibility (or probability in some denominations) that one will live on eternally in Hell after death. None of these ideas work to encourage an acceptance of death through meditation thereupon. Death is equated with sin, and as such is detestable and to be avoided; the cure is a focus on Jesus and Christian dogma instead.

In discussing the role of Catholic dogma, I will move next into a discussion of the importance of the body not only in the Christian tradition but its depiction in horror, and especially in body horror, a sub-genre of horror focusing on imaginative destruction of human bodies. Similar questions of personal identity and individual mortality appear in this genre of fiction as in Catholic reflections on the body, though the answers differ for the secularist, often resulting in such filmmakers being misunderstood as misanthropes or nihilists. Zombie fiction clearly fits into this category, with its realistic exploration of human anatomy stretched, broken, and reformed, all central to the genre. In the pages to come, I will turn to ideas about disgust and the abject in relation to the zombie to illuminate the problems posed by our own experiences and perspectives on our bodies, and ultimately upon our attitudes towards death, the self, and mortality. I will then show how a Buddhist *memento mori* much more cleanly and plainly accords with both the reality of human mortality and with what we see reflected in the zombie genre. In fact, the zombie itself is a perfect reflection of Buddhist philosophy in ways that far outstrip its relationship to Christian conceptions of the resurrection, the body, and sin.

On Catholic Interpretations of the Zombie

Certainly, the symbolism of the risen corpse as a dark and twisted resurrection of the dead relates easily to the Catholic tradition. Romero has spoken openly about his own ambivalence to his Catholic upbringing, and Romero's zombie films have been filmed largely in Western Pennsylvania, a region with a relatively large Catholic population.[10] Romero's rigid parochial-school upbringing left him with an early terror of Hell[11] that he has grown to mock contemptuously in his films. Some have argued that Italy became a hotbed of zombie film-making due to the strength of its Catholic tradition.[12] We saw earlier how African slaves salvaged their spirituality through a syncretism of their African traditions with Catholicism, which was being foisted upon them by European oppressors. While Catholicism has become the official state religion of Haiti, Vodou remains an integral part of its heritage, working for Haitians in concert with official Church doctrine. Vodou, though, includes subtle subversions of Catholic tradition in playing with its symbolism to undercut its historical colonial power. The zombie especially stands in as a parody of the resurrection, and the fear of eating the flesh of a zombie a subtle rejection of the flesh of Christ. Even removed from Haitian tradition, the risen corpse and the cannibalistic connotations of the Communion remain perceptible to anyone even loosely familiar with Christian thought.

We have also seen how the subversive spirituality of the Beat Generation entered into the horror lexicon, especially through Richard Matheson's influential works. In fact, though Romero based his monsters on the vampires of *I Am Legend*, audiences instead saw them as zombies. So confusing has been the transition for some that Tim Kane completely ignores *The Last Man on Earth* and *I Am Legend* in his history of vampires in television and film,[13] while at the other extreme, David Pirie argued that Romero's monsters should most rightly be categorized as vampires instead![14]

Though vampires have themselves been folklorically tied to Christianity as devils defeated by the power of the cross, the zombie instead subverts the very tradition from its beginnings. If the traditional vampire is a mockery of the resurrection, it is one that still demonstrates the strength of established religion in its impotence in the face of the cross. The vampire is like a dull shadow of Christ—killed by impaling, stealing blood to survive rather than offering blood to save[15]—ultimately destroyed by the light of the sun and the power of the cross. The zombie, though, recognizes no such authority, offering a resurrection without God and the much more brutal craving for raw flesh rather than the potentially more delicate sucking of blood alone.[16] The notion of vampires feeling no fear of the cross has since become an often used trope, but the newness of the idea at the time contributed to audiences' failure to see the creatures as vampires but rather as zombies with their Christian-ambivalence built in.

Much Catholic theology of the body revolves around a triune distinction in the body of Christ as it appears in the individual, in the Eucharist, and in the Church itself. The individual yearns for the *imitatio Christi*, to imitate Christ (most coarsely expressed by WWJD?—What Would Jesus Do?). The Eucharist embodies Christ in the miraculous transubstantiation whereby the very substance of the unleavened bread becomes that of the Divine Savior. Participating in Communion allows the individual Catholic to become literally one with Christ as His body joins with their own. The Eucharistic body of Christ is, before consumption, broken in sympathy with the damage done to the physical body of Jesus during His crucifixion.[17] This broken body, on one hand, comes into communion with the physical individual body through literal consumption. However, the divine One-ness in Christ is achieved as well, facilitated and engineered through the body of the Church in which individuals come together as a whole. There is, then, even at this theological level, ambivalence about bodies, physical and divine, singular and communal, broken and whole. This tension is apparent in Catholic discussions of not only the body, but of the specifically dead and broken, and yet also still communal, body.

Kim Paffenroth, beginning with his award-winning *Gospel of the Living Dead*,[18] describes Romero's zombie films as reflections of a world without God, a veritable Hell on Earth. Here, he follows the likes of the scholar of American literature, and fellow Catholic, Edward Ingebretsen, who sees modern horror as the flip-side of the sacred reality, using it to construct a vision of Paradise, arguing that "a map of Heaven could only be constructed, as it were, by inversion, beginning with Hell."[19] Seen from this perspective, zombie fiction is entirely nihilistic, representing an apocalyptic vision of life as a hopeless march towards death—a notion Paffenroth describes as "a fairly common—and straightforward and understandable—criticism of the zombie subgenre."[20] Pointing to what is essentially the existentialist problem forced upon the consumer of zombie fiction, Paffenroth says: "The enormous, worldwide popularity of such a hopeless film shows that its hopelessness struck a chord with people, said something meaningful to people about a world of meaninglessness."[21] Now, the Christian response to existentialism is, without a doubt, to reject it as nihilism and to assert that meaninglessness is a fallacy, a demonic trick, and that one need only witness the truth of God's love to know meaning. To expect that there can be found any hope or meaning within humanity itself is "a fool's hope," as banding together, those living without God cannot find "a real escape from the utterly horrifying dead world in which they are trapped."[22] In a sense, Paffenroth and others recognize the absence of God in the zombie genre, but since they believe that such an absence is a lie, they must then seek to explain how these films reflect Him, thereby mapping Heaven through understanding Hell.

Essentially, for these writers, the depth of horror is nothing more than the absence of God. They believe, though, that in reality God is not absent, and that His Love overcomes any fear. As one scholar suggests: "The 'Romero zombie' has become a representation of our greatest fears realized in an apocalyptic vision of flesh and bone—that the forces of good and evil will eventually collide in a massive conflict that threatens to consume everything we value."[23] Regardless of whether Armageddon can really be called our greatest fear or merely that of a particular ideology, such an interpretation cannot be constrained only to zombie fiction as surely any scene of utter despair and suffering must similarly call for the same. The fearful absence of God is instead an absence of faith. Timothy Beal, reflecting on the story of Job, notes that the true horror here is not an empty Nietzschean abyss of meaninglessness in the face of suffering, but rather the discovery of God within that abyss in the form of an "overwhelming [...] divine chaos," a meaningfulness beyond human comprehension.[24] Wherever there is darkness and suffering, Christian commentary sees the absence of belief in Christ, a turning away from His Love. Douglas Cowan, for instance, argues that "a multitude of cinematic horrors" are best described as commentary "on the fear of secularization, not necessarily the reality of it, and the ambivalence of our ongoing attempts to retain belief in an omnipotent and omnibenevolent deity," and that "the practical absence of benevolent deity [sic] is the linchpin that allows these films to succeed as horror."²⁵ So, why approach the zombie specifically from a Catholic perspective?

Paffenroth notes similarities between the grotesque corpses of zombie fiction and those of Dante's *Inferno*. Michael Gilmour likewise points out just how gory the Bible itself can be, especially in the context of *gehenna*, or Hell.²⁶ This brings the link between human suffering and mortality into a clearer focus, not only in the clear depiction of the literal corruption of the flesh but also in the Christian approach of positing a post-mortem reward, thereby over-riding the fear of death with the promise of eternal life—at the cost of no more than having faith in Jesus Christ, Son of God, Savior, and acting accordingly so far as one is able. Zombie fiction, in similarity with Dante's *Inferno*, uses grotesque and disturbing imagery to, according to Paffenroth, "shock us out of our sins, especially out of our violence and materialism."²⁷ And so, in this view, horror is a means of scaring us towards God; and zombies in particular connote death, resurrection, and the afterlife in their similarities to traditional depictions of Hell. That Hannah Arendt, a secular Jew, also saw reflections of medieval depictions of Hell in the bodies of the "living corpses" filling Nazi concentration camps ought to give us pause in accepting a distinctly Christian view of zombies.²⁸

The Church has long been criticized for its perspectives on the Holocaust, from the silence of Pius XII during World War II to the foundation of the Carmelite nunnery on the grounds of Auschwitz and the perceived co-opting of the martyrdom of Edith Stein to become St. Teresa Benedicta of the Cross, after it.²⁹ Pope Benedict XVI drew no small criticism to his response to his visit to Auschwitz in which he urged in the face of "this place of horror":

> Let us cry out to God, with all our hearts, at the present hour, when new misfortunes befall us, when all the forces of darkness seem to issue anew from human hearts: whether it is the abuse of God's name as a means of justifying senseless violence against innocent persons, or the cynicism which refuses to acknowledge God and ridicules faith in him. Let us cry out to God, that he may draw men and women to conversion and help them to see that violence does not bring peace, but only generates more violence—a morass of devastation in which everyone is ultimately the loser.³⁰

The suggestion here would seem to be that if only there had been more Christian converts, the horrors of the Holocaust might have been averted, and that the way to peace ultimately comes through such conversion. Likewise, Kipp Davis finds points of comparison between the Essene apocalyptic writings of the Dead Sea Scrolls and AMC's *The Walking Dead*, both offering prophetic condemnations of the present and pessimism about the future, with the core difference being that while the zombie apocalypse offers only nihilistic Hell, the Essenes predicted the coming salvation through Christ.[31]

Paffenroth contends that Romero's films are "recognizably biblical in their apocalyptic imagery, and their prophetic denunciation of the society in which their creator and audience lives."[32] Further, biblical evidence for resurrection or depictions of Hell are based on divine revelation, such as that granted to the Prophet Zechariah promising a plague upon the enemies of Israel:

> Their flesh will rot while they are still standing on their feet, their eyes will rot in their sockets, and their tongues will rot in their mouths. On that day people will be stricken by the Lord with great panic. They will seize each other by the hand and attack one another.[33]

Of course, one doesn't really need to invoke prophecy to recognize a successful social critique. Still, Paffenroth is not alone in likening Romero's work to prophecy. In his fascinating analysis, David Pagano explains that the apocalyptic writer (and the reader must remember that in its truest sense, apocalypse—from the Greek, *apo kalypsis*, to uncover—refers to the revealing of the hidden) must, in order to have truly witnessed the end of time, have experienced individual death and returned to tell the tale; as such, "a prophet is a 'reanimated corpse.'"[34] If the vision is really one of the end of time, the viewer of such a state must also exist outside of time, like imagining one's own funeral where, as object, one will be the corpse while, as observer, one is still alive beyond death. The liminality of both being and not-being, between being alive and dead, here and there, are all inherent in revelation. This liminality, being suspended between two definitive states, is also a feature of horror generally, and explicitly in the "living dead."[35] The vision presented by Romero, according to Pagano, is better described as "meta-apocalyptic" since, although prophetic in the sense that it offers a criticism of contemporary society against a glimpse of the end times, it refuses to offer "the aid of any supernatural intermediary."[36] And the zombie fiction of the likes of Lucio Fulci (*Zombie*, 1979; *City of the Living Dead*, 1980; *Zombi 3*, 1988) and Michele Soavi (*Dellamorte Dellamore*, 1994) go even further than Romero in dropping social critique altogether, and simply rending open the apocalyptic veil of a Godless present and future.[37]

Apocalyptic fiction has been popular for some time, and not all of it, or even most of it, includes zombies. Evangelical millenarianist expectations of impending end-times, as depicted in the likes of Hal Lindsey's *Late Great Planet Earth*, published in 1970, were stoked as the year 2000 approached. Likewise, the seeds for the absolute explosion of interest in the zombie were planted by Sony's 1996 video game, *Resident Evil*.[38] Interest in the zombie simmered through the turn of the century, until 2002 saw the cinematic release of both *Resident Evil* and *28 Days Later*, both of which depict experiments gone wrong resulting in a viral spread that turns people into mindlessly homicidal monsters. The modern zombie film, following the mold set by Romero, offers the imminent destruction of humankind with no salvation either divine or human (suggestions of "happy endings" are routinely undercut in sequels showing the situation to have gotten worse instead of better); a vision the Christian commentator decries as nihilistic.

Of course, much of what we call apocalyptic fiction is apocalyptic only in the sense of its representing the destruction of the world as we know it, whereas a more technical view of apocalypse requires the involvement of divine power. Recognizing an increase in what might be termed secular apocalyptic fiction through the turn of the last century, Conrad Ostwalt noted, "the modern apocalypse has replaced a sovereign God with a sovereign humanity, and instead of providing hope for an eschatological kingdom, the cinematic apocalypse attempts to provide hope for this world."[39]

According to Paffenroth, Romero's apocalyptic vision is a warning of how not to behave lest one be damned, just as were those of the early biblical prophets. Certainly, some of the characters (most often black) in zombie fiction do see the zombies as a punishment from God, as with Andre's (Mekhi Phifer) sense that he personally deserves this apocalypse in *Dawn of the Dead* (2004) to Peter's (Ken Foree) famous proverbial wisdom: "When there's no more room in Hell, the dead will walk the Earth" in *Dawn of the Dead* (1978) and John's (Terry Alexander) rumination in *Day of the Dead* (1985) that God "visited a curse on us so we might get a look at what hell was like. Maybe He didn't wanna see us blow ourselves up and put a big hole in His sky. Maybe He just wanted to show us He was still the boss man. Maybe He figured we was getting' too big for our britches tryin' to figure His shit out."

Rather than seeing the protagonists as trapped in Hell, Carole Lépinay offers the alternative, yet still Catholic, possibility that they are instead in Purgatory and so there remains hope for their salvation.[40] The mall of *Dawn of the Dead* (1978), the underground military bunker of *Day of the Dead* (1985), and even the high-rise of Fiddler's Green in *Land of the Dead* (2008) are all static way-points surrounded by the mouth of Hell in the jaws of every zombie. In her view, the characters in each film who cause the zombies to finally break down the barricades (Stephen, Miguel, and

Cholo, respectively) are actually martyrs whose sacrifices force the remaining protagonists to escape from Purgatory and move on towards Paradise. The failure of this interpretation should be apparent, though, when one recognizes that each of Lépinay's martyrs dies not for any higher purpose than for their own selfish desires—Stephen begins a disastrous war with a biker gang in order to try and hold onto the riches of the mall; Miguel opens the gates of the bunker and throws himself at the horde of zombies, clutching a crucifix, succumbing to severe depression; and Cholo is blinded by his own desire for vengeance. These men do not die to save the living, but rather their selfish deaths bring the zombies even closer. As Heath (Corey Hawkins) laments in an episode of *The Walking Dead*, "If it's you or someone else, you choose you. You take what you can, you take out who you have to, and you get to keep going. Nobody's in this together, okay? Not anymore" (S7E6: "Swear"). These are not descriptions of individuals being purged of sin leading to eventual reward.

Paffenroth correctly identifies what he calls a "fierce" and "misguided individualism"[41] at the root of the problem in zombie movies; as the crisis intensifies, the living fight amongst themselves instead of working in communal harmony. In the above-mentioned episode of *The Walking Dead*, Tara (Alanna Masterson) counters Heath's claim with, "Hey. It only hurts because you know what you just said is total bullshit. That's not you, Heath," illustrating the ambivalence individuals face in confronting personal mortality and that of others. And this struggle, between individualism and communitarianism, lies at the heart of American political philosophy, according to political scientist, Leah Murray, who argues that Romero's films (she specifically references *Night*) promote communitarianism by negating the effectiveness of individualism.[42] We root for the protagonists to work together to survive the apocalyptic struggle as infighting inevitably spells disaster and death, thereby teaching the lesson that we should work together to succeed. Of course, this misses the more important fact that however long one survives, there is never any scenario in which everyone does not end up dying. Paffenroth recognizes this overarching fact in *Night of the Living Dead*, lamenting that the death of all of the film's main characters represents "a rejection of any value for any human relationship, institution, or virtue. According to this most cynical and nihilistic of the films [...], nothing really matters, because the result is always the same—death."[43] But the film doesn't ever say that "nothing matters," it simply allows all of its characters to die. So, it isn't that the film's message is one of nihilism; it is, rather, only the viewer's perception that there can be no meaning if death is the end.

I am reminded of René Girard's theory that human society is based upon a contagious, mimetic desire leading inevitably to violence and strife. This violence begets violence as our competitive desires turn to desire simply to win the competition. According to Girard, only a scapegoat, a common target for the now-competing group's violent hatred, can bring the group together in cooperation. Collective hatred for the scapegoat finds catharsis in its death, by which the scapegoat becomes a sacrifice that is seen as the savior from strife. Essentially, in life, the scapegoat is hated, but once dead, the scapegoat may be deified. Obviously, the Christ myth provides a core example for Girard. Likewise for Paffenroth, Jesus was the necessary sacrifice to overcome the cycle of violent, individualistic desire. In this view, the returned dead are the continuation of the former strife and violence due to an absence of the salvific influence of Christ's sacrifice. Noting cultures in which the dead are believed capable of returning to torment the living, Girard notes: "The punishments that the dead inflict upon the living are indistinguishable from the consequences of wrongdoing."[44] If the resolution to violence can only be accomplished by the sacrifice of the scapegoat, and that scapegoat was Jesus Christ, then there is only one interpretation for the punishment inflicted by the dead upon the living—that the sacrifice of the scapegoat was ineffective.

Paffenroth argues that while Romero depicts a world in which both faith and reason fail to save anyone, Christian faith does not claim to *physically* save whereas secular reason aims to do just that. This is a world in which reason is defeated and faith is left unscathed—essentially, because faith can NEVER be scathed.[45] Given the facts of the films themselves, I have to agree with Robin Wood when he says: "Of one thing we may be sure: the films are not about 'punishment for sin.' Romero's universe is certainly not a Christian one (the occasional religious references are always negative)."[46] The characters in zombie films are often religious. *Night of the Living Dead* begins with two characters in a cemetery, one of whom prays solemnly at her father's grave and chastises her brother's absence from Sunday mass before being attacked by the walking dead. The original *Dawn of the Dead* includes a one-legged Catholic priest who laments the inevitable social power shift from recognized authority to zombie, and also features both a zombie-nun and a zombie–Hari Krishna. The remake of *Dawn of the Dead* (2004) includes an atheistic church organist, as well as a television evangelist (Ken Foree in a wink to the original *Dawn*) who preaches God's wrath as the meaning behind the zombie apocalypse. *Day of the Dead* (1985) includes a character who commits suicide by throwing himself to zombies while clutching his crucifix as he is devoured. And *28*

Days Later (2002) sees the protagonist's first encounter with the infected as he enters a Catholic church for help only to be attacked by a zombified priest. *Fear the Walking Dead* (2015) likewise introduces its first zombie in a church, this time one having been abandoned and used as a shooting gallery for heroin addicts before the zombie outbreak even started. There is no indication in any of these films that faith offers any sort of salvation, physical or otherwise. Gregory Waller puts it well when he notes that Barbara's faith serves only "to make her awakening to her dilemma that much more rude and catastrophic."[47] Paffenroth declares his position early on, stating that for Christians "the only way for people to be really happy is by loving God in community with other human beings, and not by selfishly loving and accumulating material possessions on their own."[48] The second part of Paffenroth's premise is supported by films like *Night*, as it is the individual desires of the living that cause in-fighting which leads quickly to death. It is the first part of the statement that goes unsupported as even religious and faithful characters not only die, but die just as horribly as others with no indication that their prayers have been answered in any way.

Not content simply with recognizing the zombie as a moral lesson for what happens without God, Paffenroth turns to AMC's series *The Walking Dead* to find his clearest example of how Love (the capitalization Paffenroth uses presumably indicating God's involvement) conquers all; in his words, "Love is also shown to be stronger than (un)death in the series."[49] In an article entitled "When All is Lost, Gather 'round: Solidarity as Hope Resisting Despair in *The Walking Dead*," theologian Ashley John Moyse argues against a nihilistic interpretation of the series along similar lines to Paffenroth's turn towards God's Love. "It is vital to recognize," Moyse says, "that not just any sort of hope is an authentic, valid, or true hope [...] the sort of hope, of which I am now speaking, is the hope embodied and enacted in Christ [....] It is the sort of hope that transforms—or rather, transfigures—our despairing existence, to one of mutual service and faithful labor toward the open, yet reconciled, future."[50] Without Christ, in other words, there is nothing but despair, as indicated by the Catholic axiom, accepted by many Protestants as well, *extra ecclesiam nulla salus*— there is no salvation outside of the Church. It is easy to see how, in the light of such black-and-white thinking, images of despair indicate the absence of Christ, while by belief in His salvific powers, and the missionary injunction to spread the Word, Christ must be brought to alleviate the suffering.

Though we must always be wary of assuming an authors' intentions because the meaning of art is in the eye of the beholder, it is worth noting that Romero, himself a lapsed Catholic, rejects a specifically Christian interpretation of his work. He has recognized the likely effects of his religious upbringing on his craft, though in a markedly negative light. "I don't believe that religion is totally absent from my films since I was immersed in it," he acknowledges, "so, in one way or another, there are definitely traces."[51] At the same time, Romero believes that religion is "not super important. I always sort of take a little jab at it whenever I can. I played a priest in *Martin* just to get back at my own confessors when I was growing up. I was raised Catholic and sort of learned early on … well, I didn't learn, I just got turned off really pretty quickly."[52] If Romero is a prophet warning modern society away from sin and into the loving arms of God, then he is a reluctant one to say the least. Regardless of Romero's intentions, the subjectivity of meaning in art allows that a Christian might find his or her faith confirmed in his films. That said, the films certainly do not demand they be seen in this light, and present features that even question the relevance.

Referencing my earlier work on the subject,[53] Seth Walker points to how the most explicitly Christian character in *The Walking Dead*, Hershel Greene, keeps zombies locked in a barn in the hopes that they may be saved despite death.[54] Both the comic and television series display this tendency to deny death in the hopes of some higher salvation as a danger that must be overcome, leading to some interesting reflections on faith and core Christian teachings. The comic book version of Hershel opines: "This could be the resurrected dead—during the rapture, we could be in the seven years of tribulation … being tested and strengthened. I'd have to ask why *we* weren't called up, good people that we are—but maybe something got lost in translation along the way." Many issues later, the comic has Father Gabriel offer a service to the people of Alexandria in which he compares their situation to the "valley of the shadow of death," of which he says, "I know it well … has there ever been a time when the Bible spoke louder to us […] are these trials? Are all our hardships brought upon us for a reason? I choose to believe that they are." The television series presents Hershel in less dogmatic fashion, facing a crisis of faith brought about by his realization that the undead cannot be saved. Ultimately, the character of Hershel demonstrates through his crisis of faith how love and compassion *are* central to the message, but the presence of a Christian God or salvific Hope are unnecessary to bring them to bear upon the world. Father Gabriel, on the other hand, though in both iterations feels compelled by God to action, shows himself to be craven and untrustworthy in his judgment of right and wrong.

In fact, at the risk of belaboring the point, discrepancies appear even in Paffenroth's own analysis as the lines blur between differing views of Christianity. The most glaring example appears in the *Dawn of the Dead* (2004) remake, which includes a cameo from Ken Foree (who played Peter in the original Romero version of the film) as a televangelist decrying homosexuality and moral degradation as the cause for the zombie apocalypse. Paffenroth denies this particular view, which he compares with similar statements actually made by the likes of Jerry Falwell (who claimed that both AIDS and 9/11 were God's punishment for a society accepting of homosexuality) and Pat Robertson (who claimed that hurricane Katrina and the Haitian earthquake of 2010 were God's punishment for legalized abortion and devil-worship respectively), as "a convenient and cost-free scapegoating, and many Christians seem eager to accept it, no matter how vengeful and unfair it makes our God seem, and *Dawn of the Dead* holds up such ignorance for the ridicule it deserves."[55] That Paffenroth feels justified in denying the existence of a God cruel enough to condemn the world for homosexuality while still suggesting that Romero reflects Dante in depicting the horrors of sin certainly recalls a Procrustean bed.

Given the relative dearth of Christian content in the zombie genre, we return to the main reason that the zombie itself should attract Catholic attention, namely the preoccupation with bodily resurrection alongside the problem of the corruptibility of the flesh. All creatures have bodies, but souls are what make one human. French essayist, François Angelier, draws the distinction between "la vie et la vivacité," between life and simply living.[56] The latter is something that all animate things have (including zombies), but the former is something that is reserved especially for those who know what it means to live a life, and moreover, those who find the true and everlasting life in Christ. Bodies simply live and die, but the soul truly lives through Christ. Christ's own suffering is a focal point in that God became flesh and thus experienced all of the suffering that this corruptible, sinful flesh is equated with. As Paul says, "the wages of sin is death,"[57] and it is this sinful death-world of pain, suffering, and decay from which Christ saved us through his sacrifice.

Mel Gibson's *The Passion of the Christ* (2004) offers an excellent illustration of the Catholic preoccupations with bodily suffering and guilt in its emphasis on the anguish inflicted upon Jesus marked, as the film is, with classic horror tropes throughout.[58] The corruptible body of sin dies and decays, to be raised up a glorified, incorruptible body upon resurrection. The questioning or lapsed Catholicism of Romero and Fulci[59] can be seen in the damage done to bodies in their vision of a resurrection without

God. And the rotting, broken, corrupt zombie bodies provide a remarkable contrast to the goal of health and fitness that has become commonplace in the so-called Health-and-Wealth movement of new millennial Prosperity Theology, wherein W. Scott Poole finds a massive interest in exercise, diet, and plastic surgery all geared towards the preparation of the body for imminent resurrection.[60] Here, secular medical efforts to delay (or prevent!) death match Christian ideals of attaining a glorified resurrected body without the intermediary death-and-resurrection—both couldn't be clearer in their denial of the reality of human mortality. And there could be no clearer antithesis to this than the decayed, corrupt, and dead body of the zombie.

Memento Mori

The tradition of *ars moriendi*, artistic representations of death, extends into pre–Christian times in the West and has parallels in other traditions as well. Reminders of personal mortality, *memento mori* (literally, remember that you will die), often appear in the context of didactic lessons on how to live life given the fact of unavoidable death. Socrates asks rhetorically of the whole field of human introspection: "For is not philosophy the study of death?"[61] In one of the earliest examples of literature ever written, the hero Gilgamesh, distraught at the death of his friend, is advised to dance, sing, and fill his belly in the face of death since it is unavoidable.[62] Epicurus, on the other hand, directs his listeners to consider death only insofar as he argues for a form of materialism in which death is nothing to fear since it does not exist while one is alive, and that one does not exist after death such that in either case death can have no negative impact on the individual.[63] The Stoic Roman philosopher, Seneca, urged his audience to be mindful of death such that it not be seen as a curse but instead a guide for making proper use of one's time. In his essay "On the Shortness of Life," he explains:

> Why do we complain of Nature? She has shown herself kindly; life, if you know how to use it, is long. But one man is possessed by an avarice that is insatiable, another by a toilsome devotion to tasks that are useless; one man is besotted with wine, another is paralyzed by sloth; one man is exhausted by an ambition that always hangs upon the decision of others, another, driven on by the greed of the trader, is led over all lands and all seas by the hope of gain; some are tormented by a passion for war and are always either bent upon inflicting danger upon others or concerned about their own; some there are who are worn out by voluntary servitude in a thankless attendance upon the great; many are kept busy either in the pursuit of other men's fortune or in

complaining of their own; many, following no fixed aim, shifting and inconstant and dissatisfied, are plunged by their fickleness into plans that are ever new; some have no fixed principle by which to direct their course, but Fate takes them unawares while they loll and yawn—so surely does it happen that I cannot doubt the truth of that utterance which the greatest of poets delivered with all the seeming of an oracle: "The part of life we really live is small." For all the rest of existence is not life, but merely time.[64]

The great Muslim theologian and philosopher Al-Ghazzali (1058–1111) notes the importance of remembering death at all times, and the judgment that will occur after that, in order to motivate oneself correctly. He notes with astonishment how a person in the midst of the finest pleasures the world can offer once expecting, in his words, "a man-at-arms who is to strike him five blows with a wooden stick," will find no pleasure to be had as he anticipates the worst; while, on the other hand, the same man might feel no such pains despite the fact that the Death may strike at any moment so long as he were kept ignorant of its imminence.[65] Bushido, the Samurai code of Japan, revolves around one's being prepared for death at all times, maintaining one's honor considered the highest of priorities. Death might strike at any time, and an honorable death was seen in and of itself to be a good death with no promise of reward in the afterlife. And preceding, and influencing, bushido, the Buddhist traditions have a rich history of meditations on death, which will be dealt with in much greater detail in the next chapter.

The Christian tradition, though, has been dominant in the West (despite Epicurean arguments still arising in defense of assisted suicide). And this tradition offers a reminder of mortality with graphic representations of the corruptibility of the human body. In this tradition, it is not simply that we are mortal, but that our bodies are profane, decaying, and ultimately abject things that die in every moment that they live. Interestingly for the topic of this book, the Vodou tradition admits the same association, reminding us not that death is a reality sometime in the future, but that death and life are intertwined to the point that they are actually one and the same: "*La mort, le visage cache de la vie.* Death, the hidden face of life!"[66] Where life is, so too there is death. The Gede are a family of spirits or divinities (called *loas*) that represent both death and fertility such that, on one hand, carnivalesque celebrations will incorporate people dressed in the characteristic black and purple attire with faces painted a ghostly white who drink to excess and dance suggestively to emulate the Gede who laughs in the face of death, while on the other hand, the catastrophic destruction of human life wrought by the Haitian earthquake in 2010 saw the whole nation embody the Gede in the bodies of over 100,000 people.[67] In contrast to traditional Christian attitudes towards death and the afterlife, the Vodou tradition again varies in incorporating elements reminiscent of pre–Christian tradition.

Unlike the sometimes-raucous juxtaposition of life and death in Vodou, the Catholic tradition has long held the body and its urges in contempt. Augustine of Hippo (354–430) is often seen as the focal point for Christian attitudes towards the body and the equation of sex with death and sin, but these connections had existed within early Christianity as well. Paul's first letter to the Corinthians exhorts its readers to avoid sex, though it admits that this may be impossible and advises that "it is better to marry than to burn,"[68] allowing sexual union within marriage to avoid the sinful fornication. The asceticism of hermits, like the Desert Fathers, also reflected a dualistic attitude that sees the suffering of the body as the strengthening of the spirit, and comforts for the body leading to the hardening of the soul. Augustine's influence, then, was in how he dealt with the notions of body and soul, and of sex, death, and sin within the contexts already established. Namely, in confronting temptation, the body was the enemy and Augustine describes a veritable war waged within each person between the body and mind, between flesh and soul.[69] At the heart of Augustine's thinking is not an anger towards the body, though, but a compassion for the tormented soul within.[70] Desires and attachments to anything within the world of finite things is the source of great suffering and dissatisfaction for Augustine, a point at which some agreement with Buddhist ideals might be reached. Finite things can never satisfy our desire for them, which leads only to a greater and greater longing after more and newer things.[71]

The sticking point between an Augustinian perspective and a Buddhist one, though, appears immediately as the former describes our longing as a misplaced longing for the Infinite, for God, which we fruitlessly seek in the myriad aspects of His creation. Instead, Augustine directs us to look inwards, not in solipsism, but into the universality of the soul and its connection to God. This looking inward leads to the understanding of the body as a reflection of one's inner nature. As sinful beings, our bodies are corrupt, subject to decay, disease, and ultimately death. This view of the body as reflection of the soul was prevalent for centuries after Augustine.

Throughout the Middle Ages, paradise was depicted in sensual terms as an idealized mirror image of life on earth without the myriad diseases and pains afflicting daily life. "Paradise was the world turned upside down: illness was banished, hunger forgotten, the flesh's corruptibility abolished, sweet scents were daily inhaled rather than stench and putrefaction."[72] The stench and putrefaction of unavoidable disease (penicillin was not discovered until the early twentieth century!) made it difficult for many to even imagine that the body was made in God's image. Instead, the corrupt body displayed the image of a sinful soul, but one that itself was made in God's image if only it could become free of the sin at the root of bodily decay. For many, the desire to free the soul from sin took on a harshness towards the body most extreme. St. John Climacus (579–649), a famed ascetic, wrote:

> Let us kill this flesh [...] let us kill it just as it has killed us with the mortal blow of sin [....] And thus did those saintly sinners behave: whose knees, through repeated and assiduous genuflexions, were dry, hard and full of callouses. Their eyes were dull, concave and sunken deeply into their heads, and all their lashes had fallen out; their cheeks were wizened, burned and full of sores from the hot and fervent tears that had coursed down them. Their faces were thin, dry and pale, not unlike the faces of the dead. Their chests likewise had sores and contusions from self-inflicted bleeding and they suffered great pain from the beatings they had given themselves [....] Having no thought or care for their bodies, they would forget to eat bread, while their tears and sighs would mingle with what they drank. They ate their bread rolled in ashes. They were dried out like hay, so their skin stuck to their skeletons.[73]

That the harsh ascetic might resemble a rotting corpse is not coincidence as, in the words of another saint, Peter Damian (1007–1072), "it could be said that human flesh, which now seems to be alive, does not in fact bring forth decay in itself after death, but only then declares itself openly to be the rottenness which it has always been."[74] And the above is not an isolated case.

Joseph of Cupertino (1603–1663), patron saint of aviators and astronauts due to his frequent miraculous levitations, was also an ardent ascetic, rarely eating and often flagellating himself bloody.

> If ever he was assailed by impure thoughts or vain fancies, or some distraction, he would flog himself to the very bone [....] His many wounds had only his rasping hairshirt to dress them; and the fearful chain that he wore about his loins made the wounds stick to his hairshirt and the hairshirt to the chain, so that his soaking and wounded body resembled more a corpse than a living human being.[75]

Likewise the Capuchin monk Carlo Girolamo Severoli (1641–1712):

> Such was the manner and number of his self-inflictions and abstinences that his appearance was completely transformed: his countenance was pallid and his bones were barely covered by his bloodless skin so had he wasted away; a few meagre hairs sprouted from his chin and his frame was bent and transfigured, so that he had become bare like a skeleton, a living image of penitence. He suffered as a consequence most grievously of languidness, fainting, swooning and a death-like pallor [...][76]

Throughout these many centuries, the body is revealed as already dead flesh, walking corpses of sin within which the soul must suffer until freed, "a putrescent and fetid yet mobile corpse."[77] These are examples to the world as to the truth of the relationship between body and soul in the context of sin and salvation. St. Bernard described the human condition so: "Man is nothing but stinking sperm, a sack of excrement and food for worms,"[78] echoing Arnobius of Sicca (c. 330) who described the body as "a disgusting vessel of urine" and a "bag of shit."[79] The one-time Archbishop of Canterbury, St. Anselm (1033–1109), advised a form of meditation on death not entirely dissimilar to those we will discuss in the following chapter:

> We should learn to contemplate in the following fashion.... In what disgusting and lamentable condition will my flesh be handed over after my death ... to be consumed by decay and worms.... Hiding, my eyes will be turned to face the inside of my head, eyes in whose empty and malicious wandering I often took delight: they will lie buried in terrible darkness which once absorbed gloatingly the hollow pleasures of the light. The ears will soon suffer an invasion of worms, ears which revel wickedly at present in the voices of slander and the rumours of the age [....] The lips crusty with a filthy scab, which used often to loosen in foolish laughter. The tongue will be bound up by a raging scum, which often proffered idle tales. The throat is constricted and the stomach stuffed full of worms, where both were stretched tight with differing foods. But why recall the individual details? The whole disposition of the body towards whose health, comfort and pleasure every concern of the mind strained itself, will dissolve in decay, worms and finally into basest dust.[80]

Such reminders of death are clearly didactic. It is not just that the body dies and decays, but there is the assumption present that this reality is caused by sin rather than something natural to life itself. The *memento mori* in this context is education through fear—a reminder not of the reality of death with a goal to acceptance, but rather an invocation of death as horror in order to promote the associated fear of sin. The gore is explicit, intended to evoke fear and horror through the association with sin.[81] In fact, that the saintly might avoid a natural physical fate of decomposition after death was evidence of their inner purity. Gerhold Scholz Williams points out:

> We need only remember St. Alexis whose body, covered with ulcers through a life of fasting and deprivation in such a way that even his parents did not recognize him, reverted in death to its erstwhile beauty. Although the Saint was not buried for several days, his body did not decompose or smell. St. Gregory, too, gives numerous examples where horrible decay and stench signal hidden sins and their just punishment.[82]

St. Gregory of Nyssa described the soul in the body as like a rope covered in mud; only through violently tugging the rope through a tight hole could the rope be cleansed.[83] So, the body reveals the sinful nature of the soul by its putrefaction, but ascetic denials acted to recognize this assumption and thereby eliminate its effect. Those not violently tugging the rope clean—the unwashed masses, so to speak—would simply continue toiling in the mud and filth to the end.

Visual depictions of death also have a strong tradition, most emphatically emerging with the *ars moriendi* of the Middle Ages, texts accompanied with graphic illustrations intended to help readers and viewers to come to grips with mortality in the midst of horrible and widespread plague.[84] A common style of painting, still-life or the related *vanitas* (empty, fleeting) art, depicts its subjects in a moment in time, recognizing the fleetingness of that now-past moment. Though many modern viewers might not immediately connect to the inherent *memento mori* of, say, a painting of a bowl of apples, even the name "still-life" connotes the paradoxical nature of the works being a moment frozen in time, the artificial stilling of life. Ageless in painting, that bowl of apples must surely now be rotten; an observation made explicit in Oscar Wilde's *The Picture of Dorian Gray* (1993 [1891]) as the eponymous Gray's portrait ages instead of he until the magic is broken and the man turns to ash leaving only his young painted image behind.

During the Renaissance, anatomists employed artistic license to bring their subject, the corpse, to life. The effort was to show that while a corpse was needed for study, the findings as to the inner workings of the body were universal and of great medical benefit to the living. Anatomy texts depict skeletons in active poses reminiscent of the *danses macabres* of earlier times, and include images in which the corpse appears to be assisting in the autopsy itself, sometimes holding back a flap of skin, or posing in such a way to expose the innards. One example offers a flayed man in a David-like pose exposing the musculature of the body while holding a knife in one hand and the entirety of his skin hanging in the other.[85] In addition to revealing the direct bodily similarities between the living and dead, many anatomists were also keen to disabuse readers of any apprehensions associated with the corpse or the inner workings of the body. Opening the body and revealing the organs inside was thought to be a useful way to assist viewers in accepting the body without turning away in abject disgust.

The philosopher, Jeremy Bentham, bequeathed his own body to be displayed for just such a purpose as he regarded the fear of the corpse a "primitive horror."[86] Bentham argued for a utilitarian approach to the body that would have all bodies donated to medicine, though he admitted that some aspect of the body might be preserved in order to console the living. This part, especially interesting in the context of modern zombie fiction, was to be the head, which alone he held to be unique among individuals.[87] Bentham bequeathed his own body to scientific dissection by friends, with the remains, including his head, to be preserved as an auto-icon; this unique memorial remains on display at the University College London to this day.[88] That modern zombie convention holds that the only way to kill a zombie is to destroy the brain at least carries some of the weight of Bentham's concession to the head as uniquely individual, though the fact that zombies are so often rotten to the point of being unrecognizable moves even further towards the blurring of individual identity. Ironically, Bentham's own head has been removed from the display of his body due to numerous attempted thefts and the fact that the process of mummification it underwent did not leave it in the life-like condition that had been hoped, thereby taking away from its usefulness as commemoration of life and into the realm of *memento mori*. Whereas Bentham hoped for the auto-icon to remain as a testament of the individual, the fate of his own head stands as yet another example of the impermanence of the body and of the individual.

    The advent of the daguerreotype opened the door to democratized photographic technology in the mid-nineteenth century. It allowed people the opportunity to take family photographs, taken for granted today, where previously only the wealthy could afford to sit for a painted portrait. Though the practice will seem odd today, recently deceased family members were among those whose portraits could be more readily captured by the new technology. Still new, a picture of a deceased loved one might actually have been the only photograph ever taken of them. Such photos acted as family mementos that allowed traveling relatives the opportunity to see their family members even if they had missed the funeral. As Western mortality rates lowered and the populations of Europe and North America began to expect long lives, the ritualization of death became almost an obsession. In fact, the modern denial of death may well be seen to have begun in earnest as people lived longer lives. Capturing photographs of the dead as mementos often served to deny that the loved one was gone, in a sense, by capturing a permanent image of them, especially when the body was posed in a lifelike manner, as was often the case. Sometimes bodies in coffins were the subject of photographs, which at least acknowledges the mortal truth.[89] Since at least the fifteenth century, artists painted post-mortem portraits as a form of *memento mori*, attempting to capture the realism of the corpse as a reminder to all of the reality of mortality, just as the writings described above had been doing for centuries earlier. Though some of the earliest photographers of the dead may have aimed for the same effect, most Victorian photographers were influenced instead by Romantic notions and, despite the obvious realism allowed by the new technology, eschewed visions of death in favor of depicting the corpse as if it were still living, whether asleep or carefully posed in a more life-like position. The purpose, then, evolved images of death from a warning of impending death to all to a source for solace against that reality.

Roland Barthes noted, "death is the *eidos* of the photograph," it is the essence of the picture.[90] With this statement, he points out that every picture that has been taken represents its subject as it was, not as it is. Even a moment after the photo is taken, the subject of the photo is already past. Every photograph captures a moment in time, but a moment that is gone, that "has been." As such, every photo evokes a sense of nostalgia for a lost past. Of course, that the subject of a photo "has been" at least asserts its existence in reality. In this way, the photograph acts both as evidence of a life lived, while also, by its nature, preserving only a memory. The photo ambiguously depicts a thing that is gone, while at the same time giving that past thing an ongoing life. In a way, the photograph is both living and dead. Barthes is explicit that even "the photograph of a corpse means that a corpse is alive *as a corpse*."[91] Zombie fiction, aside from being largely moving pictures itself, is replete with instances of survivors looking at photos of dead loved ones, thereby reinforcing the sense of loss and the fact of death as unavoidable.

The Walking Dead television series offers a number of solid examples. The show's first episode, "Days Gone Bye," depicts Rick Grimes (Andrew Lincoln) returning home to find his house deserted. He finds assurance that his wife and son, Lori and Carl, may have survived when he finds that the family photo albums have been taken. The same episode juxtaposes Rick's sense of reassurance with Morgan's (Lennie James) amusement as he notes that his own wife had done the same while he was packing survival gear; and the fact that his wife has since become a zombie. The show uses photographs as a marker of the ambiguity between life and death presented by the zombie (interestingly, the comic book makes extremely little reference to photographs, the only real example being the family portrait behind Rick's head as he first enters the family home looking for Lori and Carl). Viewers discover that Lori (Sarah Wayne Callies) and Carl (Chandler Riggs) are indeed alive before Rick Grimes himself does; but immediately after we are shown his surviving family, the scene cuts to Rick who is forced to abandon his vehicle, taking only a bag of guns, an empty gas can, and a photo of Lori, Carl, and himself.[92] Meanwhile, Morgan is shown thumbing through the family albums taken by his wife, eventually taping one particular image of her up on the window next to him as he searches for his zombified wife through a rifle's scope; ultimately, he finds her but is unable to pull the trigger. From the outset, photos are linked with survival of a kind, but the line between living and dead is indiscernible. The photograph is at once both proof of life but also a representation of a dead past, it is, like the zombie, both alive and dead. The photograph serves as a bridge between the zombie and the living, posing questions about the boundaries between life and death and between the living and the dead.

Another interesting example of the use of photographs is found throughout the show's second season, which finds the survivors holed up at Hershel Greene's (Scott Wilson) farm. The rustic farmhouse is decorated with few photographs, but those that appear are clearly old, black-and-white images of relatives from a past era. The significance of this is revealed when viewers discover that the Greenes have been storing zombies in their barn, Hershel believing his deceased family and friends might be cured. Both reflect a clinging to a dead past; from my perspective, it is also interesting that the Greenes are the first (and aside from a very flawed Catholic priest, the only) committed Christians depicted in the series. Once he realizes the true nature of the zombies, Hershel suffers a profound crisis of faith, offering yet another example of the ways in which zombie fiction moves counter to Christian tradition. The house does include some color images of more recent vintage, these crowding the face of the fridge. We are directed to these photos as Maggie Greene (Lauren Cohan) points out those family members who have been killed, and whom we later find in the barn (season two, episode three [S2E3], "Save the Last One"). By the time the series brings us to the relative safety of the walled community of Alexandria, viewers will recognize what would normally be considered a natural display of family pictures decorating the walls of houses as signs of just how insulated the community has been from the horrors of the undead beyond its walls. The pictures, like the people of Alexandria, are signs of what has been, not what is. More than once the show's protagonists remark on the fact that the suburban survivors should be dead if not for their good luck. Photographs, then, appear as markers of death, as *memento mori*, for the viewing audience even as they fulfill their everyday function as simple mementos for the characters.

All of the various images of death depicted through history find their modern parallel in the blatant representation of death that is the zombie itself. Given the instances described above of self-inflicted tortures visited upon the body in order to benefit the soul, equating the body with death and decay to the point of forcing the body to portray that state even in life, it is no wonder that Catholic interpretations of the zombie would make the connection. Without bringing Jesus into the discussion, though, a move that is in no way necessitated by the genre itself, we are left with the body as corpse as a reminder of death, a *memento mori*, without the moral to flee from this reality into the arms of a savior. Instead, we are left simply with the truth of what will happen, and what is happening, to every body that is right now and that ever has been. In cinematically exposing the material nature of the body, the zombie genre remains a part of the subset of horror fiction described as body horror. That sub-genre concerns itself with manipulations of the body, its destruction and its reassembly, essentially playing with the body in such a way to test and expose its limits, while at the same time drawing to the fore important questions about human nature and the relationship of the person to the body.

Body Horror

Among horror filmmakers, a great deal of pride resides in the capacity to create realistic gore. Many critics have routinely disregarded horror, especially gore and splatter, as sensationalist at best and pornographic at worst. In fact, a film reviewer for *Variety* magazine declared *Night of the Living Dead* (1968) "the outer-limit definition by example" of "the pornography of violence."[93] The contention that such depictions of death and bodily destruction desensitizes audiences to violence, or even promotes it, has been commonplace. Filmmakers, though, take an entirely different perspective. Lucio Fulci, for example, explains: "I portray violence in such an exaggerated way because I detest it. I am seeking to exorcise it."[94] Drawing the connection back to the *ars moriendi* with its focus on death explicitly, Greg Nicotero, the lead special effects artist for *The Walking Dead*, aims for superrealism, "so there's a weird part of the brain that registers, 'Wait a second, I saw tissue and sinew and bone and muscle all inside of that wound. How is that possible?' What the anatomy looks like as a corpse decomposes is very important."[95] With this super-realistic depiction, audiences are provided with an artistic, detailed (albeit not strictly authentic) view of the permeable body. For a modern, Western audience, the decomposition of the corpse is entirely outside of normal experience. Death itself, it has often been said, is ultimately denied in Western culture. Viewers are forced, in watching zombie fiction, to come to terms with the disgusting Otherness of one's own body in its capacity for rot and decay, "to confront the horror that lay within them, the Otherness of their own flesh," as Jamie Russell puts it.[96] When Julia Kristeva speaks of the abject, it is just this kind of uneasy tension between the self as subject and the body as object that she has in mind.[97]

Kristeva's abject has been described as "reverse *memento mori*, in a way,"[98] since we reject and turn away from the abject whereas the *memento mori* calls for attention. This misses the point of *memento mori*, though; there would be no need to urge us to remember that we will die unless it were something that we did not wish to consider naturally. The abject is not a reversal of the admonition to remember but rather it is the reason that the reminder is necessary!

According to Kristeva, that which we call abject is reviled and rejected because of its implications, troubling the neat separation imagined between self and other, between subject and object. It is difficult enough for an individual to overcome the solipsistic tendency to perceive one's self as the center of the universe. Allowing other agents to have as much subjectivity and importance relegates my own importance from center to just one among many satellites circling who knows what. It is so much easier to focus inward, on my own self and my own needs and desires and to relate to others only insofar as they act as part of the world-out-there. Much more troubling, though, is the recognition that even within my own world, I am also an object, a body that will decay.

The tension between my subjective agency as self and my objective reality as body creates anxiety. This anxiety is prominent whenever the bodily envelope is broken, suggesting the permeability of the worlds within and without, the blurred distinction between my self and other and between subject and object. This liminality is the source for our sense of abjection towards such boundary-crossing elements as saliva, excrement, or blood. A person may comfortably accept their own self's dwelling within a body, or even that they are in fact that self-same body, but this does not normally also include an acceptance of all that shares the space within the body—the piss, shit, bile, snot, blood, and pus. If I am my body, or if I dwell within it, then either I am also these other aspects or, at least, I share my space with them. When such effluvium escape the body, thus revealing that they had been me/with me all along, they are received as abject, rejected and avoided as reminders of the ambiguity of being human. The corpse itself, especially when burst open and rotten, explodes the false boundary and forces its witness to confront the abject as core to the self. As Kristeva puts it:

> The corpse (or cadaver: *cadere*, to fall), that which has irremediably come a cropper, is cesspool, and death; it upsets even more violently the one who confronts it as fragile and fallacious chance. A wound with blood and pus, or the sickly, acrid smell of sweat, of decay, does not *signify* death. In the presence of signified death—a flat encephalograph, for instance—I would understand, react, or accept. No, as in true theater, without makeup or masks, refuse and corpses *show me* what I permanently thrust aside in order to live. These body fluids, this defilement, this shit are what life withstands, hardly and with difficulty, on the part of death. There, I am at the border of my condition as a living being. My body extricates itself, as being alive, from that border. Such wastes drop so that I might live, until, from loss to loss, nothing remains in me and my entire body falls beyond the limit—*cadere*, cadaver. If dung signifies the other side of the border, the place where I am not and which permits me to be, the corpse, the most sickening of wastes, is a border that has encroached upon everything.[99]

The corpse is not only a reminder that we will die, but that we are already invested with death. It isn't that life and death are opposite things but that they are the same. If you are living, then you are also dying; it is as simple as that. People have a strong tendency to avoid this association, though, glorifying life and rejecting death despite their inextricability.

Body Horror focuses on the dissolution, destruction, and reformation of bodies, especially human bodies. Started by anatomist, Gunther von Hagens, Body Worlds preserves cadavers, whole or in parts, using plastination, allowing viewers to bear witness to the inner workings of real human bodies and for the bodies to be molded and formed into desired positions and poses. Critics deride the exhibitions as a debasement of humanity, reducing the human from an individual person to simply a body to be put on display for the titillation of curious thrill-seekers. Ethicist Thomas Hibbs likens Body Worlds to pornography in manipulating bodies at the expense of the significance of the human being.[100] One might recall St. Augustine's dim view of the body and its carnal desires. Horror and porn have often shared a dismissive contempt from intellectuals, considered either lowbrow or taboo (often both), but the two genres are linked in other ways. Often, fiction evinces an uncontrollable emotional response from the audience, and perhaps none more viscerally than the fear of horror or the arousal of pornography. Kyle Bishop argues that nudity and gore both drive home a sense of corporeality that gets to the heart of abjection.[101] And it is perhaps this troubled area that causes the likes of Hibbs and others to react as they do, unable to reconcile the relationship between mind and body. And this is exactly the tension that emerges in zombie fiction—is this corpse a person or not?

Many of the major makers of postmodern film horror—a group including George Romero, Dario Argento, John Carpenter, and David Cronenberg—are, in the words of one film scholar, "obsessed with the manufacture of the most convincing, visually explicit and fascinatingly original grotesques."[102] Carpenter, for his part, lays the foundations of graphic violence in horror squarely at the feet of George Romero, citing *Night of the Living Dead* as the turning point.[103] Though sometimes mentioned alongside Romero, the one artist whose work is most often associated with body horror is the Canadian filmmaker, David Cronenberg. Both Romero's and Cronenberg's films focus on the body as site of death, but where Cronenberg differs most emphatically is in his emphasis on sex as a natural partner to death, reflecting his clear interest in Freudian philosophy with its interconnected notions of Eros and Thanatos while again echoing views of the likes of Augustine.

Carnal Bodies, Carnal Zombies

The importance of examining the body, specifically, in this way brings to light the essential distinction between the body, most explicitly when a corpse, as an object, a thing like any other empty machine, and the meaning-making ghost that dwells within it. Philosopher, William S. Larkin makes the case that we intuitively recognize ourselves as primarily *physical* beings, and that whatever its fate, the person's locus remains in the body—even imagining a state beyond the body will involve the depiction of *some* kind of body. He notes that zombie films, in particular, bring this intuition to the fore. For example, the viewer of *Night of the Living Dead* is horrified when the zombie kills Johnny, but then recognizes the ironic tragedy of his return as a zombie who then kills his sister; though we know Johnny to have been killed, we still react to the zombified Johnny as if it remained Johnny.[104] Cronenberg, on the other hand, insists that the physical body is itself monstrous, a threat to personal identity in that "you carry the seeds of your own destruction around with you, always, and [...] they can erupt at any time."[105] The very thing that seems to allow the individual to have presence is also that thing that ultimately threatens to extinguish the self as well.

Both *Shivers* (1975) and *The Fly* (1986) show the effects of Cronenberg's experience of his father's degenerative death. Of *The Fly*, Noël Carroll notes how the film's "monster" elicits feelings of disgust and sympathy for his fate rather than fear, reflecting the experience of watching a loved one's slow and painful bodily deterioration and death.[106] *The Fly* is implicitly a film about aging, decay, and death. Seth Brundle (Jeff Goldblum) unknowingly combines his DNA with that of a fly when experimenting with a teleportation device. At first, he is filled with a drug-like euphoria that fills him with increased strength and vitality, and a significantly heightened sex-drive. Soon, though, he begins to deteriorate as he first sprouts ugly hairs in places he had previously been bare, then slowly begins to slough off body parts—teeth, hair, fingernails, and, apparently, his penis. In a last-ditch effort to preserve his humanity, Seth (now as the hybrid Brundlefly) teleports once again, this time merging himself with the teleportation equipment itself. When it would seem that all humanity has now been lost in the unrecognizable mess of mutant fly and machine parts, the tortured creature slowly reaches for the gun held by his once-lover and gently places the barrel between his own eyes, plaintively, and silently, seeking the mercy of an assisted suicide. As Cronenberg himself explains, the film is "a metaphor for ageing, a compression of any love affair that goes to the end of one of the lover's lives."[107] While the cycle of life from youthful energy to decay and death is most clearly played out in *The Fly*, death, especially in the form of cancer, is a frequent image in Cronenberg's films including *The Brood* (1979), *Videodrome* (1983), *Crimes of the Future* (1970), and *Rabid* (1977); and *Shivers* adds to the list venereal disease.[108] And Cronenberg has admitted to being "haunted" by the slow death of his father that saw his body wither but his mind remain sharp, a death which occurred during the filming of *Shivers*.[109]

For its part, *Shivers* offers an homage to Romero's *Night*, most clearly in the images of the film's climactic ending when the last "survivor" is surrounded by a mass of slow-moving sex-zombies that corral him back into the hotel pool where he finally succumbs to the parasite that has infected them all.[110] In this film, Cronenberg clearly wrestles with the relationship between sex and death. For one thing, Cronenberg seems to have been specific about his casting in bringing in Susan Petrie, whom he describes as having previously been in "a couple of the Cinépix porno films"[111] (a bit of an exaggeration, in fact, with her *Loving and Laughing* [1971] a comedic sexploitation at most). *Rabid* (1977) more successfully blurs the lines between sex and death in his casting of adult-film star Marilyn Chambers (*Behind the Green Door*, 1972; *Insatiable*, 1980) as the lead.

Both raw sex and violence, like slavery before, reduce bodies to objects, thereby moving away from recognizing the human within. Psychoanalyst Mikita Brottman makes the interesting observation that this can happen in degrees as well, drawing an association amid the distinction between mainstream horror and the extreme violence of so-called mondo horror that revels in gore and "true" death (with body horror lying somewhere in the middle of these two) and between soft- and hard-core pornography.[112] And, as Ian Conrich points out, *Fangoria* magazine took to publishing glossy centerfolds reminiscent of those in *Playboy*, but depicting favorite monsters and scenes of horror-gore, both "glossy adorations of a flesh-fantastic which leaves little unshown."[113] More explicitly even than the body horror of Cronenberg, zombie porn most fully embodies that strange connection of sex and death. As Steve Jones explains, "[z]ombie porn straddles the boundary between discourses—of philosophic concerns regarding zombies as non-conscious animated entities, of misogyny and non-consent associated with necrophilia, and of feminist concerns regarding pornographic representations."[114] In one recent article on the liminal state of zombie porn, by commodifying one's body as an object for the pleasure of strangers, "pornography is tied to both the vital and not-so-vital, that it is alive (it has the power to arouse, to affect) and dead (it is commercial, exploitative, aesthetically inert, especially for anti-porn feminists)."[115] Of course, for these and other scholars, the sex of pornography is not simply about sex but is replete with gendered power dynamics just as the undeath of zombie fiction is not purely about death and dying but embodies all manner of issues, which are reflected in socio-political turmoil. Largely following the thought of Michel Foucault, such perspectives focus on the body as the site of subjugation or resistance, among other things, but ignore the body as site of individual experience. Certainly, socio-political theory has an important place, but at the individual level, the body is the site of one's own life and, ultimately, death.

With *Shivers*, Cronenberg's purpose was "to show the unshowable, to speak the unspeakable. I was creating certain things that there was no way of suggesting because it was not common currency of the imagination."[116] In fact, Cronenberg's bodily manipulations explicitly expose aspects of the body, and by extension aspects of the human self, that are not only normally accessible only to the imagination but are more often rejected from consciousness—questions about the extent to which the human person is nothing more than raw flesh, or about how raw flesh can somehow be considered more than simply meat and instead a human being. Many, like Steven Price, see the nature of the human being as the central anxiety of horror generally, but body horror drives to the core of the mind-body split and the assumptions of our current materialist Weltanschauung much more explicitly than does the more simplistic and reactionary horror typifying the genre for most of its history. The messy problem of the "ghost in the machine" that is the person within the body is central to Cronenberg and to zombie fiction as well. His films aim at delivering his audiences to a new, and better, perspective. And Cronenberg outlines this perspective, and his goal of beautifying the unshowable, unspeakable chinks in the armor of humanist self-conception:

> When you're in the muck you can only see muck. If you somehow manage to float above it, you still see the muck but you see it from a different perspective [....] The ideal is that on your deathbed you smile and say, "Ah, yes of course," and die with a smile on your face. That's what I'd like. To deny the muck is no consolation; it's a false philosophy. The reason my films can be so dark is that I have a real compulsion to make optimism real, to have it based in reality, however tough. To tell a child, "Don't worry about death, because you'll go to heaven and we'll all be there and you'll meet all your friends"—that's a hideous thing to say if you don't believe it. And I don't. That's not optimism or a positive approach to life and death; that's pure fakery. That's useless. If I can still find beauty and grace in tears, that starts to be more real. That's something I can use, build a philosophy on.[117]

Cronenberg does not, however, offer a detailed account of this philosophy, but rather simply points to an acceptance of the realities that are so often neglected or rejected in the face of a posed optimism of Hope, not as a nihilist but as a realist. At core, his films depict, in his words, "disintegration, ageing, death, separation, the meaning of life. All that stuff,"[118] but, in the words of the fictional author of the Foreword to a biographical interview, their goal is singular: "finding the cure to a disease common to us all. It is called mortality. Knowing this disease to be incurable, and finding religious belief an unacceptable anaesthetic, each film explores an alternative way of exploring and defusing anxiety about death."[119]

In *Shivers*, the inhabitants of a yuppie condominium complex fall victim to a strange parasite that turns its hosts into sex-crazed maniacs. In the end, no one is safe from infestation, but, importantly, as the last inhabitants are infected, calm returns to the building and the people quietly, and smilingly-satisfied, drive out into the wider world, presumably to further spread the sex-zombie parasite. William Beard argues for the primacy of the mind/body split in *Shivers* because of the imbalance between rational thought and acts of passion.[120] More directly, though, the dialectic of mind and body is not as important as that of sex and death. In a pivotal scene, Nurse Forsythe (Lynn Lowry), the presumed love interest of the frigidly rationalist protagonist Roger St. Luc (Paul Hampton), describes a dream she's had before revealing that she, too, has been infected by the parasite:

> Roger, I had a very strange dream last night. In this dream, I found myself making love to a strange man. Only I'm having trouble, you see, because he's old and dying, and he smells bad, and I find him repulsive. But then he tells me that everything is

erotic, that everything is sexual. You know what I mean? He tells me that even old flesh is erotic flesh, that disease is the love of two alien creatures for each other—that even dying is an act of eroticism. That talking is sexual. That breathing is sexual. That even to physically exist is sexual. And I believe him. And we make love *beautifully*.

The concept of "beauty" takes on a different meaning in Cronenberg. That is, Cronenberg claims to want to find beauty in places where it is not normally seen—namely, he seeks beauty in some of those places that are normatively deemed ugly and abject. In his body horror, Cronenberg sees "a beauty contest for the inside of the human body."[121] In this way, body horror performs a reversal of the Catholic repulsion to the body.

According to Kristeva, "The corpse, seen without God and outside of science, is the utmost abjection. It is death infecting life."[122] Certainly, in the body horror of Cronenberg and others, the body is treated without any sense of the sacred while science is also demonized in its efforts to control and enhance the body. It is clear that body horror, at its core, places the abjection of the human body on full display. As much as the abject body presents a threat to stable notions of self, it is natural to see the degree to which so many critics and audiences react with outrage to body horror. On the other hand, though, Kristeva's observations about abjection are not intended to reflect hard-and-fast truths about how we ought to react, but rather offer an explanation for why we might react the way we do. Put another way, it isn't the case that corpses must, by their nature, cause a reaction of utter revulsion, but rather that when seen as abject, without a means of accepting or coping with what the corpse suggests about the self, one will react negatively. Just as the Christian critics seen earlier cannot find any hope in a God-less apocalypse, so too the reaction to the corpse/body as abject is one of perspective.

Mikhail Bakhtin's theorizing of the grotesque and carnivalesque provides a background to the abject, examining what he calls the classic and grotesque bodies in terms of boundaries. Specifically, he describes classical interest in the body, say, with the nude male form as in Greek statuary, depicted as it is in stone without orifice—it is solid and without boundary between inside and out. The grotesque body, on the other hand, reveals and opens the orifice, breaking the distinction between inner and outer. Where Kristeva points to our revulsion to such boundary breaking, Bakhtin frames it as comedy instead—Kristeva's pile of shit stands against Bakhtin's fart jokes. Commenting on Romero's filmography, historian Sébastien Le Pajolec interestingly notes that laughter and vomiting both serve to distance one's self from the object to which one reacts.[123] While Kristeva speaks of "death infecting life," in Bakhtin, "the reverse is true, and life infects death: 'Death is included in life.'"[124] Bakhtin is able to take a positive perspective on death, though, through denial, focusing on the survival of the community over that of the individual. He asserts, for instance, that "death brings nothing to an end, for it does not concern the ancestral body, which is renewed in the next generation."[125] The individual, with this platitude, is left to laugh in the face of death as one lives life like passing a fart that dissipates in the air. And, as comedian Louis CK says, "you don't have to be smart to laugh at farts, but you have to be stupid not to."[126] For Bakhtin, laughter lowers its subject to the level of the real, lowers the sacred to the profane—it de-crowns the king and instead crowns the fool, thereby flipping, however temporarily, the state of things and alleviating tensions in society. To laugh in the face of death disempowers it, thus alleviating our fear of it by suggesting that for every death there is new life. Still, this ignores the very real loss that occurs in individual death. Whether for the person dying, or for those immediately touched by an individual's death, the prospect that there are others being born at the same time offers little solace.

There is a rich tradition of comedy, not always completely dark, in zombie fiction. Philipe Aries described the horrifying vision of a corpse pierced with tubes and attached to monitors as the new, and terrifying, *memento mori*,[127] but films like *Weekend at Bernie's* (1989) respond with a comical abuse of the corpse as two hapless insurance actuaries try to keep up the appearance that their boss is still alive in order to stave off mobsters that he'd hired to kill them before his own death (and, of course, the sequel, *Weekend at Bernie's II*, 1993, sees the zombified CEO actually return from the dead to carry on the shenanigans)![128] Around this same time, *Return of the Living Dead* (1985) and *Return of the Living Dead Part II* (1988), received and billed as comedies, parody Romero's *Dead* films. (After accidentally losing the copyright on *Night of the Living Dead*, a legal battle between Russo and Romero ended with the former retaining the right to use the term "Living Dead" and the latter going on to use only "Dead" in his later titles). If taken as pure horror, though, the zombies depicted in *Return* are far more horrific than any others in being intelligent and capable of speech, counting among their number not only the recently dead but those long buried in cemeteries that can dig their way to the surface, and being completely indestructible. Destroying the brain does nothing to slow them down, and, in fact, severing the head or any other limb simply results in multiple moving parts that continue their efforts to kill the living. Even burning them is ineffective as, while it reduces the individual body to ash, the smoke combines with the clouds to rain zombie-producing contaminants far and wide. A nuclear bomb dropped at the end of the first film accomplishes nothing more than an even wider spread of zombies. Horror of this magnitude requires comedic balance! The sheer terror of death's unavoidability in the form of these relentless, crafty, and indestructible zombies is met here with a kind of nihilistic bemusement that reacts with a laugh at the absurdity of the predicament.

I am here reminded of Albert Camus' *Myth of Sisyphus*,[129] in which he expresses an absurdist view of life and death. In fact, I agree with philosopher, Rachel Robison-Greene, who suggests that apocalyptic horror is especially adept at presenting audiences with absurdist existentialism given the confrontation with the overwhelming force of nature and the way it puts in perspective the place of humanity in the universe.[130] Of course, one can go back to the Roman Stoic Seneca for the argument that monstrous tragedy is especially effective at delivering its lesson when a visually disturbing monster is at the heart of it.[131] Camus urges us to consider just how silly life is from its very beginnings, the sex act itself being completely ridiculous when considered technically. "Bawdy humor" is essentially "body humor" of a particularly sexual kind that recognizes exactly this absurdity. At the other extreme, death is inevitable and, Camus, argues, we live as if it won't happen to us and then react with shock and disappointment when we are touched by it.

Denying any afterlife, Camus wonders at what the point of life might be if all will ultimately result in death. And not merely individual death, but against Bakhtin, the eventual death of all humankind. In the grand scheme of the universe, eventually our sun will die and all life on this planet will cease to exist. What will have been the point of any of it then? Camus describes life in terms of the Greek myth of Sisyphus, who was forced to push a rock up a hill for all eternity. Knowing that once reaching the top, the rock would roll back down, and that he would then simply have to begin pushing the rock up once more, Sisyphus, Camus suggests, would have to at some point come to grips with this reality simply because he had no other choice. That is a reflection of life in the face of death—we live every day in the knowledge that ultimately whatever we do will be lost and forgotten in our own death and the deaths of every other human who will ever live.

It would be easy in the face of such a view to throw one's hands up and give up, but Camus argues that suicide is no solution at all. In fact, he describes what he calls bodily suicide and philosophical suicide as equally wrong-headed approaches. On one hand, recognizing the pointlessness of life in the face of the death of everything, one may choose physical death as bodily suicide, but this does not resolve the problem since death is inevitable in any event. Taking one's life now or waiting for it to happen later are effectively the same thing except for the fact that life can still be lived if one waits it out. On the other hand, ignoring the absurdity of living in the face of death, assuming that there is some greater meaning and that there is some enduring future, Camus argues, is philosophical suicide in the sense that one is purposefully being irrational and living in denial of reality. A life lived in utter ignorance is one not truly being lived just as one who would commit bodily suicide would cease to live. Instead, Camus urges a rational acceptance of the inevitability of death and the attendant absurdity of living with that knowledge, which, he argues, allows for the freedom to truly live life to its fullest, removed from denial and free of fear. Some will describe this view as nihilistic, but it is important to distinguish a passive nihilism that gives up in the face of death as opposed to an *active* nihilism that sees life as filled with possibilities for experience constrained by death.[132] The combined horror and comedy of the *Return* franchise goes to lengths to evoke the pointlessness of the fight against death while encouraging a positive response in its humor, whereas Romero's *Dead* films, themselves decried for their nihilism, similarly present an active nihilism in their prophetic call for a kinder and gentler society.[133]

Other zombie fiction takes the form of traditional comedy in the use of a happy ending alongside its humorous take on the undead. *Shaun of the Dead* (2004) most effectively skewers modern society in having its protagonists fail to recognize that a zombie apocalypse has even begun, so unaware of their surroundings and fellow humans they are. While also functioning as an effective horror, *Shaun* ends with the zombie outbreak coming under control with zombies domesticated as pets and servants, effectively trivializing death while recognizing the absurdity of life itself. A final scene has Shaun (Simon Pegg) living happily-ever-after with his girlfriend while blissfully whiling away his life playing video games with his zombified friend, Ed (Nick Frost). While the film opens with its protagonists unaware that they are surrounded by walking death, the appearance and subsequent control of the zombies seems to allow them to overcome the petty concerns of a life lived in ignorance of death in exchange for a more authentically happy life integrating death—one that allows for what we might now consider "wasted" time playing video games given the absurdity of considering some activities to be more or less meaningful than others.

Fido (2006) similarly incorporates the domesticated zombie for comedic purpose, but here more attention is given to the lives of the zombies than to the zombie as walking dead. Fido, the eponymous zombie, takes on a kind of parental role in the family by film's end. Though the connection between the living and the dead, and often the confusion between the two, has been a prominent feature of zombie fiction since its Haitian roots, in most iterations the emphasis has been on recognizing the equation between the living as *already* dead. From Ben's being shot at the conclusion of *Night* to Rick's proclamation "We ARE the Walking Dead!" in *The Walking Dead*, we are directed to recognize that as living we are also dying. *Fido*, however, lies within a small sub-category of zombie films that change the perspective to instead suggest that the dead are actually alive, a kind of continuation of the denial of death. In *Warm Bodies* (2013), for example, the audience is given insight into the undead perspective as a zombie protagonist narrates his inner thoughts and feelings as if trapped in a zombified body like a victim of locked-in syndrome. Through the film, the zombie, R (Nicholas Hoult), returns to life as his body is warmed by his love for a still-living woman, Julie (Teresa Palmer). While the film humanizes the zombie, the skeletal bonies are the true monster, intent on destroying life both human and zombie. There is a sleight of hand at play here in suggesting that the zombie (traditionally standing in for death) can return to life (thereby denying the power of death itself) while then creating a new monstrous threat that takes the place of zombies as the emblem of death, but one removed from an immediate human equation being, on one hand, without any flesh, but further being entirely CGI unlike the flesh-and-blood actors portraying zombies. *Zombies Anonymous* (2006) and *iZombie* (2015–present) both depict zombiedom as a disability against which the world remains fearfully and hatefully opposed; this concept might allow a reading encouraging death-awareness except for the fact that the "zombies" in these examples, while dead and risen, retain all of their former personality and so are not actually dead in any real sense.

Michele Soavi's *Dellamorte Dellamore* (1994), which is oddly titled *Cemetery Man* for American audiences but more accurately translates to *Of Death and Love*, offers what might be viewed, again contra Bakhtin, as a criticism of valuing social survival over the individual. In this film, considered by some to be the best Italian horror movie ever made,[134] a cemetery caretaker, named Francesco Dellamorte (Rupert Everett), discovers that the dead begin to rise from their graves but elects to deal with the problem himself lest he risk being seen as a failure. He falls in love with a grieving widow who is then killed by her zombified husband while consummating her relationship with Dellamorte. The woman returns as a zombie and is killed by Dellamorte not once but twice before she then appears in various other forms, the same actress portraying a number of identical women about town, whom Dellamorte similarly murders. His passionate excitement at seeing each iteration of his beloved is quickly replaced by the knowledge of her ever-present death. Every time he sees another version of the woman he loves, he cannot help but to realize that she will also die—"Unable to see her as herself, Francesco views each woman through a veil of immortal hopes and mortal dread."[135] Sex and death are combined here in a strange cycle played for comedic effect in the film, which ends only when Dellamorte comes to realize that, in fact, no one else in his life is even alive at all! The dead rise up as zombies, while the "living" are all actually dead from the outset. The protagonist is not afraid of dying, and the zombies do not represent a physical threat to him but rather pose the potential for embarrassment if the rest of the town were to discover they were rising in his cemetery. Dellamorte is unconcerned about his own mortality, but not because he can accept the survival of society beyond him—quite the opposite. He ends in realizing that everyone is dead and it is he alone who is left. Soavi himself explains, the film "is not about the fear of dying; its concern is the fear of living."[136] The question is one of how to fit into society while alive, the existential quest for a meaningful life in the face of personal mortality.

Slavoj Zizek, another philosopher of the psychoanalytic school, also exemplifies the scholar's capacity to identify political and social ideology in every human product, including excrement. In *The Plague of Fantasies*, Zizek explains how differences in toilet design, resulting in different manipulations of excrement, reflect distinct ideological differences across cultures.[137] The French toilet, he explains, with a hole at the back to allow the immediate removal of excrement, reflects the cultural tendency towards "revolutionary hastiness." The German toilet, by contrast, has a hole at the front, which results in the excrement being laid on a shelf before being flushed; thereby, the typical "reflective thoroughness" of German culture appears in the tendency to inspect one's feces for signs of illness. Regardless of the extent to which Zizek's analysis actually captures a snapshot of the diverse cultures of these nations, the emphasis is on social generalizations of a cultural and political kind. Whether looking at sex, food, excrement, or bodies (dead, alive, or in-between), one can certainly find cultural signs that allow for ideological criticism and understanding, but the individual experience remains.

Japanese zombie cinema offers a different perspective on the abject, while seemingly accepting Kristeva's association of shit with the corpse as the epitome of abjection. *Tokyo Zombie* (2005), for instance, has zombies emerge from a massive landfill at the base of Mount Fuji. More interesting, however ridiculous the film itself, is *Zombie Ass: Toilet of the Dead* (2011). Harkening back to *Shivers*, this film sees a mad scientist develop a zombie-making parasite in an effort to stave off the cancer that is killing his daughter. Here, rather than inciting sexual mania in its victims, this parasite induces severe abdominal pain, gas, and death-by-diarrhea, followed by the inevitable rise from death as a coprophilic zombie that hurls excrement at its victims. The film is explicit and unrelenting in its direct association of death with shit, both examples of the abject reminder that we are decaying objects while we'd prefer to think of ourselves as constant subjects.

The scientist at the root of the *Zombie Ass* outbreak, Dr. Tanaka laments of the results of his creation, "You fart and fart until you die. That's your fate." But this observation is essentially an existential reflection on reality as we all move steadily closer to death with each moment. Whereas most Western thinkers, including Zizek and Kristeva and the Christian scholars like Paffenroth above, would have us look away in horror, the Japanese perspective is different. Here, instead, the heroine of *Zombie Ass* comes to terms with the outbreak despite herself becoming infected by the parasite. She harnesses the gas building within her body, acknowledging the abject nature of her own self not as a rejected object that is ejected but as an inherent component that must be accepted.

Echoing this comfort with one's own skin and all that lies within it, Cronenberg said: "I don't think that the flesh is necessarily treacherous, evil, bad. It is cantankerous, and it is independent."[138] The body is not the site of evil to be rejected, its worst aspects seen as depictions, whether literal or metaphoric, of its sinful nature. It is not intent on destroying us, however much its tenuous structure and transformation over time leads inevitably to that end. It is malleable and changing, and yet its soft and delicate casing is all that separates us as individuals from the outside world and death. As Cronenberg notes, especially in *The Fly*,[139] as the body changes, so do we, while at the same time as the body decays aspects of the self continue to surface. This is a core component of all zombie fiction, with the zombie standing as the logical end result of the body's ongoing transformation. Of course, the corpse also literally stands before both fictional protagonists and their audience as the ongoing representation of a self in that body! It isn't just that a line between the living and the dead is blurred, but the notion that there is any permanent aspect of selfhood that can cling to a denial of the ever-changing body-towards-death is forced into stark light. This exposure might be deflected by looking instead at the ideological or political ramifications that are metaphorically present here, but most viscerally, and immediately, for consumers of zombie fiction, the immediate sense is one of the immediacy of death, reflection thereupon leading one to recognize one's own mortality. Viewers may empathize with the protagonists who struggle vainly to survive, but zombie fiction again and again reinforces the point that everyone dies and that anyone can die at any point, a point made perhaps most clearly in the ongoing serial drama of *The Walking Dead*. What is needed is exactly the kind of change of perspective seemingly embraced in some Japanese zombie cinema, however ludicrous those may be.

In a sense, then, we should see the destruction of the body in zombie fiction as a core component of the genre, the gore and decay pointing directly at its subject—the body and our personal perspectives and reactions to it, especially as it relates to our own physical being as mortal body. As film scholar, Pete Boss, notes, however useful cultural critiques of zombie fiction may be, critical interpretations which focus

> upon the figure of the monster as "Other," leaves the discourse of bodily destruction largely unexamined or taken for granted as somehow determining the extent of the monster's "monstrousness." It is the case, however, that these films are in many ways "about" this ruination of the physical subject; the fascination with this spectacle is not in any way a secondary consideration.[140]

Noël Carroll's philosophical examination of the problem of why anyone should ever elect to be scared by consuming horror fiction, in its delineation of art-horror from genuine fear of immediate danger, points to the necessity of both fear and disgust as defining characteristics. For him, though, the latter is indicative of the culturally-determined and largely symbolic "impure."[141] In what he perceived as an increasing use of gore in body horror depictions of "person-as-meat," Carroll posits various possibilities for what might be *truly* dying, from the post–1960's death of the American dream to Foucault's "death of man."[142] I prefer to look to the obvious and simply stop at what is most plainly indicated as death itself. Not the "death of man" but rather my own individual death. The ruination of bodies on display in zombie fiction elicits disgust not for being "impure," except in the sense that we see death itself as "impure" in our clinging to a denial of its reality. The disgust at seeing the pierced containers of human bodies forces us to reflect immediately on the piercing of our own containers, and the troubling thought of our own imminent, and very real, demise.

Varieties of Disgust

Zombie fiction offers multiple avenues for the elicitation of disgust beyond just blood and gore, making the genre stand apart from other splatter-horror in this regard. Yes, bodies are torn apart, heads are exploded, and much blood is splattered, but the zombie itself evinces disgust in its status as dead body, too. The living may be rent limb from limb, and the walking dead move on with gaping holes dragging entrails behind, but the fact that they ought to be dead brings with it another layer of disgust. It isn't that the disgust of the corpse is entirely different than that of blood and guts generally, since both of these relate clearly to the problem of individual frailty and mortality.

One other avenue for disgust is added in the form of the practically universal taboo against cannibalism—zombies since Romero routinely devour the flesh (or sometimes preferring just the brains) of their living victims. Being a taboo, the discomfort with cannibalism might lead us away from the core concern with immediate mortality and opens a range of metaphorical possibilities; Romero's *Dawn of the Dead* (1978) most famously made clear the association between the zombies' mindless consumption of flesh and modern consumer culture in basing its action almost entirely in a shopping mall. In the fiction, though, the eating of living flesh by the zombies is intimately tied to the cycle of life and death, as it is the sole motivating factor for the dead to do anything at all, while it is also a key vector for the creation of more zombies through the killing of their victims.

Cannibalism, along with defecation and incest, has long been among the most odious taboos in a majority of cultures.[143] It has often been applied to groups as a means of "othering" them. We've seen earlier how the Spanish used the term for the Carib people to derogatively depict them as uncivilized savages. Broadly, the term might be applied to any instance of a species eating other members of its own species. To apply the moniker to zombies is to imply that zombies must be of the same species as humans, that is, they are both the same.

Confusion emerges, though, as, firstly, protagonists in zombie fiction regularly argue about whether the zombies are, in fact, human or not, with the latter side generally winning the day in order to justify destroying the zombies. This confusion plays to critiques of colonial applications of the label, too, since in order to be a cannibal one must be of the same species (that is, human), while being a cannibal itself suggests that the eater is expressly *not* human, or sub-human. Television series, *iZombie* (2015–present), features zombies with full agency, though they are dead and have returned to life craving human brains. The protagonist, Liv Moore (Rose McIver), is shown eating a new brain in every episode, but a cooking montage shows her making intricate recipes that serve to camouflage the bits of brain that are included. On the other hand, a number of antagonistic zombies are depicted throughout the series, and these almost always eat brains without preparation of any kind. The effect is to humanize Liv while emphasizing the baser natures of the villains.

Humans can safely eat other animals, seen as beneath them, but those humans who do eat other humans then move to a state that is also less-than-human. They do not move to an animal state, though, since eating a cannibal would still be an act of cannibalism itself such that the sub-human is still human, that is, of the same species. If the zombie is a cannibal, then, it may reduce them to sub-human status, but it does not reduce them to completely un-human. Audiences, and scholars, who label the zombies as cannibal must also then agree with the ongoing connection between the living and the dead as one species, lest they apply the term inaccurately. And it is not simply the matter of referring to cannibalism as the eating of humans by anything as nobody would describe, say, the shark in *Jaws* (1975) or even the undead rodents of *Zombeavers* (2014) as cannibals![144] In fact, examples in zombie fiction of zombies eating other zombies are exceedingly rare. In one example of such an instance, surrealist author Aimee Bender describes a single zombie eating other zombies, "the latest zombie" being the only one at all interested in eating others like himself. Taking the zombie-as-consumer to an absolute extreme, this zombie "ate and ate," he became sick, died, and re-re-animated even hungrier than before and this time consuming himself "until all that was left was a mouth and a GI tract. A mouth, an esophagus, a stomach, intestines."[145] Most of the time, zombies are attracted only to living humans, while less often they're shown eating non-human animals. *The Walking Dead* allows its zombies to feast on any living creature they can catch, while Romero moved from zombies eating insects along with human flesh in *Night of the Living Dead* to needing to be trained to eat non-human animals in *Survival of the Dead* (2009). Even those quasi-zombie films where the "zombies" are not actually dead but simply infected humans, like *28 Days Later* (2002) or *Cannibal Apocalypse* (1980), the infected might even work together while potentially starving to death en masse in the absence of uninfected humans upon whom to feed.

To describe zombies as cannibals looks like a misguided application of the term, which perhaps leads to a confusion with what is exactly causing the sense of disgust in the first place. Applying a Freudian interpretation of cannibalism emphasizing the fear of being eaten as the core concern in the taboo, which when depicted is then seen as a reflection of one's struggle for autonomy in the face of one's parents, will certainly lead one far from the obvious source of disgust.[146] For one thing, calling zombies cannibals brings to the fore the ongoing confusion between the living and the dead that is core to so much zombie fiction. Are the living-dead living or dead? And what does their status, especially if the same as other humans, say about that of the living? Scott Poole suggests that zombies are "'gross,' because their appetites denigrate the human body, turning it into an abject consumable."[147] But the abject is, by definition, NOT consumable; it is the waste produced *after* consuming. More correctly, the zombie (and the cannibal) objectifies the human body by consuming it, which is what makes the eater abject in the eyes of the potentially consumable human. Thinking about the relationship between the eater and the eaten as one and the same species forces us to recognize that the zombie as dead and the victim as living are one and the same; death and life are counterparts at all times. Abjection does nothing to resolve the problem, but noting the presence of the abject in the reaction of disgust, points us directly at the heart of the problem—the denial of death.

The suggestion of cannibalism in zombie fiction may also speak against prevailing interpretations of disgust generally, which tend to point to a removal of the human from the animal, suggesting that those things which we find disgusting are also those things which remind us of our own animality.[148] And, to be sure, animality appears as a feature of some zombies as well, especially in examples like *28 Days Later*, *Pontypool* (2008), *World War Z* (2013), or Stephen King's *Cell* (2016),[149] where the zombies are not only insatiably drawn to the living, but do so with a violent rage. Since cannibalism requires intra-species consumption, the concept isn't one that easily applies to humans eating animals, or vice versa. William Miller, in his *The Anatomy of Disgust*, notes a correlation between disgust and the ageing process, pointing to the personal disgust (among other feelings including embarrassment, fear, excitement, etc.) one experiences with one's own body as it enters puberty and then gradually changes over time. He suggests that the eventual acceptance of one's ageing (and aged) state ("a giving up in the losing battle against physical deterioration") equates with an increasing tolerance for what younger people find biologically disgusting—stray hairs, unkempt nails, warts, noisy and noisome bodily functions, etc.[150] Cronenberg's interpretation of *The Fly* as a compression of the ageing process is all the more horrific in that it doesn't allow its protagonists, let alone the audience, to become accustomed to the changes over time as we would through a lifetime.

Alongside this, Miller observes, "There are few things that are more unnerving and disgust evoking than our partibility."[151] Here, he touches on Kristeva's abject as such discarded parts of the body are rejected as disgusting—hair and nail clippings, spit, snot, and other jetsam of the body. Miller emphasizes, though, our partibility on a larger scale, in the severing of limbs and dissection of the body. The severing of limbs has become something of a trope in the zombie genre, often with protagonists lopping off the arm or leg of a loved one who has been bitten in an attempt to stop the infection from killing them. *The Walking Dead* comes most immediately to mind with a number of characters enduring life-saving dismemberments (most obviously Hershel Greene [Scott Wilson] in the television show, but also Merle Dixon [Michael Rooker] in a different context, and in the examples of Allen, Dale, and Heath in the comic book), and dismemberment in the process of cannibalism or punishment of various kinds. Romero might have started the idea with an ultimately tragic amputation in *Day of the Dead*. In that movie, Miguel Salazar (Antony Dileo, Jr.) has a chunk of flesh ripped from his arm by a zombie bite and must be knocked unconscious to control his panic before having his arm amputated by friends who then work to nurse him back to health. Unfortunately, already rattled by the undead and his own brush with death, Miguel, feeling the loss of his arm as another assault on his manhood, becomes suicidal and opens the base to allow the zombies outside to take over. Essentially, Miller points to concerns for the integrity of the bodily envelope, pointing once again to the fragility of the body.

A particularly gory puncturing of the body envelope that emphasizes the viewing of the event itself occurs in instances of eyes being gouged out of the living, or hanging from the sockets of a walking corpse. *The Walking Dead* offers numerous examples of eyes being gouged out or otherwise destroyed (prime among them those of Carl, the Governor, and Glenn), providing some of the goriest images in both the comic book and television series. Perhaps the most famously gruesome instance in zombie fiction is the notorious eye scene in Fulci's *Zombie Flesh Eaters*. In this scene, the wife of a scientist tasked with researching a Caribbean zombie outbreak (played by Olga Karlatos) is stalked by a zombie that punches a hole in the door to her house. Grabbing her by the hair, the zombie pulls her slowly towards the hole it has created as Fulci forces the audience to, at turns, take on the perspective of the woman and watch a close up from the side as her eye is slowly impaled on a sharp piece of broken wood.

Another threat to the integrity of the body envelope is that of virus or infection. Many have made the erroneous assumption that zombie fiction is, at root, a plague narrative. Jennifer Cooke, in what has been described as "the first book-length study to take as its focus the relationship between the plague and psychoanalysis,"[152] delineates three types of plague genre. Among these three is the zombie genre, of which she claims: "Ever since [Romero], instead of a hypnotised slave, the zombie has been a dangerous, infectious embodiment of the living dead who cannibalistically parasitises the living: Romero made his zombies plague carriers and able to infect others, to turn them, too, into zombies."[153] While it is true that Romero's zombies are infectious, it isn't some zombie parasite or virus with which they are infected, but simply that their bites cause deadly infection to set in. The cause for the dead rising back up as zombies is left entirely ambiguous throughout Romero's cycle. Across the broad swath of zombie fiction, a range of possibilities exist, including chemical agents, radiation, alien technology, the supernatural, and, yes, a virus. Only some zombie fiction refers to the virus as cause, probably most notably with the Rage virus in *28 Days Later*, a film that can rightly be seen as sparking the most recent upswing in the monster's popularity. John Russo, seeking to carve out his own zombie narrative outside of Romero's narrative, also encourages the viral zombie germ in a litany of sub-par fiction.[154] And Cooke is not alone in ignoring the fact that no single cause is ever agreed upon in the genre; one academic wrongly claims, "It is an infection—a disease—that much seems to be clear,"[155] voicing the assumption of so many others. Some have even used zombies as an educational model for the spread of disease.[156]

While characters in *The Walking Dead* comic (namely Rick and Negan) independently come to the conclusion that everyone is infected by some zombie-virus, no justification is given. The television series makes the claim through the person of Center for Disease Control scientist, Edwin Jenner (Noah Emmerich), who tells Rick that everyone is already infected with a zombie-inducing virus, a claim which Rick then repeats in the series and is accepted as gospel truth not only by the characters in the show but by viewers as well. Of course, Jenner is also depicted as not altogether sane, choosing suicide after having failed in his attempts to understand the zombie outbreak, leaving ample room for doubt as to the veracity of his in-show claim. Moreover, the spinoff series, *Fear the Walking Dead*, has Liza Ortiz (Elizabeth Rodriguez), a nursing student conscripted by the military to help with medical treatment, explain in no uncertain terms: "I've seen it. I've seen what it does. The bites don't turn you, but the infection's not treatable. The infection kills you like anything else. Then it happens. It doesn't matter how you die, you come back. We all come back." It is as if Liza is speaking to all of those who have leapt to the assumption that we understand the cause of the zombie apocalypse and that it might be treated, cured, like any disease!

The denial of death as unavoidable appears prominently in medical expectations to cure all. Eric Cazdyn suggests that we are currently living in what he calls a "chronic time" that denies the terminal and instead wallows in a chronic state of dealing with symptoms while ignoring root causes.[157] Chronic time is a particular perspective on time, one that sees the future essentially as a continuation and extension of the present, and imagines the present as somehow permanent and continuous. This certainly relates to the prevailing Judaeo-Christian view of human life, for instance, as a permanent, individual self moving through a chronic period of sin. Moments of pain and suffering are symptomatic of the sinful chronic state, and can be alleviated only by the thought of God, lying entirely outside the system. Any true end to life's suffering is imagined to lie in a heavenly paradise that belies description or imagination except to say that it is good. That mindset, though, accepts the current state of suffering as a given, and sees any instance of suffering as a symptom to be dealt with as it arises. In terms of an attitude to death in the face of life, it is also one that refuses to see a terminal state and instead imagines that the current self will continue to exist indefinitely, despite a variety of problematic questions that arise from conceptions of heavenly resurrection. Will I still be me if I do not have the same body? Will I still be myself as I know myself if all of my negative emotions, memories, and feelings are removed? Can I be me if I no longer feel guilt for a wrong I've committed? Can I be myself if I am no longer married, or if I am reunited with partners who died before I met new ones? And what if I had died before I got old; will I then be a child forever? The tension that ought to come from the unanswerability of these, and many, many other questions normally ends in the questions simply being ignored in the chronic view of present continuity into the future.

On the flip side there are also cases where the continuity of life blurs with the certainty of death in ways that trouble this chronic view, such as the increasing prevalence of dementia like Alzheimer's disease and new research and debate about victims of coma. In both cases, the discomfort caused by such patients often places them in the context of the abject, to be removed from sight and from consideration. Recall that health care experts often find parallels between zombies as the living-dead and

Alzheimer's patients whose bodies continue to act but whose minds and personalities may be all but lost.[158]

The problem of determining an incontrovertible moment of death given the advances made by modern medicine in sustaining life in various forms now often results in arguments between family and doctors over comatose patients. Technology can keep a body alive even without signs of significant brain activity. From the materialist perspective of medicine, this indicates an opportunity for organ donation, which itself presents an interesting dilemma—organs must be alive to be suitable for transplant, whereas the comatose body must be declared dead in order for organs to be removed, leaving the patient in a gray zone between life and death.[159] On the other hand, many families will see any sign of life in the body of their loved one as an indication that they have not died. The borderline between being alive and being dead is shown to be unclear in such cases, and such a blurring of boundaries is especially problematic when one expects to see continuity clearly laid out ahead.

Cazdyn points to the Buddhist *Tibetan Book of the Dead* as a potential sign of how one might change the perspective.[160] This text is recited to a person as they are dying and continues for days after death. The book explains to the individual that they have died and that they will find themselves in a new situation, between life, death, and rebirth, called *bardo*. As a gap between death and renewed life, though, the *bardo* also mirrors the gap between life and death. As Cazdyn puts it, "Rather, the truth for the already dead is the truth for the living, and the *bardo* represents all gaps, most notably the gap between life and death in which the living always exist. It is only at the moment when the living remember that they are already dead that the possibility for liberation emerges."[161] Essentially, instead of looking at the surface current moment in which I am living and imagining that this state will continue into the future, thereby ignoring the reality of the terminal state, thinking in terms of the *bardo* "gap" forces a conflation of the future and present. Rather than extrapolating an imagined future from the present, we can accept the future reality (i.e., death) and bring that back to bear upon the present lived reality. To put it another way, instead of considering that we are living now and will continue to live tomorrow, and then imagining that even when we die we will continue to live on in life everlasting, it is more realistic to accept that we are currently *dying* and we will inevitably end in dying. As Jen Webb and Sam Byrnand put it, echoing a Buddhist maxim, "Only in finding a way to ignore, overlook or eradicate them [the dying or dead] can we forget the fact that as they are, so too I will be."[162] There is no chronic condition, then, in life, but rather a terminal one. The problems of sickness and ageing are not symptoms to be removed from life, but are intrinsic to the process of living and dying.

Conclusion

Zombies, as a modern *memento mori*, shock the viewer out of the complacency of living in a chronic condition of death denial and force the reality of impending death into the fore of one's mind. And it is not simply the effect of watching scenes of death that makes the connection explicit. The argument for simply witnessing scenes of death as a meditation on mortality has already been made by none other than Satanism's Anton LaVey in his narration of *Death Scenes* (1989), part of the long running *Faces of Death* franchise.[163] And the difference is also not simply one of true death (as in the *Faces of Death*) vs. fictional depictions, especially given the attempt at realism in zombie fiction and the general blurring of the boundary between the real and the simulacrum, following Jean Baudrillard.[164] The very features of the zombie and its history combine to provide the ideal illustration of human mortality and the means by which we might adapt to the knowledge of our own mortality without fear and denial.

It is important to note that the model of zombie as a focus of meditation works only for audiences, as protagonists in zombie fiction almost universally fight against death, thereby embodying the very death denial that zombies reveal as untenable. From *Night of the Living Dead* the tradition begins with every protagonist in the house killed by the film's end, and *The Walking Dead* continues the tradition as viewers are warned not to become too attached to any character as core characters are apt to die at any point. Many viewers may side with the protagonists in denying the inevitability of death, with many fans even devising their own personal zombie-apocalypse survival plans. To them, like the survivors in *The Walking Dead* who so wish to remove themselves from death that a prison becomes a haven, the ironic imprisonment-as-liberation-from-death goes unnoticed.[165] And, like the characters themselves, regular viewers become distressed when that haven collapses. When fan-favorite, Glenn Rhee (Steven Yeun), apparently died in season six, many threatened to stop watching the series. There was even greater reaction when Glenn was finally killed in a very brutal scene. Attachment to a favorite character led to outrage at his death, despite the facts that death is inevitable, not only in real life but also as depicted in the original source material of the comic, too. Media coverage wondered at whether the death was necessary, or too violent, and fans threatened to boycott the show.[166] What is needed is a change of perspective, new lenses through which to view the zombie and its apocalypse. Recognizing the unavoidability of death, and accepting it as a certainty, is a large part of zombie fiction.

Though it is often said that we live in a culture of death denial, Tony Walter famously differed in expressing that the modern attitude appears more clearly to present an obsession with death rather than its denial, and certainly the prevalence of zombie fiction might cause some to agree.[167] Importantly, though, even if there is an obsessive need in modern popular culture for creative expressions of death, the core denial remains in the response to such depictions. It is as though constant repetition of death is some vain attempt to cope with the fear of its inevitability. Instead of therapy, though, such representations would appear instead to simply reinforce the denial of death's power. Walter points to secularism as a turning point in our attitude towards death, and such an observation certainly meshes with the transformed zombie of Romero. The 1960s saw a massive turn away from traditional authority across the board, and Christian perspectives of death denial in the light of everlasting life came under as much scrutiny as any other institution. Though the model of death in the form of the zombie has only increased in popularity, what has been missing is the explicit framework in which to comprehend them outside of the previous traditions of death denial. I turn to Buddhist philosophy for that framework, a system that itself burst into American consciousness in the 1950s and 60s just as Christian tradition failed for many people and attitudes towards death began to change.

In *The Undead and Theology*, Jessica DeCou refers to a line from *The Walking Dead*, in which one character (Daryl Dixon, played by Norman Reedus) ruefully asks, "What, am I the only one who's Zen around here?" Jokingly, she suggests that Zen might be better suited to understanding the nature of zombies than any other system of thought "because of its insights into the nature, cause, and cure of suffering," though she demurs from pursuing it for lack of sufficient training in Buddhism.[168] Though using the line for off-hand comedic effect, the Christian theological interpretation of the zombie offered by DeCou is undermined by recognizing the context of Daryl's quote; immediately before the quoted question, Daryl adds: "It's a waste of time, all this hopin' and prayin'. We're going to locate that little girl, and she's gonna be just fine." Here, Daryl makes a call to action over passive hope and prayer, a sentiment echoed by the Dalai Lama after the recent Paris attacks when he acknowledged: "We cannot solve this problem only through prayers. I am a Buddhist and I believe in praying. But humans have created this problem, and now we are asking God to solve it. It is illogical. God would say, solve it yourself because you created it in the first place."[169] Interestingly, Kevin Wetmore notes the effect of explicit Christian imagery on the zombie as he critiques John Russo's revised *30th Anniversary Edition* (1998) of *Night of the Living Dead* (in which extra scenes are clumsily appended to the original film, adding a sinful motive to the zombie outbreak and a priest who is saved by God after having been bitten), which transforms the film into *Left Behind: The Zombies*, a "Christian horror film in which the horror no longer comes from fear of the dead but from fear of demons and evil spirits."[170]

The next chapter will show how zombies avail themselves to a Buddhist perspective quite readily, in part referencing the insatiable cravings embodied by the gluttonous zombie; cravings that not only lie at the heart of suffering in Buddhist thought, but that are analogous to the misdirected desires for unachievable bodily satisfaction attested to in the *Confessions* of St. Augustine.[171] Fiction has long been used as a teaching device for Buddhist philosophy, and, in fact, walking corpses have been a common trope in such tales for centuries.[172] In his book using a range of films as a means to teach Buddhism, scholar of religion, Ronald Green wonders openly whether film might not have replaced the mandala had it been available in earlier times, so effective is it at conveying its message even to those who are at first unaware they are being taught.[173] Likewise, Buddhist scholar Francisca Cho sees film as the perfect medium for Buddhist teaching given its "unequalled power [...] to create the illusion of 'real life,'" reflecting "the Buddhist lesson that life itself is an illusory projection."[174] I will not argue that any maker of zombie fiction has intentionally tried to depict Buddhist teachings, nor even that any of them are necessarily aware of the details of Buddhist philosophy themselves. It does seem reasonable, though, given the provenance of the zombie from its anti–Catholic history in Haiti through its development to Matheson's Theosophical leanings and 1950's Beat-Gen and later 1960s counter-cultural attitudes, that the genre should depict elements moving against the normative Christian orthodoxy, and perhaps even adopting some of the same alternative ideas that grew alongside a growing acceptance of Eastern notions of self. In any event, interpreting the zombie through a Buddhist lens will provide new avenues for understanding ourselves in the face of mortality.

CHAPTER FOUR

Zombies and the Buddhist Meditation on Death

Both Christianity and Buddhism downplay the importance of the self in a communal context to encourage selflessness, but while the former imagines an eternal persistence of the self, the other reinforces the observed reality of eternal change. While for the Christian, the latter idea suggests dark nihilism, when approached with a positive mindset the Buddhist view allows for a healthy relationship with death that is free from fear of eternal punishments for past failures. Nietzsche's observation that "God is dead" led to his viewing Christianity as a "reactive nihilism," which turns away from the realization of nothingness and imagines meaning where it cannot exist. The zombie can be seen to reflect core Buddhist teachings as an embodiment not of apocalyptic and nihilistic fears of an imagined Godless world, but rather of the world of self-inflicted suffering that we currently inhabit, but from which there is escape through understanding. Effectively, consuming zombie fiction can become a form of the Buddhist meditation on death, mortality, and impermanence when one recognizes the Buddhist imagery present. This is not to say that one cannot enjoy zombie fiction on its own terms, but understanding the Buddhist doctrines and being able to see them reflected in said fiction will allow thoughtful audiences to garner benefits from their entertainment as might be gained through meditative techniques. Namely, fear of death as some mysterious future unknown replaced instead by an acceptance that in living we are already dying and that it is our willful ignorance of that simple reality that is actually at the root of our selfish anxieties.

Dharma of the Dead: The Four Noble Truths

All of Buddhist thought traces its origins to a man named Siddhartha Gautama, the original Buddha, an honorific meaning "Awakened One," the first man to awaken to an understanding of human nature to which most of us remain blind. Though the biographical details of Gautama's life cannot be verified as established fact, tradition places his birth among the Shakya clan, another of his titles being Shakyamuni, "The Sage of the Shakya," fathered by a regional chieftain or leader in what is today modern Nepal.[1] Before becoming enlightened, Gautama was raised a spoiled prince, protected from the world by his father who had been foretold of his son's potential to become either a great ruler or a wandering mendicant, the latter, less-desirable path linked to the boy's experience of real-world suffering. Gautama was thus protected from suffering, living in a veritable bubble of riches, being lavished with everything a young man could desire and for which a wealthy ruler could provide. He had several palaces in which to live, every luxury at hand, eating the best foods, wearing the best clothes, and marrying the most beautiful woman around. Still, the story goes, Gautama felt dissatisfied with his life, feeling certain that there must be more to it than the comforts of wealth.

At the age of 29, following the birth of his first and only son, Gautama fled the palace to explore the world outside. He there experienced four crucial sights: first, he encountered an old man, hobbled and bent with age and suddenly became aware that all life decays over time; then he encountered a sick man, visibly diseased and in pain, and only then did he realize that sickness and pain were inevitable realities regardless of wealth; third, he stumbled upon a funeral and witnessed the sight of a decaying corpse, only then realizing the reality that death awaits all living things, and that the body that had been lavished with comfort would eventually grow old, get sick, and die. In the face of these realities, Gautama realized his dissatisfaction with his life was founded on the existential realization that all material wealth was naught but a distraction from the reality of an unstoppable progression through suffering and decay to death. Finally, Gautama encountered the fourth sight that would forever alter his life path—an ascetic monk who rejected all material comforts in exchange for spiritual pursuits. Gautama then decided to follow this same path of renunciation and embarked on a multi-year effort to achieve spiritual enlightenment.

At first, as the story goes on, Gautama followed traditional paths to enlightenment offered by the India of his day (circa 500 BC), but found them to be lacking. The Vedic caste system denied him access to higher spiritual learning by birthright, his being the ruling caste of Kshatriya rather than the priestly Brahmin class. At the other extreme, he pursued a kind of Jainist asceticism that denied material "comforts" to the point of, according to one tale, fainting from near-starvation, living as he had been on a single grain of rice a day. After finding failure in these systems, Gautama embarked on what would become the Buddhist "middle path," whereby he sated his bodily need to eat before simply sitting under a tree to meditate on the human condition. Through this period of contemplation, Gautama realized the truths that would form the core teachings of Buddhism—the Four Noble Truths. The structure of these four "truths" can be seen as a diagnosis for human suffering, and mark the beginning of the path of treatment advocated by the now awakened Buddha.

The core of Buddhism rests in the Four Noble Truths, central to which are the notions of attachment, impermanence, and suffering.[2] In short, the first truth is that all of life involves suffering. Even writing of Buddhism in English, it is often preferable to use the Pali term, *dukkha*, in order to emphasize that this is not simply obvious suffering like when one stubs a toe or has one's heart broken, but that suffering is intrinsic to living and colors experience even when it is not immediately felt. Certainly, obvious forms of suffering like physical, emotional, and mental anguish are all accounted for in *dukkha*. The Buddha points to the fact that suffering persists even when it is not immediately present, so that a person who has been burned might avoid fire, a person who has been wronged may avoid relationships, and a person with a fear of public speaking may avoid social gatherings. This background suffering is also encompassed by *dukkha*. Avoiding painful experiences incorporates the suffering of the pain within its avoidance. One way to talk about this is to break suffering into types where one is the experience of direct suffering of an event that we'd prefer not to experience (the stubbed toe), another is the suffering implicit in trying to avoid those experiences that we do not want. More implicit yet, though, is the tricky hidden suffering on the flip side of avoiding that which we don't want—having an experience that we do want, and the suffering that occurs when we lose it. Getting a tear in one's favorite shirt causes suffering in this category. Likewise, though, there is even more hidden suffering in our attempts to avoid suffering, in this case the effort to avoid losing those experiences that we want. Covering one's prized couch in plastic protects the couch from damage, but also takes away from the enjoyment that the couch might provide in both comfort and aesthetics! Avoiding the inevitable absence of a good thing is one of the most pernicious and surreptitious forms of suffering/*dukkha*.

I like to use chocolate cake as my example to help explain just how a thing that would at first glance appear to make me happy is, in fact, a further source of suffering. The problem is, as the saying goes, that I want my cake and to eat it, too. I love chocolate cake. Especially with thick icing. I can imagine the pleasure of having a piece of chocolate cake in front of me. In this instance, the immediate feeling of happiness may be what I most explicitly experience. But, the Buddha reminds us, in the back of my mind I know that this cake will be here only temporarily. This moment of happiness is fleeting. I may not have these thoughts immediately, and I may not want to have them for fear that even thinking thus will hamper my enjoyment. The fact is, though, it is the truth and ignoring that truth is a lie. Even as I try to hold onto my enjoyment of the cake, I might eat smaller and smaller bites. Turning the piece of cake so that I eat only a little from this side and then a little from the other in a vain effort to keep this cake-induced happiness alive a little longer. Towards the end, I may spend more time savoring each smaller and smaller bite, sucking the icing from my fork more thoughtfully. And then the plate is empty ... except for maybe these last few crumbs that I can pick up with a finger, or last scrapings of icing. Yes, I will have enjoyed eating that cake, but the Buddha's emphasis is on the fact that even as I "enjoyed" it, I also suffered through the torment of knowing that my enjoyment was fading. The more I ate, the closer I got to losing that thing that was bringing me joy.

Knowing that, in the back of my mind, the cake and the enjoyment it brought were both temporary, in itself, is *dukkha*, a suffering that detracts from full enjoyment. The fact that I might try to ignore and deny the fact that my pleasure will soon end only proves the extent to which not only the end but the drive towards the end causes suffering. More importantly than merely cake, the same applies to everything in life. In fact, the same applies directly to life itself. We all know that life will end and yet we ignore that reality as much as possible. Living and dying are the same thing, the same process, yet speaking of dying while living is often received as pessimistic or depressing. Instead, we wish to ignore the inevitability of the end as if such ignorance will enhance our enjoyment of life, when, in fact, the desire to ignore is embedded with suffering as evidenced in the reaction to being made aware of its truth. This is *dukkha*, the first noble truth described by the Buddha. In a sense, the Buddha here points to the symptom and, while the above may very well sound depressing to many, rest assured that he also presents a cure!

The second noble truth is that of what causes *dukkha*, suffering. If we focused on obvious forms of suffering, like stubbing a toe, then we might well blame aspects external to ourselves for suffering, like the table leg or the person who moved the table to vacuum and didn't put it back in its right place. We often blame others when we feel hurt, or curse fate or luck when bad things happen to us. But all of this takes the power of suffering, and more importantly the cure, out of our hands. The Buddha describes the second truth, the cause of suffering, as attachment. Specifically, we are attached to things that make us feel good. This attachment endures despite the knowledge that all things are impermanent. I'm attached to the chocolate cake as a source of pleasure; as the cake disappears, so too does my pleasure, which results in a concomitant increase in suffering and a desire to find the next source of pleasure. In my attachment to things, I ignore their impermanence, or at least I try to ignore it. The shirt that gets a tear may have been my favorite shirt, and thus my sadness at losing it. However, every time I wore that shirt, I also knew, despite my effort to ignore it, that it could get torn, that it would get worn, and that it would fade, and so I tried desperately to protect that shirt from its inevitable end. I suffered through my enjoyment of that shirt because of my attachment to it and my wish that it would never tear. It is not only inanimate objects that cause the problem here, but also everything that exists. It is all temporary, and so long as we try to hold onto a thing, anything, then we suffer as we realize that it will pass away like every other thing.

Each individual self is at the core of this attachment. I imagine myself as an ongoing, somehow permanent entity despite my knowledge that my own death is a certainty. As I try to ignore my own mortality, for fear that acknowledging it is somehow depressing, I end in perpetuating my own suffering. That suffering may become explicit in moments of reflection precipitated, say, by a near-accident, an illness, or the death of a friend, but the suffering is implicit in every action that I take as a person who wishes to, literally self-ish-ly as in to behave like a self, assert my own permanence in the world.

The Buddha came to the realization that all things come to an end, and that all that we see as real is in fact impermanent and ever-changing. The notion that reality is at all static is an illusion, a misperception that misses the slow but inevitable progress of change, and this impermanence applies to all things, including the self. In Buddhism, there is no eternal soul, but only a constantly changing state of flux, a collection of aggregates that form and reform at every moment. Reacting to the context of its Indian origins, Buddhism refers to the "self" as *anatta*, a negation of the Hindu concept of self, *atman*. In Hinduism, *atman* is a permanent aspect, like a soul, associated with an individual from conception, throughout life, and surviving the death of the body, then being reborn in new lives as part of an ongoing cycle (*samsara*) of birth, death, and rebirth. Since a core realization of Buddhism is the impossibility of a thing's ever being permanent, the *atman* of Hinduism (and, likewise, the Abrahamic soul) cannot exist. That is to say, whatever sense of self I have right now, since change is central to all that exists, simply cannot be the ongoing thing that we think ourselves to be. Instead, a new concept of self must be adopted—*anatta*, not-self.

I have the sense of having been the self-same person I was yesterday and last week. I may recognize some changes in my self over time, but there remains a sense of coherence through these changes that gives a sense of permanence. From the Buddha's perspective, however, the self that I am now is not the same self as was a moment ago, or the one that will be tomorrow. Subtle changes occur over time which make one moment's self different, if even slightly, from the next's. Change is emphasized here, with the understanding that "same" and "different" are mutually exclusive opposites. If I am now different than I was before, then I cannot also say that I am the same. The self that I was even a moment ago has already changed and so is gone forever. In a sense, we move through a continuous series of little deaths throughout life. What I was is lost, what I am will cease to be. Our "final" death is but another change like any other.

Of course, like Hinduism before it, Buddhism accepts a belief in rebirth. At death, I will likely be reborn. The new birth that I will have will be a significantly different self from the one I am now, but the self that I am now is significantly different from the one that I had upon my birth into this present life. Remember now that when I refer to myself in a Buddhist sense I am referring to that "not-self" that I really am; a forever changing, impermanent something. Descartes proffered the fact that I exist as the only thing that I can truly know based on the fact that I think, and that thinking requires a thinker—*cogito ergo sum*. That a thought occurs to me indicates the presence of a thinker having the thought, and it is that selfsame thinker with which I identify at all times that I think. Cartesian mind-body duality stems from the distrust of the senses as offering unmediated experience of the world outside of my thoughts, but the overreliance on thoughts themselves leads to an unjustified conclusion. Though Ambrose Bierce had his tongue firmly in cheek, his "improvement" to the dictum mentioned earlier, "*cogito cogito ergo cogito sum*,"[3] I think that I think, therefore I think that I am, is much more in line with Buddhist thinking here. A thought certainly appears, and the one to whom the thought appears can rightly be called the thinker, "I." At the moment a thought occurs, we might be justified in agreeing that I am if all that we mean by that is that a thinker has a thought. The problem appears when we assume that I-ness is continuous from one thought-thinker dichotomy to the next. Memory would seem to be the only thing tying my thinking now to my thinking from the past, but memory is at least as untrustworthy a source for evidence as are our senses, and it is likely much worse, especially the more time passes. We tend to accept the fact that we remember the past as evidence that we have been and will continue to be into the future. The present state of being in which we remember or think of the future becomes blurred into the past and future unless we focus on the moment as distinct from other moments. In this way, memories, whether accurate or not, can serve to inform decisions made in the moment but need not serve any other purpose.

That we are attached to permanency, especially of our selves, results in much suffering since we cannot grasp anything for more than a moment before it is gone and has been replaced by something new. When I accept the illusion of my own permanence, I am unable to accept its eventual end and so I reject death. In the Buddhist worldview, my attachment to life will be enough to have me reborn. If I do not want to end, then I will be reborn upon death. The I that is reborn, of course, is but an illusion of consistency across an ever-changing thinker. Unlike a theory of resurrection that teaches that the resurrected self will be the exact same one that lived, Buddhist rebirth is simply a continuing process of changing selves moving through *samsara*. But, as observed in the Buddha's first Noble Truth, all of existence, all of samsara, is tainted by suffering. We may very well cling to the conception of our own individual permanence, but that clinging is exactly the very thing that will force rebirth to occur in a, literally, self-fulfilling and self-perpetuating circle of suffering. The fear of accepting impermanence is exactly that thing which causes us our own suffering by perpetuating the false reality of an ongoing, unchanging self.

Recognizing the self as not-self, radically changing one's perspective on the self, and thereby becoming unattached from all of the material world as sources for pleasure are the means to overcoming suffering. The Third Noble Truth speaks to the fact that there is a means to end suffering through ending attachments. In acting like a self (a permanent, ongoing entity), one naturally behaves self-ish-ly; but acting like a not-self (a temporary, and ever-changing series of thoughts and actions) one naturally behaves self-less-ly. A self that imagines it is permanent requires maintenance and upkeep, like a favorite shirt that one does not want to wear for fear of its being torn, or a last piece of cake uneaten for fear of being without it. That self, while decaying and changing, perpetuates an illusion of permanence that requires ignorance, distraction, and deceit. Such a self lives for itself, its life a constant effort to surround itself with the luxuries once lavished on the child Buddha to buffer him from the truth of suffering. Recognizing the transitoriness of all things, the not-self can move about unperturbed by the loss of a favorite shirt for that shirt did not move from a state of permanent perfection to one of torn garbage with one act, but was constantly in a state of decay itself. Even the sense of loss that might accompany the final tear that makes the shirt unwearable is itself transitory and so cannot inflict lasting suffering—the moment of loss is felt, but passes like every other moment such that there is no lingering attachment and so no lingering suffering. Of course, one might still experience pleasure at eating the last piece of cake, but the distinction comes in the not-self's lack of attachment to the pleasure. The focus of the not-self is not on the future, of which the self is constantly aware as it wonders where its next source of pleasure will be since it expects to continue into that future requiring another "fix." The not-self recognizes that it will itself cease to be in the next moment and so there is no fear of the loss of the current source of pleasure nor any need to crave after a new source since any lack is as temporary as any gain. The moment itself is the focus.

The elimination of suffering is core to Buddhism. The recognition that everything is impermanent and ever changing provides the path to escape suffering since the source of all suffering is the attachment to things. Attachment implies a desire for permanence, a craving for a thing's ongoing existence. Of course, understanding the temporariness of all things reveals attachment to be an entirely illogical act, however much it is ingrained in human nature. If we know that we are doing something not only pointless (i.e., craving after a permanent source of pleasure that does not exist), but that actually engenders pain and suffering to self and others (through constant failure to achieve permanent happiness and selfish behavior), then there is really no reason not to change course. Recognizing that there is no permanent source of happiness allows us to take pleasure in those passing moments of pleasure that do occur, and further allows us to ignore moments of darkness as likewise passing. Put another way, every moment is itself passing and recognizing it as such allows the opportunity to greet it and dismiss it in equal measure.

A famous story tells of a monk who has exhausted all of his options to escape a hungry tiger, leaving him dangling over a precipice clutching a small bush. He cannot climb up as the tiger awaits, he cannot climb down as there is no safe path. Further, the limbs of the bush are cracking and he will soon plummet to his death. In that moment, he notices the bush holds a single strawberry, which he plucks and eats, and it is the best strawberry he has ever tasted. When I tell this story to my students, they are most often disappointed that there is no more to the tale, no resolution to the monk's fate. The point, though, is in the moment. The certainty of that monk's death is the certainty of our own deaths at some unspoken future time. Whatever we do at any moment, if we react as the monk and enjoy whatever strawberry may be present at any given moment, then we are free from the suffering of clinging to a future of illusory permanence. That strawberry may not have been particularly flavorful, but in that moment of unattachment, the monk neither wished for future strawberries nor remembered past ones that may have tasted better, and in that moment it was the only strawberry that existed to the temporary thinker of that momentary thought. In any given moment, every strawberry is the best.

Mortality Salience: Thinking About Death

Various Buddhist practices of meditation focus upon death or the dead body.[4] The goal in these efforts is to drive home the reality of personal impermanence and in so doing to expose the pointlessness of attachment to any kind of permanent self. The Buddha himself became enlightened upon his encounter with the finitude of death, and brushes with mortality are often profound occasions whether one experiences one's own fragility personally (as in a health scare or car accident, perhaps), or the loss of a loved one. Modern research shows that many people find greater meaning in life once confronted by the reality of their impending death.[5]

Current research into mortality salience, the increased awareness of one's own mortality, has been largely influenced by Ernest Becker's death-denial approach to human psychology.[6] Accordingly, scholarship emphasizes the so-called Terror Management Theory ('TMT'),[7] which postulates the fear of death as a key driver in human behavior, and that religion's function has been to buffer people from what would otherwise become a paralyzing fear.[8] Of course, as with so much modern scholarship, this theory is heavily biased towards a Judeo-Christian understanding of religion, ignoring other possibilities and generalizing beyond its capacity.[9] The promise of immortality is seen as the succor to fear of death, with the assumption that all traditions include just such a promise though that is simply not the case. One study aimed at exploring the role of religious belief in TMT, for example, used a survey that was administered to different populations including Christian and Buddhist groups, with key differences being the changing of the word "God" to the word "Buddha." The researchers then wrestled with the problematic results in which Christian respondents clearly confirmed the TMT hypotheses while the Buddhist results varied.[10] The first thing that one might point to here is a simplistic understanding of Buddhism in regard to the terms God and Buddha as synonymous. For example, a question about whether the Buddha "exists" is problematic in that the nature of existence is itself in question in Buddhism. Western logic expects that a thing either exists or it does not, and for most Christians it is a given that God exists. In Buddhism, though, given the transiency of all things it is difficult to speak of anything existing except in the most ephemeral and temporary way. So, the Buddha may have existed, and for many Buddhists may still exist in one sense, but that existence is not in a solid, permanent, ongoing form normally expected by a Western view of existence. Scholars equating a belief in the existence of a thing versus its nonexistence will inevitably be baffled by a belief in the possibility that a thing may both exist and not-exist at once.

When applied to the self, Western TMT researchers tend to view a dichotomy between the experienced "self-that-is" and the future "self-that-won't-be" after death, and theorize that the incapacity to rectify these two selves is the source of death anxiety. Much TMT research has involved reminding subjects of their eventual death, the self-that-won't-be, but it has also found that a focus on the self-that-is can be equally effective in initiating mortality salience and death anxiety. That is to say, one does not need to be reminded of one's future death to experience fear of it; simply forcing a person to consider their current existence is enough to evoke fear for that self's future death.[11] This seems paradoxical from a perspective that imagines a conception of self-that-is as necessarily ongoing as a given. As seen above, though, the Buddha's conception of self as not-self breaks that paradox in emphasizing the changingness of all things, including the self, such that the self-that-is is, at all times, also the self-that-won't-be as well as the self-that-was-not-before. The anxiety that arises when one considers either the self-that-is or the future self-that-won't-be likely emerges from the false presumptions that these are two distinct states of being, and that the former is an ongoing and continuous one that should be preferred over the other. That is not a universal conception, and is one that is countered by Buddhist philosophy.

Furthermore, assuming that a heavenly immortality is the norm across religions, and that reincarnation is simply another form of death-denying reward, is seriously flawed. As seen above, in Buddhism, rebirth is actually part of an ongoing system of suffering such that life everlasting is far from a positive but an eternal hell of its own. In fact, one recent study aimed directly at Buddhist belief as related to TMT found no support for the expected buffering effect, which the authors surmise results from the facts that Buddhists do not see reincarnation as necessarily positive and that whatever life there is to come will be temporary as well.[12] We might keep in mind the anthropological concept of sociophobics, which describes all emotion as culturally determined.[13] Fear of death need not be seen as an instinctual necessity.

Buddhist Views of Death

Much effort is spent in Buddhist meditation to remind the practitioner of the impermanence of all things, especially of the self. As one second-century Buddhist poem says:

> Don't you know, then, that the body is a storehouse of diseases?
> It is subject to old age, its existence is unsure, it is like a tree on the bank of a river.
> Don't you know, then, that the body is vulnerable as a bulb of foam on water?
> Do you really think that the force that resides in your will always remain strong?
> How can you have trust in your power?
> The body is always prone to disasters,
> It is always busy with things like too much, too little, things like eating, drinking, sitting, walking.
> How can you be proud of your forces when you are always on your way to the end?
> [....]
> Frankly, I think this body has even less essence than a pot of unfired clay, because if this pot is well stored, it will last a long time.
> This accumulation, however, will fall to pieces anyhow, even if you take utmost care of it [....]
> Even if this body is well taken care of over a long time with helpful acts such as reclining, sitting, drinking, and eating, it will not forgive even one wrong act that is performed; it is easily provoked like a great poisonous snake, were you to step on it.[14]

The meditation on death is believed to provide an especially effective means to achieving the cessation of attachment. Focusing on one's own mortality is a striking reminder of one's impermanence, limiting one's capacity to over-value the self. Much of the TMT literature emphasizes the role of self-esteem in meaning-making, but an over-valuation of the self leads naturally to selfish tendencies. The idea that we ought to accept the limited view of self-worth leads some to cry nihilism, but I have shown earlier that this is not the necessary conclusion. In Buddhist terms, recognizing the self as but a small, temporary, and ephemeral passing moment does not lead to meaninglessness. Rather, such meditation allows for a selfless reflection that accepts the reality of one's own limited existence within the grand scheme of things and moves the focus of one's actions away from the futile preservation of the self and onto compassion for everything and everyone else. Meditating on death does not lead to depression, though the process may very well be difficult, but instead leads to an acceptance of one's place in the world that moves one from the position of star in one's own movie to that of supporting cast in some much larger show in which there are no stars, only one all-encompassing chorus.

Several varieties of meditation on death appear across Buddhist traditions, some isolated to monastic life, but others practiced widely. Funerary ritual in Tibetan Buddhism, for example, incorporates a series of ritual meditations aimed at helping both the bereaved and the deceased as well. Attachment is deemed not only a problem for the living but the dead must also be encouraged to accept the change that has come with death and to loose the grip on the self and the life left behind.

Tibetan Buddhist priests, called *lamas*, will perform a ritual reading of the *Bardo-Thodol*, often translated as the *Tibetan Book of the Dead*, though a more accurate translation might read something like the *Book of the Space between Life and Death*. This ritual, called *powa*, takes place over several days and might begin while the dying person is still alive, but will certainly continue over the corpse with the aim of guiding the deceased to a realization that death has occurred and helping shift consciousness away from the dead body.[15] Following the *powa*, the corpse is prepared for disposal; while Tibetan Buddhism includes burial in the earth or water as rare possibilities, more commonly bodies are cremated (especially when the body of a lama) or a special form of disposal known as a sky burial is performed. In case of cremation, friends and family of the deceased are encouraged to imagine the body of their loved one being consumed by flames, but also devoured by the hundred Peaceful and Wrathful Deities.[16] More graphically, in sky burial the body is placed upon a rock outside where specific individuals, the body cutters (*ro-rgyah-pa*), ritually cut into the corpse under the guidance of a lama or other spiritual leader. The body is then systematically dismembered while an inevitable flock of vultures is kept at bay.

Family and friends who may be in attendance meditate on the transiency of life as the actuality of their loved one's parting is literalized before them. The skeleton and skull are pulverized to dust and mixed with barley flour (*tsam-pa*). Finally, the body and the powdered remains are fed to the anxious vultures in an act of compassion for the hungry animals. The ritual complete, there can be no denying the death of the loved one, and attachment to their physical presence is made clearly impossible.[17] Symbolically, the ever-changing cycle of everything is witnessed in the birds returning to whence they came, each having devoured some aspect of the loved one, whose form has changed while life, in another form, carries on. Vultures, in Tibetan Buddhist folklore, also stand in for the feminine divinity called *dakini*, like angels, thought to carry away the dead. Vultures, like other birds, and angels as well, appear cross-culturally in the ambivalent symbolic reflection of both mortality and fertility, as well as of the space in between them.[18]

Another form of the meditation on death simply has the individual sit alone in private contemplation of the fact of his or her eventual death. The effort is to remind one's self that death will come to everyone, including oneself. Such a practice might be helped by gazing into a mirror and imagining one's face decaying, revealing the skeletal frame currently beneath the face to which we normally identify. Following the likes of the fifth-century Buddhist scholar Buddhaghosa, meditators are further directed to reflect "on the repulsiveness of the body, in its 31 parts: head-hairs, body-hairs, nails, teeth, skin, flesh, sinews, bones, bone-marrow, kidney, heart, liver, midriff, spleen, [lungs], bowels, entrails, gorge, dung, bile, phlegm, pus, blood, sweat, fat, tears, grease, spittle, snot, oil-of-the-joints, and brain-in-the-head."[19] This kind of thinking addresses issues of the abject considered earlier, forcing the participant to recognize that whatever we might be disgusted by within our bodies remains a real and immediate component of that which we consider our selves. One powerful example appears in the story of a Thai woman named Supaporn who had been diagnosed with a breast cancer that had become necrotic, "opening her chest up into a giant black hole of putrid dead tissue."[20] A life-long meditator, Supaporn refused palliative treatment, instead remaining home, occasionally removing her bandage to observe her own horrible wound and the pain and nausea connected with it. Though her doctors were often not in agreement with her approach, she wanted to reflect on the suffering of death throughout its experience and ended her life the way she had lived it.

Yet another meditation, which corresponds more closely to the act of watching a zombie film, is that on the foulness of the corpse.[21] Here the meditator is instructed to sit next to an actual corpse, perhaps one awaiting cremation, and meditate over its state. The gory details of the body's corruption are central to the meditation. Alan Klima quotes the description of such a meditation in the words of one Buddhist nun: "This body opens up for you to see. You see bodily ooze. Clear oozelike in the brain; thick, filmy ooze and clear ooze. The body splits open into intestines, intestines the size of your wrist, *na*. Liver, kidneys, intestines, the stomach, you can see it all."[22] Certainly, such imagery is ever-present in zombie cinema.

The Pali canon (Buddhist scriptures) teaches the meditator to consider the dead body, and to think: "As this [my body] is, so that is; as that is, so this is," and further, "Indeed this [my] body is of this [foul] nature, will become like this, and cannot escape this."[23] The *Mahā-satipatthāna-sutta* guides the cemetery meditator through the stages of decomposition at length:

> And further, O Bhikkhus, while a bhikkhu sees a dead body, one day old, two days, three days, swollen, blue and festering, thrown in to the cemetery, so he applies this perception to his own body thus: "Verily, my own body, too, is of the same nature; such will it become and will not escape it." Thus he lives observing the body according to the nature of the body [....] And further, O Bhikkhus, while a bhikkhu sees a dead body thrown in to the cemetery, being eaten by crows, hawks, vultures, dogs, jackals or by different kinds of worms, so he applies this perception to his own body thus: "Verily, my own body, too, is of the same nature; such will it become and will not escape it." Thus he lives observing the body according to the nature of the body [....] And further, O Bhikkhus, while a bhikkhu sees a dead body thrown in the cemetery reduced to a skeleton with some flesh and blood attached to it, held together by the tendons [....] And further, O Bhikkhus, while a bhikkhu sees a dead body thrown in to the cemetery reduced to a skeleton blood-be-smeared and without flesh, held together by the tendons [....] And further, O Bhikkhus, while a bhikkhu sees a dead body thrown on to the cemetery reduced to a skeleton without flesh [....] And further, O Bhikkhus, while a bhikkhu sees a dead body thrown on to the cemetery reduced to disconnected bones, scattered in all directions—here a bone of the hand, there a bone of the foot, a shin bone, a thigh bone, the pelvis, spine and skull [....] And further, O Bhikkhus, while a bhikkhu sees a dead body thrown in to the cemetery reduced to bleached bones of conch-like colour [....] And further, O Bhikkhus, while a bhikkhu sees a body dead body thrown in to the cemetery reduced to bones, more than a year, old lying in a heap [....] And further, O Bhikkhus, while a bhikkhu sees a dead body thrown on to the cemetery reduced to bones rotten and become dust, so he applies this perception to his own body thus: "Verily, my own body, too, is of the same nature; such will it become and will not escape it." Thus he lives observing the nature of the body.[24]

Through observing the corpse and realizing the connection to oneself, the meditator can realize both the impermanence of things as well as the suffering inherent in attachment to the body. The foulness of the body is meant to powerfully bring home the fact that the body is in a state of perpetual dying, even throughout what we consider life. As Klima notes, "the corpse in its gory, abject, and repulsive state is the most desirable aesthetic."[25] Such meditations force the mindful to become aware of their own being-towards-death, and by accepting it realize the truth about life. Effectively, the finitude and impermanence of the self suggests that the death that one fears is in reality occurring every moment. Death is a reality not only in some unforeseen future, but is happening as we live in this very moment. I am dying, I will continue dying, and I have been dying since I was born. The more I want life, the more prolonged my dying will seem to me. By accepting the absence of a permanent self from one moment to the next, one can overcome the fear of death and so, in a sense, live free of dying. Moreover, as the Buddhist philosopher Nagarjuna put it, the body is but "an ornamented pot of filth."[26] Here, though he appears to echo Catholic sentiment expressed earlier, the sentiment sits within the tradition emphasizing the transiency of all things. The fact that remembering the disgusting elements of the body might help to reduce sensual cravings is a useful side-effect!

Zombies Embodying Buddhist Philosophy

Throughout this book, I have emphasized the need for an alternative perspective on zombie fiction in order to come to grips with the perspective on death, suffering, and human fragility without caving either to nihilism or a hope to somehow overcome the reality being depicted. Given the ambivalence towards Christianity over the history of the zombie mythos, from Haiti to its countercultural reinterpretation, with the added influence of the likes of Matheson, I have turned to Buddhism. The zombie reflects the core Buddhist perspective on the human condition as essentially one of suffering due to ignorant craving for the impossible despite rational cognizance of individual transience.

Most obviously, there is the zombie's similarity to Buddhist meditations on death and the dead body. The "living dead" zombies are literally walking corpses. These corpses appear in various forms, rotting, oozing, bleeding, covered in filth and maggots, bones emerging from peeling flesh, echoing each of Buddhaghosa's traditional set of meditation themes.[27] They are rotting bodies in various stages of damage. In their hordes, many are barely dressed, appearing ignobly in underwear, pajamas, hospital gowns, and often completely naked. The bodies are revealed both externally and internally. Many of these risen dead seem to have been disturbed from sleep and reveal the body at its most vulnerable. For a modern, Western audience, the decomposition of the corpse is entirely outside of normal experience. Death itself, it has often been said, is ultimately denied in Western culture. In traditional Western funerals, bodies are specially treated to preserve them and enhance their appearance so that they appear as lifelike as possible. They are often dressed in their finest attire for display, viewers remarking on the body as if it were still the person simply sleeping. Zombies, like the corpses at the center of Buddhist meditation, reveal the truth of bodily death in stark contrast. I am reminded of an early scene in Tom Savini's remake of *Night of the Living Dead* (1990) in which the initial zombie, mistaken for a well-dressed man in distress, stumbles towards Johnny and Barbara. The camera shifts perspective to reveal that the man is a corpse who has been only partially dressed for a funeral, his three-piece suit arranged to cover the front of his body, but a huge slit down the back revealing his naked, dead flesh. The protagonists only realize the horror of this figure as his clothing slowly sags, causing him to stumble and trip, ultimately revealing the stitches of his autopsy. Like the rotting zombie generally, the death-denying trappings of Western funerals are shown for what they are, mere decoration hiding the truth of death beneath.

Viewers are forced to come to terms with the disgusting Otherness of one's own body, "to confront the horror that lay within them, the Otherness of their own flesh."[28] This is exactly what Julia Kristeva termed the abject, that which we recognize as having been a part of, but is now rejected from, the normative order of things.[29] But this normative order is not a given, but a construct. William S. Larkin makes the case that we intuitively recognize ourselves as primarily *physical* beings, and that whatever its fate, the person's locus remains in the body. We understand ourselves to "be" our bodies in some commonsensical way, even when we accept dualistic notions of body and soul or mind. This is one reason donating an organ to another person is not an easy decision, and why receiving one often involves feelings that one has incorporated another person in accepting their organs.[30] Philosopher Stephen Braude even argues that cases of organ transplant in which the recipients feel as if they are somehow changed by the entry of bodily parts from another person might be useful evidence for personal survival beyond bodily death; here, the surviving personality is thought to *"hover"* around its former parts even when transplanted into another body.[31] In any case, zombie films bring this intuition of a primarily bodily personal identity to the fore.

For instance, the viewer is terrified when the zombie kills Johnny (in the original *Night of the Living Dead*), but recognizes the horror and tragedy of his return as a zombie who then kills his sister; despite the fact that Johnny is reduced to an animated corpse, the tendency is to recognize the corpse for what it was in life, that is the person it embodied.[32] Craig Derksen and Darren Hudson Hick similarly draw out the problem of identity confusion using the example of yet another returned loved one, this time Uncle Rege from Savini's *Night* remake.[33] Evoking the paradox of Theseus's ship (which ponders the question of whether a boat remains the same boat when a plank is changed, and another, and another, until all planks have been changed), they ask:

> You might put a new coat of paint on your house, or fix the plumbing under the sink, but we still want to say in a meaningful way that it is the same house—and so too with your body. The body can survive such small-scale changes, and insofar as you are identifiable with your body, so too can you. If this view is correct, then the matter applies as equally to Uncle Rege as it does to you—never mind that somewhere in the interim, he died. That is, because the creature before you is a continuation of the same body as Uncle Rege, that creature *is* Uncle Rege [...][34]

The error here is in assuming that similarity indicates permanence. Zombie fiction makes the tension between the identity of the zombie with the previously living person explicit.

In a season two episode of *The Walking Dead*, "Pretty Much Dead Already," survivors argue over what to do with a group of zombified loved ones being kept in Hershel's barn. Some consider the monsters simply a threat to be dealt with by a gunshot to the head, but Hershel, playing host to the group, sees the creatures as his wife and family who are sick and curable. Shane (Jon Bernthal), by this point recognized by viewers as having lost any moral compass he may have previously had, leads the charge to release the zombies and destroy them all. In an emotional scene, the doors of the barn are opened and the horde of zombies slain in a hail of bullets as they shamble into the open. Hershel struggles to stop the massacre before falling on his knees in recognition of his wife's fate after Shane mercilessly fires bullet after ineffective bullet into her zombified body before finally dealing the fatal shot to her head. On one hand, Hershel is depicted as having been proven wrong to believe that his loved ones remained in the zombies, but the show does not make it so clear cut, as it is a villain in the person of Shane who makes the case in violent fashion. Furthermore, the episode ends when the final zombie emerging from the barn is the little girl, Sophia (Madison Lintz), who had been the object of a manhunt throughout the entire season. Her zombified form emerging into the light stuns the crowd, including Shane, and requires Rick's leadership to administer the final shot to destroy her as well. Viewers and survivors alike begin with a determination that Hershel is wrong to believe that the zombies in the barn are his loved ones. In the end, they recognize that Sophia's story did not end with her death somewhere in the woods, but that she wound up a zombie in a barn being shot mercifully by Rick.

Viewers need not view the zombie as do the characters. Recognizing the zombie within the context of Buddhist meditation removes the viewer from the position of the ignorant survivors. The meditation on the corpse can help to bring home the realization of the impermanence of the self by plainly illustrating the true nature of the body as corruptible, changing, and, at its core, impermanent. The walking corpse forces itself upon the living in fiction, and its abject gruesomeness is likewise unavoidably thrust upon the viewing audience, such that recognizing the corruptibility of the flesh becomes obvious.

More than simply acting as *memento mori*, though, the zombie embodies *samsara*, the entire cycle of birth, life, death, and rebirth. In Buddhist thinking, all that exists exists in *samsara*. All things, actions, deeds; these all occur within *samsara*. It is everything, and encompasses every thing. As one dies, the reincarnation belief inherited from Hinduism explains, one is reborn in a new body. So, one lives, one dies, and one lives again. In Christian terms, this new life is a life everlasting in Heaven, but not so in Indian tradition. Living means dying, so the cycle continues. One lives, dies, is reborn to live again, and to die again, and so on indefinitely. Hindu belief, generally speaking, suggests the existence of some permanent self that moves from one body to the next with an end goal, and release from the cycle of *samsara*, in the form of a reunion with the Absolute akin to a kind of heavenly eternity.[35] The Buddha rejected this idea, though, given the evidence for the impermanence of all things. Since no thing could possibly last forever in a permanent, unchanged state, the concept of an enduring *atman*, or soul, was ridiculous. Every thing changes; all that does not change could not properly be called a thing in any sense, not a body, a mind, or a soul. If the definition of a soul or a self is that core thought to exist, unchanged, permanently through time, then, according to the Buddha, that term was inappropriate.

Instead, we must refer to that thing which we usually experience as our own self as *anatta*, not-self, simply because there is no other term available except for the negation of what we have erroneously imagined to be permanent. In the cycle of birth, life, death, and rebirth it is not a permanent self moving from one life to the next, but simply an ongoing process of change experienced by an also ever-changing not-self. The zombie shows not only that we will all die one day, but that we are all already dying presently.

In every moment that we live, we also die. Living and dying are intrinsically the same thing. We tend to emphasize the idea of living life and deny not only death but that we are dying from the moment that we are born.

The state of being for zombies is a pitiable one, recognized as one that nobody would choose for themselves. It is common in zombie fiction for a character to express his fear not of death but of returning as a zombie, truly a fate worse than death. As Rachel Robison-Greene playfully suggests, "Being a walker really screws with a person's value system [....] You no longer care about growing the best garden on the block or about getting that big promotion at work. You would sooner dine on your five-year-old's leg than teach him how to ride a bike. All you care about is consuming human flesh. And even that isn't fundamentally valuable to you. You just feel an irresistible urge to do it."[36] Destroying a zombie is often expressed as an act of mercy. Only the most odious of evil characters, like Shane and The Governor in *The Walking Dead*, purposefully kill people with the intention of seeing them turn into zombies. Shane kills a prisoner in order to set a trap for his best-friend-turned-romantic-rival Rick, a plan that ultimately fails when the zombie is destroyed first. Even more gruesome is Merle's (Michael Rooker) vindictive murder at the hands of the Governor, a death that later forces fan-favorite Daryl (Norman Reedus) to come to face-to-face with his own zombified brother in a scene both heart-wrenching and cathartic. While the Governor chose to shoot Merle through the heart instead of the head, the former meets his own demise when Michonne (Danai Gurira) later stabs the Governor through the heart with her sword; in this case, though, the Governor is immediately shot in the head by another woman he had previously deceived. The series leaves some ambiguity as to whether this act is one of mercy or vengeance, but what remains clear is that purposefully creating zombies is a horrible thing to do.

Choosing to become a zombie is equally rare. The quirky television series *iZombie* (2015–present) plays with this idea with a number of characters electing to become a zombie, then seeking to find a cure, and then becoming a zombie again. In the show, though, there is a distinction between being a functional zombie that retains its agency and what in the show is referred to as a "Romero" that devolves into a mindless, rotting monster. Nobody wants to become one of those! Ethicist Dien Ho wonders whether it might not be so bad to be a zombie. He argues that, in fact, the simplicity of the zombie's existence might be akin to the detached Zen monk without a care in the world. The cravings for flesh that plague the zombie are but bodily impulses.[37] Ho makes the assumption, though, that zombies have no awareness at all, and so experience no suffering. He then argues that it is the lack of experience itself that is the worst thing about being a zombie, then. That life requires "complex cognition" for meaning, and that part of that meaningfulness will, by definition, include suffering. He concludes by allowing that one must weigh the pros and cons of meaningfulness against suffering, and that one may choose a meaningless life without suffering over a meaningful one with it.

Ho entirely misunderstands Buddhist thinking here, though. Zen monks are *not* like zombies in being detached from material pleasures. Mindfulness is a core component of Buddhism, and the reason that meditation is held in such high regard. The hero of *iZombie*, Liv Moore (Rose McIver), often narrates her own reflections on life lessons she learns in the face of her newfound reality as a zombie. Certainly, if one were to have no cognition whatsoever, then one would lose the capacity for mindfulness, awareness of one's thoughts, actions, and surroundings. Zen mindfulness is the complete opposite of this—it is, as in Buddhist meditation universally, the effort to maintain constant awareness of the moment. Attachment to the past and to the future are avoided in a focus on the present.

Mark Siderits also engages with the equation of Buddhists and zombies, instead positing what he calls "Robo-Buddhas," as "enlightened beings act[ing] directly on their perception without any intervening thought, yet their actions are ideally suited to benefit the unenlightened."[38] The enlightened Buddha can only act self-less-ly, having realized the absence of a permanent self with which to become attached. As such, no genuine decision-making would be needed. Still, awareness of one's state, one's surroundings, and the needs of others all require some form of consciousness even if the actions of an entirely compassionate being would be largely predictable. The zombie may be living in the moment, but that existence appears, by all accounts, to be one that wavers between being entirely consumed by craving for the living and complete apathy (zombies are often depicted bumping mindlessly into each other when not aware of the living). The goal of Buddhist mindfulness is not to achieve some kind of mindless state in which one has no experience whatsoever, but rather to achieve a state of hyperawareness in which one can place experience in the proper context of transiency rather than reacting to each moment as if it were the be-all and end-all of everything.

One exception to the general rule that characters rue zombiedom comes in the person of Cholo (John Leguizamo), from *Land of the Dead* (2005); seeing that he's been bitten and will soon die from infection, he chooses to let himself turn with the statement, "I always wanted to see how the other half lives." His comment references his own ambitions of rising to the upper echelons of social life while also tying the wealthy elites to the zombies; while the circularity of the connection reinforces the conclusion that striving after material wealth and suffering are intertwined, Cholo remains selfishly attached to his cravings to the extent that he hopes his zombified body will exact revenge on the wealthy Kaufman (Dennis Hopper). Another example, this coming from *The Walking Dead*, reflects a much more common attachment in Jim's (Andrew Rothenberg) decision to be left in the woods to die in the hopes that he might reunite with his zombified family. Jim had previously been shown to be mentally unstable, having great difficulty coping with the grief over having lost his family.

Rick of *The Walking Dead* tellingly exclaims, "We are the walking dead!" *Dawn of the Dead* (1978) aimed a focus on the activity of the living dead, when not devouring the living, as akin to the aimless ambling of shoppers in a mall. Likewise, an exchange from Romero's *Land of the Dead* (2005) captures a similar sentiment. As a group of raiders seeking supplies for the living enter a small town, they witness various undead corpses shambling about town repeating actions that they performed when alive—a young couple walk hand-in-hand, a gas-station attendant pumps gas. The new guy, Mike (Shawn Roberts), blurts in surprise, "It's like they're pretending to be alive!" To which the leader, Riley Denbo (Simon Baker) replies without missing a beat, "Isn't that what we're doing? Pretending to be alive?" Audiences may react to such pronouncements with pity at the sorry postapocalyptic living conditions of the protagonists, but beyond that there is the unmistakable observation that the living dead are really not all that different from us. The dead are thought to be "pretending" to be alive, but they present the reminder that so long as we ignore the fact that we are also dying, then we too are only pretending to live. Martin Heidegger, himself influenced by Buddhist philosophy,[39] described living in ignorance of death to be inauthentic[40]; Viktor Frankl, whose ideas about life's meaning were galvanized by his incarceration in Auschwitz, explains how death "is the very factor that constitutes [life's] meaning."[41] Living and dying are two sides of the very same coin.

As the Buddha realized, suffering is intrinsic to living. The dead, in rising up from the grave, bring that suffering out in the open. As one zombie in *Return of the Living Dead* (1985) explains, "I can feel myself rot." Most zombies are not as clear in expressing their suffering, but the groans and moans issued in most zombie fiction imply discomfort to say the least. The physical state of decay, and the incapacity to move effectively because of it, further drives home the notion that this is not a preferred state of being. When shot in an empathetic light, most often with close-ups of the maudlin expression in the eyes of a zombie, the sense is that whatever intelligence remains could only be one trapped in a hellish state. Trapped in a body, incapable of communication, and single-mindedly driven to attack and devour other humans, any intelligence that remained would certainly be suffering immensely.[42]

The suffering in life stems from our attachments to things as if they were permanent, especially to the self as if it could not die. Ignoring the fact that we are dying right now is a tactic that helps to promote attachment to living, but it also causes suffering since we know that it is not true. We do not like to be reminded of our dying because that brings about a more explicit suffering, but it is not the knowledge of our dying that is the cause of the suffering—it is our wish for the illusion of not-dying that we suffer. Zombies crave but one thing—the living. Typically, the zombie seeks to actually consume the flesh of the living, but even when not driven to eat flesh, the zombie still seeks to kill the living. When there are no living humans present, the undead generally fall into a slothful, aimless meander, awakened with excitement at the sight or smell of a person. Even the "fast" zombies tend to mope when not in the presence of living humans. All zombies are driven by a craving after the living, enslaved by their cravings, just as the Buddha describes humankind when he is reported to have said: "The world lacks and hankers, and is enslaved to 'thirst' [cravings]."[43] The Buddha delineates several forms of craving, or thirst (*tanha*). The craving for sensual experience is primary among forms of attachment emphasized in the Buddha's first sermon.[44] To consume is the most sensuous of experiences, absorbing the body of the other into the self.

The zombie appetite is insatiable. Just as the Buddha predicts that our own cravings can never be satisfied, being desires after an illusion, so too the zombie is never satisfied regardless of the amount consumed. As the opening line of the parodic *Pride and Prejudice and Zombies* reads: "It is a truth universally acknowledged that a zombie in possession of brains must be in want of more brains."[45] Though winking and nodding at the unique tastes of the intelligent zombies of the *Return of the Living Dead* franchise, the irrationality of the zombie's need to constantly consume appears elsewhere as well. In one scene in *Day of the Dead* (1985), for example, Dr. Logan (Richard Liberty) demonstrates by holding his hand over the mouth of a restrained yet still jaw-snapping corpse which has had all of its organ removed save for the brain: "It wants me! It wants food! But it has no stomach, can take no nourishment from what it ingests. It's acting on instinct!" Similarly, we also crave after various sources of pleasure, imagining that somehow we can sate our desires if we could just get that one more thing, but we are always disappointed when the truth becomes apparent that every seeming satisfaction is transitory and demands that we seek another. Of course, even as we try to enjoy whatever it might be that we have at the moment, we know in the backs of our minds that it will not last and so even that temporary enjoyment is tainted. The zombie in *Return* that expressed the pain of being dead (yet another with no body below the ribcage, and so no stomach in which to digest) explains that the reason they eat brains is because "it makes the pain go away!" Of course, whatever relief there is, is fleeting at best—recall the zombies of *Return* radioed twice for "more paramedics/cops" even in the middle of feasting on the brains already present.

Not only is the suffering of insatiable craving an individual problem, but it is a self-perpetuating one. The futile avoidance of suffering is frustrating in itself, but also engenders more suffering through its very efforts. Put simply, trying to make my self happy through consumption (of material things, experiences, people, whatever) is a self-centered endeavor. If I crave a piece of chocolate cake, and so do you, but there is only one piece left then one can easily imagine the selfishness that may result regardless of who gets the cake. Zombies are self-perpetuating in that when they consume they inevitably create more zombies. In this way they illustrate just how suffering arises through craving. The cycle of life, death, and rebirth are thus tied together as suffering in terms of the craving after an impossible life of ongoing happiness, and a life without death.

The protagonists of zombie fiction are locked in an impossible effort to survive in the unavoidable face of death incarnate. Survival at all costs often becomes the basis upon which the living find meaning in the zombie apocalypse. The craving for life is central to the genre. In one telling scene in Romero's *Dawn of the Dead* (1978), Roger (Scott Reiniger), dying from the infection caused by a zombie bite, promises his friend Peter (Ken Foree), "I'm going to try not to…. I'm gonna try not to come back…. I'm gonna try…." Importantly, the assumption of one's being able to try not to return implies the ongoing presence of agency after death. Roger assumes that he will survive death as himself, able to exercise agency in "trying" to prevent the zombified return. In Buddhist thinking, though, the presumption of ongoing-ness, of permanence, is exactly the kind of attachment to self that encourages rebirth into the *samsara* world of suffering. The false dichotomy of living and dying blurs Roger's (standing in for the rest of us) view of his own relationship to change in death allowing him to maintain a false hope of his own ongoing permanence, an attachment which is then itself responsible for the very return that he wishes to prevent. The mirror image is reflected in the co-equal death scene in the *Dawn* remake (2004), when Frank (Matt Frewer), similarly bit and dying from the wound, says to his friend Kenneth (Ving Rhames) in his final moments, "You want every single second...." His attachment to life is likewise quickly rewarded by his return as a howling zombie unceremoniously shot off-screen.

Many viewers will likely empathize with the survivors' desire to carry on living, this despite the fact that so much zombie fiction reveals a largely hopeless future for them. By sheer force of numbers, the dead inherit the earth! This is the reason so many critics have seen zombie fiction as nihilistic. *The Walking Dead*, imagined as an ongoing serial exploring just what happens if a zombie movie just kept on going, has made no qualms about killing off central characters in both the comic and television series. Viewers attached to the survival of any character (be it Glenn, Daryl, or anyone else) in a series about the ubiquity of death are missing the point! Craving after life is not only the one purpose of the dead, it would seem, but rather a driving concern of the living as well. We might empathize with the survivors, but in reality they are but the flip sides of their zombie counterparts, struggling to deny the connection between themselves and the undead even when confronted by their risen loved ones, suffering defeat after defeat in their efforts to kill the already dead. Any series that goes on long enough will, inevitably, mirror the fact of living that is the fact of eventual death; zombies, embodying death, simply move the dial forward to the point where deaths happen much more quickly and frequently. Just like every person, every character will die. That is a core lesson to take away from zombie fiction.

Maggie (2015), starring Arnold Schwarzenegger and Abigail Breslin (who had previously appeared in *Zombieland*, among other things), approaches the zombie genre from a more thoughtful direction. This meditative film positions Schwarzenegger as the father to a girl who has been infected with a zombifying virus (the "necro-ambulist virus"). The plot follows the emotional journey of all involved as the virus progresses to the point of certain death, and return. Easily seen as a metaphor for the grieving in life that occurs alongside terminal illness, the film ties the zombie to its role as the embodiment of death itself. Nostalgia runs throughout the film, from the anachronistic use of cassette players and corded telephones to scenes of an aging Schwarzenegger chopping wood that recall his earlier appearance in *Commando* (1985), another film featuring at its core the relationship between a father and his daughter. The difference in tone between the two films is striking in the earlier's seeming celebration of the destruction of life, while the more recent film considers death much more existentially. In *Commando*, the father is willing to kill an army to rescue his daughter, while in *Maggie*, he is forced to deal with the possibility of euthanizing his dying daughter, a task which he is ultimately unable to perform. In fact, when Wade Vogel (Schwarzenegger) is forced to kill two zombified neighbors, he is heartbroken at being forced to murder people he had considered friends. Importantly, those same neighbors had been kept locked in their home by the mother of that family, despite government rules dictating they should have been sent to a quarantine.

When his character visits the now-abandoned house, Schwarzenegger sheds his first ever on-screen tear as he observes the disjuncture that appears between the smell of decay and the destruction of property wrought by the zombified inhabitants alongside scrawled messages of love between parent and child. The filth that remains where the family had died and returned undead stands in stark contrast to the messages of love that kept them there in the first place. The ambivalence between the selfish love that does not want to give up happiness and the selfless compassion needed to let go of that which is gone is at the heart of both this film and the Buddhist approach to death. The film further teases out the need to recognize the cyclical nature of life and death in the recurring imagery of flowers, themselves a common image in *memento mori* imagery as well, in tying the daughter, Maggie/Margueritte, to a bed of daisies growing in remembrance of her deceased mother.

More than simply the sensuality of the body, zombies represent attachment in other ways, too. The other two forms of attachment, elucidated by the Buddha in his first sermon, are those of the desire for the maintenance of positive states and the elimination of negative states. For the individual who maintains the belief in the importance of the permanent self, which is the normal state of human experience, then the ultimate maintenance of the positive is that self-same permanence achieved through life, and the opposite of life is death, which would in turn be that negative state which must ultimately be eliminated. The living dead, by definition, embody the combination of these latter two desires in that they live beyond death, having somehow overcome death. As noted earlier, however, this same attachment to the permanence of the self simply locks one into the frustrating cycle of death and subsequent rebirth. So, with the life that is thus craved comes, hand-in-hand, death. The living dead, then, illustrate the inseparability of life and death at once. These zombies stand in for the cycle of *samsara* itself, embodying the interconnection between life and death created and driven by a single-minded craving after an illusory permanently living self.

Further to the zombies themselves, the living characters in zombie fiction exemplify the human response to the struggle of life and death in ignorance of the Buddhist nirvana. In reaction to the embodied *samsara*, and antecedent suffering through frustrated cravings, the living are made to behave in negative and harmful ways. It is typically the human "survivors" who are a greater threat to themselves than are the zombies. It is regularly the interactions between the living that lead to their downfall. The Buddha explains how the ignorant attachment to the self leads to all manner of harmful behaviors. From attachment arises possessiveness, then defensiveness, which then results in lies and conflicts.[46] For example, Ben in *Night of the Living Dead* remains level-headed early on as he works to board up the abandoned farmhouse, keep the living dead at bay, and protect the hysterical Barbara. As he appears to get matters under control, the situation changes when it is revealed that a group of survivors had been hiding in the basement throughout Ben's struggles to secure the house. He immediately reacts in anger over their lack of support while he worked alone. The most nefarious of these new survivors, Harry Cooper, responds just as angrily, defensively lying about what they could or could not hear going on from their hiding place. Confronted by his own contradictory stories, Cooper blurts out: "We luck into a safe place and you're telling me we gotta risk our lives because somebody might need help, huh?" This reluctance to risk his life prompts Cooper to forcefully argue for the security of the basement over what he perceives as the dangerous open floor of the farmhouse with its loosely boarded windows.

When Cooper moves to retreat to the basement, he seeks support for his decision by trying to take others into the basement with him. He turns to take the now catatonic Barbara, which prompts Ben to reveal his interests. "Keep your hands off her," he yells, "and everything else up here, too, because if I stay up here, I'm fighting for everything up here, and the radio and the food is part of what I'm fighting for." So, while Cooper admits to his own fear for his livelihood (and perhaps that of his daughter and wife as well), Ben admits to greater attachments that would allow him to put his life at risk. The conflict between Cooper and Ben escalates to a point where Cooper's fear causes him to hesitate at a crucial point when Ben is trapped outside the farmhouse and surrounded by zombies. Cooper wavers between retreating to the cellar and moving to unlock the door to the house for Ben. Only when Ben breaks the door in himself does Cooper come to his aid in order to re-secure it, thus acting once again in his own interests. Once the door is secured, Ben responds by viciously beating Cooper. Soon after this, Cooper tries to turn the tables on Ben, only for Ben to actually shoot Cooper in cold-blood. So, despite the threat from without, it is their own competitions which result in one man's murdering the other.

Similar conflicts appear time and again in zombie fiction. Survivors battle mall cops for entry to safety in *Dawn of the Dead* (2004), which also includes a gun fight between Andre (Mekhi Phifer) and Norma (Jayne Eastwood), when she discovers, horrified, that he is keeping his zombified wife and baby secured away in the mall. The original *Dawn of the Dead* (1978) sees the survivors' safe haven destroyed when a marauding biker gang invades—in this case, the survivors had built a secure hiding space from which they could have rebuilt after the bikers moved on if not for Stephen's (David Emgee) angry decision to fight to protect everything, muttering, "It's ours. We took it. It's ours." *Day of the Dead* (1985) sees the survivors safely hidden in a military bunker, but ends with almost all of them dead due to in-fighting between scientists and military men over priorities and authority. Echoing this, *28 Days Later* (2002) begins with eco-terrorists accidentally releasing the virus into the world, and concludes with the capture of the main protagonists by a violent group of soldiers intent on rape. *Zombieland* (2009) sees Bill Murray (playing himself) tragicomically slain when he tries to prank one of the protagonists with the zombie outfit that he'd been using to survive on his own. And *The Walking Dead* is punctuated by battles between various groups of people: Rick vs. Shane; Rick's group vs. prisoners; Rick's group vs. the Governor; Rick's group vs. Negan and the Saviors; etc.

Throughout zombie fiction, time and again other people become the more serious threat than the zombies. The closest example of a Buddhist mindset in zombie fiction comes in the form of Morgan (Lennie James) in *The Walking Dead* television series (the character does not follow the same path as his comic book counterpart). In the episode, "Here Not Here" (S6E4), Morgan is taken in by a (white) man, provocatively named Eastman (John Carrol Lynch), who studied Aikido before the zombies came. Aikido, of course, is not a Buddhist practice, but a Shinto-influenced Japanese spiritual martial art style. He trains Morgan on the martial art, which focuses on preserving the life of the opponent. Morgan adopts the motto that "all life is precious." Despite carrying this message into the world, he still runs into conflict when he tries to execute the philosophy, especially in a number of confrontations with Carol, who has adapted to the new world by taking on the role of vicious defender of her friends and family.

Selfish desires trump cooperation time and again, and despite the knowledge that zombies surround them, people continue to bicker amongst themselves. Every fight between people brings the zombies closer to achieving their one goal of destroying the living. As such, human craving, attachment, desire, and ignorance drive the progress of the living not only towards death, but to their dark mirror-image in an ongoing and insatiable quest to consume in a life of unending torment. Typically, monster theorists view the monster as a threat to the social order, one that is most often conservatively beaten back to restore normativity.[47] Revolutionary horror, according to Robin Wood, allows for the monsters to institute some kind of radical change in their aftermath.[48] Zombie fiction, though, while allowing for zombies as a threat to social order, also sheds an important light on the ways in which human relationships driven by selfishness represent a more immediate threat. Romero himself has said that he sees "the longing [...] for people to get together," as a central theme of his work, and that it never ceases to bother him when critics see his films as depicting "how rotten we are."[49]

Kim Paffenroth comes to a similar conclusion in terms of the problems of individualism versus cooperation, but he errs not only in seeing the zombies as representations of sin (presumably bothering Romero himself!), but also in assuming that the message of love wins out.[50] There are plenty of examples of selfish forms of love, like "romantic love," in which individual attachments between specific people become possessive or create in-groups and outsiders; and these real-world relationships are echoed on screen, often leading to further death and destruction. We tend to celebrate romantic love, but in a Buddhist sense it represents yet another source of pain in its frustrating impermanence and changeability. As Bhikkhu Nyanasobhano (Leonard Price) puts it, "Love, or possibly the myth of love, is the first, last, and sometimes the only refuge of uncomprehending humanity."[51]

Take, for instance, Tom (Keith Wayne) and Judy (Judith Ridley) in *Night of the Living Dead* (1968). Judy's clinging love for her boyfriend causes her to behave selfishly, ultimately ending in death. She first does not want to tend to the Coopers' injured daughter, preferring instead to simply be near Tom, and she only goes to the girl when Tom asks her to do it "for him." More damaging, however, is when the men formulate a plan to facilitate their escape from the farmhouse, Judy asks Tom not to play his part for fear of his being in danger. Tom explains that his role is crucial to the success of the plan, and Judy responds that she'd simply rather hide with him than risk seeing him in danger. When Tom and Ben then leave the house to embark on their plan to retrieve gasoline for an escape, Judy impulsively runs out after them, throwing an unnecessary and ultimately deadly wrench into the plan. Both she and Tom die when she soon gets stuck in the burning truck, leaving Ben to fend for himself. Here, she is driven by her own selfish attachment to Tom. Her fear of being left without him ends in both of them being killed. Likewise, in *Dawn of the Dead* (2004), Nicole's (Linda Booth) love for the dog, Chips, results in her rashly attempting rescue, ending in her need of rescue herself. The group, mostly strongly urged by Nicole's boyfriend Terry (Kevin Zegers), then undertakes a plan to rescue Nicole which has disastrous consequences—six of the remaining ten people die in the subsequent chaos. Whatever, or whoever, the attachment, human craving results in suffering, as explained in Buddhism and exemplified in zombie fiction.

As with the meditation on the corpse, the viewer is directed to realize the similarities between the dead and the living and in so realizing to move beyond an ignorant attachment to an illusory sense of self-permanence. The rotting corpse in its abjection brings home the fact that the body is impermanent and imperfect. By understanding the walking dead as the embodiment of the suffering of *samsara*, the viewer can sympathize with the desire not to become one of them. The zombies are shown to be enslaved by their single-minded cravings, just as the Buddha teaches that all humans are slaves to attachment and desire. This enslavement to cravings keeps us all yearning after the impossible, forever hankering after an ephemeral permanence. The inevitable dissatisfaction that results from unsatisfied cravings is what the Buddha called *dukkha*, the first Noble Truth. As viewers, we can recognize their empty quest for fulfillment in our own. And we must also recognize in the zombie the fact that it is through self-delusion and ignorance that this cycle is perpetuated. The zombie mindlessly pursues its cravings only to find that once its desire has been achieved—once it has killed a person and consumed his or her flesh—the twofold result is a lack of satisfaction on the part of the zombie, and also the reproduction of a new, craving undead corpse.

Attachments and cravings are self-perpetuating; they support further attachment and craving through the production of the illusion of a self. Buddhism teaches that so long as we believe in the illusion of permanence, we will continue to experience that illusion. In the illusion, we will constantly fight for permanency and suffer over never achieving it. The solution, for the Buddha, is to eliminate our attachments, especially that to our selves. By getting over our selves, we can overcome the sufferings that result from attachments to false realities, and so achieve nirvana. If we yearn after the illusion of a permanent self, then we are already zombies, walking corpses clinging to an unsatisfactory false life. On the other hand, by realizing the impermanence of the self, one gives up attachment to the illusion of permanence, and in so doing escapes the cycle of *samsara*. One might thus reach nirvana and avoid the fate of being eternally and repeatedly reborn as one of the living dead.

Zombies in Buddhist Contexts

Fiction has been a recognized tool for conveying Buddhist teachings from the beginning. Tenzin Wangmo's collection, *The Prince and the Zombie: Tibetan Tales of Karma*,[52] represents only one example of the centuries-old *Vetalapancavimsati* tales (traditional ghost stories, including walking corpses and disembodied spirits). Though not exactly zombies in the traditional Haitian sense, nor necessarily flesh-eating Romero-zombies, walking corpses have featured in legend throughout Buddhist lands.

For instance, Tibetan Buddhism includes the possibility that a corpse may be revived as what is called a *ro-langs*.[53] This can happen either through the conjuration of a shaman or from possession by an evil spirit. Tibetan Buddhism's complex series of rituals surrounding the death of a person are intended to facilitate that person's transition from this life into the next world, leading to probable rebirth, but potentially leading instead to nirvana if the individual is able to overcome attachments. The possessing spirit represents a kind of rebirth that remains filled with cravings and so needs to incarnate by stealing a body that has recently become free, so to speak. The horror of these creatures is twofold: on one hand, there is the fear of the invading spirit, recognized as being filled with craving; on the other hand, there is also the fear for the safety of the deceased as one's spirit might be threatened by this turn of events, especially if it is viewed as having one's body stolen by another, and so may not have a successful rebirth. Here, echoing the Haitian tradition, there is both the fear of the zombie's master (in this case, the invading spirit taking possession of the body of another), but also the fear of becoming a zombie (in this case directed towards a loved one for fear that they may suffer further by not being able to move effectively towards nirvana, or at least a better life).

Warnings against zombies, and so-called half-zombies, which might be raised by evil magicians to murder people, can be found early in the Buddhist tradition as well. One text, for example, describes the strange practice of one monk raising a corpse, which is then armed with two swords and placed in a special two-wheeled wagon by which it can move itself. The text goes on to describe means by which one can ensure safety from such a monster, including prayers, offerings, and the awareness of a bodhisattva—

all of which are themselves minor forms of meditation easily accomplished by busy people not accustomed to life in a monastery!⁵⁴

Southeast Asian legend also includes similar tales, including that of King Vikramāditya who engages in a series of conversations with a corpse hung in a tree. The king sees the "zombie" as a source of power, but the crafty corpse continually tricks the king with a variety of riddles. The undead corpse is itself seen as the source of wisdom—a monster in the root sense of the word, *monstrare*, Latin to warn or to show. Modern Thai cinema continues the tendency to view the undead as sources of wisdom as well as fear.⁵⁵ *The Coffin* (2008), for instance, centers around a Thai tradition of seeking to avoid death by spending a night in a coffin. The coffins are arrayed in a circle around a large statue of the Buddha, such that the practice is a form of meditation on death. The female protagonist, Su (Karen Mok) sees her cancer go into remission after the ritual, though she also begins to have various ghostly encounters. Haunted by the spirit of her late fiancé, Su repeats the coffin ritual, during which she finally embraces her deceased love. After the ritual, her cancer returns as she comes to accept both the death of her fiancé and her own mortality, stating: "I guess the wheel is spinning, and I don't want to interrupt it." The spirit had been guiding her to this conclusion throughout, but her refusal to accept his death had resulted in fear as she wrestled with its reality.

Further examples show how such didactic tales appear across Buddhist traditions, with two Chinese stories from the eighteenth-century Chan Buddhist writer Yuan Mei. The first, "Two Scholars of Nanchang,"⁵⁶ tells of two friends who studied together. The elder of the two died, leaving his younger friend in mourning. During the night, the elder scholar visited his friend while he was in bed. At first afraid, the younger scholar was convinced that the ghost's intentions were benevolent. He came to console his still living friend but also to ask that he repay some unpaid debts for him. The elder scholar having delivered his message, intended to leave, only to have the younger scholar ask for just a little more time since they would likely not see each other again, the one being dead and the other alive. At this request, the elder scholar's face began to change, becoming ugly and decayed. The younger scholar once again became frightened and demanded that his friend leave him. Instead the corpse stood staring, and then chased the younger as he stood and ran. The corpse chased him until the younger man escaped over a wall. While he lay at the bottom of the wall, the corpse simply looked at him from the top, drool dripping on the younger man from his dead mouth. In the morning, the young man was found lying in the street, and the corpse of his friend was found on the other side of the wall.

A second story from Yuan Mei, "An Artisan Paints a Zombie (*jiangshi*),"[57] tells of a son who hires an artist to do a portrait of his recently deceased father. The painter agrees and once he begins his painting the father's corpse sits up in his bed. The painter determines to keep painting, and the corpse begins to imitate his actions, moving his hand in the air as if he were painting as well. Rather than running as the young man in the previous tale did, the painter freezes and waits for help to arrive, in response to which the corpse simply sits frozen in the same position as the painter. The corpse is returned to a dead state once again when some passersby bring brooms with which to sweep away the evil influence.

Both of these stories reflect both traditional Chinese belief and Buddhism. Traditionally, the Chinese have believed in multiple spirits. The *hun* is the seat of consciousness and the *po* the animating principle, which can be loosely compared to the Haitian conception of *gros* and *ti bon anges*. Without the *hun*, an animated corpse has no self. More interestingly for our present purposes, however, is the raison d'être for each of these zombies. In the first story, the elder scholar appears out of compassion to his younger friend and also out of duty for he asks his friend to take care of some unpaid debts for him, both of which are common tropes in ghost stories. The elder friend transforms into a walking corpse once the younger friend asks him to stay longer. Here, the elder scholar can be seen exercising the Buddhist virtue of compassion (for his friend) and perhaps a Confucian sense of duty (the repayment of debts), but things go wrong when the younger scholar is compelled to ask for more time due to his attachment to his friend's earthly existence. The lesson to avoid attachment is here taught by the dead friend's transforming into a rotting corpse and pursuing the young man through the night. Just as modern Hollywood zombies thrust themselves at a death-denying audience, so too the corpse here forces its message on the young man. In the second story, again the problem stems from attachment to the dead. The son wishes to immortalize his father in a portrait. The beginning of said portrait causes the corpse to rise. It is attachment to the deceased that results in its reanimation. Reinforcing the relationship between the living and the dead, the body then mimics the painter as if it were his reflection. The painter and the corpse are not unlike each other, just as the one meditating on a corpse will come to realize: "as that is, so this is." When corpses rise of their own accord in a Buddhist context, the cause can clearly be seen to be attachment, the root of all suffering. The fear of the reanimated corpse stems from a refusal to accept the connection, an attachment to the comfort of ignorance.

Other Buddhist practices also show how art and performance are weaved into ritual and meditation in order to assist the grieving to come to grips with death. Theravada Buddhists in Thailand and Cambodia, for example, engage in what is called a *paṃsukūla* ceremony, a term used for both the ritual and the shroud-garment central to it.[58] In this ritual, mourners turn the burial shroud of the deceased over to a monk, who then accepts the mantle as a new garb, thereby embodying the dual nature of life and death, essentially becoming a kind of living-dead himself. It is said that the Buddha himself "sought his ultimate experience of enlightenment dressed in the shroud of a deceased servant of the girl cowherd Sujata, so with his shorn hair and the clothing of a corpse he truly looked like a living dead person."[59] Upon reaching nirvana, the Buddha "awakened" to a new life that transcends the bounds of the living/dying within *samsara* and instead accepts and embraces the unity of both life and death. Temple spaces used for this ritual are typically decorated with painted murals depicting scenes of funerals, cremations, as well as the appearance of corpses, the meditation over the corpse, and scenes of birds devouring the corpse.

Some Thai temples house the mummified corpses of monks who continue to embody both life and death in their seemingly permanent state outside of living and dying.[60] Similar mummies, called *sokushinbutsu*, have been found throughout Japan as well, though in these cases practitioners actually endeavored to mummify themselves while still living, even drinking formaldehyde in order to encourage the preservation of their corpse after death.[61] In combination with the physical transference of the shroud of the dead to the living monk, the images of death and decay are all geared towards an overcoming of death through the realization that it surrounds us all and is inherent in life at every moment.[62]

In Burmese culture, a ritual play is performed at the funeral of a monk. The traditional play revolves around a particular woman who cannot bear the fact of the monk's death, and does everything in her power to try to keep the man alive somehow, even rejecting the reality of death itself. The play resolves itself when two men violently confront the woman and then teach her the lesson of impermanence. The woman offers a monologue following this harrowing encounter in which she recites what amounts to a kind of meditation on the corpse expressed in terms of the absurdity of the body's fate:

> On the first day after death, the joints can no longer move; and even though the five aromatic substances are applied, one mark, then two gradually appear on the cheekbones; the cheeks and the eyelids cave in.

On the second day, the food rots, the intestines overflow, the stomach loses its shape and swells up out of all proportion.
On the third day, it is impossible to love the deceased any longer, the heart feels only hate; the veins on the corpse swell and liquid seeps out of all the orifices.
On the fourth day, protuberances appear on the body which, through lack of air, looks like a bag of skin on the bones.
On the fifth day, it's really disgusting, the two eyes bulge from their sockets and the tongue hangs out like a monster's.
On the sixth day, pus flows out; it would be a lie to say it smells nice, it stinks, it's disgusting and you want to be sick.
On the seventh day, it is impossible to love the deceased, the kidneys and the liver mix as they decompose, the guts are in shreds, shit flows out constantly.
On the eighth day, a breath of air is enough to detach the skin, the body withers and falls away like rotten fruit before disappearing into the ground, it is written in the Dhamma that all is doomed to disappear and die.
On the ninth day, it's disgusting to see the marrow coming through the bones and these whitening in places like depigmented skin.
On the tenth day, the veins and arteries are in shreds and the body in pieces. There is no hope of escaping the endless cycle of samsara, the Buddha himself was not spared it.[63]

Ritual, art, and performance are not the only forms in which such meditations on death appear in Buddhist contexts. Role-playing is included as an active meditation on death and mortality in modern Thai palliative and end-of-life care. People are asked to adopt various roles, placing themselves in imaginary situations where they need to confront death from different perspectives and in different circumstances. In one study of such practices, participants became emotional as the characters they were meant to role-play had experiences very similar to their own lived experiences. When asked if they wished to carry on with the exercise, one participant responded immediately, echoing the desire of zombie special effects artists mentioned earlier: "It is good. We need to face reality. The closer this is to the real thing, the better."[64] The need for the confrontation with death to feel as real as possible returns us to the kinds of meditations often reserved for monks observing actual corpses, but sits within a continuum of exposure to personal mortality.

Buddhist precepts reflected in zombie cinema can also take on a similar role as these other ritualized forms of art and performance, which have themselves been adapted to clinical settings as well. Western audiences may well benefit from directly confronting personal mortality in the same way. The Donald Margulies play, *Time Stands Still* (2010), tells the story of a photographer returning to America after having covered wars in the Middle East, and how he turns to consuming horror films to help cope with his experiences, similar to Tom Savini's earlier-stated reflection on his work in special effects. In his story, "Closure Limited" (2012), Max Brooks imagines the need for a company specifically devoted to helping provide survivors of the zombie apocalypse with closure over the loss of loved ones by providing zombies, who will be dressed up to resemble those loved ones lost and can then be shot in the head by the grieving customer.[65] The story recognizes that most customers will rationally acknowledge that the zombie in question is not really their loved one, but that the fiction works.

Interestingly, proponents of the Terror Management Theory mentioned above have considered the value of film in confronting personal mortality, but zombie fiction seems to be completely off their radar. In an essay on apocalyptic cinema, TMT advocates Joel Lieberman and Mark Fergus mention zombies only once, and in a footnote that conflates *Night of the Living Dead* (1968) and *White Zombie* (1932), to remark that these represent nothing more than a subgenre of plague films.[66] The chapter does make multiple references to both *I Am Legend* (2008) and *The Last Man on Earth* (1968) as vampire films, completely ignoring the ways in which the original Matheson story, and subsequently Romero's adaptation, completely revamp (and de-vamp) the genre. The editors of the volume in which this essay appears do, at least, observe the potential for film to address death anxieties, but note that audiences must be actively engaged in the process. Daniel Sullivan and Jeff Greenberg conclude:

> In the confines of a film we can safely contemplate death, the ultimate tragedy, and feel our way through both familiar and foreign systems of meaning as we try to come to grips with it. To uncover these potentialities, however, it seems that viewers cannot be passive participants in the act of viewing. Rather, they must actively engage with films on a psychological level [... or] seek out unusual films [...] that encourage critical engagement with conventional meaning systems.[67]

Certainly, engaging in a meditation on mortality is precisely the kind of audience activation I would encourage. Their attitude that death marks "the ultimate tragedy," though, speaks volumes for just why zombie fiction and Buddhist philosophy are absent from their discussion.

Death is no tragedy, it is a simple reality. Tragedy implies an unhappy end. To describe death as, by nature, tragic implies from the outset that it is a negative. The presumption of the TMT enthusiasts is obviously one that considers death inherently fearsome, but it is difficult to imagine just how open they are to "critical engagement with conventional meaning systems" when this particular perspective is so imbedded in their own thinking.[68] Accepting death as coequal to living since one cannot happen without the other is a key to overcoming the fear of death, which engenders selfishness and only continues the cycle of suffering. Firestone is stumped by what he considers our "bipolar" attitude towards death as he admits, "Any experience that reminds an individual that he possesses strength, independence, personal power, or acknowledged value as a person will make him acutely conscious of his life and its eventual loss."[69] TMT researchers generally approach the problem from the opposite side, noting that death anxiety is buffered by stronger thoughts of self-worth and greater clinging to relationships based on romantic love. Combining Firestone's perspective on separation with the research from TMT, it would seem to be the case that recognizing one's self-importance engenders fears of death, while fear of death encourages individuals to bolster their own sense of self-worth, often through reinforcing their own worldviews at the expense of "outsiders."[70] This would have one moving in the opposite direction from an authentic confrontation with personal mortality, and one that might be better coped with by a critical engagement with conventional models.

Beyond Existential Angst

The point of confronting one's mortality within the framework of a Buddhist philosophy is not to bring about a paralyzing existential crisis or encourage a hedonistic individualism that indulges every momentary pleasure. Many Western existentialists have argued for the importance of realizing personal mortality as an integral component of a moral ethic. Some of these have inspired my own thinking, and some, like me, have been inspired by Buddhist thought as well, but none has fully realized the potential offered by a full integration of this perspective. If, as Mary Warnock suggests, existentialism aims "above all, to show people *that they are free* [her italics], to open their eyes to something which has always been true, but which for one reason or another may not always have been recognized,"[71] then Buddhism is another existentialist philosophy. On the other hand, Walter Kaufmann points to the diversity in those philosophers who have been labeled existentialists as being united most explicitly in their "perfervid individualism" and "refusal to belong to any school of thought, the repudiation of the adequacy of any body of beliefs whatever, and especially of systems, and a marked dissatisfaction with traditional philosophy as superficial, academic, and remote from life."[72] Again, the Buddha was a revolutionary thinker, and the tradition of zombies is also one of antiauthoritarianism, so both find a comfortable home alongside such thought.

Martin Heidegger described human existence as Being-toward-death.[73] For him, the individual Being, *Dasein*, comes into its own by the knowledge of its finitude. This individuation can be seen as having two components: firstly, it serves to delineate the boundaries of the self from beginning at birth to ending at death and thus creates an individual life story, but secondly, it also serves to allow the individual to function effectively, authentically, within society. The individual *Dasein* finds meaning only in relation to society and others, but it also finds form only through recognition of its own self. We are social creatures, needing community, while at the same time each of us is restricted by nature to our own individual experience. Society, for its part, seeks to ignore death as irrelevant to the big picture—individual members may die, but the community lives on. Society, in denying death, then also denies the authenticity of the self that is defined by it. From the bigger societal perspective, individual lives are as grains of sand on a beach. *Dasein*, the individual, is torn by the individuation of the self, which requires an acknowledgment of eventual cessation and the need to find meaning in a society that denies death. Heidegger describes the authentic self as that which acknowledges its own finitude and incorporates it; the inauthentic self is one that denies death and flees it. Here, Dasein sounds much like the *anatta*, a different perspective on selfhood that acknowledges the truth of its impermanence.

All of those individuals responding to death in the manner expected by the post–Becker death-denial, TMT school of thought—that is, with fear and denial—are enacting the inauthentic self, referred to by Heidegger as Das Man, "one" or "the they." Essentially, individuals in this mode then act in ways that "one" ought to act or do as "they" tell them to. The inauthentic self lives to please society, and so does not live as an individuated self at all. A society composed of inauthentic selves would be nothing more than a self-perpetuating mass existing merely to survive. The authentic self is one that is both self *and* member of society. Like the zombies in *Dawn of the Dead* (1978), a society of inauthentic selves sees its members simply stumble about a space of consumption advertised as the source for fulfillment, with each individual playing the dutiful role of consumer without questioning the system or whether it truly does provide any satisfaction at all.

More subtly, a belief in eternal life also flees from the acceptance of finitude and so prevents the individuation of selves. Paffenroth complains of a hyper*individualism* in Western culture, but this is not what Heidegger intends by the individuated *Dasein*. The hyperindividualistic person is similarly inauthentic in being unable to conceive of its own demise. It is this hyperindividual, inauthentic *Dasein* that finds horror in death and the godless resurrection of zombies. Essentially, the inauthentic *Dasein* flees from death and runs into the arms of society—not into the arms of any other people, but to the overarching system itself—thus failing to be individuated and actually fulfilled. How, then, can one come to accept death authentically and avoid a self-less state of slavery to the fear of mortality and the societal denial of death? Heidegger does not give any specific instructions on exactly what an authentic *Dasein* would behave like, except that it does so in freely choosing from its possibilities within the context of a definite individual end.

Curtis Bowman makes the equation, "Heidegger is to horror as Aristotle is to tragedy."[74] What he means to suggest is that Heidegger's philosophy encouraging individual authenticity is ideally expressed through horror fiction. For his part, Heidegger follows the likes of Søren Kierkegaard who, sometimes referred to as the father of existentialism, spoke of existential angst or dread as the "dizziness of freedom."[75] Recognizing anxiety and the uncanny as moments in which the individual's comfortable, commonplace views of the world are challenged allows one the opportunity to reflect upon one's possibilities. The various emotions evoked by horror can include real horror and fear, but are also evocative of the uncanny, or eerie.[76]

The sense of the uncanny is particularly important since it jars us out of our comfortable existence and forces us to take note—something is out of place here, and I'd better pay attention. This is not the experience of mounting fear that might be induced by an effective musical score. As Bowman puts it, it is the feeling of losing our "ontological equilibrium."

Zen Buddhist kōans, which are usually short verses used as meditative aids, are purposefully filled with ambiguity especially intended to force those considering them to think in different and contradictory ways. For example, one Zen saying runs: "one doesn't know the smell of one's own shit [*Jishi kusaki o oboezu*]."[77] The meaning of this statement is not singular. On one hand, one may take the conventional approach and interpret it in the sense that a person is never fully aware of one's own self, thereby urging self-reflection. The statement can also be expressed in Zen as, "one does not know one's own Buddha-nature." Reflection on one's self ought to lead one to an understanding of the truth of that self, which is encapsulated in the notion of no-self, or Buddha-nature. The truth within one's self-centeredness is that there is no self at all. Here, the Zen koan flips perceptions of self and self-centeredness in equating shit with the Buddha in a way that would be typically shocking to an audience that expects the sacred and profane to remain separate. If ignorance of the smell of one's own shit is akin to ignorance of the true nature of the self, then in order to recognize one's Buddha-nature, one must become familiar with one's own shit. Recognition of the shocking double-entendre is part of the process of fully understanding. Fantasy and horror are especially good venues for the evocation of this uncomfortable feeling, forcing viewers to experience the wonderment at the possibility that our world is not what we think it is.[78]

In terms of zombie fiction, the forcefulness with which the abject qualities of the human body, and its revelation of individual mortality, evoke powerful responses, mirroring the crassness of some Zen verse as well. It is not merely the fact that a body will rot that is important, though, but audience reactions to this revelation. If the experience of the uncanny can jostle the viewer even slightly into considering alternate possibilities for action in the world, then horror films can "act as aids to self-understanding. They slowly turn us toward different ways of looking at the world [....] As we watch uncanny films, we must revise or abandon the ontology that we initially used to understand what we see on the screen, and by doing so we become more explicitly aware of our own ontological commitments."[79] We find agreement here with the TMT psychotherapists who argued that audiences might benefit from film, provided that they actively engaged with the material. If horror forces the viewer to consider his or her own ontological assumptions, if even briefly, then that consideration represents at least some active participation. Providing the framework for understanding that fiction in terms of Buddhist existential philosophy can help to situate the mental ontological reworkings needed to come to grips with death anxiety and the problems of retreating into a paradoxically self-defeating selfishness. Brent Adkins phrased the possibility well: "If *Dasein* is driven to its absorption in the world by an avoidance of death, it is not really free to choose its possibilities. It is rather chained to its possibilities. Authentic *Dasein*, on the other hand, since it is not driven to its possibilities to avoid death but faces death, can choose its possibilities not out of avoidance but freedom."[80]

The choice of possibilities remains for many existentialists a personal decision. I mentioned earlier Camus' discussion of the absurdity of realizing the fruitlessness of life in the face of certain death, comparing all living to the punishment of Sisyphus, forced as he was to eternally push a rock up a hill only to see it fall back down upon reaching the peak where he would resume pushing anew. The pointlessness of the task is like that of every human, living and dreaming and building, only to die. Camus urges his readers, like Heidegger and the Buddha before him, to accept individual mortality and incorporate its reality into life, ensuring that every decision one makes is done in the full light of the knowledge that death is imminent. Again, though, Camus does not offer a system for how to make such decisions, leaving it to the individual to live life according to his or her own will. In *The Myth of Sisyphus*, Camus offers a number of biographies of the "Absurd Man"—the serial philanderer, the actor, and the unthinking soldier. None of these seems much like a role-model.

Friedrich Nietzsche offers an interesting thought experiment that may provide at least some direction towards how the authentic person might behave. In *The Gay Science*, he asks:

> What if some day or night a demon were to steal after you into your loneliest loneliness and say to you: "This life as you now live it and have lived it, you will have to live once more and innumerable times more; and there will be nothing new in it, but every pain and every joy, and every thought and sigh and everything unutterably small or great in your life will have to return to you, all in the same succession and sequence—even this spider and this moonlight between the trees, and even this moment and I myself. The eternal hourglass of existence is turned upside down again and again, and you with it, a speck of dust!" Would you not throw yourself down and gnash your teeth and curse the demon who spoke thus? Or have you experienced a tremendous moment when you would have answered him: "You are a god and never have I heard anything more divine." If this thought gained possession of you, it would change you as you are or perhaps crush you. The question in each and every thing, "Do you desire this once more and innumerable times more?" would lie upon your actions as the greatest weight. Or how well disposed would you have become to yourself and to life to crave nothing more fervently than this ultimate confirmation and seal?[81]

At first thought, the challenge appears to be twofold. One is tortured by the possibility of reliving all of the sufferings and regrets of one's life, despite whatever pleasures one will also have had. Some have noted the fact that the life relived to the detail would also be one in which there was no awareness of having lived it before.[82] Nonetheless, the thought experiment still presents a challenge. One is forced to consider one's actions in the moment in terms of whether one would be happy to relive or regret them eternally.

In the Buddhist tradition there is also a sense of reliving suffering through one's actions, described as controlled by the laws of karma. As seen above, the core of this whole system rests on the fact that my own suffering is the result of my own actions, brought upon myself by my own decisions. If I am suffering now, whatever I may point to as the immediate cause, my suffering is ultimately the result of my own attachment to some other state. It becomes a matter of perspective, and considering Nietzsche's demon is one example of an attempt to bring one to change perspective from an imagined future (without death) to an immediate present in which death is a recognized certainty.

Another way to imagine this focus on the current moment is to ask whether one might choose whatever course of action one is currently choosing if this were to be the final moment of one's life, since it may very well be. And, in fact, given the ongoing change that occurs to all of us all the time, that past moment of action was the final action of that past self. If we take Heidegger's observation that birth and death define the limits of the person, we can apply that on a smaller scale as well. On the scale of an individual lifetime, death puts the final punctuation mark at the end of a life story; there are no further potentialities, no more choices to be made. As such, the story of the person is complete. Well, every passing moment further delimits some part of that story as well. Parts of the story are written and cannot be changed. Actions taken now are living actions, and also dying actions. Having been taken, they are done. Actions done in the past are no longer alive; they do not change. Gwyneth Peaty points to the relationship of the protagonists in *The Walking Dead* to their pasts and present in pointing to a seeming "obsession with keeping time and memory 'alive.'"[83] By harking back to a time that is gone, the protagonists do not effectively recognize the reality of their current state. Characters reflect on photographs, wind watches, keep track of passing days on a calendar. Dr. Jenner (Noah Emmerich), who has given in to suicidal thoughts, has a clock that counts down to the time of his demise. Jenner and Rick argue over whether there is any hope in continuing, Jenner sensing there is none, Rick arguing that there is always hope. The concept of hope is bound with time, though, and loses meaning when one focuses on the moment. Hope directs attention to the future, but ignores the fact that death lies unavoidable in that future. Further, hope removes responsibility from the actor in the present. One simply does not need hope for change when one understands that change is inevitable, and is happening all the time.

The way to behave, then, in the face of certain death is to accept that certainty as a possibility that exists within each and every moment. As each moment passes away, it makes apparent the death that lay within it. Those past moments, as dead moments, float away from our grasp, unchangeable. There is no need to cling to them; instead, focus on the moment. If that last moment was unpleasant, make the next one pleasant. Encourage positive conditions to arise where they do not exist, and discourage negative ones from arising. This is simply the mantra of every moment. That apparent self that did those unpleasant, selfish acts is gone, along with the acts themselves. We need not forget them and the harm they did, but there is no need to cling to their existence as if they persisted. Likewise with the good that was done by the selfless person; it too is gone but need not be forgotten. The effects of a good act, or a bad one for that matter, may result after the act itself is done, allowing for new moments in which to respond again in positive or negative ways. Clinging to some past act further ignores the effects and their opportunities in the present.

If we remember that we are dying in each and every moment of living, we must also remember that every other person we meet is also dying. Everyone we meet is a dying person. There has been a lot of attention paid to the difficulties of caring for dying people, and given our death-denying culture, caring for a dying loved one is often an anxiety-laden task. Joan Halifax leads Being with Dying, a clinical training program inspired by Buddhist teachings, which is geared towards helping clinicians deal with the dying through a contemplative approach. In this practice, clinicians are encouraged in self-reflection, including in accepting one's own suffering and mortality, in order to better assist their patients through the dying process.[84] Remembering that everyone we interact with is, in fact, a dying person, will allow two core outcomes. For one thing, this might evince more care and compassion for a person recognized as dying instead of the contempt harbored for some "other" whom we see as a nameless face within the crowd of undying society. As noted when discussing Heidegger, society ignores death since it continues on regardless of and despite the individual's death. Second, we might normalize interactions with the dying to the extent that we would not feel anxiety welling up as we wish to deny mortality and push the dying out of view and away to a hospital or care facility. We might come to recognize dying as entirely natural, thereby engendering further compassion for those who might be closer to the point of death than others. Zombie fiction routinely tries to instill a sense of empathy for some zombies, but as the woman in the Burmese Buddhist ritual play described earlier asks, how can one love such a disgusting thing as a rotting corpse? When we recognize that we are all dying, moving inevitably towards the disgusting state of rot and decay, we might have increased sympathy for each other as sharing the same inevitable ongoing change. Certainly, no one could love the rotten corpse in the sense of being attached to that detestable thing. Instead, one can show compassion to all of those whose fate remains the same. This is the self-less love professed by the Buddha and learned through severing attachments to all material reality and to the self above all.

Buddhism, at its core, requires no faith. It is a simple, rational system to guide one's life. The reasons for why one might choose to follow this path stem entirely from experience. Recognizing one's mortality as a lived reality is a rational approach simply because death is an unavoidable reality. Ignoring that is unsustainable over the long run as change, ageing, and death are ever-present. Further recognizing the transitoriness of every thing in every moment helps to move away from being attached to material things as if it were all going to last forever. We can all recall instances of disappointment, suffering, and sadness resulting from wishing a thing would not have broken or ended, or that a person had not left or died. Attachment to any of these things only makes that suffering all the more palpable. Buddhism doesn't suggest that we should not have feelings, and sadness and grief are natural, but refusing to deal with the fact of temporal existence exaggerates these emotions and makes them linger. Overcoming attachments is no easy task, especially in a context of capitalist consumerism and the constant barrage of advertising aimed at making us all believe that we need more things and that the future is filled with limitless possibilities. Viewed in the right light, zombie fiction points out that we ought to be neither the survivors nor the zombies. We are not the living dead or simply the dying alive, but so long as we are truly living then we must also be dying in every moment.

Conclusion

The zombie, from its origins in Haiti, has been a product, and a representation, of slavery. Individuals who became enslaved lost their lives in the sense of being free to live a meaningful existence, replaced instead with the bare life of simply surviving. Slavers' selfish interests in capitalist and colonial consumption drove the barely alive to do their bidding. The zombie has also been a symbol of resistance, however, as a metaphorical rejection of the religious tradition of slave holders. The anti–Christian aspects reacting against such doctrines as resurrection and communion were cleverly disguised under the veneer of Christian symbolism itself. Ultimately, though, the Haitian zombie tradition set the ground for future zombies in constructing an implicitly antiauthoritarian image of the bare-life existence of individuals enslaved by greed and selfishness, which is critical of the dominant spiritual tradition while tacitly indicating assent through the adoption of those same dominant images.

Audiences that recognized the zombie in Romero's "living dead" were reacting to symbols and images from that creature's history with which they were familiar. And these images and symbols appeared in Romero's work despite his lack of conscious intent. Remember, the creatures in *Night* were never meant to be zombies in the traditional sense. Still, Romero's creatures redefined the zombie, broadening the application from its Haitian roots. Unlike the Haitian zombie, these creatures had no slave master creating or controlling them, and the craving driving them was pure and simple—the flesh of the living.

Inspired by changes to the vampire tradition, which moved that creature increasingly away from its Christian roots, especially through the work of Richard Matheson, the evolved zombie embraced the antiauthoritarian and Christian-critical elements of its origins. At a time when secularism was on the rise and alternative, largely Eastern, spiritualities were increasingly considered legitimate sources of meaning, the timing was apt for the acceptance of a monster similarly threatening the boundaries of social normativity.

Removing the slave master had a number of effects on the zombie. For one, it situated the driving force within the individual. The suggestion of one's lack of autonomy remains, to some extent; but without the clear interference of a controlling agent, the cause of a person's lost autonomy is similarly internalized. Though some versions of the zombie focus on explanations for its cause, be that scientific experimentation or, more commonly, a virus of some kind, the Romero zombie has no known cause. As such, the drive to consume is the zombie's own. And this drive is shared by all zombies, illustrating the universality of one overarching desire among all who relinquish their agency and self-control—the desire for "life" stolen from those who retain it. In thus stealing, though, the zombies remain as ignorant of their state as do the living. Both zombies and survivors have relinquished their agency as unable or unwilling to see the mortal truth before them. The living turn on each other in vain attempts at selfish self-preservation rather than adopting selfless cooperation while the zombies ignore each other and fight over scraps of living flesh.

I say that the agency is relinquished rather than stolen since zombie fiction is clear in its juxtaposition of the living and the dead as mirror images of each other. The living survivors look more familiar to the viewers, but the dead are a reflection of those same survivors. As such, the dead are reflections also of us, consumers of this fiction. The protagonists in zombie fiction are locked in a constant, but ambiguous, struggle. On one hand, they recognize the relationship they share with the walking dead, yet on the other hand they carry on the fruitless battle to destroy that reflection of themselves. As viewers, we have the opportunity to transcend this tension.

We can recognize the connections between the living and the dead, between us and them, and we can move beyond the knee-jerk reaction of denial. In a simplified way, we might overcome attachment to a character like Glenn and accept his death as a moment of drama and tragedy that fits within an overall storyline of both his character, those of the rest of the cast, and of the overall series.

Just as the agency of the modern zombie has not been stolen by some slave master, we too have control over whether we exercise our own agency or not. We have the opportunity to be mindful of our own reality, to be aware of the facts that we are both living and dying right now, at every single moment. As such, we have the possibility to transcend selfish desires for some impossible continuation into the future and instead focus on making the present moment one that is not characterized by the suffering that worrying for the future or past entails, or that searching out the next source of individual happiness engenders, but that is characterized by an understanding of the impermanence of all things such that momentary happiness is an experience best shared. It is not my happiness to cling to and hold, since it is not so much the case that my happiness is transitory as it is that I am transitory. Happiness can be seen to exist in its own right, and so long as I cling to the hope that whatever is causing that happiness is a thing that should remain unchanged, I will have it and lose it over and over again. When I realize that it is I that is the thing that changes, beginning and ending in every moment anew, then I can change my perspective such that I am aware of true happiness, a state without the suffering from fear, desire, and attachment.

Viewers of zombie fiction can see core Buddhist elements reflected on-screen. If the films jar the viewer into considering existential questions of human existence, then Buddhist concepts can help to rebuild shaken ontologies that have become ineffective in dealing with questions of death and meaning. There is even the possibility for testable hypotheses here in that I propose that viewing zombie fiction must surely intensify mortality salience, but viewing such fiction in the light of core Buddhist teachings should ameliorate the experience of anxiety. There is clearly a strong interest in being exposed to zombie fiction despite the evocation of death anxiety, and my contention is that there may well be an incipient understanding among viewers about the importance of confronting the reality of death in order to come to grips with existential angst. All that may be needed is the application of a Buddhist understanding to integrate viewer experience into a workable zombie ethic.

Chapter Notes

Introduction

1. For more on "sociophobics," see David L. Scruton (ed.), *Sociophobics: The Anthropology of Fear* (Boulder, Colorado: Westview Press, 1986).
2. Sarah Juliet Lauro, *The Transatlantic Zombie: Slavery, Rebellion, and Living Death* (New Brunswick, NJ: Rutgers University Press, 2015).
3. Kim Paffenroth, *Gospel of the Living Dead: George Romero's Visions of Hell on Earth* (Waco, TX: Baylor University Press, 2006).
4. Anthony N. Smith, "Putting the Premium into Basic: Slow-Burn Narratives and the Loss-Leader Function of AMC's Original Drama Series," *Television & New Media* 14.2 (2011): 150–166, p. 163.
5. Ulrich Beck and Elisabeth Beck-Gernsheim, *Individualization: Institutionalized Individualism and its Social and Political Consequences* (London: Sage, 2002).
6. Peter Dendle, *The Zombie Movie Encyclopedia* (Jefferson, NC: McFarland, 2000); Peter Dendle, *The Zombie Movie Encyclopedia, Vol. 2: 2000–2010* (Jefferson, NC: McFarland, 2012).
7. Christopher M. Moreman, "Why Do We Love Zombies?" *The Washington Post*, Oct. 31, 2011. Online: http://www.washingtonpost.com/blogs/guest-voices/post/why-do-we-love-zombies/2011/10/31/gIQACwBmZM_blog.html; C.M. Moreman, "What is the Most Important Thing Zombies can Teach us About Being Human?" *Science + Religion Today*, June 6, 2012. Online: http://www.scienceandreligiontoday.com/2012/06/06/what-is-the-most-important-thing-zombies-can-teach-us-about-being-human/; "Varney & Co.," Fox Business (June 24, 2013).
8. Gilles Deleuze and Felix Guattari, *Anti-Oedipus: Capitalism and Schizophrenia*, trans. Robert Hurley, Mark Seem, and Helen R. Lane (1972; Minneapolis: University of Minnesota Press, 2005), p. 335.
9. Brent Adkins, *Death and Desire in Hegel, Heidegger and Deleuze* (Edinburgh University Press, 2007), pp. 178–185.
10. Gilles Deleuze and Felix Guattari, *A Thousand Plateaus: Capitalism and Schizophrenia*, trans. Brian Massumi (Minneapolis: University of Minnesota Press, 1987).
11. Deleuze and Guattari, *A Thousand Plateaus* (1987), p. 21.
12. For more on the connections between Deleuze and Guattari and Buddhism, see: Tony See and Joff Bradley (Eds.), *Deleuze and Buddhism* (London: Palgrave, 2016).
13. Che-ming Yang, "Nietzsche, Deleuze, and Nāgārjuna: Mapping the Dialectics of Will/Desire," *Journal of Language Teaching and Research* 1.6 (2010): 842–847, p. 844.

14. Quoted in Giulia D'Agnolo-Vallan, "Let Them Eat Flesh," *Film Comment* 41: 4 (July/Aug., 2005): 23–24, p. 24.

15. Noël Carroll, "Nightmare and the Horror Film: The Symbolic Biology of Fantastic Beings," pp. 91–105 in Moshe Lazar (ed.), *The Anxious Subject: Nightmares and Daymares in Literature and Film* (Malibu: Undena Publications, 1983), p. 105.

16. Carroll, *The Philosophy of Horror or Paradoxes of the Heart* (London: Routledge, 1990).

17. Jeffrey Jerome Cohen (ed.), *Monster Theory: Reading Culture* (Minneapolis: University of Minnesota Press, 1996), p. viii.

18. Eugene Thacker, *In the Dust of This Planet* (Winchester, UK: Zero Books, 2011), p. 9.

19. Robin Wood, "An Introduction to the American Horror Film," pp. 107–141 in Barry Keith Grant and Christopher Sharrett (eds.), *Planks of Reason: Essays on the Horror Film*, rev. ed. (Lanham, MD: Scarecrow Press, 2004).

20. Robert Kirk and Roger Squires, "Zombies v. Materialists," *Proceedings of the Aristotelian Society, Supplementary Volumes* 48 (1978): pp. 135–136.

21. See especially: David Chalmers, *The Conscious Mind: In Search of a Fundamental Theory* (New York: Oxford University Press, 1996). See also: Robert Kirk, "Zombies," *The Stanford Encyclopedia of Philosophy*, Edward N. Zalta (ed.) (Summer 2012). Online: http://plato.stanford.edu/archives/sum2012/entries/zombies/. Accessed Jan. 23, 2014.

22. Daniel C. Dennett makes the same observation in one of his many critiques of the concept in his *Consciousness Explained* (Boston: Little, Brown & Co., 1991), pp. 72–73.

23. Chalmers, *The Conscious Mind* (1996), p. 95.

24. Dennett, *Consciousness Explained* (1991), pp. 310–313.

25. Chalmers, *The Conscious Mind* (1996), p. 96.

26. Daniel C. Dennett, *Sweet Dreams: Philosophical Obstacles to a Science of Consciousness* (Cambridge, MA: MIT Press, 2005), p. 13.

27. Ambrose Bierce, "Cartesian," *Devil's Dictionary* (London: Arthur F. Bird, 1906).

28. Peter Dendle, "The Zombie as Barometer of Cultural Anxiety," pp. 45–57 in Niall Scott (ed.), *Monsters and the Monstrous: Myths and Metaphors of Enduring Evil* (New York: Rodopi, 2007), pp. 47 & 48.

29. Kevin Alexander Boon, "Ontological Anxiety Made Flesh: The Zombie in Literature, Film and Culture," pp. 33–43 in Scott (ed.), *Monsters and the Monstrous* (2007), pp. 36–37.

30. Kyle Bishop, "Raising the Dead: Unearthing the Nonliterary Origins of Zombie Cinema," *Journal of Popular Film & Television* 33.4 (2006): 196–205: p. 204.

31. Catherine Belling, "The Living Dead: Fiction, Horror, and Bioethics," *Perspectives in Biology and Medicine* 53.3 (2010): 439–451.

32. Susan M. Behuniak, "The Living Dead? The Construction of People with Alzheimer's Disease as Zombies," *Ageing & Society* 31 (2011): 70–92.

33. See, for instance, Carmelo Aquilina and Julian C. Hughes, "The Return of the Living Dead: Agency Lost and Found?" pp. 143–161 in Julian C. Hughes, Stephen J. Louw, and Steven R. Sabat (eds.), *Dementia: Mind, Meaning, and the Person* (London: Oxford University Press, 2006).

34. Craig Derksen and Darren Hudson Hick, "Your Zombie and You: Identity, Emotion, and the Undead," pp. 11–23 in Christopher M. Moreman and Cory James Rushton (eds.), *Zombies are Us: Essays on the Humanity of the Walking Dead* (Jefferson, NC: McFarland, 2011).

35. Derksen and Hick, in Moreman and Rushton (eds.), *Zombies are Us* (2011), p. 21. Cf. Hamish Thompson "'She's Not Your Mother Anymore, She's a Zombie!': Zombies, Value, and Personal Identity," pp. 27–37 & William S. Larkin, "Res Corporealis: Persons, Bodies, and Zombies," pp. 15–26, both in Richard Greene and K. Silem Mohammad (eds.), *The Undead and Philosophy* (Chicago: Open Court, 2006); Brendan Riley, "Zombie People: The Complicated Nature of Personhood in The Walking Dead," pp. 82–97 in James Lowder (ed.), *Triumph of the Walking Dead: Robert Kirkman's Zombie Epic on Page and Screen* (Dallas: BenBella, 2011).

36. See both Richard Dyer, *White* (London: Routledge, 1997); and Dyer, *The Matter of Images*, 2nd ed. (London: Routledge, 2002).
37. Cf. Outi Hakola, "Exotic Primitivism of Death in Classical Hollywood Living Dead Films," *Ilha do Desterro: A Journal of English Language, Literatures in English, and Cultural Studies* 62 (2012): 219–240.
38. Hannah Arendt, *The Origins of Totalitarianism* (Oxford: Benediction Classics, 2009 [1958]).
39. Michel Foucault, *The History of Sexuality*, Vol. 1, trans. Robert Hurley (New York: Pantheon Books, 1978).
40. Giorgio Agamben, *Homo Sacer: Sovereign Power and Bare Life*, trans. Daniel Heller-Roazen (Stanford, CA: Stanford University Press, 1998).
41. As quoted in Amy J. Ransom, "Ce Zombi égaré est-il un Haïtien ou un Québécois? Le vaudou chez les écrivains haïtiano-québécois," *Canadian Literature* 203 (2009): 64–83, p. 66.
42. Jon Stratton, "Zombie Trouble: Zombie Texts, Bare Life and Displaced People," *European Journal of Cultural Studies* 14.3 (2011): 265–281.
43. See Eric Hamako, "Zombie Orientals Ate My Brain! Orientalism in Contemporary Zombie Stories," pp. 107–123 & Becki A. Graham, "Post-9/11 Anxieties: Unpredictability and Complacency in the Age of 'New Terrorism' in *Dawn of the Dead* (2004)," pp. 124–138, in Christopher M. Moreman and Cory James Rushton (eds.), *Race, Oppression and the Zombie: Essays on Cross-Cultural Appropriations of the Caribbean Tradition* (Jefferson, NC: McFarland, 2011); Cf. Nicole Birch-Bayley, "Terror in Horror Genres: The Global Media and the Millennial Zombie," *Journal of Popular Culture* 45.6 (2012): 1137–1151; Nick Muntean and Matthew Thomas Payne, "Attack of the Living Dead: Recalibrating Terror in the Post–September 11 Zombie Film," pp. 239–258 in Andrew Schopp and Matthew B. Hill (eds.), *The War on Terror and American Popular Culture: September 11 and Beyond* (Madison, NJ: Farleigh Dickinson UP, 2009).
44. Gerry Canavan, "'We Are the Walking Dead': Race, Time, and Survival in Zombie Narrative," *Extrapolation* 51.3 (2010): 431–453.
45. Ian Olney, *Euro Horror: Classic European Horror Cinema in Contemporary American Culture* (Bloomington: Indiana University Press, 2013), p. 116.
46. Elizabeth McAlister, "Slaves, Cannibals, and Infected Hyper-Whites: The Race and Religion of Zombies," *Anthropological Quarterly* 85.2 (2012): 457–486.
47. Jason Mattera, *Obama Zombies: How the Liberal Machine Brainwashed My Generation* (New York: Threshold, 2011).

Chapter One

1. Patrick Bellegarde-Smith, *Haiti: The Breached Citadel* (Toronto, ON: Canadian Scholars' Press, 2004), remains a valuable resource on the history and culture of Haiti.
2. From Alexandra Boutros, "The Spirit of Traffic: Navigating Faith in the City," pp. 118–137 in Alexandra Boutros and Will Straw (eds.), *Circulation and the City: Essays on Urban Culture* (Montreal: McGill-Queen's University Press, 2010), p. 128.
3. Christopher Columbus, *The Voyage of Christopher Columbus*, translated by John Cummins (New York: St. Martin's Press, 1992).
4. Bellegarde-Smith, *Haiti* (2004), p. 48.
5. Cilas Kemedjio, "Rape of Bodies, Rape of Souls: From the Surgeon to the Psychiatrist, from the Slave Trade to the Slavery of Comfort in the Work of Edouard Glissant," *Research in African Literatures* 25.2 (1994): 51–67.
6. Bellegarde-Smith, *Haiti* (2004), p. 59.
7. See Hubert Herring, *A History of Latin America from the Beginnings to the Present*, 3rd ed. (New York: Knopf, 1972), pp. 171–175 as cited in Anne Greene, *The Catholic Church in Haiti: Political and Social Change* (East Lansing: Michigan State University Press, 1993), p. 4.
8. Cf. Adolph Francis Bandelier, "Bartolomé de las Casas." *The Catholic Encyclopedia*. Vol. 3. (New York: Robert Appleton Company, 1908).
9. Greene, *The Catholic Church in Haiti* (1993), p. 77 here cites Adolphe Cabon, *Notes Sur L'Histoire Religieuses*

d'Haiti de la Revolution au Concordat, 1789–1860 (Port-au-Prince: Petit Séminaire Collège St. Martial, 1933), p. 9.
10. Cf. George Breathett, "Catholicism and the Code Noir in Haiti," *The Journal of Negro History* 73:1 (1988): 1–11.
11. Greene, *The Catholic Church in Haiti* (1993), p. 24.
12. J. Michael Dash, *Culture and Customs of Haiti* (Westport, CT: Greenwood, 2000), p. 52.
13. Greene, *The Catholic Church in Haiti* (1993), p. 80, quoting C.L.R. James, *Black Jacobins, Toussaint L'Ouverture and the San Domingo Revolution*, 2nd ed. (New York: Random House, 1963), p. 87.
14. Carolyn Fick, *The Making of Haiti: The San Domingue Revolution from Below* (Knoxville: University of Tennessee Press, 1990); James G. Leyburn, *The Haitian People* (New Haven, CT: Yale University Press, 1941).
15. Bellegarde-Smith, *Haiti* (2004), p. 60, translated by the author from Jan Fouchard, *Les Marrons de la liberté* (Port-au-Prince: Henri Deschamps, 1972), p. 117.
16. Bellegarde-Smith, *Haiti* (2004), 59.
17. Adam M. McGee, "Dreaming in Haitian Vodou: Vouchsafe, Guide, and Source of Liturgical Novelty." *Dreaming.* (2012, February 20). Advance online publication. doi: 10.1037/a0026691.
18. Donald J. Cosentino, "Introduction: Imagine Heaven," pp. 25–55 in D.J. Cosentino (ed.), *Sacred Arts of Haitian Vodou* (Los Angeles: UCLA Fowler Museum of Cultural History, 1995).
19. Leslie G. Desmangles, *The Faces of the Gods: Vodou and Roman Catholicism in Haiti* (Chapel Hill, NC: University of North Carolina Press, 1992), p. 27. Quoting Jean-Baptiste Labat, *Nouveaux voyages aux isles d'Amérique.* 8 vols. (Paris: Cabelier, 1722).
20. Desmangles, *The Faces of the Gods* (1992), p. 15.
21. Desmangles, *The Faces of the Gods* (1992), pp. 172–173.
22. For more on this, and exemplary images, see: Robert Farris Thompson, "From the Isle Beneath the Sea: Haiti's Africanizing Vodou Art," pp. 91–119 in Cosentino, *Sacred Arts of Haitian Vodou* (1995).

23. Quoted in Donald J. Cosentino, "Envoi: The Gedes and Bawon Samdi," pp. 399–415 in Cosentino, *Sacred Arts of Haitian Vodou* (1995).
24. Cosentino, *Sacred Arts of Haitian Vodou* (1995), p. 38.
25. Arthur C. Lehmann and James E. Myers (eds.), *Magic, Witchcraft, and Religion: An Anthropological Study of the Supernatural* (Palo Alto, CA: Mayfield Publishing Co., 1997), p. 321. See also Bryan Senn, *Drums of Terror: Voodoo in the Cinema* (Baltimore, MD: Midnight Marquee Press, Inc., 1998).
26. See Carolyn Morrow Long, *Spiritual Merchants: Religion, Magic, and Commerce* (Knoxville: University of Tennessee Press, 2001).
27. Adam M. McGee, "Haitian Vodou and Voodoo: Imagined Religion and Popular Culture," *Studies in Religion / Science Religeuses* 41.2 (2012): 231–256.
28. Pat Robertson, *The 700 Club: CBN News*, TBN, 13 Jan. 2010.
29. Karen McCarthy Brown, "Voodoo," pp. 321–326 in Lehmann and Myers, *Magic, Witchcraft, and Religion* (1997), p. 321.
30. Deut. 18:10–12; Lev. 19:31; Isa. 8:19–20; Eccl. 9:5–6.
31. John S. MBiti, *African Religions and Philosophy* (New York: Praeger, 1969), p. 83.
32. See Geoffrey Parrinder, *African Traditional Religion* (London: SPCK, 1962), pp. 134–141; MBiti, *African Religions and Philosophy* (1969), pp. 162–165.
33. Persephone Braham, "The Monstrous Caribbean," pp. 17–47 in Asa Simon Mittman and Peter J. Dendle (eds.), *The Ashgate Research Companion to Monsters and the Monstrous* (Burlington, VT: Ashgate, 2012).
34. Joan Dayan, *Haiti, History and the Gods* (Berkeley: University of California Press, 1998), pp. 37–38 as quoted in Mimi Sheller, *Consuming the Caribbean: From Arawaks to Zombies* (London: Routledge, 2003), p. 145.
35. Luise White, *Speaking with Vampires: Rumor and History in Colonial Africa* (Berkeley, CA: University of California Press, 2000).
36. Jean Comaroff and John Comaroff, "Alien-Nation: Zombies, Immigrants, and

Millennial Capitalism," *South Atlantic Quarterly* 101.4 (2002): 779–805. See also Peter Geschiere, *The Modernity of Witchcraft: Politics and the Occult in Postcolonial Africa* (Charlottesville: University of Virginia Press, 1997).

37. Hans W. Ackermann and Jeanin Gauthier, "The Ways and Nature of the Zombi," *The Journal of American Folklore* 104.414 (1991): 466–494, p. 468.

38. Isak Niehaus, "Witches and Zombies of the South African Lowveld: Discourse, Accusations and Subjective Reality," *Journal of the Royal Anthropological Institute* 11 (2005): 191–210, p. 192.

39. Louis P. Mars, "The Story of Zombi in Haiti," *Man* 45 (1945): 38–40, p. 38.

40. For a discussion of these differences, see Ackermann and Gauthier, "The Ways and Nature of the Zombi" (1991), p. 469.

41. Erika Bourguignon, "The Persistence of Folk Belief: Some Notes on Cannibalism and Zombies in Haiti," *The Journal of American Folklore* 72.283 (1959): 36–46.

42. The translation to zombies is recorded in N.V. Ralushai, M.G. Masingi, D.M.M. Madibi, et al., *Report of the Commission of Inquiry into Witchcraft Violence and Ritual Murders in the Northern Province of South Africa* (no publisher, 1996) as cited in Neuhaus, "Witches and Zombies of the South African Lowveld" (2005), p. 192.

43. Ackermann and Gauthier, "The Ways and Nature of the Zombi" (1991), p. 485.

44. For examples, see Ackermann and Gauthier, "The Ways and Nature of the Zombi" (1991), pp. 478–482.

45. Elizabeth McAlister, "Slaves, Cannibals, and Infected Hyper-Whites: The Race and Religion of Zombies," *Anthropological Quarterly* 85.2 (2012): 457–486.

46. Maximilien Laroche, "Mythe africain et mythe antillais: le personnage du zombi," *Canadian Journal of African Studies / Revue Canadienne des Études Africaines* 9.3 (1975): pp. 479–491.

47. Louis Mars, "The Story of Zombi in Haiti" (1945) describes the magicians as "Haitian medicine-men (*Nganga*)," p. 38.

48. William Seabrook, *The Magic Island* (New York: Literary Guild of America, 1929).

49. Zora Neale Hurston, *Tell My Horse: Voodoo and Life in Haiti and Jamaica* (Philadelphia: Lippincott, 1938).

50. Mars, "The Story of Zombi in Haiti" (1945).

51. Rita Keresztesi, "Hurston in Haiti: Neocolonialism and Zombification," pp. 31–41 in Christopher M. Moreman and Cory James Rushton (eds.), *Race, Oppression and the Zombie: Essays on Cross-Cultural Appropriations of the Caribbean Tradition* (Jefferson, NC: McFarland, 2011).

52. Alfred Métraux, *Voodoo in Haiti*, trans. Hugo Charteris (New York: Schocken Books, 1972), p. 281.

53. Seabrook, *The Magic Island* (1929), p. 100 as cited in Gary D. Rhodes, *White Zombie: Anatomy of a Horror Film* (Jefferson, NC: McFarland, 2001), p. 81.

54. Louis Mars, personal communication, as cited in Roland Littlewood and Chavannes Douyon, "Clinical Findings in Three Cases of Zombification," *Lancet* 350 (1997): 1094–1096.

55. Littlewood and Douyon, "Clinical Findings in Three Cases of Zombification," (1997); Mars, "The Story of Zombi in Haiti" (1945).

56. P.J. Guarnaccia and L.H. Rogler, "Research on Culture-Bound Syndromes: New Directions," *American Journal of Psychiatry* 156.9 (1999): 1322–1327. Though not about Vodou, or Haitian folklore, James Waldram's *Revenge of the Windigo: The Construction of the Mind and Mental Health of North American Aboriginal Peoples* (Toronto: University of Toronto Press, 2004) problematizes the notion of culture-bound syndromes in ways applicable to Haitian and African contexts.

57. Wade Davis, *The Serpent and the Rainbow* (New York: Simon & Schuster, 1985); Davis, *Passage of Darkness: The Ethnobiology of the Haitian Zombie* (Chapel Hill: University of North Carolina Press, 1988).

58. For an excellent overview of the criticisms of Davis, and the problems with taking them at face value as well, see David Inglis, "Putting the Undead to Work: Wade Davis, Haitian Vodou, and the Social Uses of the Zombie," pp. 42–59 in Christopher

M. Moreman and Cory James Rushton, Eds., *Race, Oppression and the Zombie: Essays on Cross-Cultural Appropriations of the Caribbean Tradition* (Jefferson, NC: McFarland, 2011).

59. Roland Littlewood, "Functionalists and Zombies: Sorcery as Spandrel and Social Rescue," *Anthropology & Medicine* 16.3 (2009): 241–252, p. 243.

60. Wade Davis, *Passage of Darkness* (1988), pp. 213–240.

61. Ackermann and Gauthier, "The Ways and Nature of the Zombi" (1991), p. 475.

62. Niehaus, "Witches and Zombies of the South African Lowveld" (2005).

63. Karen E. Richman, *Migration and Vodou* (Gainesville: University Press of Florida, 2005), pp. 163–178.

64. Jack Corzani, "West Indian Mythology and its Literary Illustrations," *Research in African Literatures* 25.2 (1994): 131–139, 134.

65. Cosentino, *Sacred Arts of Haitian Vodou* (1995), 26.

66. McAlister, "Slaves, Cannibals, and Infected Hyper-Whites" (2012).

67. W. Arens, *The Man-Eating Myth: Anthropology and Anthropophagy* (New York: Oxford University Press, 1979). See also Gannath Obeyesekere, *Cannibal Talk: The Man-Eating Myth and Human Sacrifice in the South Seas* (Berkeley: University of California Press, 2005). Contrast with Lewis Petrinovich, *The Cannibal Within* (New York: Aldine De Gruyter, 2000).

68. Sheller, *Consuming the Caribbean* (2003), p. 145.

69. See William F. Keegan, "Columbus was a Cannibal: Myth and the First Encounters," pp. 17–32 in Robert L. Paquette and Stanley L. Engerman (eds.), *The Lesser Antilles in the Age of European Expansion* (Gainesville: University Press of Florida, 1996); and Basil A. Reid, *Myths and Realities of Caribbean History* (Tuscaloosa: University of Alabama Press, 2009).

70. Mary A. Owen, "Voodoo," pp. 640–641 in James Hastings (ed.), *Encyclopedia of Religion and Ethics* (New York: Charles Scribner's Sons, 1908–1922), 640.

71. Rhodes, *White Zombie* (2001), p. 73.

72. Greene, *The Catholic Church in Haiti* (1993), p. 28 here cites Selden Rodman, *Haiti: The Black Republic* (New York: Devin-Adiar, 1984), p. 133.

73. Greene, *The Catholic Church in Haiti* (1993), p. 28.

74. Laënnec Hurbon, "American Fantasy and Haitian Vodou," pp. 181–197 in Cosentino, *Sacred Arts of Haitian Vodou* (1995), p. 186, quoting Roger Gaillard, *Les Blancs Débarquent*, 8 vols. (Port-au-Prince, 1973–1993), Vol. 7, pp. 79–80.

75. *Report of American High Commissioner, 1923*, p. 6 as cited in Arthur C. Millspaugh, *Haiti Under American Control, 1915–1930* (Boston, MA: World Peace Foundation, 1931), p. 137.

76. *Report of American High Commissioner, 1925*, p. 4 as cited in Millspaugh, *Haiti Under American Control* (1931), p. 137.

77. John H. Craige, *Cannibal Cousins* (New York: Minton, Balch, and Co., 1934). Quotation comes from the cover jacket.

78. J. Michael Dash, *Haiti and the United States: National Stereotypes and the Literary Imagination*, 2nd ed. (New York: St. Martin's Press, 1997), pp. 58 & 60.

79. See, for instance, Robert Lawless, *Haiti's Bad Press* (Rochester, VT: Schencken Books, 1992), and Amy E. Potter, "Voodoo, Zombies, and Mermaids: U.S. Newspaper Coverage of Haiti," *The Geographical Review* 99.2 (2009): 208–230.

80. See Frank Degoul, trans by Elisabeth M. Lore, "'We are the mirrors of your fears': Haitian Identity and Zombification," pp. 24–38 in Deborah Christie and Sarah Juliet Lauro (eds.), *Better off Dead: The Evolution of the Zombie as Post-Human* (New York: Fordham University Press, 2011).

81. Desmangles, *The Faces of the Gods* (1992), p. 195 n. 7. Citing Article 249.

82. Madelaine Hron, *Translating Pain: Immigrant Suffering in Literature and Culture* (Toronto, ON: University of Toronto Press, 2009), p. 142.

83. W.E.B. DuBois, *The Souls of Black Folk*, ed. by Brent Hayes Edwards (London: Oxford University Press, 2007).

84. Ransom, "Ce Zombi égaré est-il un Haïtien ou un Québécois?" (2009): 64–83.

85. Zina Saro-Wiwa, "No Going Back," pp. 17–26 in Pieter Hugo, *Nollywood* (Munich: Presetel, 2009).

86. Madelaine Drohan, "Gruesome Tales Show Nigeria's Desperate State," *Globe and Mail*, Toronto, ON, Sept. 25. 2000, p. A1. See also David McNally, *Monsters of the Market: Zombies, Vampires and Global Capitalism* (Leiden: Brill, 2011).

87. See both Richard Dyer, *White* (London: Routledge, 1997); and Dyer, *The Matter of Images*, 2nd ed. (London: Routledge, 2002); Cf. Outi Hakola, "Exotic Primitivism of Death in Classical Hollywood Living Dead Films," *Ilha do Desterro: A Journal of English Language, Literatures in English, and Cultural Studies* 62 (2012): 219–240.

88. Giorgio Agamben, *Homo Sacer: Sovereign Power and Bare Life*, trans. Daniel Heller-Roazen (Stanford, CA: Stanford University Press, 1998).

89. Michel Foucault, *The History of Sexuality*, Vol. 1, trans. Robert Hurley (New York: Pantheon Books, 1978).

90. Jon Stratton, "Zombie Trouble: Zombie Texts, Bare Life and Displaced People," *European Journal of Cultural Studies* 14.3 (2011): 265–281.

91. As quoted in Ransom, "Ce Zombi égaré est-il un Haïtien ou un Québécois?" (2009), p. 66.

92. On Romero, see: Paul R. Gagne, *The Zombies that ate Pittsburgh: The Films of George A. Romero* (New York: Dodd, Mead, and Co., 1987), p. 9; On Fulci, see John Martin, "Maestro of Maggot Mayhem: Zombie King, Lucio Fulci, Interviewed," pp. 129–134 in Allan Bryce (ed.), *Zombie: They Just Won't Stay Dead* (Liskeard, UK: Stray Cat, 1999).

93. Priscilla L. Walton, *Our Cannibals, Ourselves* (Urbana and Chicago, IL: University of Illinois Press, 2004).

94. Sarah Juliet Lauro and Karen Embry, "A Zombie Manifesto: The Nonhuman Condition in the Era of Advanced Capitalism," *boundary 2* 35.1 (2008): 85–108.

Chapter Two

1. Clyde Taylor, "Autopsy of Terror: A Conversation with Raoul Peck," *Transition* 69 (1996): 236–246, p. 244.

2. Gary D. Rhodes, *White Zombie: Anatomy of a Horror Film* (Jefferson, NC: McFarland, 2001), pp. 126–127.

3. Peter Dendle, *The Zombie Movie Encyclopedia, Vol. 2: 2000–2010* (Jefferson, NC: McFarland, 2012), p. 31.

4. All three suggested by Kim Newman, "Review of *The Last Man on Earth*," pp. 31–34 in Jay Slater (ed.), *Eaten Alive! Italian Cannibal and Zombie Movies* (London: Plexus, 2002).

5. Shawn McIntosh, "The Evolution of the Zombie: The Monster that Keeps Coming Back," pp. 1–17 in Shawn McIntosh and Marc Leverette (eds.), *Zombie Culture: Autopsies of the Living Dead* (Lanham, MD: Scarecrow, 2008).

6. Robin Wood, *Hollywood from Vietnam to Reagan ... and Beyond* (New York: Columbia University Press, 2003).

7. Roy Frumkes in his documentary, *Document of the Dead* (1989).

8. R.H.W. Dillard, "*Night of the Living Dead*: It's Not Like Just a Wind That's Passing Through," pp. 14–29 in Gregory A. Waller (ed.), *American Horrors: Essays on the Modern American Horror Film* (Chicago: University of Illinois Press, 1987).

9. Jay Slater, "Introduction: Cannibal/Zombie," pp. 12–21 in Jay Slater (ed.), *Eaten Alive! Italian Cannibal and Zombie Movies* (London: Plexus, 2002).

10. Sébastien Le Pajolec, "Zombies: de la marge au centre—La reception française des films de George Romero," pp. 155–181 in Jean-Baptiste Thoret (ed.), *Politique des zombies: L'Amérique selon George A. Romero* (Paris, France: Ellipses, 2007).

11. Jean-Baptiste Thoret, "Ils sont comme nous," pp. 5–13 in Thoret, *Politique des zombies* (2007).

12. John Hanners and Harry Kloman, "'The McDonaldization of America': An Interview with George A. Romero," *Film Criticism* 7.1 (1982): 69–81.

13. William Seabrook, *The Magic Island* (New York: Literary Guild of America, 1929).

14. Gary Rhodes gives a number of examples of where Seabrook's work clearly influenced the makers of *White Zombie*, but Seabrook's work is far from constituting literary tradition. See Rhodes, *White Zombie* (2001), pp. 30–34.

15. Kyle Bishop further argues that the cinematic experience brings the monster to life in a much more realistic fashion

than the cerebral imaginings allowed by a book, adding to the value and function of the zombie as uncanny. See: Kyle Bishop, "Raising the Dead: Unearthing the Non-literary Origins of Zombie Cinema," *Journal of Popular Film & Television* 33.4 (2006): 196–205.

16. Robin R. Means Coleman, *Horror Noire: Blacks in American Horror Films from the 1890s to Present* (London: Routledge, 2011), p. 51.

17. Jennifer Fay, "Dead Subjectivity: White Zombie, Black Baghdad," *CR: The New Centennial Review* 8.1 (2008): 81–101.

18. David J. Skal, *The Monster Show: A Cultural History of Horror* (London: W.W. Norton & Co., 1993), p. 169.

19. Chera Kee makes the case in "'They are not men ... they are dead bodies': From Cannibal to Zombie and Back Again," pp. 9–15 in Deborah Christie and Sarah Juliet Lauro (eds.), *Better Off Dead: The Evolution of the Zombie as Post-Human* (New York: Fordham University Press, 2011).

20. Fay struggles with the ambivalence throughout her piece, describing the zombie as at once both an admission and denial of the failures of American policy in Haiti, and suggests that while the film can be seen as a critique of American colonialism, it also ends in expunging any threat caused by it. Fay, "Dead Subjectivity," (2008).

21. Rhodes, *White Zombie* (2001), pp. 46–48.

22. Rhodes, *White Zombie* (2001), pp. 135–136.

23. Fay, "Dead Subjectivity," (2008).

24. Jamie Russell, *Book of the Dead: The Complete History of Zombie Cinema* (Surrey: FAB Press, 2005), p. 23.

25. The film paraphrases, likely from Legge's translation: James Legge, trans., *The Chinese Classics: The Life and Works of Mencius*, "The Works of Mencius," Bk. VII, Ch XLII, 1 (Philadelphia, PA: J.B. Lippincott and Co., 1875), p. 364.

26. Coleman, *Horror Noire* (2011), Chapter 3.

27. Russell, *Book of the Dead* (2005), 33–34.

28. Coleman, *Horror Noire* (2011), p. 67.

29. For examples, see: Wood, *Hollywood from Vietnam to Reagan* (2003); Peter Biskund, *Seeing is Believing: How Hollywood Taught Us to Stop Worrying and Love the Fifties* (London: Pluto, 1983); Andrew Tudor, *Monsters and Mad Scientists: A Cultural History of the Horror Movie* (Oxford: Blackwell, 1987).

30. Here, I agree with Juneko J. Robinson, "Immanent Attack: An Existential Take on the Invasion of the Body Snatchers Films," pp. 23–44 in Scott A. Lukas and John Marmysz (eds.), *Fear, Cultural Anxiety, and Transformation: Horror, Science Fiction, and Fantasy Films Remade* (Plymouth, UK: Lexington Books, 2009).

31. Barry Keith Grant, *Invasion of the Body Snatchers* (London: Palgrave MacMillan, 2010), p. 94.

32. Jack Finney, *The Body Snatchers* (Boston, MA: Gregg Press, 1976 [1955]), p. 152.

33. Deborah Christie, "A Dead New World: Richard Matheson and the Modern Zombie," pp. 67–80 in Bishop, Kyle William, *American Zombie Gothic: The Rise and Fall (and Rise) of the Walking Dead in Popular Culture* (Jefferson, NC: McFarland, 2010), p. 70.

34. For an overview of the most common interpretations of the film, see Grant, *Invasion of the Body Snatchers* (2010).

35. Lincoln Geraghty, "*Invasion of the Body Snatchers* (1956)," pp. 118–123 in John White and Sabine Haenni (eds.), *Fifty Key American Films* (London: Routledge, 2009).

36. Grant, *Invasion of the Body Snatchers* (2010), p. 75.

37. Finney, *The Body Snatchers* (1976 [1955]), p. 44.

38. It is worth noting that of the film adaptations made, though Hawks' is the first, John Carpenter's *The Thing* (1982) is much truer to the original text. Romero cites the Hawks film in Paul R. Gagne, *The Zombies That Ate Pittsburgh: The Films of George A. Romero* (New York: Dodd, Mead, and Co., 1987), p. 11.

39. Kendall R. Phillips, *Dark Directions: Romero, Craven, and the Modern Horror Film* (Carbondale: Southern Illinois University Press, 2012), p. 27.

40. Wood, *Hollywood from Vietnam to Reagan* (2003).

41. Mark Jancovich, *Rational Fears: American Horror in the 1950s* (Manchester, UK: Manchester University Press, 1996), p. 28.

42. For instance, Tim Kane, *The Changing Vampire of Film and Television* (Jefferson, NC: McFarland, 2006); Beth E. McDonald, *The Vampire as Numinous Experience: Spiritual Journeys with the Undead in British and American Literature* (Jefferson, NC: McFarland, 2004); William Patrick Day, *Vampire Legends in Contemporary American Culture* (Lexington: University of Kentucky Press, 2002); and Joan Gordon and Veronica Hollinger (eds.), *Blood Read: The Vampire as Metaphor in Contemporary Culture* (Philadelphia, PA: University of Pennsylvania Press, 1997) all make no reference to the seminal work whatsoever. *I Am Legend* earns a footnote in Bruce A. McClelland, *Slayers and their Vampires: A Cultural History of Killing the Dead* (Ann Arbor, MI: University of Michigan Press, 2006).

43. See also Gregory A. Waller. *The Living and the Undead; From Stoker's* Dracula *to Romero's* Dawn of the Dead (Urbana and Chicago: University of Illinois Press, 1986), p. 258.

44. James B. Twitchell, *Dreadful Pleasures: The Anatomy of Modern Horror* (New York: Oxford University Press, 1985), p. 106.

45. J. Gordon Melton, *The Vampire Book: The Encyclopedia of the Undead* (Detroit: Visible Ink Press, 1999), pp. 117–21.

46. McClelland, *Slayers and their Vampires* (2006), p. 127.

47. Richard Matheson, *I Am Legend* (New York: Tor Books, 1954), p. 21.

48. Matheson, *I Am Legend* (1954), pp. 135, 140.

49. Matheson, *I Am Legend* (1954), p. 112.

50. Matheson, *I Am Legend* (1954), p. 113.

51. Matheson, *I Am Legend* (1954), p. 115.

52. Mary Pharr, "Vampiric Appetite in *I Am Legend, 'Salem's Lot*, and *The Hunger*," pp. 93–103 in Leonard G. Heldreth and Mary Pharr, eds., *The Blood in the Life: Vampires in Literature* (Bowling Green, OH: Bowling Green State University Popular Press, 1999), p. 95.

53. Edward J. Gorman, "Ed Gorman Calling: We Talk to Richard Matheson." *Mystery*File: The Crime Fiction Research Journal.* (2006), online: http://www.mysteryfile.com/Matheson/Interview.html.

54. Jancovich, *Rational Fears* (1996) cites Max Weber, *The Protestant Ethic and the Spirit of Capitalism*, trans. by Stephen Kalberg (Los Angeles: Roxbury. 2002) for the use of this term.

55. Christopher Partridge, *The Re-Enchantment of the West*. 2 vols. (London: T & T Clark, 2004), vol. 1, p. 69.

56. Partridge, *The Re-Enchantment of the West*. (2004), vol. 1, pp. 69–70.

57. Robert S. Ellwood, *1950: Crossroads of American Religious Life* (Louisville, KY: Westminster John Knox Press, 2000).

58. After Jack Kerouac's *The Dharma Bums* (New York: Viking Press, 1958). See also Kerouac, *Wake Up: A Life of the Buddha* (New York: Viking, 2008).

59. Oswald Spengler, *The Decline of the West*, trans. Charles Francis Atkinson (New York: Alfred A. Knopf, 1926).

60. Matheson, *I Am Legend* (1954), 146–47.

61. Matheson, *I Am Legend* (1954), p. 26.

62. Matheson, *I Am Legend* (1954), p. 39.

63. Matheson, *I Am Legend* (1954), pp. 61–62.

64. Matheson, *I Am Legend* (1954), p. 140.

65. Matheson, *I Am Legend* (1954), p. 32.

66. Matheson, *I Am Legend* (1954), p. 165.

67. Gorman, "Ed Gorman Calling" (2006).

68. Matheson, *I Am Legend* (1954), 168.

69. Matheson, personal communication, telephone, 2009.

70. Paul Stuve, "Birth of a Writer: The Matheson/Peden Letters," pp. 30–46 in Stanley Wiater, Matthew R. Breadley, and Paul Stuve (eds.), *The Twilight and Other Zones: The Dark Worlds of Richard Matheson* (New York: Citadel Press, 2009), pp. 32–33.

71. William P. Simmons, "Reflections of a Storyteller: A Conversation with Richard Matheson," *Cemetery Dance* 49 (2004),

online: http://www.rodserling.com/wsimmons/Richard_Matheson.htm.

72. Richard Matheson, *What Dreams May Come* (New York: G.P. Putnam's Sons, 1978), p. 5.

73. William F. Nolan, "The Matheson Years: A Profile in Friendship," pp. 9–29 in Wiater, Bradley, and Stuve (eds.), *The Twilight and Other Zones: The Dark Worlds of Richard Matheson* (2009), p. 26.

74. Susan L. Schwartz, "I Dream, Therefore I Am: *What Dreams May Come*," *Journal of Religion and Film* 4.1 (2000), online: http://www.unomaha.edu/jrf/IDream.htm. para. [2].

75. Gorman, "Ed Gorman Calling," (2006).

76. See especially Carlos Castaneda, *The Teachings of Don Juan: A Yaqui Way of Knowledge* (Oakland: University of California Press, 1968).

77. Begin with James Redfield, *The Celestine Prophecy* (New York: Warner Books, 1993).

78. Richard Matheson, *The Path: A New Look at Reality* (New York: Tor Books, 1993).

79. Richard Matheson, *A Primer of Reality* (Springfield, PA: Edge Books, 2002).

80. Harold W. Percival, *Thinking and Destiny* (New York: The Word Foundation, 1946), p. 1.

81. Tom Weaver, *Return of the B Science Fiction and Horror Heroes: The Mutant Melding of Two Volumes of Classic Interviews*, Vol. 2 (Jefferson, NC: McFarland, 2000), p. 307.

82. Joseph P. Laycock points to other clear associations with Christ in his article, "Conversion by Infection: The Sociophobic of Cults in the Omega Man," *International Journal for the Study of New Religions* 1.2 (2010): 261–278.

83. Laycock, "Conversion by Infection" (2010), p. 262.

84. See also Christopher M. Moreman, "Review of *I Am Legend*. Dir. Francis Lawrence," *Journal of Religion and Film* 12.1 (2008), Online: http://www.unomaha.edu/jrf/vol12no1/reviews/ILegen.htm.

85. Gagne, *The Zombies That Ate Pittsburgh* (1987), p. 24.

86. Weaver, *Return of the "B" Science Fiction and Horror Heroes* (2000), p. 307.

87. One scholar detects a hint of racial tension underlying Matheson's text, pointing especially to the victory of Brown v Board of Education recognizing segregated schools as unconstitutional in 1954, the year of *I Am Legend*'s publication: Kathy Davis Patterson, "Echoes of Dracula: Racial Politics and the Failure of Segregated Spaces in Richard Matheson's *I Am Legend*," *Journal of Dracula Studies* 7 (2005): 19–28.

88. A good jumping-off point for further research can be found in Angela Ndalianis, "Why Comics Studies?" *Cinema Journal* 50.3 (2011): 113–117.

89. Digby Diehl, *Tales from the Crypt: The Official Archives* (New York: St. Martin's, 1996), 182.

90. Diehl, *Tales from the Crypt* (1996), p. 34.

91. Diehl, *Tales from the Crypt* (1996), p. 28.

92. Skal, *The Monster Show* (1993), p. 311.

93. Gerry Canavan, "'We Are the Walking Dead': Race, Time, and Survival in Zombie Narrative," *Extrapolation* 51.3 (2010): 431–453.

94. June Pulliam, "The Zombie," Vol. 2, pp. 723–753 in S.T. Joshi (ed.), *Icons of Horror and the Supernatural: An Encyclopedia of Our Worst Nightmares*, 2 Vols. (Westport, CT: Greenwood Press, 2007).

95. For more on the connection between EC Comics and the *Grand Guignol* Theatre, see Richard J. Hand and Michael Wilson, "Transatlantic Terror! French Horror Theater and American Pre-Code Comics," *Journal of Popular Culture* 45.2 (2012): 301–319.

96. Tony Williams, "An Interview with George and Christine Romero," *Quarterly Review of Film and Video* 18.4 (2001): 397–411.

97. Fredric Wertham, *Seduction of the Innocent* (New York: Rinehart & Co., 1954).

98. For more on this history, see Arnold T. Blumberg, "Four-Color Zombies: The Walking Dead in Comics History," pp. 36–52 in James Lowder (ed.), *Triumph of the Walking Dead: Robert Kirkman's Zombie Epic on Page and Screen* (Dallas, TX: BenBella, 2011).

99. For more on the history of comic

book censorship, see David Hadjou, *The Ten-Cent Plague: The Great Comic-Book Scare and How It Changed America* (New York: Farrar, Straus and Girouz, 2008).

100. Mark R. McDermott, "History of the Marvel Zombies and Colonel America among the Marvel Zombies," pp. 147–159 in Robert G. Weiner (ed.), *Captain America and the Struggle of the Superhero: Critical Essays* (Jefferson, NC: McFarland, 2009), p. 148.

101. For more on zombies in comics, see Antonio Domínguez Leiva, "Apocalypse Zombie: l'invasion des morts-vivants dans le roman graphique contemporain," *Frontières* 25.2 (2013): 93–108.

102. For more on this history, see Kevin Heffernan, *Ghouls, Gimmicks, and Gold: Horror Films and the American Movie Business, 1953–1968* (Durham, NC: Duke University Press, 2004).

103. For an interesting take on this film as a representation of unresolved Confederate grievances, see Anthony Szczesiul, "Re-Mapping Southern Hospitality: Discourse, Ethics, Politics," *European Journal of American Culture* 26.2 (2007): 127–141.

104. For instance: Le Pajolec, "Zombies," pp. 155–181 in Thoret, *Politique des zombies* (2007).

105. Philippe Rouyer, "Le gore des zombies," pp. 131–138 in Thoret, *Politique des zombies* (2007). See also Philippe Rouyer, *Le cinéma gore: une esthétique du sang* (Paris: Le cerf, 1997).

106. Slater, "Introduction" pp. 12–21 in Slater, *Eaten Alive!* (2002).

107. For instance: Thoret, "Ils sont comme nous," pp. 5–13 in Thoret, *Politique des zombies* (2007) & Newman, "Review of The Last Man on Earth," pp. 31–34 in Slater, *Eaten Alive!* (2002).

108. One paper that does take the connections seriously is Craig Fischer, "Meaninglessness: Cause and Desire in *The Birds*, *Shaun of the Dead*, and *The Walking Dead*," pp. 68–80 in Lowder, *Triumph of the Walking Dead* (2011).

109. Christopher M. Moreman, "On the Relationship Between Birds and Spirits of the Dead," *Society & Animals* 22.5 (2014): 481–502.

110. Camille Paglia, *The Birds* (London: BFI, 1998).

111. "The Birds," pp. 59–100 in Daphne Du Maurier, *Don't Look Now: Stories*, selected by Patrick McGrath (New York: NY Review of Books, 2008), pp. 59–60.

112. Gagne, *The Zombies That Ate Pittsburgh* (1987), p. 27.

113. Foreword by Robin Wood, p. xiii–xviii in Steven Jay Schneider (ed.), *Horror Film and Psychoanalysis: Freud's Worst Nightmare* (Cambridge, UK: Cambridge University Press, 2004). See also Wood, *Hollywood from Vietnam to Reagan* (2003), p. 103.

114. Sumiko Higashi, "*Night of the Living Dead*: A Horror Film about the Horrors of the Vietnam Era," pp. 175–188 in Linda Dittmar and Gene Michaud (eds.), *From Hanoi to Hollywood: The Vietnam War in American Film* (New Brunswick, NJ: Rutgers University Press, 1990); Karen Randell, "Lost Bodies/Lost Souls: *Night of the Living Dead* and *Deathdream* as Vietnam Narrative," pp. 67–76 in Stephanie Boluk and Wulie Lenz (eds.), *Generation Zombie: Essays on the Living Dead in Modern Culture* (Jefferson, NC: McFarland, 2011).

115. Coleman, *Horror Noire* (2011); Barbara S. Bruce, "Guess Who's Going to be Dinner: Sidney Poitier, Black Militancy, and the Ambivalence of Race in Romero's *Night of the Living Dead*," pp. 60–73 in Christopher M. Moreman and Cory James Rushton (eds.), *Race, Oppression and the Zombie: Essays on Cross-Cultural Appropriations of the Caribbean Tradition* (Jefferson, NC: McFarland, 2011).

116. Reynold Humphries, *The American Horror Film: An Introduction* (Edinburgh, UK: Edinburgh University Press, 2002), p. 114.

117. This seems to be the preferred vision of Romero himself as expressed in Jean-Baptiste Thoret, "Conversations avec George A. Romero," pp. 183–206 in Thoret, *Politique des zombies* (2007).

118. Bishop, "Raising the Dead," (2006): 196–205.

119. Kim Paffenroth, *Gospel of the Living Dead: George Romero's Visions of Hell on Earth* (Waco, TX: Baylor University Press, 2006); Peter Dendle, "The Zombie as Barometer of Cultural Anxiety," pp. 45–57 in Niall Scott (ed.), *Monsters and the*

Monstrous: Myths and Metaphors of Enduring Evil (New York: Rodopi, 2007).

120. Dillard, "*Night of the Living Dead,*" pp. 14–29 in Waller, *American Horrors* (1987).

121. Karl Marx, *Capital: Critique of Political Economy*, trans. Samuel Moore and Edward Aveling (London: Swan Sonnenschein, 1887), Vol. 1, p. 342. See also Mark Neocleous, "The Political Economy of the Dead: Marx's Vampires," *History of Political Thought* 24.3 (2003): 668–684.

122. Slavoj Zizek, *The Pervert's Guide to Ideology* (2012); Annalee Newitz includes robots, serial killers, and mad scientists alongside zombies as examples of "capitalist monsters," in her *Pretend We're Dead: Capitalist Monsters in American Pop Culture* (Durham, NC: Duke University Press, 2006).

123. Francis Gooding, "They Still Believe There's Respect in Dying: Wittgenstein, Tercier, Romero," *Film Quarterly* 49: 3 (Autumn, 2007): 13–30, 27.

124. For more on this, see Randell, "Lost Bodies/Lost Souls" pp. 67–76 in Boluk and Lenz, *Generation Zombie* (2011).

125. Russell, *Book of the Dead* (2005), pp. 71–75.

126. Stephen King, *Cell* (New York: Scribner, 2006).

127. For a definitive overview of the work of Lucio Fulci, see Stephen Thrower, *Beyond Terror: The Films of Lucio Fulci* (Guildford, UK: FAB, 1999).

128. Jay Slater, "Afterword," p. 236 in Slater, *Eaten Alive!* (2002).

129. John Martin, "Maestro of Maggot Mayhem: Zombie King, Lucio Fulci, Interviewed," pp. 129–134 in Allan Bryce (ed.), *Zombie: They Just Won't Stay Dead* (Liskeard, UK: Stray Cat, 1999).

130. Jay Slater, "Review of Zombie Flesh Eaters," pp. 93–99 in Slater, *Eaten Alive!* (2002).

131. Gary Anthony Surmacz, "Anatomy of a Horror Film" (A round-table with Russo, Hardman and Streiner), *Cinefantastique* 4.1 (1975): 14–27: p. 16.

132. John Russo, *Undead* (New York: Kensington, 2010), p. x. See also John Russo, *The Complete Night of the Living Dead Filmbook* (New York: Harmony Books, 1985), p. 118.

133. Thrower, *Beyond Terror* (1999), p. 23.

134. For more on the Church's influence on European zombies, see: Alan Jones, "Morti Viventi: Zombies Italian-Style," pp. 14–27 in Bryce, *Zombie* (1999). For a counter-point, see Nigel J. Burrell, "Beyond the Blind Dead," pp. 109–119 in Bryce, *Zombie* (1999); Brad O'Brien, "Vita, Amore, e Morte—and Lots of Gore: The Italian Zombie Film," pp. 55–70 in Shawn McIntosh and Marc Leverette (eds.), *Zombie Culture: Autopsies of the Living Dead* (Lanham, MD: Scarecrow, 2008).

135. Russell, *Book of the Dead* (2005), p. 88.

136. Cohen, *Monster Theory* (1996), p. 18.

137. Bruce G. Hallenbeck, *Comedy-Horror Films: A Chronological History, 1914–2008* (Jefferson, NC: McFarland, 2009), 141.

138. Caterina Fugazzola and Christopher M. Moreman, "Shugendō and *The Shining*: Liminal Space and Religious Experience in the Work of Stanley Kubrick," *Symposia* 6 (2014): 75–93. See also Larry W. Caldwell and Samuel J. Umland, "'Come and Play with Us': The Play Metaphor in Kubrick's *Shining*," *Literature Film Quarterly* 14.2 (1986): 106–111.

139. Wood, *Hollywood from Vietnam to Reagan* (2003), p. 84.

140. Maurice Yacowar, "The Comedy of Cronenberg," pp. 80–86 in Piers Handling (ed.), *The Shape of Rage: The Films of David Cronenberg* (Toronto, ON: General Publishing, 1983), p. 85.

141. https://www.youtube.com/watch?v=3ghblXfASWs.

142. Linda Badley, "Zombie Splatter Comedy from *Dawn* to *Shaun*: Cannibal Carnivalesque," pp. 35–53 in McIntosh and Leverette, *Zombie Culture* (2008); Bishop, *American Zombie Gothic* (2010), p. 187.

143. Mikhail Bakhtin, *Rabelais and his World*, p. 50, as cited in Sue Vice, *Introducing Bakhtin* (Manchester, UK: Manchester University Press, 1997), p. 175.

144. Isabel Cristina Pinedo, "Postmodern Elements of the Contemporary Horror Film," pp. 85–117 in Stephen Prince (ed.), *The Horror Film* (New York: Rutgers University Press, 2004).

145. Masahiro Mori, "The Uncanny Valley," trans. Karl F. MacDorman and Norri Kageki, *IEEE Robotics & Automation Magazine* (2012): 98–100. Trans. of: Mori, "The uncanny valley," *Energy* 7.4, pp. 33–35, 1970 (in Japanese).

146. Dave Beisecker, "A Stagger-on Role to die for," pp. 67–79 in Wayne Yuen (ed.), The Walking Dead *and Philosophy: Zombie Apocalypse Now* (Chicago: Open Court, 2012).

147. All of which are also recognized by the film's writer, Alex Garland, who also acknowledges inspiration from David Cronenberg, Stephen King, J.G. Ballard, and the *Resident Evil* franchise. See Alex Garland, "Introduction," pp. vii–viii in his *28 Days Later* (London: Faber and Faber, 2002).

148. Kurt Gray, T. Anne Knickman, and Daniel M. Wegner, "More Dead Than Dead: Perceptions of Persons in the Persistent Vegetative State," *Cognition* 121.2 (2011): 275–280.

149. Russo, *The Complete Night of the Living Dead Filmbook* (1985), p. 118.

150. http://www.cdc.gov/phpr/zombies.htm.

151. Jason Thompson, "House of 1000 Manga: 10 Great Zombie Manga," *Anime News Network*, Jan 9th, 2014. Online: http://www.animenewsnetwork.com/house-of-1000-manga/2014-01-09.

Chapter Three

1. For more on this concept, start with David Scruton, *Sociophobics: The Anthropology of Fear* (Boulder, CO: Westview Press, 1985). For its application to the post–Romero zombie, see Kevin J. Wetmore, Jr., *Back from the Dead: Remakes of the Romero Zombie Films as Markers of Their Times* (Jefferson, NC: McFarland, 2011).

2. He says as much in the following interviews: Dan Yakir, "Morning Becomes Romero: George Romero Interviewed by Dan Yakir," *Film Comment* 15.3 (May/June 1979): 60–65.

3. Paul R. Gagne, *The Zombies That Ate Pittsburgh: The Films of George A. Romero* (New York: Dodd, Mead, and Co., 1987), p. 38.

4. Giulia D'Agnolo-Vallan, "Let Them Eat Flesh," *Film Comment* 41: 4 (July/Aug., 2005): 23–24, p. 24.

5. Tony Williams (ed.), *George A. Romero: Interviews* (Jackson: University Press of Mississippi, 2011), p. 173.

6. Jay Slater, "Review of Zombie Flesh Eaters," pp. 93–99 in Jay Slater (ed.), *Eaten Alive! Italian Cannibal and Zombie Movies* (London: Plexus, 2002), p. 99.

7. Gary Anthony Surmacz, "Anatomy of a Horror Film" (a round-table with Russo, Hardman and Streiner), *Cinefantastique* 4.1 (1975): 14–27: p. 16.

8. Juneko J. Robinson, "Immanent Attack: An Existential Take on *The Invasion of the Body Snatchers* Films," pp. 23–44 in Scott A. Lukas and John Marmysz (eds.), *Fear, Cultural Anxiety, and Transformation: Horror, Science Fiction, and Fantasy Films Remade* (Plymouth, UK: Lexington Books, 2009).

9. Russo seems to recognize as much in his preface to John Russo, *Undead* (New York: Kensington, 2010), p. x.

10. The crew on *Night of the Living Dead* referred to the centrally-gory scene of Tom and Judy's being devoured by the dead as "The Last Supper," Ben Hervey, *BFI Film Classics: Night of the Living Dead* (Basingstoke, UK: Palgrave MacMillan, 2008), p. 88. For denominational statistics for Pennsylvania, see: "Religious Landscape Study," Pew Research Center, Online: http://www.pewforum.org/religious-landscape-study/state/pennsylvania/. Accessed Oct. 20, 2016.

11. Gagne, *The Zombies that ate Pittsburgh* (1987), p. 9.

12. Alan Jones, "Morti Viventi: Zombies Italian-Style," pp. 14–27 & Nigel J. Burrell, "Beyond the Blind Dead," pp. 109–119 in Allan Bryce (ed.), *Zombie: They Just Won't Stay Dead* (Liskeard, UK: Stray Cat, 1999).

13. Another possible reason for Kane's exclusion of the film is that it does not conform to his thesis for a particular chronology of vampire fiction. See Tim Kane, *The Changing Vampire of Film and Television* (Jefferson, NC: McFarland, 2006).

14. David Pirie, *The Vampire Cinema* (New York: Crescent Books, 1977), p. 141–142.

15. The contrast is drawn out more in

Lloyd Worley, "Impaling, Dracula, and the Bible," pp. 168–180 in George Aichele and Tina Pippin (eds.), *The Monstrous and the Unspeakable: The Bible as Fantastic Literature* (Sheffield, UK: Sheffield Academic Press, 1997).

16. For the record, John Russo claims this particular innovation as his own contribution to the genre: Russo, *Undead* (2010), p. ix.

17. See Andrew Louth, "The Body in Western Catholic Christianity," pp. 111–130 in Sarah Coakley (ed.), *Religion and the Body* (Cambridge, UK: Cambridge University Press, 1997), pp. 126–127.

18. Kim Paffenroth, *Gospel of the Living Dead: George Romero's Visions of Hell on Earth* (Waco, TX: Baylor University Press, 2006).

19. Edward J. Ingebretsen, S.J., *Maps of Heaven, Maps of Hell: Religious Terror as Memory from the Puritans to Stephen King* (Armonk, NY: M.E. Sharpe, 1996), p. ix.

20. Kim Paffenroth, "'For Love is Strong as Death': Redeeming Values in The Walking Dead," pp. 218–230 in James Lowder (ed.), *Triumph of the Walking Dead: Robert Kirkman's Zombie Epic on Page and Screen* (Dallas, TX: BenBella, 2011) : p. 218.

21. Paffenroth, *Gospel of the Living Dead* (2006), p. 34.

22. Kipp Davis, "Zombies in America and at Qumran: AMC's The Walking Dead, the Dead Sea Scrolls, and Apocalyptic Redux," *Journal of Religion and Popular Culture* 27.2 (2015): 148–163, p. 152.

23. Davis, "Zombies in America and at Qumran" (2015), p. 149.

24. Timothy K. Beal, *Religion and Its Monsters* (London: Routledge, 2002), pp. 54–55.

25. Douglas E. Cowan, *Sacred Terror: Religion and Horror on the Silver Screen* (Waco, TX: Baylor University Press, 2008), p. 90.

26. Michael Gilmour, "The Living Word Among the Living Dead: Hunting for Zombies in the Pages of the Bible," pp. 87–99 in Christopher M. Moreman and Cory James Rushton (eds.), *Zombies are Us: Essays on the Humanity of the Walking Dead* (Jefferson, NC: McFarland, 2011): pp. 94–96.

27. Paffenroth, *Gospel of the Living Dead* (2006), p. 70.

28. Hannah Arendt, *The Origins of Totalitarianism* (Oxford: Benediction Classics, 2009 [1958]), p. 447.

29. For a detailed criticism of the co-option of the Holocaust to Christian ideologies, see Bernhard H. Rosenberg and Chaim Z. Rozwaski, *Contemplating the Holocaust* (Jerusalem: Jason Aronson, 1999), Chapt. 2.

30. "Address by the Holy Father—Visit to the Auschwitz Camp," *Libreria Editrice Vaticana* (May 28, 2006), Online: http://w2.vatican.va/content/benedict-xvi/en/speeches/2006/may/documents/hf_ben-xvi_spe_20060528_auschwitz-birkenau.html.

31. Davis, "Zombies in America and at Qumran" (2015).

32. Kim Paffenroth, "Apocalyptic Images and Prophetic Function in Zombie Films," pp. 145–164 in Kim Paffenroth and John W Morehead (eds.), *The Undead and Theology* (Eugene, OR: Pickwick, 2012): p. 145. Cf. Charles P. Mitchell, *A Guide to Apocalyptic Cinema* (London: Greenwood Press, 2001), p. 30.

33. Zech. 14: 12–13.

34. David Pagano, "The Space of Apocalypse in Zombie Cinema," pp. 71–86 in Shawn McIntosh and Marc Leverette (eds.), *Zombie Culture: Autopsies of the Living Dead* (Lanham, MD: Scarecrow, 2008)., p. 74.

35. Cf. Judith Lee, "Sacred Horror: Faith and Fantasy in the Revelation of John," pp. 220–239 in George Aichele and Tina Pippin (eds.), *The Monstrous and the Unspeakable: The Bible as Fantastic Literature* (Sheffield, UK: Sheffield Academic Press, 1997).

36. Pagano, "The Space of Apocalypse in Zombie Cinema," in McIntosh and Leverette, *Zombie Culture* (2008), p. 75.

37. Pagano, "The Space of Apocalypse in Zombie Cinema," in McIntosh and Leverette, *Zombie Culture* (2008), p. 85.

38. Though outdated, the following offers decent coverage of the franchise as of 2004: Richard J. Hand, "Proliferating Horror: Survival Horror and the *Resident Evil* Franchise," pp. 117–134 in Steffen Hantke (ed.), *Horror Film: Creating and Marketing Fear* (Jackson: University Press of Mississippi, 2004). See also Scott A. Lukas, "Hor-

ror Video Game Remakes and the Question of Medium: Remaking *Doom*, *Silent Hill*, and *Resident Evil*," pp. 221–242 in Scott A. Lukas and John Marmysz (eds.), *Fear, Cultural Anxiety, and Transformation: Horror, Science Fiction, and Fantasy Films Remade* (Plymouth, UK: Lexington Books, 2009).

39. Conrad E. Ostwalt, "Hollywood and Armageddon: Apocalyptic Themes in Recent Cinematic Presentation," pp. 55–63 in Joel W. Martin and Conrad E. Ostwalt jr. (eds.), *Screening the Sacred* (Oxford: Westview Press, 1995): p. 62. Cf. Conrad Ostwalt, "Apocalyptic," pp. 368–383 in John Lyden (ed.), *The Routledge Companion to Religion and Film* (London: Routledge, 2009).

40. Carole Lépinay, "À l'ouest d'Éden," pp. 101–119 in Jean-Baptiste Thoret (ed.), *Politique des zombies: L'Amérique selon George A. Romero* (Paris, France: Ellipses, 2007).

41. Paffenroth, *Gospel of the Living Dead* (2006), pp. 21–22.

42. Leah A. Murray, "When They Aren't Eating Us, They Bring Us Together: Zombies and the American Social Contract," pp. 211–220 in Richard Greene and K. Silem Mohammad (eds.), *The Undead and Philosophy* (Chicago: Open Court, 2006).

43. Paffenroth, *Gospel of the Living Dead* (2006), p. 40.

44. René Girard, *Violence and the Sacred*, trans. Patrick Gregory (Baltimore, MD: Johns Hopkins University Press, 1972), pp. 254–255.

45. Paffenroth, *Gospel of the Living Dead* (2006), p. 41–43.

46. Robin Wood, "Fresh Meat: *Diary of the Dead* May Be the Summation of George A. Romero's Zombie Cycle (at Least Until the Next Installment)," *Film Comment* 44: 1 (Jan./Feb., 2008): pp. 28–31, p. 29.

47. Gregory A. Waller, "The Living and the Undead; From Stoker's *Dracula* to Romero's *Dawn of the Dead*" (Urbana and Chicago, IL: University of Illinois Press, 1986), p. 283.

48. Paffenroth, *Gospel of the Living Dead* (2006), p. 22.

49. Paffenroth, "'For Love is Strong as Death,'" in Lowder, *Triumph of the Walking Dead* (2011): p. 226.

50. Ashley John Moyse, "When All Is Lost, Gather 'Round: Solidarity as Hope Resisting Despair in *The Walking Dead*," pp. 124–144 in Paffenroth and Morehead, *The Undead and Theology* (2012): p. 137.

51. Jean-Baptiste Thoret, "Conversations avec George A. Romero," pp. 183–206 in Thoret, *Politique des zombies* (2007): p. 197.

52. Williams, *George A. Romero* (2011), p. 173.

53. Christopher M. Moreman, "Dharma of the Living Dead: A Meditation on the Meaning of the Hollywood Zombie," *Studies in Religion/Sciences Religieuses* 39.2 (2010): 263–281; Moreman, "A Modern Meditation on Death: Identifying Buddhist Teachings in George A. Romero's *Night of the Living Dead*," *Contemporary Buddhism* 9.2 (2008): 151–165.

54. Seth M. Walker, "'Whatever it is, we all carry it': Tanhā and AMC's *The Walking Dead*," *Nomos Journal* (2012), Online: http://nomosjournal.org/2012/10/whatever-it-is-we-all-carry-it/. Accessed Nov. 8, 2013.

55. Paffenroth, *Gospel of the Living Dead* (2006), p. 105.

56. François Angelier, "À leurs corps defendant..." pp. 15–23 in Thoret, *Politique des zombies* (2007).

57. Rom. 6:23.

58. For example, see Mark Kermode, "Drenched in the Blood of Christ," *The Guardian* (Feb. 29, 2004), online: https://www.theguardian.com/film/2004/feb/29/melgibson.markkermode. Accessed Sept. 9, 2017.

59. Fulci discusses the influence of his own spiritual doubts as a Catholic on his interest in zombie fiction here: John Martin, "Maestro of Maggot Mayhem: Zombie King, Lucio Fulci, Interviewed," pp. 129–134 in Allan Bryce (ed.), *Zombie: They Just Won't Stay Dead* (Liskeard, UK: Stray Cat, 1999).

60. W. Scott Poole, *Monsters in America: Our Historical Obsession with the Hideous and the Haunting* (Waco, TX: Baylor University Press, 2011), pp. 204–206.

61. Plato, *The Dialogues of Plato*, trans. B. Jowett, 5 vols. (Oxford: Clarenden Press, 1892), Vol. 2, p. 222.

62. John Gardner and John Maier, *Gilgamesh* (New York: Vintage, 1985).
63. Epicurus, *Letter to Menoeceus*, trans. Robert Drew Hicks, *The Internet Classics Archive*, Online: http://classics.mit.edu/Epicurus/menoec.html.
64. Seneca, *On the Shortness of Life*, trans. John W. Basore (London: William Heinemann, 1932), par. 2.
65. Al-Ghazali, *The Remembrance of Death and the Afterlife*, trans. T.J. Winter (Cambridge, UK: The Islamic Texts Society, 1989), p 37.
66. Claudine Michel and Patrick Bellegarde-Smith, "*Koko Na Pa Pwèl: Marasa* Reflection on Gede," pp. 13–16 in Donald J. Cosentino (ed.), *In Extremis: Death and Life in 21st-Century Haitian Art* (Los Angeles: Fowler Museum at UCLA, 2012), p. 15.
67. For more on this, see Patrick A. Polk, "Remember You Must Die! Gede Banners, Memento Mori, and the Fine Art of Facing Death," pp. 115–141 and Katherine Smith, "Genealogies of Gede," pp. 85–99 in Cosentino, *In Extremis* (2012).
68. 1 Cor. 7: 9.
69. See St. Augustine, *The Confessions of St. Augustine*, trans. John K. Ryan (New York: Image Books, 1960).
70. For the detailed argument, see Beverley Clack, *Sex and Death: A Reappraisal of Human Mortality* (Cambridge, UK: Polity Press, 2002).
71. Slavoj Zizek marks another pivot in this connection between Christian theology, Buddhism, and Marxism: Ola Sigurdson, "Slavoj Zizek, the Death Drive, and Zombies: A Theological Account," *Modern Theology* 29.3 (2013): 361–380.
72. Piero Camporesi, *The Incorruptible Flesh: Bodily Mutation and Mortification in Religion and Folklore*, trans. Tania Croft-Murray (Cambridge, UK: Cambridge University Press, 1988), p. 25.
73. Camporesi, *The Incorruptible Flesh* (1988), p. 45, quoting from Johannes Climacus, *Sermoni di S. Giovanni Climaco* (Venezia, 1570), 19.
74. Camporesi, *The Incorruptible Flesh* (1988), p. 78, quoting St. Peter Damian, *Institutio monialis*, in *Opera omnia* (Bassano, 1783).
75. Camporesi, *The Incorruptible Flesh* (1988), p. 56.
76. Camporesi, *The Incorruptible Flesh* (1988), 43–44.
77. Camporesi, *The Incorruptible Flesh* (1988), p. 106.
78. Camporesi, *The Incorruptible Flesh* (1988), p. 78, quoting St. Bernard, *Meditationes*.
79. Ariel Glucklich, *Sacred Pain: Hurting the Body for the Sake of the Soul* (London: Oxford University Press, 2001), p. 27.
80. Camporesi, *The Incorruptible Flesh* (1988), p. 154, quoting St Anselm, *Meditationes*.
81. For more on the structure and purpose of *memento mori* literature, see Gerhild Scholz Williams, *The Vision of Death: A Study of the "Memento Mori" Expressions in Some Latin, German, and French Didactic Texts of the 11th and 12th Centuries* (Göppingen, DE: Verlag Alfred Kümmerle, 1976).
82. Williams, *The Vision of Death* (1976), pp. 53–54.
83. Glucklich, *Sacred Pain* (2001), p. 27.
84. For examples of these and other visual representations of death, see Enrico De Pascale, *Death and Resurrection in Art*, translated by Anthony Shugaar (Los Angeles, CA: J. Paul Getty Museum, 2007).
85. For more on this, and for some great illustrations, see Monique Kornell, "The Eternal Cadaver: Anatomy and Its Representation," pp. 209–226 in Mitchell, Margaret (ed.), *Remember Me: Constructing Immortality* (London: Routledge, 2007).
86. Kornell, "The Eternal Cadaver: Anatomy and Its Representation," in Mitchell, *Remember Me: Constructing Immortality—Beliefs on Immortality, Life, and Death* (2007), p. 223.
87. Jeremy Bentham, *Auto-Icon and Related Writings*, ed. James E. Crimmins (Bristol, UK: Thoemmes Press, 2002 [1842?]).
88. UCL Bentham Project, Online: http://www.ucl.ac.uk/Bentham-Project/who/autoicon/Virtual_Auto_Icon.
89. Audrey Linkman, *Photography and Death* (Islington, UK: Reaktion Books, 2011).
90. Roland Barthes, *Camera Lucida:*

Reflections on Photography, trans. Richard Howard (New York: Farrar, Strauss and Giroux, 1981), p. 85.

91. Barthes, *Camera Lucida* (1981), p. 79. See also Halla Beloff, "Immortality Work: Photographs as *Memento Mori*," pp. 179–192 in Mitchell, *Remember Me* (2007).

92. An interesting fact is that the three-person nuclear-family photo appears often throughout the series: Rick's original photo is of this type and makes a number of appearances including a copy's being discovered by strangers in a self-storage unit (Webisode 2: Cold Storage, E2, "Keys to the Kingdom"), as is the one Carl later retrieves from the café after his mother is killed, also occurring in the return appearance of Morgan to the series (S3E12, "Clear"); later, the Governor also gazes at just such a photo when he reminisces about his own daughter (S3E3, "Walk with Me," and S4E6, "Live Bait"), and then he finds yet another version in the hands of a survivalist who shot himself in the head (S4E7, "Dead Weight").

93. Beau, "Review of *Night of the Living Dead*," *Variety* Wed., Oct 16, 1968, pp. 6–7.

94. Martin, "Maestro of Maggot Mayhem," in Bryce, *Zombie* (1999), p. 131.

95. Michael Mechanic, "The Brains of the Operation: Makeup Master Greg Nicotero Knows How to Freak You Out," *Mother Jones* (March/April 2014): 53–54; David Roche cites Zack Snyder's repeated emphasis on the need for realism in his, "'That's real! That's what you want!': Producing Fear in George A. Romero's *Dawn of the Dead* (1978) vs. Zack Snyder's Remake (2004)," *Horror Studies* 2.1 (2011): 75–87.

96. Russell, *Book of the Dead* (2005), p. 70.

97. Julia Kristeva, *Powers of Horror: An Essay on Abjection* (New York: Columbia University Press, 1982).

98. Laura Kremmel, "Rest in Pieces: Violence in Mourning the (Un)Dead," pp. 80–94 in Dawn Keetley (ed.), *"We're All Infected": Essays on AMC's* The Walking Dead *and the Fate of the Human* (Jefferson, NC: McFarland, 2014), p. 84.

99. Kristeva, *Powers of Horror* (1982), p. 3.

100. Hibbs, interestingly, is also moved to invoke Dante as he sees the corpses of Body Worlds reflected in the *Inferno*. Thomas S. Hibbs, "Dead Body Porn," *The New Atlantis* 15 (Winter 2007): 128–131.

101. Kyle William Bishop, *American Zombie Gothic: The Rise and Fall (and Rise) of the Walking Dead in Popular Culture* (Jefferson, NC: McFarland, 2010), pp. 164–166.

102. Ian Conrich, "An Aesthetic Sense: Cronenberg and Neo-Horror Film Culture," pp. 35–49 in Michael Grant (ed.), *The Modern Fantastic: The Films of David Cronenberg* (Westport, CT: Praeger, 2000), p. 36.

103. Gagne, *The Zombies That Ate Pittsburgh* (1987), p. 21.

104. William S. Larkin, "*Res Corporealis*: Persons, Bodies, and Zombies," pp. 15–26 in Greene and Mohammad, *The Undead and Philosophy* (2006); and William Larkin, "Persons, Animals and Bodies," *Southwest Philosophical Review* 20: 2 (2004).

105. Rodley, *Cronenberg on Cronenberg* (1992), p. 58.

106. Noël Carroll, *The Philosophy of Horror or Paradoxes of the Heart* (London: Routledge, 1990), pp. 39–40.

107. Rodley, *Cronenberg on Cronenberg* (1992), p. 125.

108. On this point, see Beard, *The Artist as Monster* (2006), p. 218.

109. Rodley, *Cronenberg on Cronenberg* (1992), p. 4.

110. Adam Lowenstein, *Shocking Representation: Historical Trauma, National Cinema, and the Modern Horror Film* (New York: Columbia University Press, 2005), pp. 159–164.

111. Rodley, *Cronenberg on Cronenberg* (1992), p. 48.

112. Mikita Brottman, "Mondo Horror: Carnivalizing the Taboo," pp. 167–188 in Stephen Prince (ed.), *The Horror Film* (New York: Rutgers University Press, 2004).

113. Conrich, "An Aesthetic Sense," in Grant, *The Modern Fantastic* (2000).

114. Steve Jones, "*Porn of the Dead*: Necrophilia, Feminism, and Gendering the Undead," in Christopher M. Moreman and Cory James Rushton (eds.), *Zombies Are Us: Essays on the Humanity of the*

Walking Dead (Jefferson, NC: McFarland, 2011), p. 40.

115. McGlotten, Shaka, and Sarah Vangundy, "Zombie Porn 1.0: Or, Some Queer Things Zombie Sex Can Teach Us," *Qui Parle: Critical Humanities and Social Sciences* 21.2 (2013): 101–125, p. 115.

116. Rodley, *Cronenberg on Cronenberg* (1992), p. 43.

117. Rodley, *Cronenberg on Cronenberg* (1992), p. 20.

118. Rodley, *Cronenberg on Cronenberg* (1992), p. 19.

119. Dr. Martyn Steenbeck (presumably Cronenberg himself), "Foreword," Rodley, *Cronenberg on Cronenberg* (1992), p. xii.

120. William Beard, "The Visceral Mind: The Major Films of David Cronenberg," pp. 1–79 in Handling, *The Shape of Rage* (1983).

121. Anne Billson, "Cronenberg on Cronenberg: A Career in Stereo," *Monthly Film Bulletin* 56.660 (1989): 5.

122. Kristeva, *Powers of Horror* (1982), p. 4.

123. Sébastien Le Pajolec, "Zombies: de la marge au centre—La reception française des films de George Romero," pp. 155–181 in Thoret, *Politique des zombies* (2007), p. 158. Cf. similar observations in Isabel Cristina Pinedo, "Postmodern Elements of the Contemporary Horror Film," pp. 85–117 in Prince, *The Horror Film* (2004), p. 112.

124. Sue Vice, *Introducing Bakhtin* (Manchester, UK: Manchester University Press, 1997), p. 175, quoting from Bakhtin's *Rabelais and His World*, p. 50.

125. Vice, *Introducing Bakhtin* (1997), p. 174, quoting from Bakhtin's *Rabelais and His World*, p. 322.

126. http://www.cc.com/video-clips/5xsjqu/the-daily-show-with-jon-stewart-louis-c-k-.

127. Philippe Aries, *The Hour of Our Death*, 2nd ed., trans. Helen Weaver (New York: Vintage Books, 2008), p. 614.

128. Cf. Peter Dendle, "The Zombie as Barometer of Cultural Anxiety," pp. 45–57 in Niall Scott, ed., *Monsters and the Monstrous: Myths and Metaphors of Enduring Evil* (New York: Rodopi, 2007), p. 52.

129. Albert Camus, *The Myth of Sisyphus*, Trans. Justin O'Brien (New York: Knopf, 1958).

130. Rachel Robison-Greene, "Better Off Undead," pp. 119–128 in Wayne Yuen (ed.), *The Walking Dead and Philosophy: Zombie Apocalypse Now* (Chicago: Open Court, 2012), p. 122.

131. Gregory A. Staley, *Seneca and the Idea of Tragedy* (New York: Oxford University Press, 2010), p. 113.

132. John A. Marmysz makes the distinction in his "From *Night* to *Day*: Nihilism and the Walking Dead," *Film & Philosophy* 3 (1996): 138–144, but he fails to apply the concept adequately as he ends in valorizing the failed struggle against passive nihilism in the absence of any true active nihilism.

133. For further discussion, see John A. Marmysz, "From *Night* to *Day*: Nihilism and the Walking Dead," *Film & Philosophy* 3 (1996): 138–144.

134. Bruce G. Hallenbeck, *Comedy-Horror Films: A Chronological History, 1914–2008* (Jefferson, NC: McFarland, 2009), p. 183.

135. Douglas Keesey, "Intertwinings of Death and Desire in Michele Soavi's *Dellamorte Dellamore*," *Horror Studies* 2.1 (2011): 105–114, p. 112.

136. *Fangoria*, number 149, January 1996, pp. 54–5, quoted by Donato Totaro, "Review of *Dellamorte Dellamore*," pp. 231–235 in Slater, *Eaten Alive!* (2002), p. 231.

137. Slavoj Zizek, *The Plague of Fantasies* (London: Verso, 1997), pp. 3–4.

138. Rodley, *Cronenberg on Cronenberg* (1992), p. 80.

139. He says as much in Rodley, *Cronenberg on Cronenberg* (1992), 82.

140. Pete Boss, "Vile Bodies and Bad Medicine," *Screen: The Journal of the Society for Education in Film and Television* 27.1 (1986): 14–25, p. 18.

141. Noël Carroll, *The Philosophy of Horror or Paradoxes of the Heart* (London: Routledge, 1990), p. 28.

142. Carroll, *The Philosophy of Horror* (1990), pp. 211–213.

143. Robert Kaster, *Emotion, Restraint, and Community in Ancient Rome* (Oxford: Oxford University Press, 2005), p. 111.

144. A fascinating irony exists in medical history as the practice of corpse medicine, and the ingestion of mummy parts for medicinal purposes was hugely popu-

lar just as colonialists were denigrating purported savages for their cannibalism. See Richard Sugg, *Mummies, Cannibals and Vampires: The History of Corpse Medicine from the Renaissance to the Victorians* (London: Routledge, 2011).

145. Aimee Bender, "Among Us," pp. 257–262 in Christopher Golden (ed.), *The New Dead: A Zombie Anthology* (New York: St. Martin's Press, 2010).

146. See Sigmund Freud, *Totem and Taboo*, trans. James Strachey (London: Routledge & Paul, 1961); Cf. Bruno Bettelheim, *The Uses of Enchantment: The Meaning and Importance of Fairy Tales* (New York: Knopf, 1976), p. 196.

147. W. Scott Poole, *Monsters in America: Our Historical Obsession with the Hideous and the Haunting* (Waco, TX: Baylor University Press, 2011), p. 206.

148. Especially, Paul Rozin, J. Haidt, and C.R. McCauley, "Disgust," pp. 757–776 in Michael Lewis and Jeannette M. Haviland-Jones (eds.), *Handbook of Emotions*, 3rd edition (New York: Guilford, 2008).

149. Cf. Dawn Keetley, "Zombie Evolution: Stephen King's *Cell*, George Romero's *Diary of the Dead*, and the Future of the Human," *Americana: The Journal of American Popular Culture* 11.2 (Fall 2012): Online: http://www.americanpopularculture.com/journal/articles/fall_2012/keetley.htm.

150. William Ian Miller, *The Anatomy of Disgust* (Cambridge: Harvard University Press, 1997), p. 15.

151. Miller, *The Anatomy of Disgust* (1997), p. 27.

152. Rebecca Totaro, "Review of Cooke, Jennifer, *Legacies of Plague in Literature, Theory and Film*," *Social History of Medicine* 23.1 (2010): 208–209.

153. Jennifer Cooke, *Legacies of Plague in Literature, Theory and Film* (New York: Palgrave MacMillan, 2009), p. 165.

154. See John Russo (Story), Dheeraj Verma (Pencils), Lalit (Inks), *Escape of the Living Dead* (Rantoul, IL: Avatar, 2006); Russo, *Undead* (2010).

155. Sean Moreland, "Shambling Towards Mount Improbable to Be Born: American Evolutionary Anxiety and the Hopeful Monsters of Matheson's *I Am Legend* and Romero's *Dead* Films," pp. 77– 89 in Stephanie Boluk and Wulie Lenz (eds.), *Generation Zombie: Essays on the Living Dead in Modern Culture* (Jefferson, NC: McFarland, 2011), p. 77; Cf. Stephanie Boluk and Wylie Lenz, "Infection, Media, and Capitalism: From Early Modern Plagues to Postmodern Zombies," *Journal for Early Modern Cultural Studies* 10.2 (2010): 126–147.

156. Melissa Nasiruddin, Monique Halabi, Alexander Dao, Kyle Chen, and Brandon Brown, "Zombies—A Pop Culture Resource for Public Health Awareness," *Emerging Infectious Diseases* 19.5 (2013): 809–813.

157. Eric Cazdyn, *The Already Dead: The New Time of Politics, Culture, and Illness* (Durham, NC: Duke University Press, 2012).

158. i.e., Carmelo Aquilina and Julian C. Hughes, "The Return of the Living Dead: Agency Lost and Found?" pp. 143–161 in Julian C. Hughes, Stephen J. Louw, and Steven R. Sabat (eds.), *Dementia: Mind, Meaning, and the Person* (London: Oxford University Press, 2006); Susan M. Behuniak, "The Living Dead? The Construction of People with Alzheimer's Disease as Zombies," *Ageing & Society* 31 (2011): 70–92.

159. Catherine Belling, "The Living Dead: Fiction, Horror, and Bioethics," *Perspectives in Biology and Medicine* 53.3 (2010): 439–451.

160. Cazdyn, *The Already Dead* (2012), pp. 189–190.

161. Cazdyn, *The Already Dead* (2012), p. 189.

162. Jen Webb and Sam Byrnand, "Some Kind of Virus: The Zombie as Body and as Trope," *Body & Society* 14.2 (2008): 83–98, p. 86.

163. Mikita Brottman, "Mondo Horror," pp. 167–188 in Prince, *The Horror Film* (2004).

164. Jean Baudrillard, *Simulacra and Simulation* (Ann Arbor: University of Michigan Press, 1994).

165. See Lisa Morton, "The Walking Dead and Dance of Death: Or, Why the Zombies Are Always on the Other Side of the Fence," pp. 174–184 in James Lowder (ed.), *Triumph of the Walking Dead: Robert Kirkman's Zombie Epic on Page and Screen* (Dallas, TX: BenBella, 2011).

166. Bruce Y. Lee, "Was Glenn's Violent Death on '*The Walking Dead*' Too Much?," *Forbes.com* (Oct. 30, 2016): Online: https://www.forbes.com/sites/brucelee/2016/10/30/was-glenns-violent-death-on-the-walking-dead-too-much/#6e865d343adb; Paul Tassi, "AMC Has an Explanation for *The Walking Dead*'s Ratings Being Down," *Forbes.com* (May 20, 2017): Online: https://www.forbes.com/sites/insertcoin/2017/05/20/amc-has-an-explanation-for-the-walking-deads-ratings-being-down/#16d8e9598d44.

167. Tony Walter, *The Revival of Death* (London: Routledge, 1994).

168. Jessica DeCou, "The Living Christ and the Walking Dead: Karl Barth and the Theological Zombie," pp. 79–100 in Kim Paffenroth and John W. Morehead (eds.), *The Undead and Theology* (Eugene, OR: Pickwick, 2012), pp. 79–80.

169. Michael McLaughlin, "Dalai Lama: Humans Created Terrorism, So Stop Praying To God For A Solution," *Huffington Post*, Nov. 17, 2015, Online: http://www.huffingtonpost.com/entry/dalai-lama-terrorism_564b8975e4b045bf3df16e75.

170. Wetmore, Jr., *Back from the Dead* (2011), p. 73.

171. For further discussion of the latter, see Sigurdson, "Slavoj Zizek, The Death Drive, and Zombies," (2013): 361–380.

172. Martin Roos, Hans Nugteren, and Zhong Jinwén have compiled a bibliography of these *Vetalapancavimsati* stories, what they call "Tales of the Bewitched Corpse," Online: http://members.home.nl/marcmarti/yugur/folktale/bewitchedcorpse.htm.

173. Ronald S. Green, *Buddhism Goes to the Movies: An Introduction to Buddhist Thought and Practice* (London: Routledge, 2014).

174. Francisca Cho, "Buddhism," pp. 162–177 in John Lyden (ed.), *The Routledge Companion to Religion and Film* (London: Routledge, 2009), p. 163.

Chapter Four

1. For a readable overview, see Hammalawa Saddhatissa, *The Life of the Buddha* (New York: Harper & Row, 1976).

2. Walpola Rahula's, *What the Buddha Taught*, 2nd ed. (New York: Grove Press, 1974), remains the most accessible introduction to core Buddhist teachings.

3. Ambrose Bierce, "Cartesian," *Devil's Dictionary* (London: Arthur F. Bird, 1906).

4. For a good over-view of such forms of meditation in the Theravadin Buddhist tradition, see George D. Bond, "Theravada Buddhism's Meditations on Death and the Symbolism of Initiatory Death," *History of Religions* 19: 3 (Feb., 1980): 237–258.

5. Orit Taubman-Ben-Ari, "Is the Meaning of Life Also the Meaning of Death? A Terror Management Perspective Reply," *Journal of Happiness Studies* 12 (2011): 385–399.

6. Ernest Becker, *The Denial of Death* (New York: Free Press, 1973).

7. Jeff Greenberg, Tom Pyszczynski, and Sheldon Solomon, "The Causes and Consequences of a Need for Self-Esteem: A Terror Management Theory," pp. 189–212 in R.F. Baumeister (ed.), *Public Self and Private Self* (New York: Springer-Verlag, 1986).

8. M. Deschesne, T. Pyszczynski, J. Arndt, S. Ransom, K.M. Sheldon, A. van Knippenberg, et al., "Literal and Symbolic Immortality: The Effect of Evidence of Literal Immortality on Self-Esteem Striving in Response to Mortality Salience," *Journal of Personality and Social Psychology* 84 (2003): 722–737; Sheldon Solomon, Jeff Greenberg, and Tom Pyszczynski, "A Terror Management Theory of Social Behavior: The Psychological Functions of Self-Esteem and Cultural Worldviews," pp. 91–159 in Mark Zanna (ed.), *Advances in Experimental Social Psychology*, Vol. 24 (Orlando, FL: Academic Press, 1991).

9. See, for example, Kenneth E. Vail III, Zachary K. Rothchild, David R. Weise, Sheldon Solomon, Tom Pyszczynski, and Jeff Greenberg, "A Terror Management Analysis of the Psychological Functions of Religion," *Personality and Social Psychology Review* 14.1 (2010): 84–94.

10. Ara Norenzayan and Ian G. Hansen, "Belief in Supernatural Agents in the Face of Death," *Personality & Social Psychology Bulletin* 32.2 (2006): 174–187.

11. Paul J. Silvia, "Nothing or the Opposite: Intersecting Terror Management

and Objective Self-Awareness," *European Journal of Personality* 15 (2001): 73–82.

12. Victoria Ka-Ying Hui and Peter G. Coleman, "Do Reincarnation Beliefs Protect Older Adult Chinese Buddhists Against Personal Death Anxiety?," *Death Studies* 36.10 (2012): 949–958.

13. David L. Scruton (ed.), *Sociophobics: The Anthropology of Fear* (Boulder, CO: Westview Press, 1986).

14. *Saundarananda* IX, 6–16, as quoted in Paul van der Velde, "Over My Dead Buddha! Death and Buddhism," pp. 239–258 in Eric Venbrux, Thomas Quartier, Claudia Venhorst, and Brenda Mathijssen (eds.), *Changing European Death Ways* (Zurich: Lit, 2013), p. 243.

15. Robert E. Goss and Dennis Klass, "Tibetan Buddhism and the Resolution of Grief: The *Bardo-Thodol* for the Dying and the Grieving," *Death Studies* 21 (1997): 377–395.

16. Goss and Klass, "Tibetan Buddhism and the Resolution of Grief," (1997), p. 384.

17. Goss and Klass, "Tibetan Buddhism and the Resolution of Grief," (1997), p. 385.

18. Christopher M. Moreman, "On the Relationship Between Birds and Spirits of the Dead," *Society & Animals* 22.5 (2014): 481–502.

19. Steven Collins, "The Body in Theravāda Monasticism," pp. 185–204 in Sarah Coakley (ed.), *Religion and the Body* (Cambridge, UK: Cambridge University Press, 1997), pp. 192–193.

20. Scott Stonington, "Facing Death, Gazing Inward: End-of-Life and the Transformation of Clinical Subjectivity in Thailand," *Culture, Medicine, and Psychiatry* 35 (2011): 113–133, p. 131.

21. Buddhaghossa outlines what are termed the Ten Foul Objects of meditation, which include the various forms of decaying corpse found in zombie cinema *Visuddhimagga: The Path of Purification*, trans. Bhikkhu Nanamoli (Sri Lanka: Buddhist Publication Society, 2011).

22. Alan Klima, *The Funeral Casino: Meditation, Massacre, and Exchange with the Dead in Thailand* (Princeton, NJ: Princeton University Press, 2002), p. 6.

23. Bond, "Theravada Buddhism's Meditations on Death," (1980), p. 247, here cites first the *Smyutta-Nikaya* (203) and secondly both the *Digha-Nikaya* (2.295) and the *Angutta-Nikaya* (3.324).

24. Mohan Wijayaratna, "Funerary Rites in Japanese and Other Asian Buddhist Societies," *Japan Review* 8 (1997): 105–125, p. 111.

25. Klima, *The Funeral Casino* (2002), p. 199.

26. Paul Williams, "Some Mahāyāna Buddhist Perspectives on the Body," pp. 205–230 in Sarah Coakley (ed.), *Religion and the Body* (Cambridge, UK: Cambridge University Press, 1997), p. 210.

27. *Visuddhimagga* (2011).

28. Jamie Russell, *Book of the Dead: The Complete History of Zombie Cinema* (Surrey: FAB Press, 2005).

29. Julia Kristeva, *Powers of Horror: An Essay on Abjection* (New York: Columbia University Press, 1982).

30. Fredrik Svenaeus, "Organ Transplantation and Personal Identity: How Does Loss and Change of Organs Affect the Self?" *Journal of Medicine and Philosophy* 37.2 (2012): 139–158.

31. Stephen E. Braude, *Immortal Remains: The Evidence for Life After Death* (Lanham, MD: Rowman & Littlefield, 2003), pp. 236–244.

32. William S. Larkin, "*Res Corporealis*: Persons, Bodies, and Zombies," pp. 15–26 Richard Greene and K. Silem Mohammad (eds.), *Zombies, Vampires, and Philosophy: New Life for the Undead* (Chicago: Open Court, 2010); and William Larkin, "Persons, Animals and Bodies," *Southwest Philosophical Review* 20: 2 (2004).

33. Craig Derksen and Darren Hudson Hick, "Your Zombie and You: Identity, Emotion, and the Undead," pp. 11–23 in Christopher M. Moreman and Cory James Rushton (eds.), *Zombies are Us: Essays on the Humanity of the Walking Dead* (Jefferson, NC: McFarland, 2011).

34. Derksen and Hick, "Your Zombie and You," in Moreman and Rushton, *Zombies Are Us* (2011), p. 18.

35. See Christopher M. Moreman, *Beyond the Threshold: Afterlife Beliefs and Experiences in World Religions*, 2nd edition (Lanham, MD: Rowman & Littlefield, 2018), chapter five.

36. Rachel Robison-Greene, "Better Off Undead," pp. 119–128 in Wayne Yuen (ed.),

The Walking Dead and Philosophy: Zombie Apocalypse Now (Chicago: Open Court, 2012), p. 119.

37. Dien Ho, "What's So Bad About Being a Zombie?" *Philosophy Now* 96 (May/June, 2013), Online: http://philosophynow.org/issues/96/Whats_So_Bad_About_Being_A_Zombie.

38. Mark Siderits, "Buddhas as Zombies: A Buddhist Reduction of Subjectivity," pp. 309–332 in Mark Siderits, Evan Thompson, and Dan Zahavi (eds.), *Self, No Self?: Perspectives from Analytical, Phenomenological, and Indian Traditions* (London: Oxford University Press, 2011), p. 328.

39. Reinhard May, *Heidegger's Hidden Sources: East Asian Influences on His Work*, trans. Graham Parkes (London: Routledge, 1996); Graham Parkes (ed.), *Heidegger and Asian Thought* (Honolulu, HI: University of Hawaii Press, 1987).

40. Martin Heidegger, *Being and Time*, trans. Joan Stambaugh (Albany, NY: State University of New York Press, 1996).

41. Viktor E. Frankl, *The Doctor and the Soul* (New York: Alfred A. Knopf, 1965), p. 69.

42. Dale Jacquette wrestles with the problem of zombie suffering in an essay on the morality of potential zombie gladiators in "Zombie Gladiators," in Richard Greene and K. Silem Mohammad (eds), *The Undead and Philosophy*. Chicago: Open Court, 2006.

43. Rahula, *What the Buddha Taught* (1974), p. 30. See also Seth M. Walker, "'Whatever it is, we all carry it': Tanhā and AMC's The Walking Dead," *Nomos Journal* (2012), Online: http://nomosjournal.org/2012/10/whatever-it-is-we-all-carry-it/. Accessed Sep. 10, 2017.

44. DN 15; SN 56.11. See also MN 44; SN 22.22.

45. Seth Grahame-Smith, *Pride and Prejudice and Zombies* (Philadelphia: Quirk Books, 2009). Also adapted to the screen in 2016.

46. DN 15.

47. Douglas E. Cowan, *Sacred Terror: Religion and Horror on the Silver Screen* (Waco, TX: Baylor University Press, 2008).

48. Robin Wood, "An Introduction to the American Horror Film," pp. 107–141 in Barry Keith Grant and Christopher Sharrett (eds.), *Planks of Reason: Essays on the Horror Film*, rev. ed. (Lanham, MD: Scarecrow Press, 2004); Robin Wood, *Hollywood from Vietnam to Reagan ... and Beyond* (New York: Columbia University Press, 2003).

49. Dan Yakir, "Knight after Night with George Romero," *American Film* 6 (1981): 42–45, 69: p. 43.

50. Kim Paffenroth, *Gospel of the Living Dead: George Romero's Visions of Hell on Earth* (Waco, TX: Baylor University Press, 2006).

51. Bhikkhu Nyanasobhano (Leonard Price), "Nothing Higher to Live For: A Buddhist View of Romantic Love," *Bodhi Leaves* 124 (Kandy: Buddhist Publication Society, 1985), online at: Access to Insight (2005), Online: http://www.accesstoinsight.org/lib/authors/price/bl124.html, Accessed July 19, 2016.

52. Tenzin Wangmo, *The Prince and the Zombie: Tibetan Tales of Karma* (Boston: Shambhala, 2014).

53. Turrell Wylie, "Ro-Langs: The Tibetan Zombie," *History of Religions* 4.1 (Summer, 1964): 69–80; Michael Walter, "Of Corpses and Gold: Materials for the Study of the Vetala and the Rolangs," *The Tibet Journal* 29.2 (2004): 13–46.

54. Peter Skilling, "Zombies and Half-Zombies: Mahāsūtras and Other Protective Measures," *Journal of the Pali Text Society* 29 (2007): 313–330.

55. Justin T. McDaniel, "Encountering Corpses: Notes on Zombies and the Living Dead in Buddhist Southeast Asia," *Kyoto Review of Southeast Asia* 12 (2012), Online: http://kyotoreview.org/wp-content/uploads/Justin-McDaniels_full-version.pdf. Accessed Nov. 8, 2013.

56. Sing-chen Lydia Francis, "'What Confucius Wouldn't Talk About': The Grotesque Body and Literati Identities in Yuan Mei's *Zi buyu*," *Chinese Literature: Essays, Articles, Reviews (CLEAR)* 24 (2002): 129–160, pp. 138–139 citing *Yuan Mei quan ji*, vol. 4, p. 3.

57. Francis, "'What Confucius Wouldn't Talk About,'"(2002), pp. 141–142 citing *Yuan Mei quan ji*, vol. 4, pp. 93–94. It is worth noting that the term "*jiangshi*" is sometimes also translated as "vampire,"

though the creature behaves like neither zombie nor vampire as conceived of in the West.

58. Erik W. Davis, "Weaving Life out of Death: The Craft of the Rag Robe in Cambodian Funerary Ritual," pp. 59–78 in Paul Williams and Patrice Ladwig (eds.), *Buddhist Funeral Cultures of Southeast Asia and China* (Cambridge: Cambridge University Press, 2012).

59. van der Velde, "Over My Dead Buddha!" in Venbrux, Quartier, Venhorst, and Mathijssen, *Changing European Death Ways* (2013), p. 240.

60. van der Velde, "Over My Dead Buddha!" in Venbrux, Quartier, Venhorst, and Mathijssen, *Changing European Death Ways* (2013), p. 245.

61. Ken Jeremiah, *Living Buddhas: The Self-Mummified Monks of Yamagata, Japan* (Jefferson, NC: McFarland, 2010).

62. M.L. Pattaratorn Chirapravati, "Corpses and Cloth: Illustrations of the Paṃsukūla Ceremony in Thai Manuscripts," pp. 79–98 in Williams and Ladwig (eds.), *Buddhist Funeral Cultures of Southeast Asia and China* (2012).

63. François Robinne, "Theatre of Death and Rebirth: Monks' Funerals in Burma," pp. 165–191 in Williams and Ladwig, *Buddhist Funeral Cultures of Southeast Asia and China* (2012).

64. Stonington, "Facing Death, Gazing Inward," (2011), p. 128.

65. Max Brooks, *Closure Limited and Other Zombie Tales* (London, UK: Duckworth Overlook, 2012).

66. Joel D. Lieberman and Mark Fergus, "The End is Near: Mortality Salience in Apocalyptic Films," pp. 37–52 in Daniel Sullivan and Jeff Greenberg (eds.), *Death in Classic and Contemporary Film* (New York: Palgrave Macmillan, 2013).

67. Daniel Sullivan and Jeff Greenberg, "Conclusion: Cinematic Death Benefits," pp. 231–245 in Sullivan and Greenberg, *Death in Classic and Contemporary Film* (2013).

68. Robert W. Firestone, "Psychological Defenses Against Death Anxiety," pp. 217–241 in Robert A. Neimeyer (ed.), *Death Anxiety Handbook: Research, Instrumentation, and Application* (Washington, DC: Taylor & Francis, 1994), p. 233.

69. R.W. Firestone, "The Bipolar Causality of Regression," *American Journal of Psychoanalysis* 50 (1990): 121–135, p. 127.

70. Cf. Jonathan F. Bassett, "Psychological Defense Against Death Anxiety: Integrating Terror Management Theory and Firestone's Separation Theory," *Death Studies* 31 (2007): 727–750.

71. Mary Warnock, *Existentialism* (Oxford: Oxford University Press, 1970), p. 1.

72. Walter Kaufmann, *Existentialism from Dostoevsky to Sartre* (New York: Meridian Books, 1956), pp. 11–12.

73. Heidegger, *Being and Time* (1996).

74. Curtis Bowman, "Heidegger, the Uncanny, and Jacques Tourneur's Horror Films," pp. 65–83 in Steven Jay Schneider and Daniel Shaw (eds.), *Dark Thoughts: Philosophic Reflections on Cinematic Horror* (Lanham, MD: The Scarecrow Press, 2003), p. 67.

75. Søren Kierkegaard, *The Concept of Dread*, trans. By Walter Lowrie (Princeton, NJ: Princeton University Press, 1944), p. 55.

76. See Noël Carroll, *The Philosophy of Horror or Paradoxes of the Heart* (London: Routledge, 1990) for more discussion on the paradoxical qualities of our experience of horror.

77. Steven Heine and Dale S. Wright (eds.), *The Kōan: Texts and Contexts in Zen Buddhism* (Oxford: Oxford University Press, 2000), p. 303.

78. S.L. Varnado, *Haunted Presence: The Numinous in Gothic Fiction* (Tuscaloosa: University of Alabama Press, 1987); cf. H.P. Lovecraft, *The Annotated Supernatural Horror in Literature*, S.T. Joshi (ed.) (New York: Hippocampus Press, 2000); Eugene Thacker, *In the Dust of This Planet* (Winchester, UK: Zero Books, 2011).

79. Curtis Bowman, "Heidegger, the Uncanny, and Jacques Tourneur's Horror Films," pp. 65–83 in Schneider and Shaw (eds.), *Dark Thoughts* (2003), pp. 81–82.

80. Brent Adkins, *Death and Desire in Hegel, Heidegger and Deleuze* (Edinburgh: Edinburgh University Press, 2007), p. 33.

81. Friedrich Nietzsche, *The Gay Science*, trans. Walter Kaufmann (New York: Vintage, 1974), p. 341.

82. For example, Aaron Ridley, "Niet-

zsche's Greatest Weight," *Journal of Nietzsche Studies* 14 (1997): 19–25.

83. Gwyneth Peaty, "Zombie Time: Temporality and Living Death," pp. 186–199 in Dawn Keetley (ed.), *"We're All Infected": Essays on AMC's* The Walking Dead *and the Fate of the Human* (Jefferson, NC: McFarland, 2014).

84. See Joan Jiko Halifax, "Being with Dying: The Upaya Institute Contemplative End-of-Life Training Program," pp. 209–228 in Jonathan S. Watts and Yoshiharu Tomatsu (eds.), *Buddhist Care for the Dying and Bereaved* (Boston: Wisdom Publications, 2012).

Bibliography

Ackermann, Hans W., and Jeanin Gauthier. "The Ways and Nature of the Zombi." *The Journal of American Folklore* 104.414 (1991): 466–494.

Adkins, Brent. *Death and Desire in Hegel, Heidegger and Deleuze*. Edinburgh: Edinburgh University Press, 2007.

Agamben, Girogrio. *Homo Sacer: Sovereign Power and Bare Life*. Trans. Daniel Heller-Roazen. Stanford, CA: Stanford University Press, 1998.

Aichele, George, and Tina Pippin (eds.). *The Monstrous and the Unspeakable: The Bible as Fantastic Literature*. Sheffield, UK: Sheffield Academic Press, 1997.

Al-Ghazali. *The Remembrance of Death and the Afterlife*. Trans. T.J. Winter. Cambridge: The Islamic Texts Society, 1989.

Angelier, François. "À leurs corps defendant..." pp. 15–23 in Jean-Baptiste Thoret (ed.), *Politique des zombies: L'Amérique selon George A. Romero*. Paris: Ellipses, 2007.

Aquilina, Carmelo, and Julian C. Hughes. "The Return of the Living Dead: Agency Lost and Found?" Pp. 143–161 in Julian C. Hughes, Stephen J. Louw, and Steven R. Sabat (eds.). *Dementia: Mind, Meaning, and the Person*. Oxford: Oxford University Press, 2006.

Arendt, Hannah. *The Origins of Totalitarianism*. Oxford: Benediction Classics, 2009 [1958].

Arens, W. *The Man-Eating Myth: Anthropology & Anthropophagy*. Oxford: Oxford University Press, 1979.

Aries, Philippe. *The Hour of Our Death*, 2nd ed. Trans. Helen Weaver. New York: Vintage Books, 2008.

Badley, Linda. "Zombie Splatter Comedy from *Dawn* to *Shaun*: Cannibal Carnivalesque." Pp. 35–53 in Shawn McIntosh and Marc Leverette (eds.), *Zombie Culture: Autopsies of the Living Dead*. Lanham, MD: Scarecrow Press, 2008.

Bandelier, Adolph Francis. "Bartolomé de las Casas." *The Catholic Encyclopedia*. Vol. 3. New York: Robert Appleton Company, 1908.

Barthes, Roland. *Camera Lucida: Reflections on Photography*. Trans. Richard Howard. New York: Farrar, Strauss and Giroux, 1981.

Bassett, Jonathan F. "Psychological Defense Against Death Anxiety: Integrating Terror Management Theory and Firestone's Separation Theory." *Death Studies* 31 (2007): 727–750.

Bauby, Jean-Dominique. *The Diving Bell and the Butterfly*. New York: Alfred A. Knopf, 1997.

Baudrillard, Jean. *Simulacra and Simulation*. Ann Arbor: University of Michigan Press, 1994.

Baumeister, R.F. (ed.). *Public Self and Private Self*. New York: Springer-Verlag, 1986.

Beal, Timothy K. *Religion and Its Monsters*. London: Routledge, 2002.

Beard, William. *The Artist as Monster: The Cinema of David Cronenberg*. Toronto: University of Toronto Press, 2006.

_____. "The Visceral Mind: The Major Films of David Cronenberg." Pp. 1–79 in Piers Handling (ed.). *The Shape of Rage: The Films of David Cronenberg*. Toronto: General Publishing, 1983.

Beau. "Review of *Night of the Living Dead*." *Variety*. Wed., Oct 16, 1968, p. 6–7.

Beck, Ulrich, and Elisabeth Beck-Gernsheim. *Individualization: Institutionalized Individualism and Its Social and Political Consequences*. London: SAGE, 2002.

Becker, Ernest. *The Denial of Death*. New York: Free Press, 1973.

Behuniak, Susan M. "The Living Dead? The Construction of People with Alzheimer's Disease as Zombies." *Ageing & Society* 31 (2011): 70–92.

Beisecker, Dave. "A Stagger-On Role to Die For." Pp. 67–79 in Wayne Yuen (ed.), *The Walking Dead and Philosophy: Zombie Apocalypse Now*. Chicago: Open Court, 2012.

Bellegarde-Smith, Patrick. *Haiti: The Breached Citadel*. Toronto: Canadian Scholars' Press, 2004.

Belling, Catherine. "The Living Dead: Fiction, Horror, and Bioethics." *Perspectives in Biology and Medicine* 53.3 (2010): 439–451.

Beloff, Halla. "Immortality Work: Photographs as *Memento Mori*." Pp. 179–192 in Margaret Mitchell, (ed.), *Remember Me: Constructing Immortality*. London: Routledge, 2007.

Bender, Aimee. "Among Us." Pp. 257–262 in Christopher Golden (ed.), *The New Dead: A Zombie Anthology*. New York: St. Martin's Press, 2010.

Benedict XVI. "Address by the Holy Father—Visit to the Auschwitz Camp." *Libreria Editrice Vaticana*. May 28, 2006. Online: http://w2.vatican.va/content/benedict-xvi/en/speeches/2006/may/documents/hf_ben-xvi_spe_20060528_auschwitz-birkenau.html.

Bentham, Jeremy. *Auto-Icon and Related Writings*. Ed. James E. Crimmins. Bristol, UK: Thoemmes Press, 2002 [1842?].

Bettelheim, Bruno. *The Uses of Enchantment: The Meaning and Importance of Fairy Tales*. New York: Alfred A. Knopf, 1976.

Bhikkhu Nyanasobhano (Leonard Price). "Nothing Higher to Live For: A Buddhist View of Romantic Love." *Bodhi Leaves* 124. Kandy, Sri Lanka: Buddhist Publication Society, 1985.

Bierce, Ambrose. "Cartesian." *Devil's Dictionary*. London: Arthur F. Bird, 1906.

Billson, Anne. "Cronenberg on Cronenberg: A Career in Stereo." *Monthly Film Bulletin* 56.660 (1989): 5.

Birch-Bayley, Nicole. "Terror in Horror Genres: The Global Media and the Millennial Zombie." *Journal of Popular Culture* 45.6 (2012): 1137–1151.

Bishop, Kyle. *American Zombie Gothic: The Rise and Fall (and Rise) of the Walking Dead in Popular Culture*. Jefferson, NC: McFarland, 2010.

_____. "Raising the Dead: Unearthing the Nonliterary Origins of Zombie Cinema." *Journal of Popular Film & Television* 33.4 (2006): 196–205.

Biskund, Peter. *Seeing is Believing: How Hollywood Taught Us to Stop Worrying and Love the Fifties*. London: Pluto, 1983.

Blumberg, Arnold T. "Four-Color Zombies: The Walking Dead in Comics History." Pp. 36–52 in James Lowder (ed.), *Triumph of the Walking Dead: Robert Kirkman's Zombie Epic on Page and Screen*. Dallas, TX: BenBella, 2011.

Boluk, Stephanie, and Wylie Lenz. "Infection, Media, and Capitalism: From Early Modern Plagues to Postmodern Zombies." *Journal for Early Modern Cultural Studies* 10.2 (2010): 126–147.

Boluk, Stephanie, and Wulie Lenz (eds.). *Generation Zombie: Essays on the Living Dead in Modern Culture*. Jefferson, NC: McFarland, 2011.

Bond, George D. "Theravada Buddhism's Meditations on Death and the Symbolism of Initiatory Death." *History of Religions* 19:3 (Feb., 1980): 237–258.

Boon, Kevin Alexander. "Ontological Anxiety Made Flesh: The Zombie in Literature, Film and Culture." Pp. 33–43 in Niall Scott (ed.), *Monsters and the Monstrous: Myths and Metaphors of Enduring Evil*. New York: Rodopi, 2007.

Boss, Pete. "Vile Bodies and Bad Medicine." *Screen: The Journal of the Society for Education in Film and Television* 27.1 (1986): 14–25.

Bourguignon, Erika. "The Persistence of Folk Belief: Some Notes on Cannibalism and Zombis in Haiti." *The Journal of American Folklore* 72.283 (1959): 36–46.

Boutros, Alexandra. "The Spirit of Traffic: Navigating Faith in the City," pp. 118–137 in Alexandra Boutros and Will Straw (eds.), *Circulation and the City: Essays on Urban Culture*. Montreal: McGill-Queen's University Press, 2010.

Boutros, Alexandra, and Will Straw (eds.). *Circulation and the City: Essays on Urban Culture*. Montreal: McGill-Queen's University Press, 2010.

Bowman, Curtis. "Heidegger, the Uncanny, and Jacques Tourneur's Horror Films." Pp. 65–83 in Steven Jay Schneider and Daniel Shaw (eds.), *Dark Thoughts: Philosophic Reflections on Cinematic Horror*. Lanham, MD: Scarecrow Press, 2003.

Braham, Persephone. "The Monstrous Caribbean." Pp. 17–47 in Asa Simon Mittman and Peter J. Dendle (eds.), *The Ashgate Research Companion to Monsters and the Monstrous*. Burlington, VT: Ashgate, 2012.

Braude, Stephen E. *Immortal Remains: The Evidence for Life After Death*. Lanham, MD: Rowman & Littlefield, 2003.

Breathett, George. "Catholicism and the Code Noir in Haiti." *The Journal of Negro History* 73:1 (1988): 1–11.

Brooks, Max. *Closure Limited and Other Zombie Tales*. London: Duckworth Overlook, 2012.

Brottman, Mikita. "Mondo Horror: Carnivalizing the Taboo." Pp. 167–188 in Stephen Prince (ed.), *The Horror Film*. New York: Rutgers University Press, 2004.

Brown, Karen McCarthy. "Voodoo." Pp. 321–326 in Arthur C. Lehmann and James E. Myers (eds.), *Magic, Witchcraft, and Religion: An Anthropological Study of the Supernatural*. Palo Alto, CA: Mayfield Publishing Co., 1997.

Bruce, Barbara S. "Guess Who's Going to be Dinner: Sidney Poitier, Black Militancy, and the Ambivalence of Race in Romero's *Night of the Living Dead*." Pp. 60–73 in Christopher M. Moreman and Cory James Rushton (eds.), *Race, Oppression, and the Zombie: Essays on Cross-Cultural Appropriations of the Caribbean Tradition*. Jefferson, NC: McFarland, 2011.

Bryce, Allan (ed.). *Zombie: They Just Won't Stay Dead*. Liskeard, UK: Stray Cat, 1999.

Buddhaghossa. *Visuddhimagga: The Path of Purification*. Trans. Bhikkhu Nanamoli. Kandy, Sri Lanka: Buddhist Publication Society, 2011.

Burrell, Nigel J. "Beyond the Blind Dead." Pp. 109–119 in Allan Bryce (ed.), *Zombie: They Just Won't Stay Dead*. Liskeard, UK: Stray Cat, 1999.

Caldwell, Larry W., and Samuel J. Umland. "'Come and Play with Us': The Play Metaphor in Kubrick's *Shining*." *Literature Film Quarterly* 14.2 (1986): 106–111.

Camporesi, Piero. *The Incorruptible Flesh: Bodily Mutation and Mortification in Religion and Folklore*. Trans. Tania Croft-Murray. Cambridge: Cambridge University Press, 1988.

Camus, Albert. *The Myth of Sisyphus*. Trans. Justin O'Brien. New York: Alfred A. Knopf, 1958.

Canavan, Gerry. "'We Are the Walking Dead': Race, Time, and Survival in Zombie Narrative." *Extrapolation* 51.3 (2010): 431–453.

Carroll, Noël. "The Fear of Fear Itself: The Philosophy of Halloween." Pp. 223–236 in Richard Greene and K. Silem Mohammad (eds.), *The Undead and Philosophy*. Chicago: Open Court, 2006.

_____. "Nightmare and the Horror Film: The Symbolic Biology of Fantastic Beings." Pp. 91–105 in Moshe Lazar (ed.), *The Anxious Subject: Nightmares and Daymares in Literature and Film*. Malibu: Undena Publications, 1983.

_____. *The Philosophy of Horror or Paradoxes of the Heart*. London: Routledge, 1990.

Castaneda, Carlos. *The Teachings of Don Juan: A Yaqui Way of Knowledge*. Oakland: University of California Press, 1968.

Cazdyn, Eric. *The Already Dead: The New Time of Politics, Culture, and Illness.* Durham, NC: Duke University Press, 2012.

Chalmers, David. *The Conscious Mind: In Search of a Fundamental Theory.* Oxford: Oxford University Press, 1996.

Chirapravati, M.L. Pattaratorn. "Corpses and Cloth: Illustrations of the Paṃukūla Ceremony in Thai Manuscripts." Pp. 79–98 in Paul Williams and Patrice Ladwig (eds.), *Buddhist Funeral Cultures of Southeast Asia and China.* Cambridge: Cambridge University Press, 2012.

Cho, Francisca. "Buddhism." Pp. 162–177 in John Lyden (ed.), *The Routledge Companion to Religion and Film.* London: Routledge, 2009.

Christie, Deborah. "A Dead New World: Richard Matheson and the Modern Zombie." Pp. 67–80 in Kyle William Bishop, *American Zombie Gothic: The Rise and Fall (and Rise) of the Walking Dead in Popular Culture.* Jefferson, NC: McFarland, 2010.

Christie, Deborah, and Sarah Juliet Lauro (eds.). *Better Off Dead: The Evolution of the Zombie as Post-Human.* New York: Fordham University Press, 2011.

Clack, Beverley. *Sex and Death: A Reappraisal of Human Mortality.* Cambridge: Polity Press, 2002.

Clark, Simon. "The Undead Martyr: Sex, Death, and Revolution in George Romero's Zombie Films." Pp. 197–209 in Richard Greene and K. Silem Mohammad (eds.), *The Undead and Philosophy.* Chicago: Open Court, 2006.

Coakley, Sarah (ed.). *Religion and the Body.* Cambridge: Cambridge University Press, 1997.

Cohen, Jeffrey Jerome (ed.). *Monster Theory: Reading Culture.* Minneapolis: University of Minnesota Press, 1996.

Coleman, Robin R. Means. *Horror Noire: Blacks in American Horror Films from the 1890s to Present.* London: Routledge, 2011.

Collins, Steven. "The Body in Theravāda Monasticism." Pp. 185–204 in Sarah Coakley (ed.), *Religion and the Body.* Cambridge: Cambridge University Press, 1997.

Columbus, Christopher. *The Voyage of Christopher Columbus.* Translated by John Cummins. New York: St. Martin's Press, 1992.

Comaroff, Jean, and John Comaroff. "Alien-Nation: Zombies, Immigrants, and Millennial Capitalism." *South Atlantic Quarterly* 101.4 (2002): 779–805.

Condon, Richard. *The Manchurian Candidate.* New York: McGraw-Hill, 1959.

Conrich, Ian. "An Aesthetic Sense: Cronenberg and Neo-Horror Film Culture." Pp. 35–49 in Michael Grant (ed.), *The Modern Fantastic: The Films of David Cronenberg.* Westport, CT: Praeger, 2000.

Cooke, Jennifer. *Legacies of Plague in Literature, Theory and Film.* London: Palgrave Macmillan, 2009.

Corzani, Jack. "West Indian Mythology and its Literary Illustrations." *Research in African Literatures* 25.2 (1994): 131–139.

Cosentino, Donald J. "Envoi: The Gedes and Bawon Samdi." Pp. 399–415 in D.J. Cosentino (ed.). *Sacred Arts of Haitian Vodou.* Los Angeles: UCLA Fowler Museum of Cultural History, 1995.

_____. "Introduction: Imagine Heaven." Pp. 25–55 in D.J. Cosentino (ed.), *Sacred Arts of Haitian Vodou.* Los Angeles: UCLA Fowler Museum of Cultural History, 1995.

_____. (ed.) *In Extremis: Death and Life in 21st-Century Haitian Art.* Los Angeles: Fowler Museum at UCLA, 2012.

_____. (ed.). *Sacred Arts of Haitian Vodou.* Los Angeles: UCLA Fowler Museum of Cultural History, 1995.

Cowan, Douglas E. *Sacred Terror: Religion and Horror on the Silver Screen.* Waco, TX: Baylor University Press, 2008.

Craige, John H. *Cannibal Cousins.* New York: Minton, Balch, and Co., 1934.

Creed, Barbara. *The Monstrous Feminine: Film, Feminism, Psychoanalysis.* London: Routledge, 1993.

D'Agnolo-Vallan, Giulia. "Let Them Eat Flesh." *Film Comment* 41: 4 (July/Aug., 2005): 23–24.

Dash, J. Michael. *Culture and Customs of Haiti.* Westport, CT: Greenwood, 2000.

_____. *Haiti and the United States: National Stereotypes and the Literary Imagination*, 2nd ed. New York: St. Martin's Press, 1997.

Davis, Erik W. "Weaving Life out of Death: The Craft of the Rag Robe in Cambodian Funerary Ritual." Pp. 59–78 in Paul Williams and Patrice Ladwig (eds.), *Buddhist Funeral Cultures of Southeast Asia and China*. Cambridge: Cambridge University Press, 2012.

Davis, Kipp. "Zombies in America and at Qumran: AMC's *The Walking Dead*, the Dead Sea Scrolls, and Apocalyptic Redux." *Journal of Religion and Popular Culture* 27.2 (2015): 148–163.

Davis, Wade. *Passage of Darkness: The Ethnobiology of the Haitian Zombie*. Chapel Hill: University of North Carolina Press, 1988.

_____. *The Serpent and the Rainbow*. New York: Simon & Schuster, 1985.

Day, William Patrick. *Vampire Legends in Contemporary American Culture*. Lexington: University of Kentucky Press, 2002.

DeCou, Jessica. "The Living Christ and the Walking Dead: Karl Barth and the Theological Zombie." Pp. 79–100 in Kim Paffenroth and John W Morehead (eds.), *The Undead and Theology*. Eugene, OR: Pickwick, 2012.

Degoul, Frank. Trans. by Elisabeth M. Lore. "'We are the mirrors of your fears': Haitian Identity and Zombification." Pp. 24–38 in Deborah Christie and Sarah Juliet Lauro (eds.), *Better off Dead: The Evolution of the Zombie as Post-Human*. New York: Fordham University Press, 2011.

Deleuze, Gilles, and Felix Guattari. *Anti-Oedipus: Capitalism and Schizophrenia*. Trans. Robert Hurley, Mark Seem, and Helen R. Lane. Minneapolis: University of Minnesota Press, 2005 [1972].

_____. *A Thousand Plateaus: Capitalism and Schizophrenia*. Trans. Brian Massumi. Minneapolis: University of Minnesota Press, 1987.

Dendle, Peter. "The Zombie as Barometer of Cultural Anxiety." Pp. 45–57 in Niall Scott (ed.), *Monsters and the Monstrous: Myths and Metaphors of Enduring Evil*. New York: Rodopi, 2007.

_____. *The Zombie Movie Encyclopedia*. Jefferson, NC: McFarland, 2000.

_____. *The Zombie Movie Encyclopedia, Vol. 2: 2000–2010*. Jefferson, NC: McFarland, 2012.

Dennett, Daniel C. *Consciousness Explained*. Boston: Little, Brown, 1991.

_____. *Sweet Dreams: Philosophical Obstacles to a Science of Consciousness*. Cambridge, MA: MIT Press, 2005.

De Pascale, Enrico. *Death and Resurrection in Art*. Translated by Anthony Shugaar. Los Angeles: J. Paul Getty Museum, 2007.

Derksen, Craig, and Darren Hudson Hick. "Your Zombie and You: Identity, Emotion, and the Undead." Pp. 11–23 in Christopher M. Moreman and Cory James Rushton (eds.), *Zombies Are Us: Essays on the Humanity of the Walking Dead*. Jefferson, NC: McFarland, 2011.

Deschesne, M., T. Pyszczynski, J. Arndt, S. Ransom, K.M. Sheldon, A. van Knippenberg, et al. "Literal and Symbolic Immortality: The Effect of Evidence of Literal Immortality on Self-Esteem Striving in Response to Mortality Salience." *Journal of Personality and Social Psychology* 84 (2003): 722–737.

Desmangles, Leslie G. *The Faces of the Gods: Vodou and Roman Catholicism in Haiti*. Chapel Hill: University of North Carolina Press, 1992.

Diehl, Digby. *Tales from the Crypt: The Official Archives*. New York: St. Martin's, 1996.

Dillard, R.H.W. "*Night of the Living Dead*: It's Not Like Just a Wind That's Passing Through." Pp. 14–29 in Gregory A. Waller (ed.), *American Horrors: Essays on the Modern American Horror Film*. Chicago: University of Illinois Press, 1987.

Dittmar, Linda, and Gene Michaud (eds.). *From Hanoi to Hollywood: The Vietnam War in American Film*. New Brunswick, NJ: Rutgers University Press, 1990.

Drohan, Madelaine. "Gruesome Tales Show Nigeria's Desperate State." *Globe and Mail*. Toronto, ON, Sept. 25. 2000, p. A1.

DuBois, W.E.B. *The Souls of Black Folk*. Edited by Brent Hayes Edwards. Oxford: Oxford University Press, 2007.

Du Maurier, Daphne. "The Birds." Pp. 59–100 in *Don't Look Now: Stories*. Selected by Patrick McGrath. New York: NY Review of Books, 2008.

Dyer, Richard. *The Matter of Images*, 2nd ed. London: Routledge, 2002.

_____. *White*. London: Routledge, 1997.
Ellwood, Robert S. *1950: Crossroads of American Religious Life*. Louisville, KY: Westminster John Knox Press, 2000.
Epicurus. *Letter to Menoeceus*. Trans. Robert Drew Hicks. *The Internet Classics Archive*. Online: http://classics.mit.edu/Epicurus/menoec.html.
Fay, Jennifer. "Dead Subjectivity: White Zombie, Black Baghdad." *CR: The New Centennial Review* 8.1 (2008): 81–101.
Fick, Carolyn. *The Making of Haiti: The San Domingue Revolution from Below*. Knoxville: University of Tennessee Press, 1990.
Finney, Jack. *The Body Snatchers*. Boston: Gregg Press, 1976 [1955].
Firestone, Robert W. "The Bipolar Causality of Regression." *American Journal of Psychoanalysis* 50 (1990): 121–135.
_____. "Psychological Defenses Against Death Anxiety." Pp. 217–241 in Robert A. Neimeyer (ed.), *Death Anxiety Handbook: Research, Instrumentation, and Application*. Washington, D.C.: Taylor & Francis, 1994.
Fischer, Craig. "Meaninglessness: Cause and Desire in *The Birds*, *Shaun of the Dead*, and *The Walking Dead*." Pp. 68–80 in James Lowder (ed.), *Triumph of the Walking Dead: Robert Kirkman's Zombie Epic on Page and Screen*. Dallas, TX: BenBella, 2011.
Foucault, Michel. *The History of Sexuality*, Vol. 1. Trans. Robert Hurley. New York: Pantheon Books, 1978.
Francis, Sing-chen Lydia. "'What Confucius Wouldn't Talk About': The Grotesque Body and Literati Identities in Yuan Mei's *Zi buyu*." *Chinese Literature: Essays, Articles, Reviews (CLEAR)* 24 (2002): 129–160.
Frankl, Viktor E. *The Doctor and the Soul*. New York: Alfred A. Knopf, 1965.
Freud, Sigmund. *Totem and Taboo*. Trans. James Strachey. London: Routledge, 1961.
Fugazzola, Caterina, and Christopher M. Moreman. "Shugendō and *The Shining*: Liminal Space and Religious Experience in the Work of Stanley Kubrick." *Symposia* 6 (2014): 75–93.
Gagne, Paul R. *The Zombies That Ate Pittsburgh: The Films of George A. Romero*. New York: Dodd, Mead, and Co., 1987.
Gardner, John, and John Maier. *Gilgamesh*. New York: Vintage, 1985.
Garland, Alex. *28 Days Later*. London: Faber & Faber, 2002.
Geraghty, Lincoln. "*Invasion of the Body Snatchers* (1956)." Pp. 118–123 in John White and Sabine
Geschiere, Peter. *The Modernity of Witchcraft: Politics and the Occult in Postcolonial Africa*. Charlottesville: University of Virginia Press, 1997.
Gilmour, Michael. "The Living Word Among the Living Dead: Hunting for Zombies in the Pages of the Bible." Pp. 87–99 in Christopher M. Moreman and Cory James Rushton (eds.), *Zombies Are Us: Essays on the Humanity of the Walking Dead*. Jefferson, NC: McFarland, 2011.
Girard, René. *Violence and the Sacred*. Trans. Patrick Gregory. Baltimore, MD: Johns Hopkins University Press, 1972.
Glucklich, Ariel. *Sacred Pain: Hurting the Body for the Sake of the Soul*. Oxford: Oxford University Press, 2001.
Golden, Christopher (ed.). *The New Dead: A Zombie Anthology*. New York: St. Martin's Press, 2010.
Gooding, Francis. "They Still Believe There's Respect in Dying: Wittgenstein, Tercier, Romero." *Film Quarterly* 49: 3 (Autumn, 2007): 13–30.
Gordon, Joan, and Veronica Hollinger (eds.). *Blood Read: The Vampire as Metaphor in Contemporary Culture*. Philadelphia: University of Pennsylvania Press, 1997.
Gorman, Edward J. "Ed Gorman Calling: We Talk to Richard Matheson." *Mystery*File: The Crime Fiction Research Journal*. (2006). Online: http://www.mysteryfile.com/Matheson/Interview.html.
Goss, Robert E., and Dennis Klass. "Tibetan Buddhism and the Resolution of Grief: The *Bardo-Thodol* for the Dying and the Grieving." *Death Studies* 21 (1997): 377–395.
Graham, Becki A. "Post-9/11 Anxieties: Unpredictability and Complacency in the Age of 'New Terrorism' in *Dawn of the Dead* (2004)." Pp. 124–138 in Christopher M. Moreman and Cory James Rushton (eds.), *Race, Oppression and the*

Zombie: Essays on Cross-Cultural Appropriations of the Caribbean Tradition. Jefferson, NC: McFarland, 2011.

Grahame-Smith, Seth. *Pride and Prejudice and Zombies.* Philadelphia: Quirk Books, 2009.

Grant, Barry Keith. *Invasion of the Body Snatchers.* London: Palgrave Macmillan, 2010.

Grant, Barry Keith, and Christopher Sharrett (eds.). *Planks of Reason: Essays on the Horror Film,* rev. ed. Lanham, MD: Scarecrow Press, 2004.

Grant, Michael (ed.). *The Modern Fantastic: The Films of David Cronenberg.* Westport, CT: Praeger, 2000.

Gray, Kurt, T. Anne Knickman, and Daniel M. Wegner. "More Dead Than Dead: Perceptions of Persons in the Persistent Vegetative State." *Cognition* 121.2 (2011): 275–280.

Green, Ronald S. *Buddhism Goes to the Movies: An Introduction to Buddhist Thought and Practice.* London: Routledge, 2014.

Greenberg, Jeff, Tom Pyszczynski, and Sheldon Solomon. "The Causes and Consequences of a Need for Self-Esteem: A Terror Management Theory." Pp. 189–212 in R.F. Baumeister (Ed.), *Public Self and Private Self.* New York: Springer-Verlag, 1986.

Greene, Anne. *The Catholic Church in Haiti: Political and Social Change.* East Lansing: Michigan State University Press, 1993.

Greene, Richard, and K. Silem Mohammad (eds.). *The Undead and Philosophy.* Chicago: Open Court, 2006.

Guarnaccia, P.J., and L.H. Rogler. "Research on Culture-Bound Syndromes: New Directions." *American Journal of Psychiatry* 156.9 (1999): 1322–1327.

Hadjou, David. *The Ten-Cent Plague: The Great Comic-Book Scare and How It Changed America.* New York: Farrar, Straus and Giroux, 2008.

Haenni (eds.). *Fifty Key American Films.* London: Routledge, 2009.

Hakola, Outi. "Exotic Primitivism of Death in Classical Hollywood Living Dead Films." *Ilha do Desterro: A Journal of English Language, Literatures in English, and Cultural Studies* 62 (2012): 219–240.

Halifax, Joan Jiko. "Being with Dying: The Upaya Institute Contemplative End-of-Life Training Program." Pp. 209–228 in Jonathan S. Watts and Yoshiharu Tomatsu (eds.), *Buddhist Care for the Dying and Bereaved.* Boston: Wisdom Publications, 2012.

Hallenbeck, Bruce G. *Comedy-Horror Films: A Chronological History, 1914–2008.* Jefferson, NC: McFarland, 2009.

Hamako, Eric. "Zombie Orientals Ate My Brain! Orientalism in Contemporary Zombie Stories." Pp. 107–123 in Christopher M. Moreman and Cory James Rushton (eds.), *Race, Oppression and the Zombie: Essays on Cross-Cultural Appropriations of the Caribbean Tradition.* Jefferson, NC: McFarland, 2011.

Hand, Richard J. "Proliferating Horror: Survival Horror and the *Resident Evil* Franchise." Pp. 117–134 in Steffen Hantke (ed.), *Horror Film: Creating and Marketing Fear.* Jackson: University Press of Mississippi, 2004.

Hand, Richard J., and Michael Wilson. "Transatlantic Terror! French Horror Theater and American Pre-Code Comics." *Journal of Popular Culture* 45.2 (2012): 301–319.

Handling, Piers (ed.). *The Shape of Rage: The Films of David Cronenberg.* Toronto: General Publishing, 1983.

Hanners, John, and Harry Kloman. "'The McDonaldization of America': An Interview with George A. Romero." *Film Criticism* 7.1 (1982): 69–81.

Hantke, Steffen (ed.). *Horror Film: Creating and Marketing Fear.* Jackson: University Press of Mississippi, 2004.

Hastings, James (ed.). *Encyclopedia of Religion and Ethics.* New York: Charles Scribner's Sons, 1908–1922.

Heffernan, Kevin. *Ghouls, Gimmicks, and Gold: Horror Films and the American Movie Business, 1953–1968.* Durham, NC: Duke University Press, 2004.

Heidegger, Martin. *Being and Time.* Trans. Joan Stambaugh. Albany: State University of New York Press, 1996.

Heine, Steven, and Dale S. Wright (eds.). *The Kōan: Texts and Contexts in Zen Buddhism.* Oxford: Oxford University Press, 2000.

Heldreth, Leonard G., and Mary Pharr

(eds.). *The Blood in the Life: Vampires in Literature*. Bowling Green, OH: Bowling Green State University Popular Press, 1999.

Hervey, Ben. *BFI Film Classics: Night of the Living Dead*. London: Palgrave Macmillan, 2008.

Hibbs, Thomas S. "Dead Body Porn." *The New Atlantis* 15 (Winter 2007): 128–131.

Higashi, Sumiko. "*Night of the Living Dead*: A Horror Film about the Horrors of the Vietnam Era." Pp. 175–188 in Linda Dittmar and Gene Michaud (eds.), *From Hanoi to Hollywood: The Vietnam War in American Film*. New Brunswick, NJ: Rutgers University Press, 1990.

Ho, Dien. "What's So Bad About Being a Zombie?" *Philosophy Now* 96 (May/June, 2013). Online: http://philosophynow.org/issues/96/Whats_So_Bad_About_Being_A_Zombie.

Hron, Madelaine. *Translating Pain: Immigrant Suffering in Literature and Culture*. Toronto: University of Toronto Press, 2009.

Hughes, Julian C., Stephen J. Louw, and Steven R. Sabat (eds.). *Dementia: Mind, Meaning, and the Person*. Oxford: Oxford University Press, 2006

Hugo, Pieter. *Nollywood*. Munich: Presetel, 2009.

Hui, Victoria Ka-Ying, and Peter G. Coleman. "Do Reincarnation Beliefs Protect Older Adult Chinese Buddhists Against Personal Death Anxiety?" *Death Studies* 36.10 (2012): 949–958.

Humphries, Reynold. *The American Horror Film: An Introduction*. Edinburgh: Edinburgh University Press, 2002.

Hurbon, Laënnec. "American Fantasy and Haitian Vodou." Pp. 181–197 in D.J. Cosentino, *Sacred Arts of Haitian Vodou*. Los Angeles: UCLA Fowler Museum of Cultural History, 1995.

Hurston, Zora Neale. *Tell My Horse: Voodoo and Life in Haiti and Jamaica*. Philadelphia: Lippincott, 1938.

Ingebretsen, Edward J., S.J. *Maps of Heaven, Maps of Hell: Religious Terror as Memory from the Puritans to Stephen King*. Armonk, NY: M.E. Sharpe, 1996.

Inglis, David. "Putting the Undead to Work: Wade Davis, Haitian Vodou, and the Social Uses of the Zombie." Pp. 42–59 in Christopher M. Moreman and Cory James Rushton (eds.), *Race, Oppression and the Zombie: Essays on Cross-Cultural Appropriations of the Caribbean Tradition*. Jefferson, NC: McFarland, 2011.

Jacobs, W.W. "The Monkey's Paw." In *The Lady of the Barge*. London: Alan Rodgers Books, 1902.

Jacquette, Dale. "Zombie Gladiators." In Richard Greene and K. Silem Mohammad (eds), *The Undead and Philosophy*. Chicago: Open Court, 2006.

Jancovich, Mark. *Rational Fears: American Horror in the 1950s*. Manchester, UK: Manchester University Press, 1996.

Jeremiah, Ken. *Living Buddhas: The Self-Mummified Monks of Yamagata, Japan*. Jefferson, NC: McFarland, 2010.

Jones, Alan. "Morti Viventi: Zombies Italian-Style." Pp. 14–27 in Allan Bryce (ed.), *Zombie: They Just Won't Stay Dead*. Liskeard, UK: Stray Cat, 1999.

Jones, Steve. "*Porn of the Dead*: Necrophilia, Feminism, and Gendering the Undead." In Christopher M. Moreman and Cory James Rushton (eds.), *Zombies Are Us: Essays on the Humanity of the Walking Dead*. Jefferson, NC: McFarland, 2011.

Joshi, S.T. (ed.). *Icons of Horror and the Supernatural: An Encyclopedia of Our Worst Nightmares*. 2 Vols. Westport, CT: Greenwood Press, 2007.

Kane, Tim. *The Changing Vampire of Film and Television*. Jefferson, NC: McFarland, 2006.

Kaster, Robert. *Emotion, Restraint, and Community in Ancient Rome*. Oxford: Oxford University Press, 2005.

Kaufmann, Walter. *Existentialism from Dostoevsky to Sartre*. New York: Meridian Books, 1956.

Kee, Chera. "'They are not men ... they are dead bodies': From Cannibal to Zombie and Back Again." Pp. 9–15 in Deborah Christie and Sarah Juliet Lauro (eds.), *Better Off Dead: The Evolution of the Zombie as Post-Human*. New York: Fordham University Press, 2011.

Keegan, William F. "Columbus was a Cannibal: Myth and the First Encounters." Pp. 17–32 in Robert L. Paquette and Stanley L. Engerman (eds.), *The Lesser*

Antilles in the Age of European Expansion. Gainesville: University Press of Florida, 1996.

Keesey, Douglas. "Intertwinings of Death and Desire in Michele Soavi's *Dellamorte Dellamore*." *Horror Studies* 2.1 (2011): 105–114.

Keetley, Dawn. *"We're All Infected": Essays on AMC's* The Walking Dead *and the Fate of the Human*. Jefferson, NC: McFarland, 2014.

____ (ed.). "Zombie Evolution: Stephen King's *Cell*, George Romero's *Diary of the Dead*, and the Future of the Human." *Americana: The Journal of American Popular Culture* 11.2 (Fall 2012): Online: http://www.americanpopularculture.com/journal/articles/fall_2012/keetley.htm.

Kemedjio, Cilas. "Rape of Bodies, Rape of Souls: From the Surgeon to the Psychiatrist, from the Slave Trade to the Slavery of Comfort in the Work of Edouard Glissant." *Research in African Literatures* 25.2 (1994): 51–67.

Keresztesi, Rita. "Hurtson in Haiti: Neocolonialism and Zombification." Pp. 31–41 in Christopher M. Moreman and Cory James Rushton (eds.), *Race, Oppression and the Zombie: Essays on Cross-Cultural Appropriations of the Caribbean Tradition*. Jefferson, NC: McFarland, 2011.

Kermode, Mark. "Drenched in the Blood of Christ." *The Guardian* (Feb. 29, 2004). Online: https://www.theguardian.com/film/2004/feb/29/melgibson.markkermode. Accessed Sept. 9, 2017.

Kerouac, Jack. *The Dharma Bums*. New York: Viking Press, 1958.

____. *Wake Up: A Life of the Buddha*. New York: Viking Press, 2008.

Kierkegaard, Søren. *The Concept of Dread*. Trans. By Walter Lowrie. Princeton, NJ: Princeton University Press, 1944.

King, Stephen. *Cell*. New York: Charles Scribner's Sons, 2006.

Kirk, Robert. "Zombies." *The Stanford Encyclopedia of Philosophy*. Edward N. Zalta (ed.) (Summer 2012). Online: http://plato.stanford.edu/archives/sum2012/entries/zombies/. Accessed Jan. 23, 2014.

Kirk, Robert, and Roger Squires. "Zombies v. Materialists." *Proceedings of the Aristotelian Society, Supplementary Volumes* 48 (1978): 135–163.

Klima, Alan. *The Funeral Casino: Meditation, Massacre, and Exchange with the Dead in Thailand*. Princeton, NJ: Princeton University Press, 2002.

Kornell, Monique. "The Eternal Cadaver: Anatomy and Its Representation." Pp. 209–226 in Margaret Mitchell (ed.), *Remember Me: Constructing Immortality—Beliefs on Immortality, Life, and Death*. London: Routledge, 2007.

Kremmel, Laura. "Rest in Pieces: Violence in Mourning the (Un)Dead." Pp. 80–94 in Dawn Keetley, (ed.), *"We're All Infected": Essays on AMC's* The Walking Dead *and the Fate of the Human*. Jefferson, NC: McFarland, 2014.

Kristeva, Julia. *Powers of Horror: An Essay on Abjection*. New York: Columbia University Press, 1982.

Larkin, William. "Persons, Animals and Bodies." *Southwest Philosophical Review* 20: 2 (2004).

____. "*Res Corporealis*: Persons, Bodies, and Zombies." Pp. 15–26 in Richard Greene and K. Silem Mohammad (eds.), *The Undead and Philosophy*. Chicago: Open Court, 2006.

Laroche, Maximilien. "Mythe africain et mythe antillais: le personnage du zombie." *Canadian Journal of African Studies / Revue Canadienne des Études Africaines* 9.3 (1975): p. 479–491.

Lauro, Sarah Juliet. *The Transatlantic Zombie: Slavery, Rebellion, and Living Death*. New Brunswick, NJ: Rutgers University Press, 2015.

Lauro, Sarah Juliet, and Karen Embry. "A Zombie Manifesto: The Nonhuman Condition in the Era of Advanced Capitalism." *boundary 2* 35.1 (2008): 85–108.

Lawless, Robert. *Haiti's Bad Press*. Rochester, VT: Schencken Books, 1992.

Laycock, Joseph P. "Conversion by Infection: The Sociophobic of Cults in the Omega Man." *International Journal for the Study of New Religions* 2.1 (2010): 261–278.

Lazar, Moshe (ed.). *The Anxious Subject: Nightmares and Daymares in Literature and Film*. Malibu: Undena Publications, 1983.

Lee, Bruce Y. "Was Glenn's Violent Death on 'The Walking Dead' Too Much?" *Forbes.com*. Oct. 30, 2016. Online: https://www.forbes.com/sites/brucelee/2016/10/30/was-glenns-violent-death-on-the-walking-dead-too-much/#6e865d343adb.

Lee, Judith. "Sacred Horror: Faith and Fantasy in the Revelation of John." Pp. 220–239 in George Aichele and Tina Pippin (eds.), *The Monstrous and the Unspeakable: The Bible as Fantastic Literature*. Sheffield, UK: Sheffield Academic Press, 1997.

Legge, James (trans.). *The Chinese Classics: The Life and Works of Mencius*. Philadelphia: J.B. Lippincott and Co., 1875.

Lehmann, Arthur C., and James E. Myers (eds.). *Magic, Witchcraft, and Religion: An Anthropological Study of the Supernatural*. Palo Alto, CA: Mayfield Publishing Co., 1997.

Leiva, Antonio Domínguez. "Apocalypse Zombie: l'invasion des morts-vivants dans le roman graphique contemporain." *Frontières* 25.2 (2013): 93–108.

Le Pajolec, Sébastien. "Zombies: de la marge au centre—La reception française des films de George Romero." Pp. 155–181 in Jean-Baptiste Thoret (ed.), *Politique des zombies: L'Amérique selon George A. Romero*. Paris: Ellipses, 2007.

Lépinay, Carole. "À l'ouest d'Éden." Pp. 101–119 in Jean-Baptiste Thoret (ed.), *Politique des zombies: L'Amérique selon George A. Romero*. Paris: Ellipses, 2007.

Levina, Marina, and Diem-My T. Bui (eds.). *Monster Culture in the 21st Century: A Reader*. London: Bloomsbury, 2013.

Lewis, Michael, and Jeannette M. Haviland-Jones (eds.). *Handbook of Emotions*, 3rd edition. New York: Guilford, 2008.

Leyburn, James G. *The Haitian People*. New Haven, CT: Yale University Press, 1941.

Lieberman, Joel D., and Mark Fergus. "The End is Near: Mortality Salience in Apocalyptic Films." Pp. 37–52 in Daniel Sullivan and Jeff Greenberg (eds.), *Death in Classic and Contemporary Film*. London: Palgrave Macmillan, 2013.

Linkman, Audrey. *Photography and Death*. Islington, UK: Reaktion Books, 2011.

Littlewood, Roland. "Functionalists and Zombis: Sorcery as Spandrel and Social Rescue." *Anthropology & Medicine* 16.3 (2009): 241–252.

Littlewood, Roland, and Chavannes Douyon. "Clinical Findings in Three Cases of Zombification." *Lancet* 350 (1997): 1094–1096.

Long, Carolyn Morrow. *Spiritual Merchants: Religion, Magic, and Commerce*. Knoxville: University of Tennessee Press, 2001.

Louth, Andrew. "The Body in Western Catholic Christianity." Pp. 111–130 in Sarah Coakley (ed.), *Religion and the Body*. Cambridge: Cambridge University Press, 1997.

Lovecraft, H.P. *The Annotated Supernatural Horror in Literature*. S.T. Joshi (ed.). New York: Hippocampus Press, 2000.

Lowder, James (ed.). *Triumph of the Walking Dead: Robert Kirkman's Zombie Epic on Page and Screen*. Dallas, TX: BenBella, 2011.

Lowenstein, Adam. *Shocking Representation: Historical Trauma, National Cinema, and the Modern Horror Film*. New York: Columbia University Press, 2005.

Lukas, Scott A. "Horror Video Game Remakes and the Question of Medium: Remaking *Doom*, *Silent Hill*, and *Resident Evil*." Pp. 221–242 in Scott A. Lukas and John Marmysz (eds.), *Fear, Cultural Anxiety, and Transformation: Horror, Science Fiction, and Fantasy Films Remade*. Plymouth, UK: Lexington Books, 2009.

Lukas, Scott A., and John Marmysz (eds.). *Fear, Cultural Anxiety, and Transformation: Horror, Science Fiction, and Fantasy Films Remade*. Plymouth, UK: Lexington Books, 2009.

Lyden, John (ed.). *The Routledge Companion to Religion and Film*. London: Routledge, 2009.

Marmysz, John A. "From *Night* to *Day*: Nihilism and the Walking Dead." *Film & Philosophy* 3 (1996): 138–144.

Mars, Louis P. "The Story of Zombi in Haiti." *Man* 45 (1945): 38–40.

Marsh, Richard. *Locked In: One Man's Miraculous Escape from the Terrifying Confines of Locked-In Syndrome*. London: Piatkus, 2014.

Martin, Joel W., and Conrad E. Ostwalt, Jr.

(eds.). *Screening the Sacred*. Oxford: Westview Press, 1995.

Martin, John. "Maestro of Maggot Mayhem: Zombie King, Lucio Fulci, Interviewed." Pp. 129–134 in Allan Bryce (ed.), *Zombie: They Just Won't Stay Dead*. Liskeard, UK: Stray Cat, 1999.

Marx, Karl. *Capital: Critique of Political Economy*. Trans. Samuel Moore and Edward Aveling. London: Swan Sonnenschein, 1887.

Matheson, Richard. *I Am Legend*. New York: Tor Books, 1954.

_____. *The Path: A New Look at Reality*. New York: Tor Books, 1993.

_____. *A Primer of Reality*. Springfield, PA: Edge Books, 2002.

_____. *What Dreams May Come*. New York: G.P. Putnam's Sons, 1978.

Mattera, Jason. *Obama Zombies: How the Liberal Machine Brainwashed My Generation*. New York: Threshold, 2011.

May, Reinhard. *Heidegger's Hidden Sources: East Asian Influences on His Work*. Trans. Graham Parkes. London: Routledge, 1996.

MBiti, John S. *African Religions and Philosophy*. New York: Praeger, 1969.

McAlister, Elizabeth. "Slaves, Cannibals, and Infected Hyper-Whites: The Race and Religion of Zombies." *Anthropological Quarterly* 85.2 (2012): 457–486.

McClelland, Bruce A. *Slayers and Their Vampires: A Cultural History of Killing the Dead*. Ann Arbor: University of Michigan Press, 2006.

McDaniel, Justin T. "Encountering Corpses: Notes on Zombies and the Living Dead in Buddhist Southeast Asia." *Kyoto Review of Southeast Asia* 12 (2012). Online: http://kyotoreview.org/wp-content/uploads/Justin-McDaniels_fullversion.pdf. Accessed Sep. 12, 2017.

McDermott, Mark R. "History of the Marvel Zombies and Colonel Am Erica Among the Marvel Zombies." Pp. 147–159 in Robert G. Weiner (ed.), *Captain America and the Struggle of the Superhero: Critical Essays*. Jefferson, NC: McFarland, 2009.

McDonald, Beth E. *The Vampire as Numinous Experience: Spiritual Journeys with the Undead in British and American Literature*. Jefferson, NC: McFarland, 2004.

McGee, Adam M. "Dreaming in Haitian Vodou: Vouchsafe, Guide, and Source of Liturgical Novelty." *Dreaming*. (2012, February 20). Advance online publication. doi: 10.1037/a0026691.

_____. "Haitian Vodou and Voodoo: Imagined Religion and Popular Culture." *Studies in Religion / Science Religeuses* 41.2 (2012): 231–256.

McGlotten, Shaka, and Sarah Vangundy. "Zombie Porn 1.0: Or, Some Queer Things Zombie Sex Can Teach Us." *Qui Parle: Critical Humanities and Social Sciences* 21.2 (2013): 101–125.

McIntosh, Shawn. "The Evolution of the Zombie: The Monster That Keeps Coming Back." Pp. 1–17 in Shawn McIntosh and Marc Leverette (eds.), *Zombie Culture: Autopsies of the Living Dead*. Lanham, MD: Scarecrow Press, 2008.

McIntosh, Shawn, and Marc Leverette (eds.). *Zombie Culture: Autopsies of the Living Dead*. Lanham, MD: Scarecrow Press, 2008.

McLaughlin, Michael. "Dalai Lama: Humans Created Terrorism, So Stop Praying to God for a Solution." *Huffington Post*, Nov. 17, 2015. Online: http://www.huffingtonpost.com/entry/dalai-lama-terrorism_564b8975e4b045bf3df16e75.

McNally, David. *Monsters of the Market: Zombies, Vampires and Global Capitalism*. Leiden, Netherlands: Brill, 2011.

Mechanic, Michael. "The Brains of the Operation: Makeup Master Greg Nicotero Knows How to Freak You Out." *Mother Jones* (March/April 2014): 53–54.

Melton, J. Gordon. *The Vampire Book: The Encyclopedia of the Undead*. Detroit: Visible Ink Press, 1999.

Mendik, Xavier. "Logic, Creativity and (Critical) Misinterpretations: An Interview with David Cronenberg." Pp. 168–185 in Michael Grant (ed.), *The Modern Fantastic: The Films of David Cronenberg*. Westport, CT: Praeger, 2000.

Métraux, Alfred. *Voodoo in Haiti*. Trans. Hugo Charteris. New York: Schocken Books, 1972.

Michel, Claudine, and Patrick Bellegarde-Smith. "*Koko Na Pa Pwèl: Marasa* Reflection on Gede." Pp. 13–16 in Donald J. Cosentino (ed.), *In Extremis: Death* and *Life in 21st-Century Haitian Art*. Los Angeles: Fowler Museum at UCLA, 2012.

Miller, William Ian. *The Anatomy of Disgust*. Cambridge, MA: Harvard University Press, 1997.

Millspaugh, Arthur C. *Haiti Under American Control, 1915–1930*. Boston: World Peace Foundation, 1931.

Mitchell, Charles P. *A Guide to Apocalyptic Cinema*. London: Greenwood Press, 2001.

Mitchell, Margaret (ed.), *Remember Me: Constructing Immortality—Beliefs on Immortality, Life, and Death*. London: Routledge, 2007.

Mittman, Asa Simon, and Peter J. Dendle (eds.). *The Ashgate Research Companion to Monsters and the Monstrous*. Burlington, VT: Ashgate, 2012.

Moreland, Sean. "Shambling Towards Mount Improbable to Be Born: American Evolutionary Anxiety and the Hopeful Monsters of Matheson's *I Am Legend* and Romero's *Dead* Films." Pp. 77–89 in Stephanie Boluk and Wulie Lenz (eds.), *Generation Zombie: Essays on the Living Dead in Modern Culture*. Jefferson, NC: McFarland, 2011.

Moreman, Christopher M. *Beyond the Threshold: Afterlife Beliefs and Experiences in World Religions*, 2nd edition. Lanham, MD: Rowman & Littlefield, 2018.

_____. "Dharma of the Living Dead: A Meditation on the Meaning of the Hollywood Zombie." *Studies in Religion/Sciences Religieuses* 39.2 (2010): 263–281.

_____. "A Modern Meditation on Death: Identifying Buddhist Teachings in George A. Romero's *Night of the Living Dead*." *Contemporary Buddhism* 9.2 (2008): 151–165.

_____. "On the Relationship Between Birds and Spirits of the Dead." *Society & Animals* 22.5 (2014): 481–502.

_____. "Review of *I Am Legend*. Dir. Francis Lawrence." *Journal of Religion and Film* 12.1 (2008): http://www.unomaha.edu/jrf/vol12no1/reviews/ILegen.htm.

_____. "What is the Most Important Thing Zombies Can Teach us About Being Human?" *Science + Religion Today*, June 6, 2012. Online: http://www.scienceandreligiontoday.com/2012/06/06/what-is-the-most-important-thing-zombies-can-teach-us-about-being-human/.

_____. "Why Do We Love Zombies?" *The Washington Post*, Oct. 31, 2011. Online: http://www.washingtonpost.com/blogs/guest-voices/post/why-do-we-love-zombies/2011/10/31/gIQACwBmZM_blog.html.

Moreman, Christopher M., and Cory James Rushton (eds.). *Race, Oppression and the Zombie: Essays on Cross-Cultural Appropriations of the Caribbean Tradition*. Jefferson, NC: McFarland, 2011.

_____. *Zombies Are Us: Essays on the Humanity of the Walking Dead*. Jefferson, NC: McFarland, 2011.

Mori, Masahiro. "The Uncanny Valley." Trans. Karl F. MacDorman and Norri Kageki. *IEEE Robotics & Automation Magazine* (2012): 98–100. Translation of: Mori, "The Uncanny Valley." *Energy* 7.4 (1970): 33–35 (in Japanese).

Morton, Lisa. "The Walking Dead and Dance of Death: Or, Why the Zombies Are Always on the Other Side of the Fence." Pp. 174–184 in James Lowder (ed.), *Triumph of the Walking Dead: Robert Kirkman's Zombie Epic on Page and Screen*. Dallas, TX: BenBella, 2011.

Moyse, Ashley John. "When All is Lost, Gather 'Round: Solidarity as Hope Resisting Despair in *The Walking Dead*." Pp. 124–144 in Kim Paffenroth and John W Morehead (eds.), *The Undead and Theology*. Eugene, OR: Pickwick, 2012.

Muntean, Nick, and Matthew Thomas Payne. "Attack of the Living Dead: Recalibrating Terror in the Post–September 11 Zombie Film." Pp. 239–258 in Andrew Schopp and Matthew B. Hill (eds.), *The War on Terror and American Popular Culture: September 11 and Beyond*. Madison, NJ: Fairleigh Dickinson University Press, 2009.

Murray, Leah A. "When They Aren't Eating Us, They Bring Us Together: Zombies and the American Social Contract." Pp. 211–220 in Richard Greene and K. Silem Mohammad (eds.), *The Undead and Philosophy*. Chicago: Open Court, 2006.

Nasiruddin, Melissa, Monique Halabi, Alexander Dao, Kyle Chen, and Brandon Brown. "Zombies—A Pop Culture Resource for Public Health Awareness." *Emerging Infectious Diseases* 19.5 (2013): 809–813.

Ndalianis, Angela. "Why Comics Studies?" *Cinema Journal* 50.3 (2011): 113–117.

Neimeyer, Robert A. (ed.). *Death Anxiety Handbook: Research, Instrumentation, and Application*. Washington, D.C.: Taylor & Francis, 1994.

Neocleous, Mark. "The Political Economy of the Dead: Marx's Vampires." *History of Political Thought* 24.3 (2003): 668–684.

Newitz, Annalee. *Pretend We're Dead: Capitalist Monsters in American Pop Culture*. Durham, NC: Duke University Press, 2006.

Newman, Kim. "Review of *The Last Man on Earth*." Pp. 31–34 in Jay Slater (ed.). *Eaten Alive! Italian Cannibal and Zombie Movies*. London: Plexus, 2002.

Niehaus, Isak. "Witches and Zombies of the South African Lowveld: Discourse, Accusations and Subjective Reality." *Journal of the Royal Anthropological Institute* 11 (2005): 191–210.

Nietzsche, Friedrich. *The Birth of Tragedy*. Oxford: Oxford University Press, 2000.

_____. *The Gay Science*. Trans. Walter Kaufmann. New York: Vintage, 1974.

Nolan, William F. "The Matheson Years: A Profile in Friendship." Pp. 9–29 in Stanley Wiater, Matthew R. Breadley, and Paul Stuve (eds.), *The Twilight and Other Zones: The Dark Worlds of Richard Matheson*. New York: Citadel Press, 2009.

Norenzayan, Ara, and Ian G. Hansen. "Belief in Supernatural Agents in the Face of Death." *Personality & Social Psychology Bulletin* 32.2 (2006): 174–187.

Obeyesekere, Gannath. *Cannibal Talk: The Man-Eating Myth and Human Sacrifice in the South Seas*. Berkeley: University of California Press, 2005.

O'Brien, Brad. "Vita, Amore, e Morte—and Lots of Gore: The Italian Zombie Film." Pp. 55–70 in Shawn McIntosh and Marc Leverette (eds.), *Zombie Culture: Autopsies of the Living Dead*. Lanham, MD: Scarecrow Press, 2008.

Olney, Ian. *Euro Horror: Classic European Horror Cinema in Contemporary American Culture*. Bloomington: Indiana University Press, 2013.

Ostwalt, Conrad. "Apocalyptic." Pp. 368–383 in John Lyden (ed.), *The Routledge Companion to Religion and Film*. London: Routledge, 2009.

Ostwalt, Conrad E. "Hollywood and Armageddon: Apocalyptic Themes in Recent Cinematic Presentation." Pp. 55–63 in Joel W. Martin and Conrad E. Ostwalt, Jr., (eds.), *Screening the Sacred*. Oxford: Westview Press, 1995.

Owen, Mary A. "Voodoo." Pp. 640–641 in James Hastings (ed.), *Encyclopedia of Religion and Ethics*. New York: Charles Scribner's Sons, 1908–1922.

Paffenroth, Kim. "Apocalyptic Images and Prophetic Function in Zombie Films." Pp. 145–164 in Kim Paffenroth and John W Morehead (eds.), *The Undead and Theology*. Eugene, OR: Pickwick, 2012.

_____. "'For Love is Strong as Death': Redeeming Values in *The Walking Dead*." Pp. 218–230 in James Lowder (ed.), *Triumph of the Walking Dead: Robert Kirkman's Zombie Epic on Page and Screen*. Dallas, TX: BenBella, 2011.

_____. *Gospel of the Living Dead: George Romero's Visions of Hell on Earth*. Waco, TX: Baylor University Press, 2006.

Pagano, David. "The Space of Apocalypse in Zombie Cinema." Pp. 71–86 in Shawn McIntosh and Marc Leverette (eds.), *Zombie Culture: Autopsies of the Living Dead*. Lanham, MD: Scarecrow Press, 2008.

Paglia, Camille. *The Birds*. London: BFI, 1998.

Paquette, Robert L., and Stanley L. Engerman (eds.). *The Lesser Antilles in the Age of European Expansion*. Gainesville: University Press of Florida, 1996.

Parkes, Graham (ed.). *Heidegger and Asian Thought*. Honolulu: University of Hawaii Press, 1987.

Parrinder, Geoffrey. *African Traditional Religion*. London: SPCK, 1962.

Partridge, Christopher. *The Re-Enchantment of the West*. 2 vols. London: T & T Clark, 2004.

Patterson, Kathy Davis. "Echoes of Dracula: Racial Politics and the Failure of Segregated Spaces in Richard Matheson's *I Am Legend*." *Journal of Dracula Studies* 7 (2005): 19–28.

Peaty, Gwyneth. "Zombie Time: Temporality and Living Death." Pp. 186–199 in Dawn Keetley, (ed.), *"We're All Infected": Essays on AMC's* The Walking Dead *and the Fate of the Human*. Jefferson, NC: McFarland, 2014.

Percival, Harold W. *Thinking and Destiny*. New York: The Word Foundation, 1946.

Petrinovich, Lewis. *The Cannibal Within*. New York: Aldine De Gruyter, 2000.

Pharr, Mary. "Vampiric Appetite in *I Am Legend, 'Salem's Lot,* and *The Hunger*." Pp. 93–103 in Leonard G. Heldreth and Mary Pharr (eds.), *The Blood in the Life: Vampires in Literature*. Bowling Green, OH: Bowling Green State University Popular Press, 1999.

Phillips, Kendall R. *Dark Directions: Romero, Craven, and the Modern Horror Film*. Carbondale: Southern Illinois University Press, 2012.

Pinedo, Isabel Cristina. "Postmodern Elements of the Contemporary Horror Film." Pp. 85–117 in Stephen Prince (ed.), *The Horror Film*. New York: Rutgers University Press, 2004.

Pirie, David. *The Vampire Cinema*. New York: Crescent Books, 1977.

Pistorius, Martin. *Ghost Boy*. New York: Simon & Schuster, 2011.

Plato. *The Dialogues of Plato*. Trans. B. Jowett, 5 vols. Oxford: Clarenden Press, 1892.

Polk, Patrick A. "Remember You Must Die! Gede Banners, Memento Mori, and the Fine Art of Facing Death." Pp. 115–141 in Donald J. Cosentino (ed.), *In Extremis: Death and Life in 21st-Century Haitian Art*. Los Angeles: Fowler Museum at UCLA, 2012.

Poole, W. Scott. *Monsters in America: Our Historical Obsession with the Hideous and the Haunting*. Waco, TX: Baylor University Press, 2011.

Potter, Amy E. "Voodoo, Zombies, and Mermaids: U.S. Newspaper Coverage of Haiti." *The Geographical Review* 99.2 (2009): 208–230.

Prince, Stephen (ed.). *The Horror Film*. New York: Rutgers University Press, 2004.

Pulliam, June. "The Zombie." Vol. 2, pp. 723–753 in S.T. Joshi (ed.), *Icons of Horror and the Supernatural: An Encyclopedia of Our Worst Nightmares*, 2 Vols. Westport, CT: Greenwood Press, 2007.

Rahula, Walpola. *What the Buddha Taught*, 2nd ed. New York: Grove Press, 1974.

Randell, Karen. "Lost Bodies/Lost Souls: *Night of the Living Dead* and *Deathdream* as Vietnam Narrative." Pp. 67–76 in Stephanie Boluk and Wulie Lenz (eds.), *Generation Zombie: Essays on the Living Dead in Modern Culture*. Jefferson, NC: McFarland, 2011.

Ransom, Amy J. "Ce Zombi égaré est-il un Haïtien ou un Québécois? Le vaudou chez les écrivains haïtiano-québécois," *Canadian Literature* 203 (2009): 64–83.

Redfield, James. *The Celestine Prophecy*. New York: Warner Books, 1993.

Reid, Basil A. *Myths and Realities of Caribbean History*. Tuscaloosa: University of Alabama Press, 2009.

"Religious Landscape Study." Pew Research Center. Online: http://www.pewforum.org/religious-landscape-study/state/pennsylvania/. Accessed Sep. 10, 2017.

Rhodes, Gary D. *White Zombie: Anatomy of a Horror Film*. Jefferson, NC: McFarland, 2001.

Richman, Karen E. *Migration and Vodou*. Gainesville: University Press of Florida, 2005.

Ridley, Aaron. "Nietzsche's Greatest Weight." *Journal of Nietzsche Studies* 14 (1997): 19–25.

Robinne, François. "Theatre of Death and Rebirth: Monks' Funerals in Burma." Pp. 165–191 in Paul Williams and Patrice Ladwig (eds.). *Buddhist Funeral Cultures of Southeast Asia and China*. Cambridge: Cambridge University Press, 2012.

Robinson, Juneko J. "Immanent Attack: An Existential Take on *The Invasion of the Body Snatchers* Films." Pp. 23–44 in Scott A. Lukas and John Marmysz (eds.), *Fear, Cultural Anxiety, and Transformation: Horror, Science Fiction, and Fantasy Films Remade*. Plymouth, UK: Lexington Books, 2009.

Robison-Greene, Rachel. "Better Off Undead." Pp. 119–128 in Wayne Yuen (ed.), *The Walking Dead and Philosophy: Zombie Apocalypse Now*. Chicago: Open Court, 2012.

Roche, David. "'That's real! That's what you want!': Producing Fear in George A. Romero's *Dawn of the Dead* (1978) vs. Zack Snyder's Remake (2004)." *Horror Studies* 2.1 (2011): 75–87.

Rodley, Chris (ed.). *Cronenberg on Cronenberg*. London: Faber & Faber, 1992.

Roos, Martin, Hans Nugteren, and Zhong Jinwén. "Tales of the Bewitched Corpse." Online: http://members.home.nl/marcmarti/yugur/folktale/bewitchedcorpse.htm. Accessed Sept. 10, 2017.

Rosenberg, Bernhard H., and Chaim Z. Rozwaski. *Contemplating the Holocaust*. Jerusalem: Jason Aronson, 1999.

Rouyer, Philippe. *Le cinéma gore: une esthétique du sang*. Paris: Le cerf, 1997.

_____. "Le gore des zombies." Pp. 131–138 in Jean-Baptiste Thoret (ed.), *Politique des zombies: L'Amérique selon George A. Romero*. Paris: Ellipses, 2007.

Rozin, Paul, J. Haidt, and C.R. McCauley. "Disgust." pp. 757–776 in Michael Lewis and Jeannette M. Haviland-Jones (eds.), *Handbook of Emotions*, 3rd edition. New York: Guilford, 2008.

Russell, Jamie. *Book of the Dead: The Complete History of Zombie Cinema*. Surrey, UK: FAB Press, 2005.

Russo, John. *The Complete Night of the Living Dead Filmbook*. New York: Harmony Books, 1985.

_____. *Undead*. New York: Kensington, 2010.

Russo, John (Story), Dheeraj Verma (Pencils), Lalit (Inks). *Escape of the Living Dead*. Rantoul, IL: Avatar, 2006.

Saddhatissa, Hammalawa. *The Life of the Buddha*. New York: Harper & Row, 1976.

St. Augustine. *The Confessions of St. Augustine*. Trans. John K. Ryan. New York: Image Books, 1960.

Saro-Wiwa, Zina. "No Going Back." Pp. 17–26 in Pieter Hugo, *Nollywood*. Munich: Presetel, 2009.

Schneider, Steven Jay (ed.). *Horror Film and Psychoanalysis: Freud's Worst Nightmare*. Cambridge: Cambridge University Press, 2004.

Schopp, Andrew, and Matthew B. Hill (eds.). *The War on Terror and American Popular Culture: September 11 and Beyond*. Madison, NJ: Fairleigh Dickinson University Press, 2009.

Schwartz, Susan L. "I Dream, Therefore I Am: *What Dreams May Come*." *Journal of Religion and Film* 4.1 (2000). Online: http://www.unomaha.edu/jrf/IDream.htm.

Scott, Niall (ed.). *Monsters and the Monstrous: Myths and Metaphors of Enduring Evil*. New York: Rodopi, 2007.

Scruton, David L. (ed.). *Sociophobics: The Anthropology of Fear*. Boulder, CO: Westview Press, 1986.

Seabrook, William. *The Magic Island*. New York: Literary Guild of America, 1929.

See, Tony, and Joff Bradley (eds.). *Deleuze and Buddhism*. London: Palgrave Macmillan, 2016.

Seneca. *On the Shortness of Life*. Trans. John W. Basore. London: William Heinemann, 1932.

Senn, Bryan. *Drums of Terror: Voodoo in the Cinema*. Baltimore, MD: Midnight Marquee Press, Inc., 1998.

Sheller, Mimi. *Consuming the Caribbean: From Arawaks to Zombies*. London: Routledge, 2003.

Siderits, Mark, Evan Thompson, and Dan Zahavi (eds.), *Self, No Self?: Perspectives from Analytical, Phenomenological, and Indian Traditions*. Oxford: Oxford University Press, 2011.

Sigurdson, Ola. "Slavoj Zizek, The Death Drive, and Zombies: A Theological Account." *Modern Theology* 29.3 (2013): 361–380.

Silvia, Paul J. "Nothing or the Opposite: Intersecting Terror Management and Objective Self-Awareness." *European Journal of Personality* 15 (2001): 73–82.

Simmons, William P. "Reflections of a Storyteller: A Conversation with Richard Matheson." *Cemetery Dance* 49 (2004). Online: http://www.rodserling.com/wsimmons/Richard_Matheson.htm.

Skal, David J. *The Monster Show: A Cultural History of Horror*. London: W.W. Norton & Co., 1993.

Skilling, Peter. "Zombies and Half-Zombies: Mahāsūtras and Other Protective Measures." *Journal of the Pali Text Society* 29 (2007): 313–330.

Slater, Jay (ed.). *Eaten Alive! Italian Cannibal and Zombie Movies*. London: Plexus, 2002.

Smith, Anthony N. "Putting the Premium into Basic: Slow-Burn Narratives and the Loss-Leader Function of AMC's Original Drama Series." *Television & New Media* 14.2 (2011): 150–166.

Smith, Katherine. "Genealogies of Gede." Pp. 85–99 in Donald J. Cosentino (ed.), *In Extremis: Death and Life in 21st-Century Haitian Art*. Los Angeles: Fowler Museum at UCLA, 2012.

Solomon, Sheldon, Jeff Greenberg, and Tom Pyszczynski. "A Terror Management Theory of Social Behavior: The Psychological Functions of Self-Esteem and Cultural Worldviews." Pp. 91–159 in Mark Zanna (Ed.), *Advances in Experimental Social Psychology*, Vol. 24. Orlando, FL: Academic Press, 1991.

Spengler, Oswald. *The Decline of the West*. Trans. Charles Francis Atkinson. New York: Alfred A. Knopf, 1926.

Staley, Gregory A. *Seneca and the Idea of Tragedy*. New York: Oxford University Press, 2010.

Stonington, Scott. "Facing Death, Gazing Inward: End-of-Life and the Transformation of Clinical Subjectivity in Thailand." *Culture, Medicine, and Psychiatry* 35 (2011): 113–133.

Stratton, Jon. "Zombie Trouble: Zombie Texts, Bare Life and Displaced People." *European Journal of Cultural Studies* 14.3 (2011): 265–281.

Stuve, Paul. "Birth of a Writer: The Matheson/Peden Letters." Pp. 30–46 in Stanley Wiater, Matthew R. Breadley, and Paul Stuve (eds.), *The Twilight and Other Zones: The Dark Worlds of Richard Matheson*. New York: Citadel Press, 2009.

Sugg, Richard. *Mummies, Cannibals and Vampires: The History of Corpse Medicine from the Renaissance to the Victorians*. London: Routledge, 2011.

Sullivan, Daniel, and Jeff Greenberg. *Death in Classic and Contemporary Film*. London: Palgrave Macmillan, 2013.

Surmacz, Gary Anthony. "Anatomy of a Horror Film." (A round-table with Russo, Hardman and Streiner). *Cinefantastique* 4.1 (1975): 14–27.

Svenaeus, Fredrik. "Organ Transplantation and Personal Identity: How Does Loss and Change of Organs Affect the Self?" *Journal of Medicine and Philosophy* 37.2 (2012): 139–158.

Szczesiul, Anthony. "Re-Mapping Southern Hospitality: Discourse, Ethics, Politics." *European Journal of American Culture* 26.2 (2007): 127–141.

Tassi, Paul. "AMC Has an Explanation for *The Walking Dead*'s Ratings Being Down." *Forbes.com*. May 20, 2017. Online: https://www.forbes.com/sites/insertcoin/2017/05/20/amc-has-an-explanation-for-the-walking-deads-ratings-being-down/#16d8e9598d44.

Taubman-Ben-Ari, Orit. "Is the Meaning of Life Also the Meaning of Death? A Terror Management Perspective Reply." *Journal of Happiness Studies* 12 (2011): 385–399.

Taylor, Clyde. "Autopsy of Terror: A Conversation with Raoul Peck." *Transition* 69 (1996): 236–246.

Thacker, Eugene. *In the Dust of This Planet*. Winchester, UK: Zero Books, 2011.

Thompson, Hamish. "'She's not your mother anymore, she's a zombie!': Zombies, Value, and Personal Identity." Pp. 27–37 in Richard Greene and K. Silem Mohammad (eds.), *Zombies, Vampires, and Philosophy: New Life for the Undead*. Chicago: Open Court, 2010.

Thompson, Jason. "House of 1000 Manga: 10 Great Zombie Manga." *Anime News Network*, Jan 9th, 2014. Online: http://www.animenewsnetwork.com/house-of-1000-manga/2014-01-09.

Thompson, Robert Farris. "From the Isle Beneath the Sea: Haiti's Africanizing Vodou Art." Pp. 91–119 in D.J. Cosentino (ed.), *Sacred Arts of Haitian Vodou*. Los Angeles: UCLA Fowler Museum of Cultural History, 1995.

Thoret, Jean-Baptiste (ed.). *Politique des zombies: L'Amérique selon George A. Romero*. Paris: Ellipses, 2007.

Thrower, Stephen. *Beyond Terror: The Films of Lucio Fulci*. Surrey, UK: FAB, 1999.

Totaro, Donato. "Review of *Dellamorte Dellamore*." Pp. 231–235 in Jay Slater (ed.), *Eaten Alive! Italian Cannibal and Zombie Movies*. London: Plexus, 2002.

Totaro, Rebecca. "Review of Coke, Jennifer, *Legacies of Plague in Literature, Theory and Film*." *Social History of Medicine* 23.1 (2010): 208–209.

Tudor, Andrew. *Monsters and Mad Scientists: A Cultural History of the Horror Movie*. Oxford: Blackwell, 1987.

Twitchell, James B. *Dreadful Pleasures: The Anatomy of Modern Horror*. Oxford: Oxford University Press, 1985.

Vail III, Kenneth E., Zachary K. Rothchild, David R. Weise, Sheldon Solomon, Tom Pyszczynski, and Jeff Greenberg. "A Terror Management Analysis of the Psychological Functions of Religion." *Personality and Social Psychology Review* 14.1 (2010): 84–94.

van der Velde, Paul. "Over My Dead Buddha! Death and Buddhism." Pp. 239–258 in Eric Venbrux, Thomas Quartier, Claudia Venhorst, and Brenda Mathijssen (eds.). *Changing European Death Ways*. Zurich: Lit, 2013.

Varnado, S.L. *Haunted Presence: The Numinous in Gothic Fiction*. Tuscaloosa: University of Alabama Press, 1987.

Venbrux, Eric, Thomas Quartier, Claudia Venhorst, and Brenda Mathijssen (eds.). *Changing European Death Ways*. Zurich: Lit, 2013.

Vice, Sue. *Introducing Bakhtin*. Manchester, UK: Manchester University Press, 1997.

Waldram, James. *Revenge of the Windigo: The Construction of the Mind and Mental Health of North American Aboriginal Peoples*. Toronto: University of Toronto Press, 2004.

Walker, Seth M. "'Whatever it is, we all carry it': Tanhā and AMC's *The Walking Dead*." *Nomos Journal* (2012). Online: http://nomosjournal.org/2012/10/whatever-it-is-we-all-carry-it/. Accessed Sept. 10, 2017.

Waller, Gregory A. *American Horrors: Essays on the Modern American Horror Film*. Chicago: University of Illinois Press, 1987.

_____ (ed.). *The Living and the Undead: From Stoker's* Dracula *to Romero's* Dawn of the Dead. Urbana and Chicago: University of Illinois Press, 1986.

Walter, Michael. "Of Corpses and Gold: Materials for the Study of the Vetala and the Rolangs." *The Tibet Journal* 29.2 (2004): 13–46.

Walter, Tony. *The Revival of Death*. London: Routledge, 1994.

Walton, Priscilla L. *Our Cannibals, Ourselves*. Urbana and Chicago, IL: University of Illinois Press, 2004.

Wangmo, Tenzin. *The Prince and the Zombie: Tibetan Tales of Karma*. Boston: Shambhala, 2014.

Warnock, Mary. *Existentialism*. Oxford: Oxford University Press, 1970.

Watts, Jonathan S., and Yoshiharu Tomatsu (eds.). *Buddhist Care for the Dying and Bereaved*. Boston: Wisdom Publications, 2012.

Weaver, Tom. *Return of the B Science Fiction and Horror Heroes: The Mutant Melding of Two Volumes of Classic Interviews*. Jefferson, NC: McFarland, 2000.

Webb, Jen, and Sam Byrnand. "Some Kind of Virus: The Zombie as Body and as Trope." *Body & Society* 14.2 (2008): 83–98.

Wertham, Fredric. *Seduction of the Innocent*. New York: Rinehart & Co., 1954.

Wetmore, Kevin J., Jr. *Back from the Dead: Remakes of the Romero Zombie Films as Markers of Their Times*. Jefferson, NC: McFarland, 2011.

White, John, and Sabine Haenni (eds.). *Fifty Key American Films*. London: Routledge, 2009.

White, Luise. *Speaking with Vampires: Rumor and History in Colonial Africa*. Berkeley, CA: University of California Press, 2000.

Wiater, Stanley, Matthew R. Breadley, and Paul Stuve (eds.). *The Twilight and Other Zones: The Dark Worlds of Richard Matheson*. New York: Citadel Press, 2009.

Wijayaratna, Mohan. "Funerary Rites in Japanese and Other Asian Buddhist Societies." *Japan Review* 8 (1997): 105–125.

Wilde, Oscar. *The Picture of Dorian Grey*. Mineola, NY: Dover Thrift, 1993 [1891].

Williams, Gerhild Scholz. *The Vision of Death: A Study of the "Memento Mori" Expressions in Some Latin, German, and French Didactic Texts of the 11th and 12th Centuries*. Göppingen, DE: Verlag Alfred Kümmerle, 1976.

Williams, Paul. "Some Mahāyāna Buddhist Perspectives on the Body." Pp. 205–230 in Sarah Coakley (ed.), *Religion and the Body*. Cambridge: Cambridge University Press, 1997.

Williams, Paul, and Patrice Ladwig (eds.). *Buddhist Funeral Cultures of Southeast Asia and China*. Cambridge: Cambridge University Press, 2012.

Williams, Tony. *George A. Romero: Interviews*. Jackson: University Press of Mississippi, 2011.

____ (ed.). "An Interview with George and Christine Romero." *Quarterly Review of Film and Video* 18.4 (2001): 397–411.

Wood, Robin. "Cronenberg: A Dissenting View." Pp. 115–135 in Piers Handling (ed.). *The Shape of Rage: The Films of David Cronenberg*. Toronto: General Publishing, 1983.

____. "Fresh Meat: *Diary of the Dead* May Be the Summation of George A. Romero's Zombie Cycle (at Least Until the Next Installment)." *Film Comment* 44: 1 (Jan./Feb., 2008): pp. 28–31.

____. *Hollywood from Vietnam to Reagan ... and Beyond*. New York: Columbia University Press, 2003.

____. "An Introduction to the American Horror Film." Pp. 107–141 in Barry Keith Grant and Christopher Sharrett (eds.), *Planks of Reason: Essays on the Horror Film*, rev. ed. Lanham, MD: Scarecrow Press, 2004.

Worley, Lloyd. "Impaling, Dracula, and the Bible." Pp. 168–180 in George Aichele and Tina Pippin, (eds.), *The Monstrous and the Unspeakable: The Bible as Fantastic Literature*. Sheffield, UK: Sheffield Academic Press, 1997.

Wylie, Turrell. "Ro-langs: The Tibetan Zombie." *History of Religions* 4.1 (Summer, 1964): 69–80.

Yacowar, Maurice. "The Comedy of Cronenberg." Pp. 80–86 in Piers Handling (ed.), *The Shape of Rage: The Films of David Cronenberg*. Toronto: General Publishing, 1983.

Yakir, Dan. "Knight After Night with George Romero." *American Film* 6 (1981): 42–45, 69.

____. "Morning Becomes Romero: George Romero Interviewed by Dan Yakir." *Film Comment* 15.3 (May/June 1979): 60–65.

Yang, Che-ming. "Nietzsche, Deleuze, and Nāgārjuna: Mapping the Dialectics of Will/Desire." *Journal of Language Teaching and Research* 1.6 (2010): 842–847.

Yuen, Wayne (ed.). The Walking Dead *and Philosophy: Zombie Apocalypse Now*. Chicago: Open Court, 2012.

Zanna, Mark (ed.). *Advances in Experimental Social Psychology*, Vol. 24. Orlando, FL: Academic Press, 1991.

Zizek, Slavoj. "Is the Quest for Good a Road to Evil? Spring, Summer, Autumn, Winter ... and Spring." *The Guardian*. April 14, 2015. Online: http://www.theguardian.com/film/2015/apr/14/force-majeure-films-philosophy-memento-ida-its-a-wonderful-life.

____. *The Plague of Fantasies*. London: Verso, 1997.

Filmography

Attack Girls' Swim Team vs. Undead. Dir. Koji Kawano. 2007. Video.
Battle Girl: The Living Dead in Tokyo Bay. Dir. Kazuo Komizu. 1991. Video.
Behind the Green Door. Dir. Artie & Jim Mitchell. 1972. Film.
Big Tits Zombie. Dir. Takao Nakano. 2010. Film.
The Birds. Dir. Alfred Hitchcock. 1963. Film.
Blacula. Dir. William Crain. 1972. Film.
Blood Feast. Dir. Herschell Gordon Lewis. 1963. Film.
Blue Sunshine. Dir. Jeff Lieberman. 1977. Film.
Body Snatchers. Dir. Abel Ferrara. 1993. Film.
Bordello of Blood. Dir. Gilbert Adler. 1996. Film.
The Brood. Dir. David Cronenberg. 1979. Film.
Cannibal Apocalypse. Dir. Antonio Margheriti. 1980. Film.
Carnival of Souls. Dir. Herk Harvey. 1962. Film.
Cell. Dir. Tod Williams. 2016. Film.
Children Shouldn't Play with Dead Things. Dir. Benjamin Clark. 1972. Film.
A Christmas Story. Dir. Bob Clark. 1983. Film.
City of the Living Dead. Dir. Lucio Fulci. 1980. Film.
The Coffin. Dir. Ekachai Uekrongtham. 2008. Film.
Color Me Blood Red. Dir. Herschell Gordon Lewis. 1965. Film.
Commando. Dir. Mark L. Lester. 1985. Film.
The Crazies. Dir. Breck Eisner. 2010. Film.
The Crazies. Dir. George A. Romero. 1973. Film.
Creature with the Atom Brain. Dir. Edward L. Cahn. 1955. Film.
Creepshow. Dir. George A. Romero. 1982. Film.
Crimes of the Future. Dir. David Cronenberg. 1970. Film.
Dawn of the Dead. Dir. George A. Romero. 1978. Film.
Dawn of the Dead. Dir. Zack Snyder. 2004. Film.
Day of the Dead. Dir. George A. Romero. 1985. Film.
Day of the Dead. Dir. Steve Miner. 2008. Video.
Day the World Ended. Dir. Roger Corman. 1955. Film.
Death Scenes. Dir. Nick Bougas. 1989. Video.
Deathdream. Dir. Bob Clark. 1974. Film.
Dellamorte Dellamore. Dir. Michele Soavi. 1994. Film.
Diary of the Dead. Dir. George A. Romero. 2007. Film.
The Diving Bell and the Butterfly. Dir. Julian Schnabel. 2007. Film.
Dr. Jekyll and Mr. Hyde. Dir. Rouben Mamoulian. 1931. Film.

Doomsday Preppers. National Geographic. 2011–2014. Television.
Dracula. Dir. Tod Browning. 1931. Film.
The Earth Dies Screaming. Dir. Terence Fisher. 1964. Film.
Evil Dead. Dir. Sam Raimi. 1981. Film.
Evil Dead II. Dir. Sam Raimi. 1987. Film.
Faces of Death. Dir. Conan Le Cilaire. 1978. Video.
Faces of Death II. Dir. Conan Le Cilaire. 1981. Video.
Faces of Death III. Dir. Conan Le Cilaire. 1985. Video.
Faces of Death IV. Dir. Conan Le Cilaire. 1990. Video.
Faces of Death V. Dir. Conan Le Cilaire. 1995. Video.
Fear the Walking Dead. AMC. 2015– . Television.
Fido. Dir. Andrew Currie. 2006. Film.
The Fly. Dir. David Cronenberg. 1986. Film.
Frankenstein. Dir. James Whale. 1931. Film.
Friday the 13th. Dir. Sean S. Cunningham. 1980. Film.
The Frozen Dead. Dir. Herbert J. Leder. 1966. Film.
Garden of the Dead. Dir. John Hayes. 1972. Film.
The Ghost Breakers. Dir. George Marshall. 1940. Film.
Ghost Ship of the Blind Dead. Dir. Amando de Ossorio. 1974. Film.
The Ghoul. Dir. T. Hayes Hunter. 1933. Film.
Halloween. Dir. John Carpenter. 1978. Film.
I Am Legend. Dir. Francis Lawrence. 2007. Film.
I Walked with a Zombie. Dir. Jacques Tourneur. 1943. Film.
Insatiable. Dir. Godfrey Daniels. 1980. Film.
The Invasion. Dir. Oliver Hirschbiegel. 2007. Film.
Invasion of the Body Snatchers. Dir. Don Siegel. 1956. Film.
Invasion of the Body Snatchers. Dir. Philip Kaufman. 1978. Film.
Invisible Invaders. Dir. Edward L. Cahn. 1959. Film.
iZombie. The CW. 2015– . Television.
Jaws. Dir. Steven Spielberg. 1975. Film.
The Killer Shrews. Dir. Ray Kellogg. 1959. Film.
King Kong. Dir. Merian C. Cooper. 1933. Film.
King of the Zombies. Dir. Jean Yarbrough. 1941. Film.
Land of the Dead. Dir. George A. Romero. 2005. Film.
The Last Man on Earth. Dir. Ubaldo B. Ragona. 1964. Film.
Left Behind. Dir. Vic Armstrong. 2014. Film.
Left Behind: The Movie. Dir. Vic Sarin. 2000. Video.
Left Behind II: Tribulation Force. Dir. Bill Corcoran. 2002. Film.
Left Behind: World at War. Dir. Craig R. Baxley. 2005. Film.
The Living Dead. Dir. Thomas Bentley. 1936. Film.
The Living Dead at Manchester Morgue. Dir. Jorge Grau. 1974. Film.
Loving and Laughing. Dir. J. Johnson. 1971. Film.
Maggie. Dir. Henry Hobson. 2015. Film.
The Man They Could Not Hang. Dir. Nick Grinde. 1939. Film.
Michael Jackson: Thriller. Dir. John Landis. 1983. Video.
Night of the Living Dead. Dir. George A. Romero. 1968. Film.
Night of the Living Dead. Dir. Tom Savini. 1990. Film.
Night of the Living Dead: 30th Anniversary Edition. Dir. John A. Russo. 1998. Video.
Night of the Seagulls. Dir. Amando de Ossorio. 1975. Film.
Nightmare City. Dir. Umberto Lenzi. 1980. Film.
Nightmare on Elm Street. Dir. Wes Craven. 1984. Film.
The Omega Man. Dir. Boris Sagal. 1971. Film.
The Passion of the Christ. Dir. Mel Gibson. 2004. Film.
The Pervert's Guide to Ideology. Dir. Sophie Fiennes. 2012. Documentary.
The Plague of Zombies. Dir. John Gilling. 1966. Film.
Plan 9 from Outer Space. Dir. Ed Wood. 1958. Film.
Pontypool. Dir. Bruce McDonald. 2008. Film.
Porky's. Dir. Bob Clark. 1981. Film.
Pride and Prejudice and Zombies. Dir. Burr Steers. 2016. Film.
Psycho. Dir. Alfred Hitchcock. 1960. Film.
Rabid. Dir. David Cronenberg. 1977. Film.

Resident Evil. Dir. Paul W.S. Anderson. 2002. Film.
Return of the Blind Dead. Dir. Amando de Ossorio. 1973. Film.
Return of the Living Dead. Dir. Dan O'Bannon. 1985. Film.
Return of the Living Dead: Part II. Dir. Ken Wiederhorn. 1988. Film.
Revenge of the Zombies. Dir. Steve Sekely. 1943. Film.
Revolt of the Zombies. Dir. Victor Halperin. 1936. Film.
Ritual. Dir. Michael Evanichko. 2001. Film.
Scream, Blacula, Scream. Dir. Bob Kelljan. 1973. Film.
The Serpent and the Rainbow. Dir. Wes Craven. 1988. Film.
The 700 Club. CBN. 1966– . Television.
Shaun of the Dead. Dir. Edgar Wright. 2004. Film.
The Shining. Dir. Stanley Kubrick. 1980. Film.
Shivers. Dir. David Cronenberg. 1975. Film.
Slaves. Dir. Herbert J. Biberman. 1969. Film.
Spider Baby. Dir. Jack Hill. 1964. Film.
Survival of the Dead. Dir. George A. Romero. 2009. Film.
Tales from the Crypt. HBO. 1989–1996. Television.
Tales from the Crypt: Demon Knight. Dir. Ernest Dickerson. 1995. Film.
Terror-Creatures from the Grave. Dir. Massimo Pupillo. 1965. Film.
The Texas Chainsaw Massacre. Dir. Tobe Hooper. 1974. Film.
They Live. Dir. John Carpenter. 1988. Film.
The Thing. Dir. John Carpenter. 1982. Film.
The Thing from Another World. Dir. Christian Nyby & Howard Hawks. 1951. Film.
Tokyo Zombie. Dir. Sakichi Sato. 2005. Film.
Tombs of the Blind Dead. Dir. Amando de Ossorio. 1972. Film.
Toxic Zombies. Dir. Charles McCrann. 1980. Film.

28 Days Later. Dir. Danny Boyle. 2002. Film.
Two Thousand Maniacs! Dir. Herschell Gordon Lewis. 1964. Film.
Vault of Horror. Dir. Roy Ward Baker. 1973. Film.
Videodrome. Dir. David Cronenberg. 1983. Film.
Voodoo Island. Dir. Reginald LeBorg. 1957. Film.
Voodoo Man. Dir. William Beaudine. 1944. Film.
The Walking Dead. Dir. Michael Curtiz. 1936.
The Walking Dead. AMC. 2010– . Television.
Warm Bodies. Dir. Jonathan Levine. 2013. Film.
Weekend at Bernie's. Dir. Ted Kotcheff. 1989. Film.
Weekend at Bernie's II. Dir. Robert Klane. 1993. Film.
What Dreams May Come. Dir. Vincent Ward. 1998. Film.
White Zombie. Dir. Victor Halperin. 1932. Film.
World War Z. Dir. Marc Forster. 2013. Film.
Z Nation. Syfy. 2014– . Television.
Zombeavers. Dir. Jordan Rubin. 2014. Film.
Zombi 2. Dir. Lucio Fulci. 1979. Film.
Zombi 3. Dir. Lucio Fulci. 1988. Film.
Zombie Ass: Toilet of the Dead. Dir. Noboru Iguchi. 2011. Film.
Zombie Honeymoon. Dir. David Gebroe. 2004. Film.
Zombie Strippers. Dir. Jay Lee. 2008. Film.
Zombieland. Dir. Ruben Fleischer. 2009. Film.
Zombies Anonymous. Dir. Marc Fratto. 2006. Film.
The Zombies of Sugar Hill. Dir. Paul Maslansky. 1974. Film.

Index

abject 20, 79, 88, 93, 105, 109, 114, 115, 120, 125, 126, 130, 131, 133, 150, 152, 153, 155, 166, 176
absurd/aburdity 77, 79, 80, 88, 122, 123, 170, 176, 177
Adam (biblical) 27
Africa/n 8, 9, 15, 16, 21–24, 26–30, 32, 34, 35, 37, 38–40, 42, 45, 47, 50, 93
African-American 16, 28
afterlife 29, 60, 61, 96, 105, 106, 122
Agamben 16, 39
aggregates 5, 142
aging 4, 13, 117, 119, 130, 135, 161, 180
AIDS 1, 103
Aikido 164
Al-Ghazzali 105
Aliens (extraterrestrial) 11, 43, 50–53, 65, 68, 72, 120, 132
Alzheimer's 13, 69, 85, 86, 133, 134
anatomy 92, 109, 113, 115
anatta 19, 142, 143, 155, 174
ancestors, spiritual 28, 29–32
angel 26, 31, 150, 169
angst 2, 3, 77, 79, 80, 173, 175, 182
animal 1, 31, 58, 129, 130, 150
Anselm, Saint 108
apocalypse 3, 4, 15, 67, 74, 76, 77, 81, 86–88, 97, 98, 100, 103, 120, 123, 129, 133, 136, 160, 172
apocalyptic 2, 7, 58, 63, 65, 74, 87, 95–99, 122, 138, 172
apparitions 3
Arawak 22, 30
Arendt, Hannah 16, 96
Argento, Dario 116
Aries, Philipe 121

Aristotle 175
Armageddon 95
Arnobius of Sicca 108
ars moriendi 92, 104, 109, 113
art-horror 127
ascetic 107, 109, 139
asceticism 106, 140
Atlas Comics 67
atman 29, 143, 155
attached 28, 40, 52, 121, 135, 142, 144, 151, 157, 158, 161, 179, 180
attachment 19, 52, 75, 106, 135, 140, 142, 144–146, 148–151, 157–163, 165–167, 169, 177, 179, 180, 182
Augustine, Saint 106, 115, 116, 137
Auschwitz 96, 158
auto-icon 110
autopsy 109, 153
awakened 139, 140, 170

baby-boom 4, 13
Bakhtin, Mikhail 79, 120–122, 124
bamboo 5
bardo 134
Bardo-Thodol 149
bare-life 39, 50, 180
Baron Samedi 27, 74
Barrymore, John 68
Barthes, Roland 111
Baudrillard, Jean 135
Beal, Timothy 95
Beat Generation 57, 64, 93, 137
Becker, Ernest 146, 174
Beckett, Samuel 79
Bellegarde-Smith, Patrick 23, 25
Benedict, Pope 96

229

Index

Benin 28
Bentham, Jeremy 109, 110
bhikkhu 151, 165
Bible 63, 96–98, 102
Bierce, Ambrose 12, 143
birds 70, 149–151, 170
The Birds 43, 69, 70
Bishop, Kyle 13, 115
Bizango 34
Blackgas 67
Blacula 74, 183
Blaxploitation 74, 75
bodhisattva 167
Body Worlds 115, 199n100
bokor 31–36, 45
Boukman, Dutty 23, 25
Boyle, Danny 81
Bradbury, Ray 65
Brahmin 140
brain: destroyed 10, 71, 110, 121; eating 9, 10, 74, 78, 128, 129, 159, 160
brain-death 13, 85, 86, 134
Braude, Stephen 153
Brazil 64
bread, as flesh of Christ 36, 94, 107
Brooks, Max 87, 172
Brundlefly 117
Buddha 5, 12, 68, 139–147, 155, 157–159, 162, 163, 166, 168, 170, 171, 173, 175–177, 179
Buddhaghosa 150–152
Buddhism 2–4, 6, 19, 61, 67, 78, 136–138, 140, 142, 143, 145, 147–149, 152, 157, 166, 167, 169, 173, 179, 180
Burmese 170, 179
bushido 105

Cambodia 47, 170
Cameroon 30
Campagne anti-superstitieuse 40
Campbell, John 43, 52
Camus, Albert 19, 80, 122, 123, 176, 177
Canada 48, 116
cancer 88, 117, 126, 150, 168
Candomblé 28
Cannibal Apocalypse 77, 129
cannibalism 8, 15, 36–38, 40, 69, 77, 84, 93, 128–132
Carib 37, 128
Caribbean 15, 22, 29, 36, 37, 42, 76, 131
Carnival of Souls 44, 69
carnivalesque 79, 105, 120
Carpenter, John 72, 116, 190n38
Carroll, Noël 6, 116, 127
Cartesian 12, 143
Casas, Bartolomé de las 23, 24
Castaneda, Carlos 61

caste 140
Catholicism 3, 15, 18, 21, 23–29, 35–37, 39, 40, 55, 76, 86, 91–94, 96, 98, 100–103, 106, 112, 113, 120, 152
Cell 73, 130
cemetery 3, 27, 73, 100, 121, 124, 125, 151
Chalmers, David 10, 11
Chan 168; *see also* Zen
children 23, 31, 28, 29, 37, 38, 58, 62, 64, 66, 72, 74, 83, 119, 133, 145, 162
Christ 15, 27, 35, 36, 61–63, 92–97, 100, 101, 103
Christianity 1, 3, 15, 17–20, 23–28, 29, 31, 35–37, 40, 42, 53–57, 60–64, 84, 86, 88, 89, 92–96, 98, 100, 102–106, 112, 120, 126, 136–138, 147, 152, 155, 180, 181, 183
chronic time 133–135
church 23–26, 35, 37, 55, 62, 63, 76, 81, 93, 94, 96, 100, 101
Churchianity 56
Clark, Bob 72, 73
clinging 51, 55, 64, 73, 83, 112, 127, 144, 146, 165, 166, 173, 178, 179, 182
Code noir 24
The Coffin 168
Cohen, Jeffrey 6, 78
Columbus, Christopher 15, 22, 24, 36, 37
coma 13, 33, 81, 85, 86, 133, 134
comedy 48, 71, 77–80, 83–86, 88, 117, 120–125, 136
comic books 4, 17, 44, 64–67, 75, 85, 102, 111, 131, 132, 136, 161, 164
Comics Code 66–68
Commando 161, 162
compassion 3, 20, 53, 57, 102, 106, 149, 150, 157, 162, 169, 179
consciousness 10–14, 18, 31, 42, 56, 61, 85, 86, 118, 136, 149, 157, 169, 173, 181
counter-culture 18, 20, 43, 54, 64, 137, 152
Cowan, Douglas 95
cravings 74, 94, 129, 137, 145, 152, 156–167, 177, 181
The Crazies 73, 74, 81, 82
Creepshow 66
cremation 55, 149, 151, 170
Creole 30
Cronenberg, David 18, 19, 77, 79, 116–120, 126, 130, 183
crucifix 54, 55, 99, 100
crucifixion 94
cruciform 63
Cuba 30

Dahomey 28
dakini 150

Dalai Lama 136
Damballah 27
danses macabres 109
Dante 3, 86, 96, 103
Dasein 174–176
Davis, Wade 33, 34, 38, 187n58
Dawn of the Dead (1978) 9, 16, 63–65, 71, 72, 75, 81–84, 98, 100, 128, 158, 160, 164, 174
Dawn of the Dead (2004) 82–84, 98, 100, 103, 161, 164, 166
Day of the Dead (1985) 9, 13, 63, 70, 71, 77, 78, 81, 84, 98, 100, 159, 164
Deadworld 67
death-denial 146, 148, 153, 169, 174, 179
death drive 5, 88, 116
Deathdream 73
Deleuze, Gilles 5, 6, 35
Dellamorte Dellamore 97, 124, 125
dementia 13, 85, 133
demons 25, 26, 31, 35, 66, 77, 95, 120, 137, 177, 183
Dendle, Peter 12, 43
Dennett, Daniel 11, 12
Descartes, Rene 10, 143
desirable 2, 29, 35, 152
desire 9, 34, 47, 70, 74, 80, 83–85, 99–101, 106, 107, 114, 115, 137, 139, 141, 142, 145, 159, 161, 162, 164–166, 171, 177, 181, 182
devil-worship 37, 73, 103
devils 28, 30, 55, 94
dharma 57, 139, 171
Diary of the Dead 71, 82
disease 2, 13, 38, 87, 88, 91, 106, 107, 117, 119, 120, 132, 133, 139, 148
disgust 6, 18, 68, 78, 93, 108, 109, 114, 116, 127, 128, 130, 131, 150, 152, 153, 171, 179
dispensationalism 87
The Diving Bell and the Butterfly 85
Dixon, Daryl 136, 156, 161
Dixon, Merle 131, 156
Doomsday Preppers 88
double-consciousness 39, 40
Dracula 44, 45, 55
DuBois, W.E.B. 39
dukkha 140–142, 166
DuMaurier, Daphne 43
Dyer, Richard 16, 39

EC Comics 44, 65, 66, 192n95
Emgee, David 164
emotions 11, 13, 51, 53, 54, 115, 133, 140, 148, 161, 171, 175, 180
enlightenment 61, 139, 170

enslavement 9, 14, 15, 22, 30, 31, 33, 35, 36, 43, 47, 51, 82, 166, 180
Epicurus 104, 105
epiphenomenalism 10–12
Eros 5, 88, 116
eschatology 8, 98
Essenes 96, 97
evangelism 25, 28, 97, 100
Evil Dead 77
existential 2–5, 18–20, 51, 71, 77, 79, 80, 87, 89, 91, 95, 122, 125, 126, 139, 162, 173, 175, 176, 182
eyes 11, 33, 49, 56, 75, 80, 84, 97, 107, 108, 117, 130, 131, 159, 170, 171, 173

Faces of Death 135
Fangoria 118
farts 88, 120, 121, 126
fast zombies 82, 83, 159
Fear the Walking Dead 101, 132
Felix-Mentor, Felicia 32
Fido 84, 123, 124
Finney, Jack 43, 50, 52
The Fly 116, 117, 126, 130, 131
Foree, Ken 64, 83, 98, 100, 103, 160
Foucault, Michel 16, 39, 118, 127
Frankenstein 44, 46
Frankl, Viktor 158
Freud 5, 88, 116, 130
Friday the 13th 7
Fulci, Lucio 40, 75, 76, 81, 90, 97, 103, 113, 131, 183
funerals 97, 110, 139, 149, 153, 170

Gandhi 57
Gautama 139, 140
Gede 105
gehenna 96
The Ghost Breakers 48
ghosts 3, 30, 46, 116, 118, 167–169
The Ghoul 46
ghouls 3, 43, 66, 67, 76
Gibson, Mel 103
Gilgamesh 51, 104
Girard, René 100
Godzilla 66
Goldblum, Jeff 51, 117
gore 10, 16, 17, 44, 63, 68, 73, 75, 76, 90, 96, 108, 113, 115, 118, 127, 128, 131, 151, 152
Governor 84, 131, 156, 164
govi 32
Grand Guignol 65, 66, 68, 192n95
Grant, Barry Keith 52
graves 8, 14, 27, 54, 55, 68, 71, 73, 74, 100, 124, 158, 183
Greene, Hershel 84, 102, 112, 131, 154, 155

Grimes, Carl 111, 112, 131
Grimes, Rick 111, 123, 132, 154–156, 158, 164, 178, 199*n*92
grotesque 79, 96, 116, 120
Guattari, Felix 5, 6, 35

Haiti 2, 3, 8–11, 14–16, 18, 19, 21–49, 64, 68, 70–74, 82, 89, 92, 93, 103, 105, 124, 137, 152, 167, 169, 180, 181
Halloween 7
Hammer Films 68
Hawks, Howard 44, 52, 190*n*38
heaven 27, 31, 36, 61, 94, 95, 119, 133, 147, 155
Hegelian 41
Heidegger 19, 158, 174, 175, 177–179
hell 3, 27, 60, 61, 64, 86, 92–98, 148, 159
Heston, Charlton 62, 63
Hinduism 29, 55, 61, 142, 143, 155
Hispaniola 21, 22, 24
Hitchcock, Alfred 67, 69, 70, 79
Hoodoo 28
Hopper, Dennis 158
houngans 31
humanism 1, 2, 79, 119, 129
hunger 43, 70, 84, 106
Hurston, Zora Neale 32, 38

I Am Legend (film) 53, 61, 63, 83, 172
I Am Legend (novel) 9, 17, 44, 53–64, 93, 191*n*42, 192*n*87
I Walked with a Zombie 48, 49
Imitatio Christi 94
impermanence 110, 138, 140, 142–146, 148, 151, 152, 155, 165, 166, 170, 174, 182
individual 5, 10, 11, 16, 52, 55, 60, 61, 79, 83, 92, 94, 97, 101, 104, 108, 110, 114–116, 118, 121, 122, 124, 125, 127, 128, 133, 134, 142–144, 150, 152, 160, 162, 165, 167, 173–178, 181, 182
individuation 174, 175
insatiable 104, 117, 130, 137, 159, 160, 165
Invasion of the Body Snatchers 11, 43, 50–53
Israel 97
Italy 76, 93, 124
iZombie 85, 124, 128, 156, 157

Jackson, Michael 77
Jainism 140
Jamaica 30
Jancovich, Mark 56
Japan 47, 67, 88, 105, 125–127, 164, 170
Jaws 129
Jesus 13, 27, 35, 36, 86, 92, 94, 96, 100, 103, 113

jiang-shi 169
Jones, Duane 16
Juju cinema 39
jumbie 30

Karloff, Boris 46, 50
karma 167, 177
Kierkegaard, Søren 175
King, Martin Luther, Jr. 16
King, Stephen 66, 73, 130
King Kong 44
King of the Zombies 48
Kirkman, Robert 10, 65, 67, 82
koan 175
Kongo 27
Krishna 100
Kristeva, Julia 79, 114, 115, 120, 125, 126, 131, 153
Kshatriya 140
Kübler-Ross, Elizabeth 91
Kubrick, Stanley 78

LaHaye, Tim 87
lama 149
Land of the Dead 63, 71, 82, 84, 98, 157, 158
The Last Man on Earth 44, 53, 62, 70, 93, 172
Lauro, Sarah Juliet 2, 40
LaVey, Anton 135
Lazarus 13
Left Behind 87, 137
Legba 27
Leguizamo, John 99, 157, 158
Lewis, Herschell Gordon 68, 69
liminal 14, 27, 41, 60, 70, 97, 114, 118
Lincoln, Andrew *see* Grimes, Rick
The Living Dead at Manchester Morgue 74
loas 26, 27, 29, 31, 32, 105
locked-in syndrome 13, 85, 86, 124
London 81, 110
lougawou 30
Louisiana 30
Lugosi 15, 44, 45

Macumba 64
Maggie 161, 162
maggots 75, 152
magic 9, 28, 30–32, 34, 37–39, 42–50, 109
magician 9, 31, 32, 44, 167
Mahā-satipatthāna-sutta 151
mall 72, 75, 84, 98, 99, 128, 158, 164
manbo 31
The Manchurian Candidate 47
mandala 137

manga 67, 88
Manson, Charles 63
mantra 178
Mars, Louis 31–33
Marvel Comics 65–67
Marx, Karl 72
Marxism 1, 14, 72
materialism 10, 12, 56, 73, 77, 96, 104, 118, 134
Matheson, Richard 9, 17–19, 44, 53, 55–57, 59–64, 70, 71, 84, 93, 137, 152, 172, 181
MBiti, John 29
McCarthyism 52, 56, 65
McMath, Jahi 86
meditation 3, 19, 20, 65, 73, 92, 105, 108, 135, 138, 140, 146, 148–153, 155, 157, 161, 166, 168–172, 175, 202*n*4, 203*n*21
memento mori 18, 19, 85, 91–93, 104, 108–110, 112–114, 121, 135, 155, 162, 198*n*81
Mencius 47
meta-apocalyptic 97
military 22, 37, 38, 63, 71, 74, 78, 81, 98, 132, 164
millenarianism 87, 97
millennial 81, 87, 104
mindfulness 6, 104, 152, 157, 182
missionaries 25, 26, 101
misté 29
mondo 118
monks 47, 107, 139, 145, 146, 156, 157, 167, 170, 171
monstrare 168
Montreal 39
mortality salience 146, 147, 182
Mozambique 30
mummies 3, 8, 9, 10, 110, 170, 200*n*144
Murphy, Cillian 81
mvumbi 30

Nagarjuna 152
National Geographic 37, 87
Nazis 68, 96
ndzumbi 30
necrophilia 118
necropolitics 50
Nicotero, Greg 113
Nietzsche, Friedrich 19, 95, 138, 177
Nigeria 39
Night of the Living Dead (1968) 9, 10, 13, 15–17, 42–44, 53, 63, 64, 68, 69–72, 75–78, 84, 90, 91, 99–101, 113, 116, 117, 121, 124, 129, 135, 153, 163, 165, 172, 181, 195*n*10
Night of the Living Dead (1990) 153, 154

nihilism 58, 71, 79, 92, 95, 97–99, 101, 119, 122, 123, 138, 148, 152, 161
Nimoy, Leonard 51
9/11 4, 16
nirvana 163, 166, 167, 170
Nollywood 39
nostalgia 52, 111, 161
not-self 19, 143–145, 147, 155, 175; *see also anatta*
nsumbi 30
nvumbi 30
nzambi 30

Obama, Barack 17
O'Bannon, Dan 78, 183
oboezu 175
occulture 57, 60, 61, 76, 88, 89
The Omega Man 53, 61–63
Ossorio, Amando de 76, 183
Ostwalt, Conrad 98

p-zombie 10–12
Paffenroth, Kim 3, 18, 77, 86, 91, 92, 94–101, 103, 126, 165, 174
paganism 57
palliative 150, 171
parasite 88, 117, 119, 126, 132
Paris 137
parody 15, 67, 78, 79, 92, 93, 121, 159
Partridge, Christopher 57
The Passion of the Christ 103
patients 13, 50, 69, 85, 86, 133, 134, 179
Paul, St. 103, 106
Pegg, Simon 84, 123
Percival, Harold 61
photograph 28, 32, 109–112, 171, 178
plague 68, 97, 109, 125, 132, 156, 172
The Plague of Zombies 43, 68
Plan 9 from Outer Space 49, 70
plastination 115
Plato 29
pod-people 11, 14, 51–53
Pontypool 130
pornography 113, 115, 117, 118
possession, by demons/spirits 26, 31, 77, 167
posthumanism 1, 2, 40
postmodernism 1, 69, 116
powa 149
Pride and Prejudice and Zombies 159
priest 23–25, 31, 37, 64, 76, 81, 100–102, 112, 137, 140, 149
priestess 31
prophet 96–98, 102, 123
Protestantism 25, 101
Psycho 43, 67, 79

psychoanalysis 6, 70, 117, 125, 132
purgatory 98, 99

Rabid 117
radiation 9, 49, 66, 70, 132
rage 73, 81, 130, 132
Raimi, Sam 77
rape 23, 164
rapture 87, 88, 102
reactionary 7, 52, 56, 118
rebirth 29, 79, 134, 143, 144, 148, 155, 160, 162, 167; *see also* reincarnation
Reedus, Norman 136, 156
reincarnation 29, 60, 61, 148, 155; *see also* rebirth
religion 8, 15, 17–18, 22–28, 35, 37, 38, 40, 48, 50, 54–58, 60, 62–64, 82, 86, 91, 93, 94, 100–102, 119, 137, 146–148, 180
repulsion 36, 119, 120, 150, 152
Resident Evil 81, 83, 87, 98, 195n147
resurrection 3, 8, 9, 13, 15, 19, 27, 35, 36, 43, 45, 55, 76, 89, 92–94, 96, 97, 102–104, 133, 144, 175, 180
Return of the Living Dead 9, 13, 74, 77, 78, 82–84, 121, 123, 158–160
revelation 26, 97, 176
Rhames, Ving 161
Rhee, Glenn 131, 135, 161, 182
rhizome 5, 6
Rhodes, Gary 45
Riggs, Chandler *see* Grimes, Carl
ro-langs 167
ro-rgyah-pa 149
Robo-Buddhas 157
Romero, George 1, 6, 7, 9, 10, 13, 15–19, 21, 30, 39, 40, 42–44, 49, 50, 52, 53, 60, 63, 64, 66–73, 75, 76–78, 81–84, 90, 91, 93–95, 97–100, 102, 103, 116, 117, 120, 121, 123, 128, 129, 131, 132, 136, 156, 158, 160, 165, 172, 180–183
Rooker, Michael *see* Dixon, Merle
Russell, Jamie 43, 73, 114
Russo, John 75–78, 87, 90, 121, 132, 137

salvation 15, 23, 36, 37, 56, 61, 63, 82, 86, 87, 97, 98, 100–102, 108
samsara 19, 143, 144, 155, 160, 162, 163, 166, 167, 170, 171
Santeria 28
Santo-Domingo 22
Satan 72–74, 135
Savini, Tom 65, 77, 153, 154, 171
scapegoat 55, 74, 100, 103
Schiavo, Terri 86
Schwarzenegger, Arnold 161, 162
Seabrooke, William 32, 44

Seneca 104, 122
The Serpent and the Rainbow 33
sex-drive 5, 88, 116
sexploitation 117
Shakyamuni 139
The Shining 78
Shinto 67
Shivers 116–119, 126, 183
Siddhartha 139
Sisyphus 122, 176, 177
sky burial 149, 150
slave 8–10, 14, 15, 18, 21–47, 64, 70, 72, 74, 82, 93, 117, 132, 166, 175, 180–183
Soavi, Michele 97, 124, 125
sociophobics 1, 2, 76, 90, 148
Socrates 104
sokushinbutsu 170
soucouyants 30
souls 9, 10, 29–32, 35, 44, 58, 61, 69, 103, 106–109, 113, 142, 143, 153, 155
Spain 22, 30, 76, 128
spirit 9, 12, 26–32, 35, 48, 58, 60, 65, 105, 106, 137, 167–169
spirit-mediums 28
spiritualism 28, 57, 61
still-life 109
Stoker, Bram 55
Survival of the Dead 71, 82, 129
Sutherland, Donald 51
syncretism 15, 21, 26–28, 36, 39, 40, 57, 64, 76, 93

Taino 22, 36
Tales from the Crypt 17, 65, 66, 183
tanha 159
terminal 133–135, 161
terror management theory 146–148, 172–174, 176
terrorism 1, 2, 81, 87, 91
The Texas Chainsaw Massacre 69, 78
Thailand 150, 168, 170, 171
Thanatos 5, 88, 116
theology 20, 24, 29, 86, 91, 94, 101, 104, 105, 136
theosophy 17, 18, 53, 57, 58, 61, 137
Theravada Buddhism 170
They Live 72
The Thing 52, 190n38
The Thing from Another World 43, 52
thirst 25, 68, 159
Tibetan Buddhism 134, 149, 150, 167
TMT *see* terror management theory
Tokyo 88, 126, 183
tombs 35, 76
Torah 55
transmigration 29; *see also* rebirth; reincarnation

transubstantiation 15, 36, 94
Trinidad 30, 64
Trioxin 74
tsam-pa 150
28 Days Later 73, 81, 82, 87, 98, 100, 101, 129, 130, 132, 164
Two Thousand Maniacs! 44, 68

uncanny 51, 52, 80, 175, 176
utilitarianism 109

valley of the shadow of death 102
vampire 3, 4, 8–10, 17, 30, 46, 53–66, 70, 72, 74, 84, 93, 94, 172, 181
Vampirella 66
vanitas 109
Vatican 24, 55
Vedic 140
vekongi 30
venereal disease 117
Vetalapancavimsati 167
Videodrome 117, 183
videogame 4, 81–83, 87, 98, 123
Vietnam 1, 65, 71, 73, 77
Vikings 22
Vikramāditya 168
virus 9, 51, 53, 54, 56, 57, 62–64, 68, 73, 74, 81, 82, 85–87, 98, 132, 161, 164, 181
vivacité 103
Vodou 15, 18, 21–23, 25–28, 31, 35, 38–40, 42–44, 48, 64, 73, 76, 93, 105, 106
vodu 28, 29
vomit 39, 88, 120
voodoo 9, 15, 25, 27, 28, 37, 39, 42–50, 64, 67, 68, 70, 73, 74, 183
vultures 149–151

The Walking Dead 4, 5, 10, 65, 67, 82, 84, 96, 99, 101, 102, 111, 113, 124, 127, 129, 131, 132, 135, 136, 154, 156, 158, 161, 164, 178
Walter, Tony 136
Warm Bodies 85, 124

Weekend at Bernie's 121
Welles, Orson 44
werewolf 30
What Dreams May Come 60, 61
White Zombie 15, 42, 44–49, 172
Whitegod 25
witchcraft 26, 31, 37, 55
Wittgenstein, Ludwig 19
wizard 68
women 23, 27, 45, 47, 48, 50, 53, 54, 57, 74, 75, 85, 96, 124, 125, 131, 139, 150, 156, 170, 179
Wood, Robin 7, 52, 78, 100, 165
World War I 30, 47
World War II 57, 65, 96
World War Z 83, 87, 130
worms 108, 151

X-Men 66

Yacawar 79
Yeun, Steven *see* Rhee, Glenn
yuppie 119

Z Nation 86
Zechariah 97
Zemeckis, Robert 65
zemi 30
Zen 78, 88, 136, 156, 157, 175, 176
zimbo 11
Zizek, Slavoj 72, 125, 126
Zombeavers 129
Zombi 2/3 16, 29–32, 35, 75, 82, 97, 183
Zombie Ass: Toilet of the Dead 88, 126
Zombie Honeymoon 84
Zombie Strippers 85
Zombieland 161, 164
Zombies Anonymous 84, 124
The Zombies of Sugar Hill 74, 75
zombification 16, 33, 34, 36, 38, 40, 43, 45, 50, 77, 84, 161
zumbi 30

www.ingramcontent.com/pod-product-compliance
Ingram Content Group UK Ltd.
Pitfield, Milton Keynes, MK11 3LW, UK
UKHW041943140426
5217IPUK00014B/625